Artist-Parents in Contemporary Art

This book examines the increasing intersections of art and parenting from the late 1990s to the early 2010s, when constructions of masculine and feminine identities, as well as the structure of the family, underwent radical change.

Barbara Kutis asserts that the championing of the simultaneous linkage of art and parenting by contemporary artists reflects a conscientious self-fashioning of a new kind of identity, one that she calls the 'artist-parent.' By examining the work of three artists—Guy Ben-Ner, Elżbieta Jabłońska, and the collective Mothers and Fathers—this book reveals how these artists have engaged with the domestic and personal in order to articulate larger issues of parenting in contemporary life.

This book will be of interest to scholars in art and gender, gender studies, contemporary art, and art history.

Barbara Kutis is Associate Professor at Indiana University Southeast, USA.

Routledge Research in Gender and Art

Routledge Research in Gender and Art is a new series in art history and visual studies, focusing on gender, sexuality, and feminism. Proposals for monographs and edited collections on this topic are welcomed.

For a full list of titles in this series, please visit https://www.routledge.com/Rout ledge-Research-in-Gender-and-Art/book-series/RRGA

Representing Duchess Anna Amalia's Bildung
A Visual Metamorphosis from Political to Personal in Eighteenth-Century Germany
Christina K. Lindeman

Virgin Sacrifice in Classical Art
Women, Agency, and the Trojan War
Anthony F. Mangieri

Emma Hamilton and Late Eighteenth Century European Art
Agency, Performance, and Representation
Ersy Contogouris

Female Body Image in Contemporary Art
Dieting, Eating Disorders, Self-Harm, and Fatness
Emily L. Newman

Class, Gender and Sexuality in Thomas Gainsborough's *Blue Boy*
Valerie Hedquist

Feminist Subjectivities in Fiber Art and Craft
Shadows of Affect
John Corso Esquivel

Artist-Parents in Contemporary Art
Gender, Identity, and Domesticity
Barbara Kutis

Artist-Parents in Contemporary Art
Gender, Identity, and Domesticity

Barbara Kutis

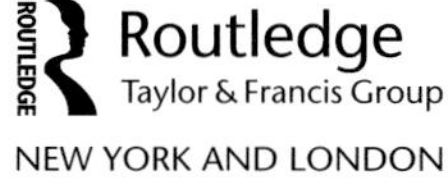

Routledge
Taylor & Francis Group

NEW YORK AND LONDON

First published 2020
by Routledge
52 Vanderbilt Avenue, New York, NY 10017

and by Routledge
2 Park Square, Milton Park, Abingdon, Oxon, OX14 4RN

Routledge is an imprint of the Taylor & Francis Group, an informa business

Library of Congress Cataloging-in-Publication Data
Names: Kutis, Barbara, author.
Title: Artist-parents in contemporary art: gender, identity, and domesticity / Barbara Kutis.
Description: New York: Routledge, 2020. | Includes bibliographical references and index.
Identifiers: LCCN 2020003174 (print) | LCCN 2020003175 (ebook) | ISBN 9781138605664 (hardback) | ISBN 9780429467981 (ebook)
Subjects: LCSH: Art and society. | Parenting. | Mothers in art. | Fathers in art. | Ben-Ner, Guy, 1969–Criticism and interpretation. | Jabłońska, Elżbieta, 1958–Criticism and interpretation. |
MESH: Mothers and Fathers (Art collective)
Classification: LCC N72.S6 K88 2020 (print) | LCC N72.S6 (ebook) | DDC 701/.03–dc23
LC record available at https://lccn.loc.gov/2020003174
LC ebook record available at https://lccn.loc.gov/2020003175

ISBN: 978-1-138-60566-4 (hbk)
ISBN: 978-0-429-46798-1 (ebk)

Typeset in Sabon
by Deanta Global Publishing Services, Chennai, India

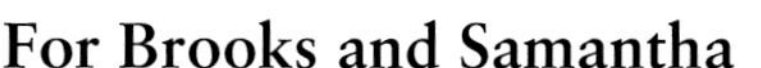

For Brooks and Samantha

Contents

List of Figures   viii
List of Plates   x
Acknowledgments   xii

1 The Artist-Parent Identity   1

2 A History of Art and Parenting from the Second-Wave to the
   Second Millennium   8

3 Superwoman, Supermother, or Polish Mother? Elżbieta
   Jabłońska's Artistic Negotiation of Motherhood   26

4 Articulating the Artist-Father: Guy Ben-Ner   66

5 A Collective Artist-Parent Identity: Mothers and Fathers   115

6 The Future of Artist-Parents in Contemporary Art   154

Bibliography   157
Index   168

Figures

2.1 Louise Bourgeois, *Autobiographical Series* (detail), 1994. Portfolio of 14 etchings with drypoint and aquatint on paper. 58.4 × 40.6 × 1.9 cm. Photo: Christopher Burke. © The Easton Foundation/VAGA at ARS, NY   12

2.2 Vance and Carl Gellert, Untitled, 1983, from *Carl Vision*, 1983–96. Color Photograph. Courtesy Vance Gellert   13

2.3 Adam Rzepecki, *Project of the Father Pole Memorial*, 1981. Photograph. Courtesy Dawid Radziszewski Gallery, Warsaw   17

2.4 Martha Rosler, *Born to Be Sold: Martha Rosler Reads the Strange Case of Baby $/M*, 1988. Color video with sound, 35 minutes, 18 seconds. © Martha Rosler. Courtesy the artist and Mitchell-Innes & Nash, New York   18

3.1 Elżbieta Jabłońska, *Supermother*, 2002. Photographic series. Courtesy the artist   34

3.2 Elżbieta Jabłońska, *Supermother*, *Home Games* exhibition, 2002. AMS Outdoor Gallery, 400 billboards in Poland. Courtesy the artist   37

3.3 Elżbieta Jabłońska, *Through the Stomach to the Heart*, 1999–2005 Performance at the exhibition *Masquerades*, Inner Spaces Gallery, Poznan, 2001. Courtesy the artist   39

3.4 Elżbieta Jabłońska, *Through the Stomach to the Heart*, 1999–2005. Performance at exhibition *Architectures of Gender*, SculptureCenter, Long Island City, New York, 2003. Courtesy the artist   44

3.5 Elżbieta Jabłońska, *83 Waiters and a Helper*, 2006. Atlas Sztuki, Łódź, Poland. Courtesy the artist   48

3.6 Elżbieta Jabłońska, *New Life*, 2010. Neon. Collection Nomus Nowe Muzeum Sztuki, Gdansk. Courtesy the artist   57

4.1 Guy Ben-Ner, still from *Berkeley's Island*, 1999. Single channel video with sound, 15 minutes. Courtesy the artist   72

4.2 Guy Ben-Ner, still from *Moby Dick*, 2000. Single channel video, 12 minutes, 35 seconds. Courtesy the artist   81

4.3 Guy Ben-Ner, still from *Wild Boy*, 2004. Single channel video, 17 minutes. Courtesy the artist   91

4.4 Dennis Oppenheim, *2-Stage Transfer Drawing. (Advancing to a Future State)*, 1971. Boise, Idaho. Erik to Dennis Oppenheim As Erik runs a marker along my back, I attempt to duplicate the movement on the wall. His activity stimulates a kinetic response from my sensory system. He is, therefore, drawing through me. Sensory retardation or disorientation makes up the discrepancy between the two drawings, and could be seen as elements that are activated during this procedure. Because Erik is my offspring, and we share similar biological ingredients, my back (as surface) can be seen as a mature version of his own ... in a sense, he contacts a future state. *2-Stage Transfer Drawing. (Returning to a Past State)*, 1971. Boise, Idaho. Dennis to Erik Oppenheim. As I run a marker along Erik's back, he attempts to duplicate the movement on the wall. My activity stimulates a kinetic response from his memory system. I am, therefore, drawing through him. Sensory retardation or disorientation makes up the discrepancy between the two drawings, and could be seen as elements that are activated during this procedure. Because Erik is my offspring, and we share similar biological ingredients, his back (as surface) can be seen as an immature version of my own ... in a sense, I make contact with a past state. Copyright Dennis Oppenheim Estate   93

4.5   Guy Ben-Ner, still from *Wild Boy*, 2004. Single channel video, 17 minutes. Courtesy the artist   94

4.6   Guy Ben-Ner, still from *Elia: A Story of an Ostrich Chick*, 2003. Single channel video with sound, 17 minutes. Courtesy the artist   101

4.7   Guy Ben-Ner, still from *Stealing Beauty*, 2007. Single channel video with sound, 17 minutes 40 seconds. Courtesy the artist   103

5.1   Mothers and Fathers, *Bread*, 2008, foam. Courtesy the artists   117

5.2   Mothers and Fathers, *Father: Decoration* and *Mother*, from *Mothers and Fathers Offer*, 2002. Plastic vacuum-formed molds. Courtesy the artists   128

5.3   Mothers and Fathers, *Family Art Crimes*, 2006, digital prints. ArtWall public art installation, Prague, CZ. Courtesy the artists   134

5.4   Mothers and Fathers, *Mop*, from *Bared!*, 2009, photographic project for *Fotograf* magazine. Courtesy the artists   141

5.5   Mothers and Fathers, *Mop*, from *Bared!*, 2009, photographic project for *Fotograf* magazine. Courtesy the artist   141

5.6   Mothers and Fathers, *Plug*, from *Bared!*, 2009, photographic project for *Fotograf* magazine. Courtesy the artists   143

5.7   Mothers and Fathers, *Report Card (front)*, from *Bared!*, 2009, photographic project for Fotograf magazine. Courtesy the artists   144

Plates

1   Elizabeth Murray, *Beam*, November 1982. Oil on canvas, four panels. 9' 2" × 6' 3 7/8" × 3 7/8." Collection Museum of Modern Art, New York. © 2019 The Murray-Holman Family Trust / Artists Rights Society (ARS), New York

2   Elżbieta Jabłońska, *Supermother*, 2002. Photographic series. Courtesy the artist.

3   Elżbieta Jabłońska, *Kitchen,* 2004, from *Through the Stomach to the Heart,* 1999–2005. Performance at exhibition, "Under the White-and-Red Flag," CAC Wilno, Lithuana. Courtesy the artist.

4   Elżbieta Jabłońska, *Kitchen,* 2003, from *Through the Stomach to the Heart,* 1999–2005. Performance at exhibition, "Biały Mazur," NBK, Neuer Berliner Kunstverein, Berlin, Germany. Courtesy the artist

5   Elżbieta Jabłońska, *Untitled,* from *Zasiedzenie,* 2004, photograph. Courtesy the artist.

6   Elżbieta Jabłońska, *Kitchen,* 2007. Performance. Courtesy the artist.

7   Guy Ben-Ner, still from *Berkeley's Island,* 1999. Single channel video with sound, 15 minutes. Courtesy the artist.

8   Guy Ben-Ner, still from *Moby Dick,* 2000. Single channel video, 12 minutes, 35 seconds. Courtesy the artist.

9   Guy Ben-Ner, still from *Wild Boy,* 2004. Single channel video, 17 minutes. Courtesy the artist.

10   Guy Ben-Ner, still from *Wild Boy,* 2004. Single channel video, 17 minutes. Courtesy the artist

11   Guy Ben-Ner, still from *Elia: A Story of an Ostrich Chick,* 2003. Single channel video with sound, 17 minutes. Courtesy the artist

12   Guy Ben-Ner, still from *Stealing Beauty,* 2007. Single channel video with sound, 17 minutes 40 seconds. Courtesy the artist

13   Mothers and Fathers, *What Would We Be Without Children?,* 2007. Plaster casts of the artists' bodies. Installation at C2C Gallery, Prague. Courtesy the artists

14   Mothers and Fathers, detail, *What Would We Be Without Children?,* 2007. Plaster casts of the artists' bodies. Installation at C2C Gallery, Prague. Courtesy the artists

15   Mothers and Fathers, *Mothers and Fathers Offer,* 2002. Exhibition poster. Courtesy the artists

16   Mothers and Fathers, *Dishes (to Wash)* from *Mothers and Fathers Offer,* 2002. Shrink-wrapped porcelain dishes. Courtesy the artists

17 Mothers and Fathers, *Father from Family Art Crimes*, 2006, digital print. *ArtWall* public art installation, Prague, CZ. Courtesy the artists

18 Mothers and Fathers, *Duck* from *Bared!,* 2009, photographic project for *Fotograf* magazine. Courtesy the artists

19 Mothers and Fathers, *Report Card (back)*, from *Bared!,* 2009, photographic project for *Fotograf* magazine. Courtesy the artists

Acknowledgments

This book is the product of over a decade of research and thinking about the practice of artists who are parents and choose to represent their children and their imagined or actual domestic lives within their practice. When I initiated this project, I was a single and childless woman who thought she could break ground on a fascinating and understudied topic in art's history. Now, as a parent of fraternal twins, the field has grown considerably with several texts, conferences, and exhibitions on the topic of maternal art, the balance of art and motherhood, and the struggles of the artist-parent-academic. Thus, in many ways, this project has come full circle. I now live, research, and write on something that has become much more personal. As such, the works discussed within are seen with new eyes—those of an art historian-parent-academic.

This project would not have been possible without the support of my peers, mentors, and the faculty at the University of Delaware. Ann E. Gibson and Ikem Okoye provided insightful feedback at the early stages of this project and my external reader, Joan C. Marter, pointed out some key connections in my project. From my time at Pennsylvania State University, Leo G. Mazow has continued to be both a mentor and friend. Emily L. Newman is a wonderful peer, providing encouragement, support, and always responds to my queries. At Delaware, Nikki A. Greene, Isabelle Havet, Elizabeth Melanson, and Ashley Rye-Kopec were an instrumental support group and helped me persevere through the final stages of the dissertation project. Many thanks to Rachel Schwartz Sirota for introducing me to Guy Ben-Ner's work and taking that road trip to Mass MoCA all those years ago to see the work.

My institution, Indiana University Southeast, provided funding to support the final research stages of this project. All of my colleagues at IU Southeast have been thoughtful and supportive, but especially Anne Allen, Samantha Earley, and Leigh Viner. I thank them for their willingness to listen and provide support as I balanced teaching, research, motherhood, and the completion of this manuscript. I also would like to thank the University of Arkansas Press for granting me permission to reprint a revised section of Chapter Three on Elżbieta Jabłońska, which was previously published as "Elżbieta Jabłońska's Kitchen Interventions: Food, Art, and Maternal Identity" in *The Taste of Art: Cooking, Food, and Counterculture in Contemporary Practices*, edited by Silvia Bottinelli and Margherita D'Ayala Valva (2017). Many thanks go to my editor, Isabella Vitti, and editorial assistant, Katie Armstrong for their assistance with this project. I also thank Sarah Irvin, Rachel Epp Buller, Kaylan Buteyn, Cayla Skillin-Brauchle, and Danielle Wyckoff for their collegiality and conversation at the 2019 SECAC in Chattanooga, TN. Sarah, Cayla, and Danielle's presentations at the conference enriched my thinking about artist-parents as I completed this manuscript.

Certainly, I must thank the artists and their estates for permitting me to reproduce their work in this book. I especially thank Guy Ben-Ner, Elżbieta Jabłońska, Lenka Klodova, Lucie Nepasická, Martin Péč, and Marek Rejent for their time and sharing their work as artist-parents.

And last, but definitely not least, the completion of this manuscript would not have been possible without the support and encouragement of Jason W. Brandt—thank you for being my crew.

1   The Artist-Parent Identity

This book examines examples of the increasing intersections of art and parenting from the late 1990s to the early 2010s, when constructions of masculine and feminine identities, as well as the structure of the family, have undergone radical change. Artists have long been parents but rarely have they dealt with it as the subject matter of their art. I call attention to artists' representations of parenting, their children, and the domestic as a critical and much needed reflection on contemporary life. The simultaneous championing of art and parenting reflects a conscientious self-fashioning of a new kind of identity, one that I term the 'artist-parent.' Artists have been particularly attuned to the visual documentation of contemporary issues, though at the height of the women's movement, motherhood (and fatherhood) were largely avoided as artistic subject-matter, and thereby scholarship, for fear of being labeled saccharine, sentimental, and kitschy. However, the contemporary period has witnessed a significant shift in topics explored by artists and new critical perspectives are brought to issues of children and parenting. By closely examining the work of three artists—Elżbieta Jabłońska, Guy Ben-Ner, and Mothers and Fathers—this project reveals how these artists have engaged with the domestic and personal in order to articulate larger, perhaps universal, issues of parenting in contemporary life.

Building on ideas articulated and explored in maternal studies, gender studies, and postcolonial theory, I examine how the contemporary familial structure, marked by the greater emphasis on women in the work force and the shift to male parenting, reveals a multi-faceted but persistent conflict within gender constructions of mothers and fathers. As such, many factors have influenced this project. First, several exhibits dedicated to the art of women, such as *Global Feminisms* at the Brooklyn Museum of Art (2007), *WACK! Art and the Feminist Revolution* at MOMA PS.1 (2007), *Mother/Mother* at the A.I.R. Gallery (2009), and *Elles* at the Centre Pompidou (2009), spurred renewed interest in the art of women, and included the work of Elżbieta Jabłońska and Mothers and Fathers within their shows. Similarly, a rise of exhibitions and conferences focused on the intersection of art and motherhood, specifically, *Maternal Metaphors I* (2004) and *Maternal Metaphors II* (2006) which brought together a variety of maternal voices. Since 2010, there has been an explosion in the discourse of maternal art: Natalie Loveless' *New Maternalisms* (2012, 2014, and 2016) brought together practice, theory, and history as a means to articulate the maternal as a political and ethical position in both North America and Chile. Lise Haller Baggesen's *Mothernism* (2013), a traveling multimedia tent-installation and book, that according to the artist is "dedicated to staking out and making speakable the 'mother-shaped hole in contemporary art discourse.'"[1] Baggesen co-organized with Deirdre Donoghue a three-day international conference of the same name in 2015 and 2017, which discussed the "topic of caring, labor, and cultural re-production."[2] And this is not to forget to mention the many conferences organized by Andrea O'Reilly through the Association for Research on Mothering and the Motherhood Initiative for Research on Mothering and Community Involvement, which brought together interdisciplinary voices—authors, activists, historians, critics, and artists to exchange ideas about the maternal. Additional evidence of this growing field is found in exhibitions such as *The Art of Breastfeeding: Modern Narratives of Motherhood* (2018) and *M/Other* (2019). These are just two of many exhibitions held on the topic of the maternal in art. In addition, the symposia such as Oxytocin: Birthing the World, and Oxytocin: Mothering the World organized by the Procreate Project in London reveal the growing critical discourse on art and a variety of aspects of lived maternal realities. And while not specifically labeled as exhibitions about fatherhood, in 2009, MassMoCA presented a survey of Guy Ben-Ner's work, *Friday the 12th*; and in 2019, Gallery 400 in Chicago held Alberto Aguilar's first largescale survey, *Moves on a Human Scale*. Both exhibitions revealed the importance of the artists' roles as fathers within their work, and thus reinforced the need to explore art and parenting, beyond the parameters of the maternal body.

Second, several important texts about feminism, maternity, and art underpin this project. Marianne Hirsch's 1997 study, *Family Frames: Photography, Narrative, and Postmemory*, provides the groundwork for the importance of the mother-artist-photographer in the operation of the familial gaze and memory. As she focuses her discussion on women artists, such as Jo Spence, Carrie Mae Weems, and Sally Mann, Hirsch suggests male artists, such as Vance Gellert, usurp the maternal through their own paternal photographs, which provides an interesting counter-perspective to the work of Guy Ben-Ner.[3] In 1999, Hirsch edited an anthology of texts, *The Familial Gaze*, which emerged from an exhibition and conference of the same name at Dartmouth College. With essays focused on the presentation and re-presentation of the family, the anthology reveals the importance that photographs hold on the social construct of the family and cultural memory, and thereby maternity. In 2009, Andrea Liss published her important text, *Feminist Art and the Maternal,* one of the first texts to explore the work of women artists who engage with issues surrounding motherhood.[4] Then, in 2011, Demeter Press published *The M Word: Real Mothers in Contemporary Art*, which is an expanded text associated with an exhibition curated by Myrel Chernick and Jennie Klein in 2004 at the Rochester Contemporary. What these texts and exhibitions have in common is their focus on women artists and mothering as it is articulated through the artists' work. Similarly, Bracha Ettinger's *The Matrixial Borderspace* explores, through psychoanalysis, how the subject and its other can be reformulated through written and visual texts by emphasizing "intrauterine feminine prenatal encounters."[5] In 2012, Rachel Epp Buller edited a collection of essays titled, *Reconciling Art and Motherhood* and in 2019, co-edited with Charles Reeve, *Inappropriate Bodies: Art, Design, and Maternity,* which are in line with Rosemary Betterton's *Maternal Bodies in the Visual Arts*, exploring the relation of the maternal, its embodiment, and art. These volumes unify many disparate voices, incorporating discussions of the maternal at the intersection of race, gender, and sexuality, but largely do not consider fatherhood. Strides are being made to be more inclusive of the non-female voice in parenting, as such artist Sarah Irvin launched the online database project *Artist Parent Index* in 2016 to create a dynamic tool that could be utilized by artists, art historians, and curators.[6] Included in this database are artists such as Alberto Aguilar, whose video and photographic work often documents or reflects his life as an artist-parent. However, male parenting experiences and fatherhood continue to be lacking from this growing critical discourse which fundamentally relies on practices of care. Recognizing that women do not solely perform mothering or parenting, this project considers both men and women artists as parents, and thus posits the term artist-parents to characterize an identity assumed by both men and women who engage in art about parenting.[7]

Nonetheless, it is necessary to recount the rise in maternal theory, masculinity, and paternity to understand how the artist-parent is distinct from, yet overlaps with, the mother-artist. As such, I begin with Sara Ruddick. In her text, *Maternal Thinking: Toward a Politics of Peace* (1989), Ruddick concentrates not on the biological or sociological aspects of motherhood, but on the diurnal activity—thinking—in regard to raising and educating one's children. Ruddick argued that, "the work of mothering demands that mothers think."[8] This perspective, according to maternal scholar, Andrea O'Reilly, "enabled future scholars to analyze the experience and work or practice of mothering as distinct from the identity of the mother," or in other words, that "mothering may be performed by anyone who commits him—or her—self to the demands of maternal practice."[9] Through this distinction, Ruddick argues that by thinking *maternally* nonviolent action will replace collective violence and therefore, as her title suggests, creates a 'politics of peace.'[10] This notion is poignant in relation to Jabłońska's art practice as she carefully and thoughtfully considers the historical, political, and social implications of her actions and how it may change conversations regarding motherhood in Poland.

Adopting the definition of mother articulated by Lisa Baraitser as a woman who chooses to care for another, whom she defines as 'child,' I define the parent as a person of any position within the sex and gender identity spectrum, who chooses to care for another whom they identify as 'child.'[11] Artist-parents, therefore, need not to be biological or cis-gendered parents, though as Shelley Park has acknowledged, the choice of non-heteronormative gender-conforming individuals to parent a child often places them into heteronormative constructs of family.[12] Basically, the perception is that if one is queer and chooses to become a parent, they are seen as engaging in the nuclear family structure—mother, father, and child/children. For this reason, J. Jack Halberstam advocates for *gaga feminism*, a "withering away of old social models of desire, gender, and sexuality, and as a channel for potent new forms of relation, intimacy, technology, and embodiment."[13] As Halberstam has argued, everything in our contemporary society has changed our daily experiences of sex and gender and it would "be weirder if our ideas of family, desire, the normal, the ordinary, the extraordinary did *not* change as everything else around us shifted, evolved, developed, and collapsed."[14] The notion that domestic work is performed by the female, the breadwinner of the family is the male, and that the family requires two parents—a male and a female—are ideas that are visible and challenged within this text.

While the artists discussed herein generally conform to heteronormativity, those constructs do not necessarily conform to the mother–father–child triad either. As such, in *Revolutionary Mothering*, a collection of writings by radical and queer black feminists, editors Alexis Pauline Gumbs and China Martens, advance a theory of mothering as an act of "creating, nurturing, affirming, and supporting life."[15] This text takes that final clause, 'supporting life,' as key to the artist-parent. While scholars such as

Ruddick and Baraitser shy away from collapsing the masculine and feminine modes of childrearing into parenting because of the historical burden placed on women in terms of care, I, like artist Sarah Irvin, argue this is only conditionally true.[16] This 'second shift,' as Arlie Hochschild termed it in 1989, is not always the unwritten second job of the working woman, as there has been a contemporary shift of men in providing care to their children.[17] Furthermore, in Halberstam's articulation of *gaga feminism,* the division of domestic labor does not need to be equal, but must be "acknowledged and chosen."[18] Care, as Milton Mayeroff articulated in 1971, is 'the antithesis of simply using another person to satisfy one's own needs. … Caring, as helping another grow and actualize himself, is a process, a way of relation to someone that involves development, in the same way that friendship can only emerge in time through mutual trust and a deepening and qualitative transformation of the relationship."[19] Caring, according to Mayeroff, is not predicated on gender identity nor sex. Rather it is the approach one takes toward another. Similarly, the activist artist project, *Reproductive Media,* founded by Cayla Skillin-Brauchle and Danielle Wyckoff, recognizes an "inclusive definition of family and remember that people receive and provide vital support from partners, elders, children, siblings, lovers, pets, friends, and more."[20] These definitions demonstrate a growing trend in the understanding and recognition of care as performed by a wide variety of persons to a wide variety of bodily entities.

I utilize the term 'artist-parent' to connote the non-exclusive relationship between the two roles of the artist and parent that constructs one's identity. In other words, a hybrid identity that signifies an artist who, as a biological parent or not, chooses to use parenting as his or her critical voice to engage issues of social relationships, space, and ultimately, gender. Identity politics of the 1960s and 1970s, along with the rise of postcolonial discourse in the 1980s, draw the subject as unfixed, plural, and temporal. While often regarded in terms of the 'other' or the 'periphery' in relation to the dominant and mainstream (typically white, middle- or upper-class, and male), the arguments of the mestiza, hybrid, queer, and subaltern articulated by Gloria Anzaldúa, Homi Bhabha, Audre Lorde, and Gayatri Spivak, among others, inform the particular understanding of hybrid artist-parent identity I am asserting within these pages.[21] As I stated above, the artist-parent identity is focused on the aspect of care toward another, and thus incorporates and is inclusive of individuals of any race, sexual orientation, and gender.

Focusing on artists who have (and have not) received heightened critical attention from scholars and critics within the last decade may seem ahistorical or misguided within the field of art history, but recent studies of the field reveal it as apt, even necessary.[22] As Terry Smith has argued, the study of contemporary art is necessary for understanding contemporaneity. As he determines, contemporaneity is a series of modes, or "distinct but connected clusters" that circumscribe modernity, transnationality, and temporality.[23] This project explores the mode in which artists, who individually and collectively "meditate on the changing nature of time, place, media and mood in the world around them."[24] As evinced in the chapters to follow, the artists discussed—Guy Ben-Ner, Elżbieta Jabłońska, and the collective Mothers and Fathers—embody a critical meditation on parenting, parenthood, and artistic production that asserts a very specific formation of one's self-identity—an identity that could only be possible in their present temporalities. While these artists may be biological parents, their work highlights issues of ideal motherhood, the ideal father, and post-communist gender constructions. When brought together, these artists provide insights about parenting and art in the new millennium that are not bound to specific cultures or disciplines, but serve as a window to more universal changes in the conditions of parenthood.

Nevertheless, one might question why these three examples were chosen. For one, the study of these particular artists reveals that each artist had a desire to explore issues of parenting within their artistic practice. They similarly chose to engage the artist-parent identity when their children were young—particularly beginning when the child was an infant and lasting at least until the child attended primary school. The emphasis on art about parenting during these key childcare years suggests that questions of one's identity are particularly resonant in this period of one's life. In tracing the circumstances of the creation of this imagery and the reaction to its viewing, we can gain a better insight into the relationship between parenthood, artistic identity, and gender construction.

To better frame the work of these artists, the second chapter provides a history of maternal and paternal artists. In it I trace the history of the feminist art movement, but concentrate on its role in producing the concept of the artist-parent, and artists' troubled engagement with parenting. This history, while admittedly mostly Euro-North American, has had a significant impact on how ideas of parenting and art are reflected in the work the artists examined in this text.

The third chapter explores the work of Elżbieta Jabłońska. Her photographic series *Supermother* (2002), the photographic and performance project *Through the Stomach to the Heart*, (1999–2005), and the actions that occur in *Helping* (2004–2009), transform the domestic spaces and activities of the home into artistic endeavors. Challenging the stereotypes of artist, mother, and Catholicism in her home country (Poland), Jabłońska engages with feminism, the myth of the Polish Mother, and ironically asserts herself as a *supermother artist* or artist-parent, quite literally in her art.

The subject of the fourth chapter, Guy Ben-Ner, similarly transforms the domestic space into a place of art activity in his videos. Almost exclusively staged within the artist's Tel Aviv apartment, the work of Ben-Ner depicts his children in fantastic roles to explore the role of parents in children's cognitive development, social interaction, and morality. Ben-Ner's work holds a significant place in this project, as the discussion of artistic identity is decidedly and typically directed at male artists. But rarely does it consider the artist as father, at least in the contemporary period.[25] Children are often listed in artist biographies, along with exhibitions and major works, but perhaps even more rarely do men depict their own children, their parenting, in their art. Again, video, either due to their potentially lower production costs or desire for a recording of action on part of the artist, appears to be the one avenue of art that allowed for children to be present without attracting pejorative charges of sentimentality. Ben-Ner constructs narrative videos that intentionally and unintentionally represent the difficulty of balancing parenting and art production, private home-life and public art-life.

Chapter Five focuses closely on the activities of Mothers and Fathers, who transposes the private and public spaces of the family and artmaking much like Jabłońska and Ben-Ner. Like the previous artists, Mothers and Fathers recognizes the problems of both the artistic and parental roles and attempts to collaboratively address such issues in their art. By finding opportunity in, and exploiting, the post-studio condition of the artist-parent, Mothers and Fathers reveals that the studio can never be completely isolated from family, but instead, can become one with it.

While this is not a new concept, the attempt to publicly and purposefully expand the identity of the artist-parent in a positive way, and therefore the idea of art itself, is. The roots of traditional notions of artistic isolation, however, are old and firm. As Baudelaire stigmatized them in 1863, the perpetual threats to the island of the studio were society, city, family, and money.[26] Mothers and Fathers takes the menaces of such views encroaching upon the artist and parent, and embraces them wholeheartedly—their resulting projects reveal an unflinching and non-idealized view of the maternal and paternal, as well as the artistic, dilemma.

Together the artists discussed in this book reveal a growing discourse of artistic exploration. They largely omit the voice of the child in favor of engaging with issues of gender, care, domesticity, and their artistic identities. The works staged, created, and performed by Elżbieta Jabłońska, Guy Ben-Ner, Mothers and Fathers, and their families reflect the interests of our contemporary moment.

Notes

1 Lise Haller Baggesen, "UMAMI," *Mothernism* (Chicago and Oak Park, Illinois: Green Lantern Press and Poor Farm Press, 2014), 17.
2 "The Mothernists," Conference Program, June 5–7, 2015, Rotterdam, Netherlands.
3 Marianne Hirsch, *Family Frames: Photography, Narrative, and Postmemory* (Cambridge: Harvard University Press, 1997), 172.
4 Liss' study focuses on the American artists Catherine Opie, Renée Cox, Mary Kelly, and Mierle Laderman Ukeles, among others. See Andrea Liss, *Feminist Art and the Maternal* (Minneapolis: University of Minnesota Press, 2009).
5 Bracha Ettinger, *The Matrixial Borderspace* (Minneapolis: University of Minnesota Press, 2006), 1.
6 Sarah Irvin, *Artist Parent Index,* artistparentindex.com.
7 It is important to acknowledge that a dissertation completed in 2011 also used the term artist-parents, suggesting a growing interest in this area of study. The author, Gayle Clemans, discusses artists who as parents created photographic works of art that engaged with the family or recorded the individual *as a parent*. Clemans argues that this mode of art making connotes a 'parental gaze,' which akin to notions of the 'male gaze,' places the spectator in the position of a parent. Clemans' project has a wider scope in terms of artists—she discusses at least fourteen American artists, but she limits her discussion to only works of photography and film/video. In her articulation of a "parental gaze," she argues that it "reflects the ideological and literal position of the parent who has picked up a camera to capture images of his or her family, or him- or her-self *as a parent.*" Organizing her study according to various functions and tropes of photography (such as the home movie), each chapter enables Clemans to discuss a variety of artists, including one featured in this book—Guy Ben-Ner. Our discussions of Ben-Ner, however, are distinctly different due to the works chosen for analysis. See Gayle Clemans, "Parental Points of View: Photographic and Filmic Acts in Contemporary Art" (PhD diss., University of Washington, 2011).
8 Sara Ruddick, *Maternal Thinking: Toward a Politics of Peace* (New York: Ballantine Books, 1989), 24.
9 See Andrea O'Reilly, "'I Envision a Future in Which Maternal Thinkers Are Respected and Self-Respecting': The Legacy of Sara Ruddick's 'Maternal Thinking,'" *Women's Studies Quarterly* 37 no. 3/4 (Fall–Winter 2009): 296; Barbara J. Risman, "Can Men 'Mother'? Life as a Single Father," *Family Relations* 35 no. 1 (January 1986): 85–102.
10 Sara Ruddick, "On 'Maternal Thinking,'" *Women's Studies Quarterly* 37 no. 3/4, Mother (Fall–Winter 2009): 308.
11 Lisa Baraitser, *Maternal Encounters: The Ethics of Interruption* (London and New York: Routledge, 2009), 7.
12 Shelley Park, *Mothering Queerly, Queering Motherhood: Resisting Monomaternalism in Adoptive, Lesbian, Blended, and Polygamous Families* (Albany: State University of New York Press, 2013), 18.

13 J. Jack Halberstam, *Gaga Feminism: Sex, Gender, and the End of Normal* (Boston: Beacon Press, 2012), 25.

14 Ibid., xix–xx.

15 Loretta J. Ross, "Preface," in *Revolutionary Mothering: Love on the Front Lines*, eds. Alexis Pauline Gumbs, China Martens, and Mai'a Williams (Oakland, CA: PM Press, 2016), xv.

16 Sarah Irvin, "Time, Gender, and Care," SECAC presentation, October 19, 2019.

17 See Arlie Hochschild, *The Second Shift* (New York: Avon Books, 1989).

18 Halberstam, *Gaga Feminism*, 61.

19 Milton Mayeroff, *On Caring* (New York: Harper Row, 1971), 1.

20 Cayla Skillin-Brauchle and Danielle Wyckoff, "Reproductive Media: A Project about Sex, Gender, Family and Reproduction," SECAC presentation, October 19, 2019.

21 See Gloria Anzaldúa, *Borderlands: The New Mestiza,* Fourth edition (San Francisco: Aunt Lute Books, 2007); Homi Bhabha, *The Location of Culture* (London: Routledge, 1994); Audre Lorde, *Sister Outsider* (Berkeley: Crossing Press, 1984); Gayatri Spivak, *A Critique of Postcolonial Reason: Toward a History of the Vanishing Present* (Cambridge: Harvard University Press, 1999).

22 The "turn towards the contemporary" been traced in the writings of Alex Alberro, Nicholas Bourriaud, Richard Meyer, Peter Osborne, and Terry Smith.

23 Terry Smith, "The State of Art History: Contemporary Art," *The Art Bulletin* 92 no. 4 (December 2010): 380.

24 Ibid.

25 The artist as father has been explored in terms of Dutch artists such as Jan Steen. See H. Perry Chapman, "Jan Steen as Family Man: Self-Portrayal as an Experiential Mode of Painting," *Nederlands Kunsthistorisch Jaarboek* 46 (1996): 368–393.

26 Charles Baudelaire, "The Painter of Modern Life," *Figaro* (1863); anthologized in Jonathan Mayne, ed., *The Painter of Modern Life and Other Essays* (London: Phaidon Press, 1964), 1–40.

2 A History of Art and Parenting from the Second-Wave to the Second Millennium

In 1971, in the wake of second-wave feminism, Linda Nochlin published her landmark essay, "Why Have There Been No Great Women Artists?," bringing to light several factors that contributed, or rather deterred, women from being included in the canon of nineteenth-century art history.[1] Primarily noting the exclusion of women from education and the art institution (the academy), Nochlin's essay was one of only ten articles on women published in an art journal that year, itself revealing the dearth of attention paid to women artists at the time.[2] As Nochlin noted in 2001, things have changed considerably—women artists, art historians, and critics have transformed the nature of the discourse to be more open and inclusive of women and their art—at least to some extent.[3] Until somewhat recently, women, not just artists, but also curators, critics, and art historians, tended to sequester and elide their roles as mothers for the sake of their practice and success in the art world. Lucy Lippard's 1964 cover letter to the editor of *Art International* reveals the delicate balance between professional and mother: "Herewith the twenty-two reviews. Hope they make whatever the deadline is. Slight delay as I had a baby last week."[4] Being her first and only reference to her role as a mother, Lippard hid her pregnancy from journal editor Jim Fitzsimmons, fearing, "that her work as a mother might be seen as an impediment to her work as a writer."[5] But to attribute this solely to social acceptability would be remiss. There was also a financial reasoning behind many such decisions—Lippard was a single mother and needed to provide for her family.[6] To admit pregnancy, her motherhood, would be to distance herself even further from her male colleagues and place her job—the only economic support she had—in jeopardy.[7]

There was an expectation, espoused by popular programming, magazines, and medical journals, that women, upon giving birth, would stay at home and raise their family.[8] Likewise, the art world required women artists to choose between motherhood and their careers. To publicly have a child was to demonstrate one's lack of commitment. As such, Alice Neel's status as a mother proved her "dilettante" nature.[9] Both Neel and Barbara Hepworth believed that a woman could not seriously return to the art world if she halted her activities for parenting. Andrea Liss similarly recounts the negative reaction Renée Cox garnered from her peers at the Whitney Museum of American Arts Graduate Studies Program when they learned that she was pregnant with her second child—by 1993, Cox was the first woman in twenty-five years to become a mother (again) while enrolled in the program.[10] Conversely, Emma Amos articulated the boredom that can be experienced in being a mother, thus implying that there is a wastefulness in parenting without art making.[11] Thus women needed to balance the public perception of the unforgiving line between art and motherhood.

For Grace Hartigan, the challenges of this dual identity proved too much—while initially she had grandparents providing childcare, they could only help for so long. In addition, she claimed that her son was "bitterly opposed" to her painting, causing her a dilemma. Ultimately, when her ex-husband remarried, she sent her son to live with him in California while she continued her career in New York.[12] Neel, on the other hand, raised several children but her first husband, Carlos Enríquez, took their child, Isabetta, to Cuba to live with her grandparents.[13] Neel's complicated relationship with mothering led to very few portraits of her children during their youth, but notably transformed as her sons, and their friends, began having families in the mid-1960s. As Pamela Allara has noted, between 1964 and 1978, Neel dedicated nearly half of her work to depictions of parents and children, painting seven monumental canvases of pregnant women.[14] Significantly, in the 1970s, Neel became adopted by the feminist movement as a sort of foremother and thus her attention to the female reproductive process can be read in terms of the doting grandmother, rather than an artist-mother.[15] Anne Wagner recently characterized these works as representing "an opposition, an inhabiting, with the female body all but taken over by the alien within."[16] Wagner's reading is attuned to Neel's recognition that being cast primarily as a mother and inherently as a sentimental artist would be detrimental to her career. Children were painful and alien entities in her life and she, like Hartigan, refused to be limited by them.

Reinforcing this mentality, the founding statement of the National Organization of Women in 1966 articulates this rationale: "It is no longer necessary or possible for women to devote the greater part of their lives to childrearing; yet childbearing and rearing ... [are still] used to justify barring women from equal professional and economic advance."[17] The price women artists had to pay, in terms of their career, by having families was overwhelming to more than just American artists like Hartigan. French artist Niki de Saint Phalle notably rejected her domestic life in 1953, after a nervous breakdown in which she claimed that she realized that her husband and two children epitomized the domestic and cultural hegemony she had tried to reject throughout her youth.[18] Saint Phalle went on to make her *Shoot Paintings*, from 1960 through 1961, which symbolized her frustration with traditional gender roles. But, interestingly, the artist ultimately turned to maternal imagery. Like Neel, Saint Phalle became inspired by the pregnancy of another woman, her friend Clarice Rivers (Larry Rivers' wife), and began creating her three-dimensional *Nanas*, 1963–80s.[19] In these curvaceous female bodies the artist began to see pregnancy as a symbol of female strength and self-confidence.[20]

Thus while Hartigan, Neel, and Saint Phalle had contentious relationships to motherhood, several women artists managed to keep this part of their lives secret or avoided motherhood altogether. Barbara Hepworth, as Anne M. Wagner has noted in her book *Mother Stone: The Vitality of Modern British Sculpture*, skillfully crafted her public persona and managed to always be referred to as "Miss," despite being married and having children. She ultimately dismissed the importance of raising her own children, placing her triplets in the care of nursing sisters a few months after their birth. This was a decision that Hepworth later regretted.[21] And, in her enlightening series of interviews, *Originals: American Women Artists*, Eleanor Munro remarks that she interviewed several women artists who had multiple abortions, avoiding the "family way" at all costs—a trend that continues to this day.

From 1990, one can argue that the British artist Tracey Emin has made her mother-hood, or her lack of it, a primary part of her practice. She publicly acknowledged her two abortions in the work, *Every Person I Have Ever Slept With 1963–1995* (1995), in which the aborted fetuses are listed among the men and women with whom Emin has shared a bed. Then in her late forties, Emin found herself struggling with the desire to be a mother and a grandmother. In her January 29, 2009 column for the UK news-paper *The Independent*, Emin's headline read: "I felt that, in return for my children's souls, I had been given my success." Emin clearly deemed her lack of procreation as a trade for a different sort of creation—her art, noting, "I felt so grateful not to be the kind of mother who gave birth to a human being, but the kind of mother who gives birth to a creative notion, a creative idea, something that isn't evil and could never have that capacity."[22] But at the same time, Emin realized that although she had achieved financial security, and even artistic acclaim in some circles, she had nothing left, as illustrated in her photographic self-portrait, *I've Got It All*, 2000. In this image, Emin gives birth to nothing more than materialistic things—money. Emin remarked that she was not part of the "raw stuff, the thing that propels people through life."[23] What Emin seemed to be experiencing was the opposite of the problem of having chil-dren: that avoiding motherhood for fear of destroying her own life may have 'ruined' her life anyway.[24]

But some artists consistently valued family life, even in the sixties and seventies, to some negative outcomes. Munro quotes one of her interviewees, Patricia Johanson, as stating, "Pregnancy is a magical time for me, during which I work the hardest, am happiest and seem to get the most done."[25] Johanson admitted that she attempted to be a "super-mom," taking her son with her into the woods as she created her site-specific land formations.[26] Similarly, the San Francisco-based artist Joan Brown pro-claimed in a 1975 interview for the Archives of American Art that she preferred family life despite the repercussions it had on her career.[27]

Brown, at the age of twenty-two, had her first New York show in 1960 at the George Staempfli Gallery to considerable acclaim. She became the youngest person included in the Whitney Museum of American Art's "Young America" exhibition and subsequently was featured in the popular magazines *Look*, *Cosmopolitan*, and *Mademoiselle*, receiving their "merit award" for her accomplishments as an artist.[28] In 1962, Brown gave birth to her only child, Noel, and through 1964 primarily painted large-scale canvases depicting this important aspect of her life, much to critics' dis-dain. Works such as *Noel and Bob*, 1964, drew uncritical or negative responses. Critic Jane Harrison, in her *Arts Magazine* review, stated that she "couldn't help wondering whether Miss Brown also hope[d] that the crudeness of pigment [would] act as an antidote for the excess sweetness of subject matter" and James H. Beck derided the same show in *Art News*, as a "homey affair," immediately relegating the work to the domestic and inferior space of women.[29] Such criticism, and her general disdain for the New York art world, caused Brown to break from dealer George Staempfli in 1965 and more or less abandon painting for a short time. This decision also may be due to the fact, that in the same year, Brown separated from sculptor Manuel Neri (Noel's father) and needed to find a consistent source of income that the art market did not provide.

This need is not unique, as several women artists needed to remove themselves somewhat from their artistic pursuits to support their families—regardless of whether or not they would be seen as "dilettantes." Elizabeth Murray, for example, stopped attending the few exhibitions and events to which artists were invited after the birth of her son Dakota in 1969. She noted, "I stayed home and had dinner with Dakota. That was the one thing clear in my mind that I had to do, or should do."[30] To support her son, she had two, maybe three teaching jobs that left little time for her art.[31] Regardless of her remote standing from art-related events, she found the years between her birth of her daughter Sophie in 1982 and Daisy in 1985 to be a "very fruitful time" in terms of her painting, noting that her paintings "got more and more pregnant" as they came off the wall, abstractly relating to her body and her full-fledged status as a mother.[32] Works such as *Beam*, 1982, prefigures Murray's trademark three-dimensional shape paintings, yet alludes to the interior female body (the uterus) and was created in the year of her daughter's, Daisy's, birth (Plate 1). This large-scale (*Beam* reaches a height over nine feet) pieced canvas monumentalizes the reproductive system, through abstraction and a bright color palette, but Murray leaves them open to plural inter-pretations.[33] One could interpret this openness in terms of Julia Kristeva's concept of the pluralistic maternal body that occludes the repression of the Symbolic.[34] However, even to thus pluralize a pregnant body as the work's subject matter would be to essen-tialize the work and reaffirm the staid relation of the feminine with the body.[35] Murray began receiving critical attention in the mid-1970s, although it varied throughout the years, and she did sometimes even reference her children, or parenting in the titles of her works—for example, *Dakota's Red*, 1971–72, and *Children Meeting*, 1978, but her canvases always retained a whimsical abstract nature. This, to some degree, sug-gests that allusions to one's parenting can become incorporated in one's work and be accepted into the institution, yet, as demonstrated through the case of Joan Brown, direct figuration resulted in reviews that undermined her artistic merit.

It was not unusual for women artists to ignore or otherwise omit one's motherhood from their art. To be considered a serious artist, women needed to create work that was 'interesting' but remained divorced from their domestic concerns and biological nature—it had to be 'cool' or removed from those aspects of the personal. As has been noted, it should have been no surprise to Lucy Lippard, that "no women deal-ing with their own bodies and biographies have introduced pregnancy or childbirth as a major image," when she constructed her survey of body art in 1976.[36] Lippard cites a few "cases" of parent related imagery, such as Mary Beth Edelson and Dennis Oppenheim, who performed ritual pieces with their children; the *Womanhouse* group performance of childbirth; and vaguely refers to women photographers who have cap-tured pregnant nudes. But, in sum, Lippard finds that these are the exceptions; thus she proposes that the "biological aspect of female creation is anathema to women who want to be recognized for their art."[37] To this day, works such as Judy Chicago's *The Dinner Party*, 1974–79, with its overt vaginal forms, is sometimes criticized for the reduction of women's accomplishments to female biology.[38] Chicago's subsequent *The Birth Project*, 1980–85, consisted of embroidered, stitched, and quilted images of birth designed by Chicago. Part of the process consisted of receiving birthing testi-monials from the women who took part in the project, but ultimately the goal of the project was to redress the omission of such images from art, and communicate the spiritual and natural power of woman as a collective entity. Chicago acknowledged, "I have come to recognize my destiny as an artist is tied up with the destiny of my sex," revealing that the struggle that many women artists faced was to some degree accepted by Chicago.[39] But it is necessary to point out that Chicago never experienced the birth process herself, as she remarked in a 1999 interview, "[women artists] talked about the conflicts that they experienced, conflicts that I myself didn't want to have to deal with, which is one of the reasons I never had children."[40] Considering how much criticism has been leveled at Chicago for her "womanly forms," it comes as both a surprise and yet is not unexpected that her feminist ideals precluded the presence of children in her life. Motherhood is generally understood as the ultimate embodiment of femininity, yet it can often be perceived, and physically become, limiting.

But these boundaries are relative to one's age and point in one's career. As Marie-Laure Bernadac has remarked, Louise Bourgeois was able to reference her role as mother quite directly, and even represent herself giving birth in an untitled work in 1941 because she worked in relative obscurity until the 1980s. Being 'discovered' later in life, this initial distance from the art world gave her the freedom to create art as she desired and raise a family, adopting an attitude towards artist-mothering that could only prove to be inspirational to the artists of later generations. As may be expected, Bourgeois' image of birth is much more psychologically charged than Chicago's later renditions. Bourgeois prominently figures the face, of both herself and her child as two individuals intertwined through the hair and body, rather than one that splits the maternal body in half, leaving nothing but an interior void (Figure 2.1).[41] Adopted into feminism as a grand matriarch of the movement, Bourgeois' perspective of mothering, and art, as seen in this early work, reveals the hybrid nature of artist-parents. Notably, Bourgeois once remarked that she considered her domestic life—her role as a spouse and a mother—as making her a better person and a better artist.[42] Indicating, perhaps, a potential for a critical edge, a standpoint from which to view the world and from which to create art that lies in the realm of the domestic.

In her reconsideration of "Why Have There Been No Great Women Artists?," Nochlin suggests the feminist movement altered the way that men approached art as well. She writes, "the recent emphasis on the body, the rejection of phallic control, the exploration of psychosexuality, and the refusal of the perfect, the self-expressive, the fixed, and the domineering are certainly to some degree implicated … with what women have been doing."[43] To consider the male artist as unfixed, imperfect, and as a parent concerned with the balance between family and professional life is to suggest,

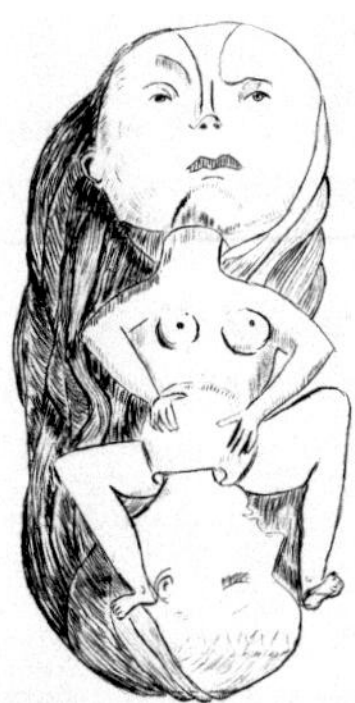

Figure 2.1 Louise Bourgeois, *Autobiographical Series* (detail), 1994. Portfolio of 14 etchings with drypoint and aquatint on paper. 58.4 × 40.6 × 1.9 cm. Photo: Christopher Burke. © The Easton Foundation/VAGA at ARS, NY.

and maybe even argue, that the binary relationship between artist and non-artist, man versus woman, has been upended by the feminist movement. The consideration of men as parents and artists has been somewhat obscured from the art world as well. Men have sometimes also found their children as a burden and a hindrance to their productivity—a prominent example is provided by Philip Guston, whose daughter, Musa Mayer, notably recounted her father's disdain of her presence in his studio in her memoir, *The Night Studio* (1988).[44] While Guston's own feelings about being a father are not the subject of the text, Mayer does suggest that the issue of fatherhood may be even more firmly rooted in stereotypes of artistic identity, rather than his unwillingness to be a 'good' father.

Mayer's statement is not to suggest that male artists universally conformed to artist stereotypes. For example, in 1983, Vance Gellert began the thirteen-year project,

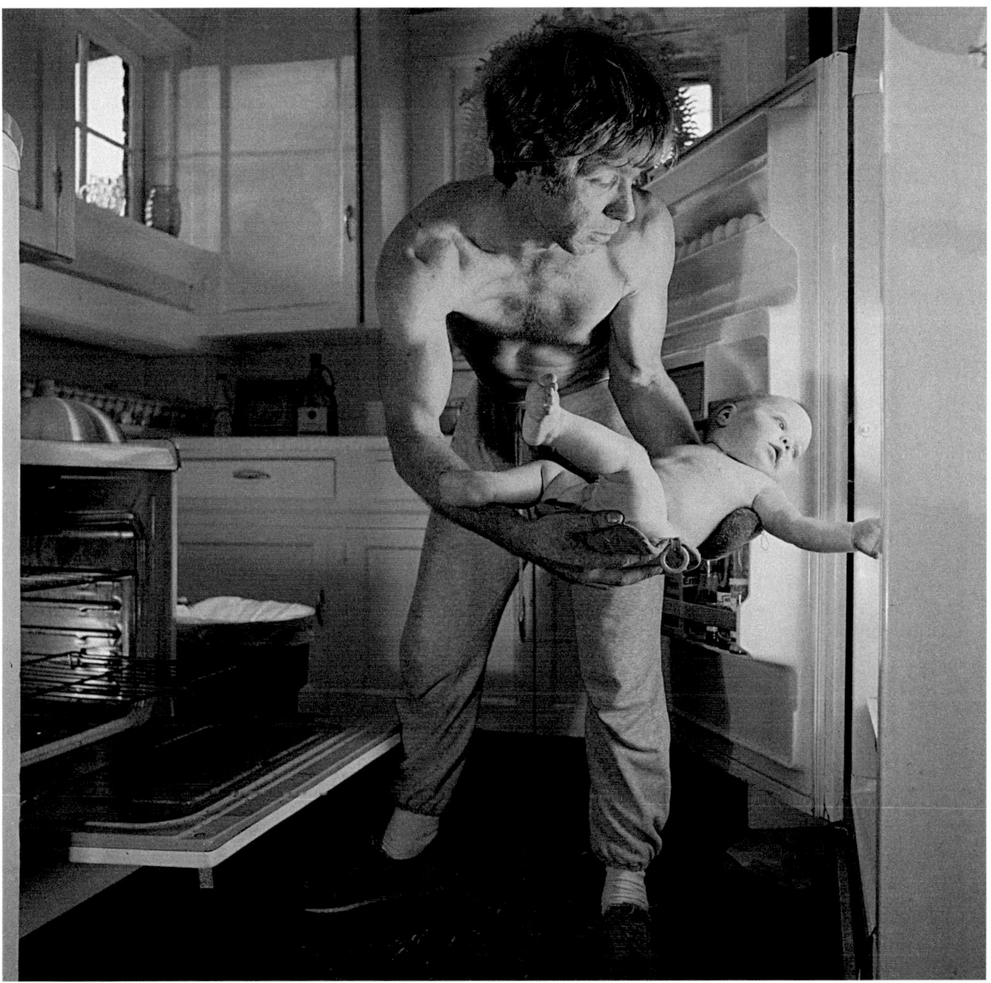

Figure 2.2 Vance and Carl Gellert, Untitled, 1983, from *CarlVision*, 1983–96. Color Photograph. Courtesy Vance Gellert.

CarlVision, which articulates his role as an artist and father. The series was prompted by the artist becoming the primary caregiver to his son while the child's mother was in medical school. Gellert asserts that the project was prompted by feelings of boredom and entrapment, but gave way to fun as "they collaborated to create fantasy from the real experience of being a dad, and of being a son."[45] The resulting images, taken primarily in the confined space of the home, poke fun at the stigmas of fathering, and often feature a television—one of the primary ways in which stereotypes about fatherhood are disseminated. In one particularly humorous untitled image, Gellert is shown in the kitchen between an open oven and refrigerator. Bent over and holding his son Carl with oven mitts, it appears as if Gellert has just taken him out of the oven—an allusion to gestation and birth—and is ready to chill him in the fridge (Figure 2.2). While Hirsch has interpreted this series as the photographer's erasure and replacement of the mother through the media of photography, I rather see this series as an artist-father's negotiation of paternity, domesticity, and caregiving and over time, the articulation of the father–son relationship.[46]

Dennis Oppenheim notably employed his children in his multi-part video-based project, *Transfer Drawings*, 1971, in which either he or his children drew on the back of the other, who then tried to mime—through the sense of touch—the image drawn on his or her own back, or a piece of paper. His incorporation of the family, and dissolution between the public artwork and private family life, serves nicely as a precursor to the videos of Guy Ben-Ner. Oppenheim believed that working with his children was a means of visually engaging the transfer of genetic data, as his children have some of his genetic traits, but these videos also reflect the father's role in children's education and learning.[47]

Thinking of the Child and Parenting

When considering the artist-parent, there may be some tendencies to read the term as suggesting a focus on the parents of artists and how parents have shaped the development of their talented children.[48] But this is not the scope of this project. Perhaps this misinterpretation occurs because there is an existing body of scholarship that considers the role of the father and the role of the mother in the development of an artist's identity, and has been applied to artists after the fact as much as it has been self-applied, as in the work of the late Louise Bourgeois, who herself was trained in psychoanalysis.[49] This discourse, while fruitful in certain contexts, often fails to include the relationship the artist has to her own child. Bourgeois herself highlights the popular and cultural interest in the family and parenting in the 2000s. In Bourgeois' work, *The Reticent Child* (2003), the artist reflects upon a lifetime of parenting and the disillusionment it garners for the entire family through the use of knit sculptures of a male, pregnant female, woman giving birth, and a child trapped in netting. An homage to her son Alain, whom she considered reticent, Bourgeois visualizes a retrospective view of family life, the pain of birth, for both the male and female, as well as the illusion of unity that the term 'family' creates. The inclusion of a distortion mirror reiterates the psychological charge and reinforces how changes in one's family life affect one's own art practice as well. For Bourgeois, it also reminds the viewer that the past often becomes distorted through memory.

Of course, there are earlier examples of psychoanalytic-based investigations, such as Mary Kelly's *Post-Partum Document* (1973–79), which explored the dissolution of the mother-child dyad through various artifacts, including her child's vests, fecal stains, feeding patterns, recorded speech, scribbles, and imprints of his hand. Through these 'documents,' Kelly indexically recorded the practical, social, and psychological relationship between mother and son, cast it, and presented it in the realm of the analyst, in a valiant attempt to remove all associations of sentimentality and kitsch from the relationship. *Documentation I*, for example, pairs her son's stained diaper liners with the meticulous documentation of the times, amounts, and types of food ingested, and an analysis of the stools according to the following key: 1- constipated, 2- normal, 3- not homogeneous, 4- loose, 5- diarrhoeal.[50] Kelly's systematic recording presents the mother as a scientist analyzing her experiment, notably lacking any external or visible emotional bond.

The denial of sentiment was a key strategy for women artists in the 1970s who desired to address their domestic labor. Conceptualism provided a means for artists such as Kelly and Martha Wilson to escape the overly sentimental and essentializing elements of art deemed "feminist" and epitomized by feminists like Judy Chicago. Wilson's *Chauvinistic Pieces* (1971), like Kelly's *Post-Partum Document*, avoided direct representation of the child and instead based the project in linguistic systems. For example:

Determined Piece: A woman selects a couple on the basis of I.Q. test scores (high or low) and raises their baby.
Unknown Piece: A woman under ether has a child in a large hospital. When she comes to, she is permitted to select the child she thinks is hers from among the babies in the nursery.
Double Piece: Two couples agree to have babies and trade them. The real parents are in no way permitted to interfere with the upbringing of their child.

Presented on two pages of typescript in the exhibition "Conceptual Art … The NSCAD Connection, 1967–73" at the Anna Leonowens Gallery at the Nova Scotia College of Art and Design, these three propositions (of eight total) reflect upon the alienation Wilson felt as a woman and an artist, articulating questions of genetics, gender roles, proprietary rights, and parental "authorship."[51] Because of their relation to the tangible world of parents and children, scholar Jayne Wark interprets these *Pieces* as Wilson's departure from the introspective nature of conceptual art and the metaphorical beginning of Wilson's interrogation of identity, both artistic and gendered. While this argument may hold true for Wilson's larger oeuvre, Wilson's own parenting does not seem to figure into the equation—establishing a line Wilson apparently refuses to cross.[52] To suddenly relate this work to the personal life would to some degree discredit the original intention of the work. However, some conceptual strategies did intentionally cross the boundaries of artist/mother. For example, in 1969, Mierle Laderman Ukeles proposed one part of her "Maintenance Art" exhibition *CARE* in a manifesto which highlighted the plural nature of her identity and labor:

A. *Part One: Personal*
I am an artist. I am a woman. I am a wife.
I am a mother. (Random order).
I do a hell of a lot of washing, cleaning, cooking,
renewing, supporting, preserving, etc. Also,
(up to now separately) I 'do' Art.

Now, I will simply do these maintenance everyday things, and flush them up to consciousness, exhibit them, as Art. I will live in the museum [as] I customarily do at home with my husband and my baby, for the duration of the exhibition. (Right? Or if you don't want me around at night I would come in every day) and do all these things as public Art activities: I will sweep and wax floors, dust everything, wash the walls (i.e. 'floor paintings, dust works, soap sculpture, wall-paintings') cook, invite people to eat, make agglomerations and dispositions of all functional refuse.

The exhibition area might look 'empty' of art, but it will be maintained in full public view.

MY WORKING WILL BE THE WORK

Published in the January 1971 issue of *Artforum*, this manifesto caught the eye of Lucy Lippard who then invited Ukeles to carry out some of the duties she proposed in the Wadsworth Atheneum in Hartford, Connecticut. The performance *Hartford Wash: Washing, Tracks, Maintenance*, 1973, consisted of Ukeles working both inside and outside of the museum—she dusted display cases, scrubbed floors and mopped stairs. She performed these duties on her hands and knees yet did nothing to announce that this was a performance, putting the very question of public versus private labor at the forefront of her work. However, it is prudent to note that Ukeles' desire to create "Maintenance Art" stemmed from an unseemly bit of advice she received from a male mentor while she was a student at the Pratt Institute—because she was pregnant and about to become a mother, this mentor said Ukeles could no longer be an artist.[53] Confronted with another's opinion that she could only be a mother, Ukeles' "Maintenance Art Manifesto," linguistically, if not practically, enmeshed her role as an artist and a mother.

In 1968, the year that Ukeles gave birth to her first child Yael, Léa Lublin, a Polish-born artist working in Paris, physically enacted what Ukeles would later propose. In *Mon Fils*, 1968, Lublin invited the public to witness her tend to her seven-month-old son, Nicholas, in the gallery of the Musée d'Art Moderne de la Ville de Paris. As one of her first performance works, Lublin effectively broke the barrier between art and mothering and suggested that childcare itself could be considered an art form. This act has recently been read as aligned with the emergence of second-wave feminism in France and the student revolts of May 1968.[54] Lublin described the work as "moving a moment of my daily life to an artistic venue."[55] But, this instance seems to be an anomaly within feminist art history, and completely absent from the artistic practices of Eastern and Central European artists.

Under the Soviet regime, artists such as Rimma Gerlovina and Valery Gerlovin broached issues of gender identity in works like *Zoo—Homo Sapiens* (1977). In this project the Gerlovins caged themselves as representatives of the male and female species to explore what Kati Chukhrov terms a "paradisiacal unit."[56] Exploring the issues of motherhood and parenthood, however, seemed to be of little interest to these and other artists whose political and social circumstances were dominated by totalitarian forces, at least until the late 1980s. There are exceptions of course. In the 1970s, Czech sculptor Kurt Gebauer incorporated his eldest son into his work, both through sculpture and photography.[57] But in some instances the propaganda machine of late communism caused artists to respond with more gusto. For example, in a series of photographs from 1980–81, Polish artist Adam Rzepecki investigated the male body in relation to maternity. In one, titled *Double Pregnancy*, 1980, Rzepecki poses with his belly exaggerated and touching the pregnant belly of his wife. Through the black and white image and their dark clothing, their bodies temporality merge and unify. But, perhaps the most compelling image from this period of his work is *Project of the Father Pole Memorial*, 1981 (Figure 2.3). In this photograph, Rzepecki is barechested, seated with his infant child attempting to latch to his non-lactating nipple. As he gazes down on this child in the fashion of the *Madonna lactans*, the artist makes a poignant statement about the absurdity of the expectations demanded of the Polish Mother as propagated by the late communist regime in Poland.[58] The push for women to embody and perform the Polish Mother, as discussed in Chapter Three, affected not only women but also men well into the twenty-first century.

Similarly, beginning in 1985, the Slovakian artist Ľubo Stacho began to turn to photographs of his parents, his own young children, and other families to stage new portraits that explore the multigenerational and complex relationship one develops within and with other families. His work *Family IV 1983–1995* (1995) depicts the artist, his wife, and two children standing before a wall that has photographs of the family at previous times (including one in which his wife is pregnant with their second child),

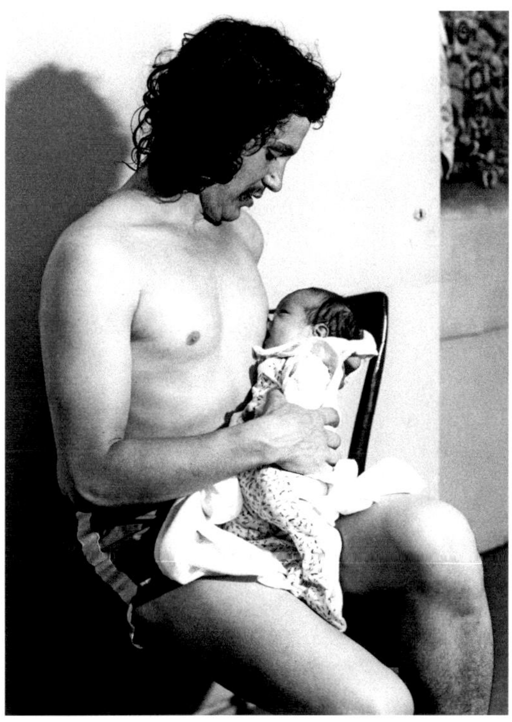

Figure 2.3 Adam Rzepecki, *Project of the Father Pole Memorial*, 1981. Photograph. Courtesy Dawid Radziszewski Gallery, Warsaw.

while Stacho holds a reproduction of Picasso's late Blue Period painting, *La Vie*, 1903. Stacho clearly draws an association between his own family and the complicated relationship of the individuals depicted in *La Vie*. The work depicts Picasso's best friend, Carlos Casagemas and his lover, Germaine, who eventually rejects him on the left and spurs him to suicide, and an image of a woman holding a child on the right, suggesting Germaine's future motherhood. Stacho's inclusion of this loaded work certainly evokes the cycle of life and death that accompany the structure of the family.

The 2009 exhibition catalog for the Museum Moderner Kunst Stiftung Ludwig Wien, *Gender Check: Femininity and Masculinity in the Art of Eastern Europe*, reveals that images of mothers and children were not completely absent from art prior to the 1980s in Eastern Europe. Artists such as Zenta Dzividzinska, Zorka Ságlová, and Moysey Vainstein prominently featured women and children in their paintings and photographs and thus engaged with personal and broader cultural ideas about motherhood.[59]

By the late eighties, the experimental medium of video art allowed American artists such as Martha Rosler to confront issues of parenting, whether or not the artist was a parent herself, head on. Rosler's *Born to Be Sold: Martha Rosler Reads the Strange Case of Baby $/M*, 1988, took surrogate motherhood and parental authorship as its subject, recounting the very public court case of Mary Beth Whitehead (Figure 2.4).[60]

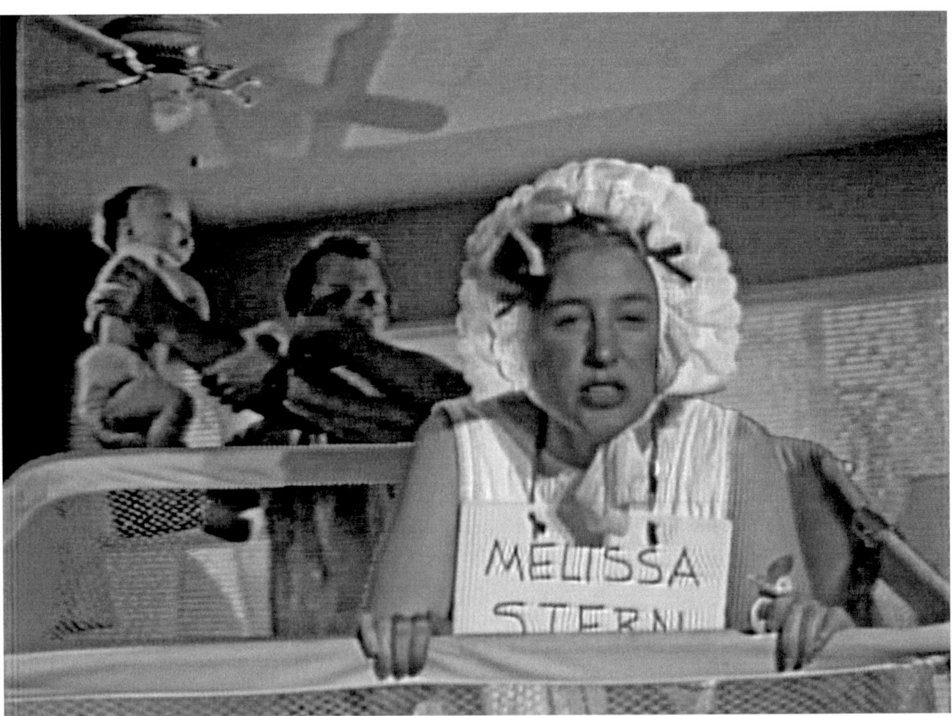

Figure 2.4 Martha Rosler, *Born to Be Sold: Martha Rosler Reads the Strange Case of Baby $/M*, 1988. Color video with sound, 35 minutes, 18 seconds. © Martha Rosler. Courtesy the artist and Mitchell-Innes & Nash, New York.

Whitehead was hired to be a surrogate by William and Elizabeth Stern. In less than twenty-four hours after giving birth to a girl, Whitehead regretted the arrangement and asked for the baby back, threatening suicide. The Sterns provided Whitehead the baby. Whitehead then subsequently refused to return the child, leaving the state of New Jersey. This situation, taken to the New Jersey Superior Court in 1987, and the Supreme Court of New Jersey in 1988, marks one of the first cases exploring the sale of children under the guise of surrogacy, the familial identity of children born under surrogacy, and the class issues inherent in the regime of parenting—Whitehead, from a working-class background, named the baby Sarah, while the Sterns, an upper-class couple, named her Melissa, and she was identified as "Baby M" for the court case. Rosler's reading of the case, recorded in collaboration with the media-activist collective Paper Tiger Television, marks one of the first artistic reflections on the politics of parenting in the contemporary period. Posing as various key players in the controversy, and reading the various statements made in the media, newspapers, and courtrooms, Rosler demonstrates sympathy for the birth mother, viewing the case as much about social class as it was about legal parenting rights. Interestingly, this led to accusations of Rosler's essentialism and Luddism.[61] Rosler, making no remarks about her own relationship to parenting, garnered pejoratives for her acknowledgment of the social and class issues tied to parenthood. According to Rosler, the video has aired among medical and nursing communities as well as in the art world and classroom environment, who generally "appreciate the defense of the 'poor woman' and woman of color," though "relatively few applaud the work for its class analyses in respect to norms, moves, access to resources, identification, and legal and journalistic bias."[62] Rosler was able to investigate in this video the transformation of the political and social structures of parenting in the 1980s and reveals the heightened mass media appeal of childcare issues, heralding a new generation of artists who examine the political debates of the family.

While Rosler investigated these issues from a distanced perspective (neither she nor anyone she knew was directly involved with the agreement or the trials that followed), Sally Mann, on the other hand, received very direct personal criticism from the media and institutions of parenting for her series of photographs, *Immediate Family*, 1984–91. To Mann, *Immediate Family* was a series of photographs representing the summertime activities of her children, Emmett, Jessie, and Virginia. To the public, they were pornographic for their nudity, for the children's dirtiness, and most provocatively, their sensuousness. Mann clearly avoided the stigma that Joan Brown encountered but, in its stead, received much worse criticism; that of the irresponsible mother. The name-calling endured by Mann demonstrates the other end of the kitsch/sentiment spectrum—if one's depiction of one's one child does not conform with general standards of public display, the artist is a "bad" parent.[63] These notions of good and bad parenting are caught between the cultural contexts of each artist, and the perspective of the viewing public. For the artists discussed in this project, nationalism is closely tied to stereotypes of motherhood and, more broadly, gender roles. For Elżbieta Jabłońska, the dominant Catholic presence in Poland directly affects how she represents and performs motherhood in her artistic practice; for Guy Ben-Ner, the avoidance of a strict Israeli nationalism propels him to turn to foreign examples of fatherhood as evinced through mostly American and French artists and filmmakers.

Shifting Identities and Spaces

The aseptic artistic relationship to parenting must be partly attributed to shifting definitions of what it meant to be an artist. This can be traced to clichéd notions of artistic genius throughout art history, and specifically in relation to the old masters. But more relevantly, revisions of the artist's identity burgeoned in the postwar period. While somewhat simplistic, for better or worse, Jackson Pollock has historically epitomized the 'cool' and troubled artist, who spent time drinking and conversing, free of practical concerns, and his image often remains fixed in the popular culture's imagination when thinking of the 'artist.'[64] This and the changes in the definition of what could constitute a studio—the place of one's artistic creativity and invention—are two underlying factors in the formulation of artist-parent identity. With the rise of alternative and avant-garde art practices, the art studio was no longer a requirement for an artist to be considered serious. Artists, especially those who were parents, could use a space within the home as their creative space as conceptual and performance artists moved outside and into non-traditional spaces.

Avoiding figuration, Pollock represented the artist whose artistic merits could be only realized in the solitary confines of his studio. It is notable that what critics considered his greatest works were created at his Springs, Easthampton, Long Island studio, a converted barn removed from every possible distraction of the home and city. The concept of the studio, the isolating and enjoyable zone traditionally marked as exclusive for men, originates from Enlightenment humanism, and derives from the Latin *studium*, to connote a "special space as well as a contemplative activity or a concentrated frame of mind."[65] It is a space of individuality, of a singular creation, that becomes tied to the artist's name, his identity. This notion becomes problematized under feminism, for, as Virginia Woolf has written, women's lack of a "room of one's own" reinforced their inferior statuses as artists.[66] As Anna Chave has noted in the case of Lee Krasner, women artists had to find a different space for their creative endeavors that did not always condone the unbridled activity of the studio.[67] Jackson Pollock, the space of the studio, and the potentiality of a specific space for artistic activity was inherent to the success of the artist. To lack proper space for artistic labor complicated the relationship between what was life and art. As Ann E. Gibson has noted, both male and female artists encountered difficulties maintaining their artistic labor and domestic duties. For example, Richard Pousette-Dart had Betty Parsons and the other painters in her gallery turn a cold shoulder to him when he began raising a family. In an interview with Gibson, Pousette-Dart recounted that Parsons told him that he had "no right having children," that he should sit in his studio and "devote everything" to his painting. Of course, Pousette-Dart did not follow this advice; he became a father, moved to the country, and subsequently was excluded from the inner circle of Abstract Expressionism.[68]

Artists transformed the studio and idea of the artistic identity in the 1960s, and again in the new millennium. This rationale is inspired by Caroline Jones' important text, *Machine in the Studio: Constructing the Postwar American Artist*, in which she recounts the antiquated romance of the studio, and the identity it garnered, in the early postwar years. Jones asserts how these ideas and spaces were changed, both verbally and nonverbally, by artists such as Frank Stella who alternately postured himself as an executive and a housepainter; Andy Warhol who wanted to be, and claimed he was, a "machine" with his formation of The Factory; and Robert Smithson, whose post-studio practices presented the artist as an "industrial-scale geological agent," transforming the concept of the studio eternally.[69] The studio, as Jones and others have noted, contributes largely to romantic notions of the artist and his genius and has its origins in nineteenth-century Romanticism. Scholars have attempted to document the artist, whether it be Picasso, Matisse, or Duchamp, in the space where "it" happens—unbridled creativity, passion, genius. Jones' study, focusing on the sixties, notes the transformation the studio underwent in terms of mechanization, industry, and conceptions of the "artist" in postwar America. As this study does not focus exclusively on American artists, it is important to understand that the unhinging of the studio similarly occurred in Europe and elsewhere, though often under much different pretenses. The Moscow-based group, Collective Actions, forewent the studio to stage performances and actions in somewhat remote fields in hope of evading the social regime. Elsewhere in Europe, the Situationist International produced interventions to evoke revolutionary thought and commentary on everyday actions. These artistic goals could only be realized outside of the conventional artist's studio.

To this end, the critically acclaimed video artist Pierre Huyghe asserted in an interview with Hans-Ulrich Obrist, "The studio is everywhere. It is with me. I am working in my studio right now as we are speaking."[70] The studio is no longer exclusively a space of one's own, but can be, rather, a state of mind that co-exists with all of one's actions.[71] This idea, which was seen to some degree in the feminist projects of Ukeles and Lublin, is interrogated fully by Elżbieta Jabłońska.

The tasks of artists, much like parents, are traditionally considered to be quite autonomous, private, and individual. Conveying the price of maintaining the charade of the 'artist' in the 1940s, Harold Rosenberg asserted that artists had no community and were isolated to an extreme that was unlike any other field of cultural production.[72] While Rosenberg's statement is problematic, at least, and completely erroneous, at worst, artist-parents are often doubly excluded as they often deal with the stigma of asserting a specific artistic identity, the isolating nature of parenting, and struggle with the demands or lack of appropriate child-care.

In 1974, a group of artist-mothers who met via their involvement with the Women's Building in Los Angeles formed the collective Mother Art. Minus a brief mention in Lucy Lippard's, "The Pains and Pleasures of Rebirth," it has been rarely discussed until Andrea Liss's study, *Feminist Art and the Maternal* (2009). Liss recounts the installation and performance activities of these mother-artists in the 1970s and their alliance to its current iteration—M.A.M.A., Mother Artists Making Art.[73] Joining together to "support each other in salvaging, theorizing, and representing through artworks, [their] experience of being mothers," M.A.M.A. attempts to publicly transform conceptions of that artist and mother through its actions in the Los Angeles area. Focused solely on women's experience, M.A.M.A. is an important counterpoint to the Prague collective of both male and female artists who call themselves Mothers and Fathers.

Political change and the culture wars of the late 1980s and early 1990s ushered many more artistic voices expressing their maternal and paternal status. Artists such as Renée Cox redefined the family image, and mother and son imagery through her monumental *Yo Mama!* series (1993) and later, through *The American Family Series* of photographs (2001). In these images Cox presents her own nude black body and proudly asserts her own identity as a black mother of mixed-race sons. However, one of the most iconic images of the artist mother of the contemporary period is probably Catherine Opie's *Self-Portrait/Nursing* (2004).[74] In this image, Opie harkens to her earlier work *Self-Portrait/Pervert* (1994), in which she had the word "pervert" carved into her chest. While the latter work reflected her queer identity and engagement in San Francisco's queer leather subculture, the former reflects her new identity as a queer mother. The image asserts a transformed domestic model of the family, a subject which she previously explored in the series *Domestic* (1995–98), which documented the lives of lesbian couples and families from diverse background and locations across the United States to articulate the new family structure.

It is in this landscape of feminist, collective, and queer makers that Elżbieta Jabłońska, Guy Ben-Ner, and Mothers and Fathers assert their work as artist-parents. As the identity of the artist and the spaces of art-making shift, these artists articulate artist-parenting as a practice of self-inquiry, of demonstrating care toward others, sometimes poking fun at static gender roles, and at others, deeply investigating what it means to care for another human and help them grow.

Notes

1   Nochlin notes that a woman artist "must in any case have a good strong streak of rebellion in her to make her way in the world of art at all, rather than submitting to the socially approved role of wife and mother, the only role to which every social institution consigns her automatically. It is only by adopting, however covertly, the 'masculine' attributes of single-mindedness, concentration, tenaciousness and absorption in ideas and craftsmanship for their own sake, that women have succeeded, and continue to succeed, in the world of art." Linda Nochlin, "Why Have There Been No Great Women Artists?" *Art News* 69 (January 1971): 22–39.

2   Nochlin notes that in 1971, ten out of eighty-four articles in art periodicals were dedicated to women, nine of which were included in the special Woman Issue in *Art News*. See Nochlin, "'Why Have There Been No Great Women Artists?' Thirty Years After," in *Women Artists at the Millennium*, ed. Carol Armstrong and M. Catherine de Zegher (Cambridge: The MIT Press, 2006), 21.

3   Ibid., 21–28.

4   Lucy Lippard to Jim Fitzsimmons, December 11, 1964, Lucy Lippard Papers, AAA. Quoted in Julia Bryan-Wilson, *Art Workers: Radical Practice in the Vietnam Era* (Berkeley: University of California Press, 2009), 127.

5   Ibid., 127.

6   Ibid., 154.

7   The problem of financial compensation and women's work was of great interest in the 1970s, being a primary focus of radical feminists. In addition, the International Coalition for Wages for Housework demanded a socialized economy that paid women for housework, noting that two-thirds of the world's work was performed by women, and with only about five percent of it compensated. For more information, see Ibid., 128–30.

8   Television programs such as *Romper Room* and domestic magazines *Ladies Home Journal*, *Parents Magazine*, and *Better Homes and Gardens* both verbally and visually construct the place of the woman in the home through their articles and advertisements. Similarly, childrearing experts, pediatricians, and family practice doctors typically assumed, if not opined, that the woman should stay home to raise her children and should only work if she had an "ideal arrangement for her child's care," meaning a grandmother or other close female figure could assume her duties. See, for example, Benjamin Spock, *The Common Sense Book of Baby and Child Care* (New York: Duell, Sloan, and Pearce, 1957), 771.

9   As Alice Neel complained, a woman who halted her artistic activity for motherhood lost her art or "just [became] a dilettante." See Alice Neel interview with Cindy Nemser, in *Art Talk: Conversations with 12 Women Artists* (New York: Charles Scribner's Sons, 1975), 125.

10   Andrea Liss, "Black Bodies in Evidence: Maternal Visibility in Renée Cox's Family Portraits," in *The Familial Gaze*, ed. Marianne Hirsch (Hanover: Dartmouth College, 1999), 281.

11 Emma Amos, "Forum on Motherhood, Art, and Apple Pie," in *M/E/A/N/I/N/G: An Anthology of Artist's Writings, Theory, and Criticism*, eds. Susan Bee, Mira Schor, and Amelia Jones (Durham: Duke University Press, 2000), 254.

12 Grace Hartigan, interview with Cindy Nemser, *Art Talk*, 154.

13 Ann Temkin, "Alice Neel: Self and Others," in *Alice Neel* (New York: Harry N. Abrams in association with the Philadelphia Museum of Art, 2000), 15. See also, Neel, interview with Eleanor Munro, *Originals: American Women Artists* (New York: Da Capo Press, 2000), 128.

14 Pamela Allara, "'Mater' of Fact: Alice Neel's Pregnant Nudes," *American Art* 8 no. 2 (Spring 1994): 6.

15 Carolyn Carr attributes this phase to Neel not being "burdened or overwhelmed by motherhood herself," and in her master's thesis, "Images of Pregnancy in Alice Neel's Paintings," Juliea Shriver claims that Neel painted her pregnant daughters-in-law because they were able to fill "a void in Neel's life" that stemmed from her inability to raise her daughters. See Carolyn Carr, *Alice Neel: Women* (New York: Rizzoli Publishing, 2002), 13; and, Juliea Shriver, "Images of Pregnancy in Alice Neel's Paintings," (MA Thesis, California State University, Fullerton, 2004), 97–99.

16 Anne M. Wagner, "'Alice Neel: Painted Truths' Whitechapel Gallery, London," *Artforum International* 49 no. 4 (December 2010): 207.

17 Statement quoted in Allara, "'Mater' of Fact," 9.

18 Susan Jenkins, "Niki de Saint Phalle," in *WACK! Art and the Feminist Revolution*, ed. Cornelia Butler (Cambridge: The MIT Press, 2007), 292.

19 Larry Rivers' daughters were recently in the news for their request to suppress videos from their father's archive at New York University. Rivers, who died in 2002, made videos and films of his adolescent daughters while naked or topless and according to the *New York Times* report, interviewed them about their budding breasts and took close-up shots of their genitals—from 1976 to 1981 for a work he called "Growing." According to Clarice, "What Larry said was that it would belong to them, as a record that when they got older they could look back at. It wasn't a huge thing. It's become huge, because they can't get back what was given to them." Kate Taylor, "Artist's Daughter Wants Videos Back," *New York Times*, July 8, 2010, C1.

20 Jenkins, "Niki de Saint Phalle," 293.

21 Anne M. Wagner, *Mother Stone: The Vitality of Modern British Sculpture* (New Haven and London: Yale University Press, 2005), 168–69; originally noted in Margaret Gardiner, *Barbara Hepworth: A Memoir* (London: Lund Humphries, 1994), 11.

22 Emin makes this statement in light of the recent atrocities in Palestine and the masses of children being buried every day. Tracey Emin, "I felt that, in return for my children's souls, I had been given my success," *The Independent*, January 29, 2009.

23 Stefanie Marsh, "Tracey Emin: Why I Dread a Childless, Sexless Future," *Times Online*, July 16, 2008.

24 Marsh, "Tracey Emin: Why I Dread a Childless, Sexless Future." See also Rebecca Baillie, "Tracey Emin: Ideas of Melancholy and Maternity," *Studies in the Maternal* 3 no. 1 (2011), www.mamsie.bbk.ac.uk.

25 Eleanor Munro, *Originals: American Women Artists* (New York: Da Capo Press, 2000), 36.

26 Patricia Johanson, interview with Munro, *Originals*, 467.

27 Joan Brown, transcribed interview with Paul Karlstrom, 1 July 1975, *Archives of American Art*, Smithsonian Institution, Washington, DC, 25.

28 Charlotte Wilard, "Women of American Art," *Look* 24 (27 September 1960): 70–74; Jean Lipman and Cleve Gray, "The Amazing Inventiveness of Women Painters," *Cosmopolitan* 151 (October 1961): 68; and "Mlle's Next Word: Speculations," *Mademoiselle* 55 no. 3 (January 1963): 29.

29 Jane Harrison, "Joan Brown," *Arts Magazine* 38 (March 1964): 64; and James H. Beck, "Joan Brown," *Art News* 63 no. 1 (March 1964): 10.

30 Elizabeth Murray, interview with Robert Storr, *Elizabeth Murray* (New York: Museum of Modern Art, 2005), 127.

31 Ibid., 190.

32 Ibid., 188.
33 Murray asserted that to read only uterine shapes in her work would be to "close it down" and that is "not what [she] want[s]." Ibid., 188.
34 Reading *Beam* in Kristeva's terms, I see Murray's use of multiple conjoined panels to create the complete uterine shape as a means of unfixing the perceived singularity of the maternal body. See Julia Kristeva, "Motherhood According to Giovanni Bellini," *Desire in Language: A Semiotic Approach to Literature and Art*, ed. Leon S. Roudiez (New York: Columbia University Press, 1980), 237–70.
35 Ann Eden Gibson articulates Kristeva's postulation of the maternal body in order to fully explore the gendered readings of monochrome painting. See Ann Eden Gibson, "Color and Difference in Abstract Painting: The Ultimate Case of Monochrome," in *The Feminism and Visual Culture Reader*, ed. Amelia Jones (New York: Routledge, 2003), 192–204. For Gibson's discussion of Kristeva, see pp. 200–01.
36 Lucy Lippard, "The Pains and Pleasures of Rebirth: European and American Women's Body Art," *Art in America* 64 no. 3 (May–June 1976): 73–81.
37 Ibid.
38 See Amelia Jones, ed. *Sexual Politics: Judy Chicago's Dinner Party in Feminist Art History* (Los Angeles: University of California Press, 1996).
39 The Birth Project Newsletter, Fall 1981, Judy Chicago Papers, The Schlesinger Library on the History of Women in America, Radcliffe Institute for Advanced Study, Harvard University, Cambridge, MA, 57.28.
40 Judy Chicago, interview with John W. Whitehead, "Women and Art," *Gadfly*, online magazine (Nov./Dec. 1999).
41 Bourgeois used the 1941 drawing as material for the prints, *Autobiographical Series*, 1993–94.
42 Bourgeois' response to "Sixty-One Questions" from Alex Rafael Krasilovsky as student research in Dr. Lenore Weitzman's course at Yale University, 1971, reprinted in *Louise Bourgeois: Destruction of the Father Reconstruction of the Father: Writings and Interviews 1923–1997*, eds. Marie-Laure Bernadac and Hans-Ulrich Obrist (Cambridge: The MIT Press, 1998; second printing, 2000), 95. Bourgeois added that as a part of this hybrid role, "it has kept me away from [her children]."
43 Nochlin, "'Why Have There Been No Great Women Artists?' Thirty Years Later," 28.
44 Mayer includes several passages that recount her memories of exclusion from and by her father. See Musa Mayer, *The Night Studio: A Memoir of Philip Guston by his Daughter* (New York: Knopf, 1988).
45 Vance and Carl Gellert, *CarlVision* Project Statement, 2014, www.vancegellert.com/projects3.php#
46 Hirsch, *Family Frames*, 172.
47 Dennis Oppenheim, *Dennis Oppenheim: Retrospective-Works 1967–77* (Montreal: Musée d'art contemporain, 1978), 62.
48 See for example, Lisa Tickner, "Mediating Generation: The Mother–Daughter Plot," in *Women Artists at the Millennium*, eds., Carol Armstrong and M. Catherine de Zegher (Cambridge, MA: The MIT Press, 2006), 85–120.
    85–120, which discusses the role of paternity, both familial and artistic, in the life and work of Rachel Whiteread.
49 See Mignon Nixon, *Fantastic Reality: Louise Bourgeois and a Story of Modern Art* (Cambridge: The MIT Press, 2005), 4–7.
50 Mary Kelly, *Post-Partum Document*, Documentation I: Analyzed fecal stains and feeding charts, Ref. 1–28F (London, Boston, Melbourne and Henley: Routledge & Kegan Paul, 1983), 9.
51 Wilson's project is discussed in terms of conceptual art and feminism by Jayne Wark. See Jayne Wark, "Conceptual Art and Feminism: Martha Rosler, Adrian Piper, Eleanor Antin, and Martha Wilson," *Woman's Art Journal* 22 no. 1 (Spring–Summer 2001): 48; and, Jayne Wark, "Martha Wilson: Not Taking It at Face Value," *Camera Obscura* 15, no. 3 (2000): iv–33.
52 Wark, "Martha Wilson: Not Taking It at Face Value," 5.
53 Liss, *Feminist Art and the Maternal*, 51.

54 Catherine Spencer, "Acts of Displacement: Lea Lublin's *Mon fils*, May '68, and Feminist Psychosocial Revolt," *Oxford Art Journal* 40 no.1 (March 2017): 69.

55 Linda Theung, "Léa Lublin," in *WACK!*, 262.

56 Keti Chukhrov, "In the Trap of Utopia's Sublime: Between Ideology and Subversion," in *Gender Check: Femininity and Masculine in the Art of Eastern Europe* (Cologne: Walther König, 2009), 34.

57 See Lenka Klodová, "About Children," *Umělec* 1 (2005).

58 Adam Rzepecki, *Adam Rzepecki, 2016 Portfolio* (Dawid Radziszewski Gallery, 2016), np.

59 In particular, Zenta Dzividzinska, an artist from Latvia, produced a series of photographs titled *Melnbaltais (Black & White)*, 1966–70, which featured a woman breastfeeding and interacting with her child in a rural setting.

60 The first incarnation of Rosler's interest in this case occurred in 1987 when Rosler gave a keynote speech on motherhood and representation, focusing on the case of "Baby M" at the Society for Photographic Education—an event that was sponsored by the Women's Caucus. See Catherine de Zegher, ed., *Martha Rosler: Positions in the Life World* (Cambridge: The MIT Press, 1998), 103.

61 Martha Rosler, "Place, Position, Power, Politics," in *Decoys and Disruptions: Selected Writings 1975–2001* (Cambridge: The MIT Press, 2004), 365.

62 Ibid.

63 This is an important and complicated issue that is beyond the scope of this project. 'Dirty' children can be cute, but sexuality, on the other hand, is not considered 'natural' and thus suggests the imposition of the photographer.

64 Caroline Jones identifies the postwar American artist as "an isolated, angst-ridden man, whose solitude in the studio was an article of faith (for artist, critic, and viewer), crucial to the experience of the work of art and the cultural construction of the artist." Caroline Jones, *The Machine in the Studio: Constructing the Postwar American Artist* (Chicago: University of Chicago Press, 1996), xiv.

65 Ibid., 3.

66 See Virginia Woolf, *A Room of One's Own* (London: Leonard and Virginia Woolf at the Hogarth Press, 1929).

67 Anna Chave, "Pollock and Krasner: Script and Postscript," *Res* 24 (Autumn 1993): 95–111.

68 Ann E. Gibson, *Abstract Expressionism: Other Politics* (New Haven: Yale University Press, 1997), 143.

69 Jones, *Machine in the Studio*, xvi.

70 Pierre Huyghe, interview with Hans-Ulrich Obrist, "I Jedi," *Point of View: An Anthology of the Moving Image*. Electronic Arts Intermix. DVD, 2004.

71 Feminist scholarship often cites Virginia Woolf's essay, "A Room of One's Own" in terms of thinking about the studio and women. This concept is still important, but not as much as it once was.

72 Rosenberg wrote: "Attached neither to a community not to one another, these painters experience a unique loneliness of a depth that is reached perhaps nowhere else in the world." See Harold Rosenberg, "Introduction to 'Six American Artists,'" *Possibilities* 1 no. 1 (Winter 1947–48): 75.

73 Liss, *Feminist Art and the Maternal*, 75.

74 As such, the work was used as the cover art for Liss' *Feminist Art and the Maternal* and is referenced in many exhibitions on maternal art.

3 Superwoman, Supermother, or Polish Mother? Elżbieta Jabłońska's Artistic Negotiation of Motherhood

Elżbieta Jabłońska's career as an artist has been considerably intertwined with her identity as a woman and her role as a parent. She presents an ironic commentary on the situation and status of women in Poland through her art, which includes photographs, installations, sculptures, and performances—and many of those incorporate or negotiate the circumstances of people living in Poland and can be interpreted as containing a maternal element—with either direct references or suggestions of it. Born in 1970, Jabłońska attended Nicholas Copernicus University in Torun, Poland, receiving her Master of Arts degree in 1995. It was during her studies that she became aware of the early feminist works by artists like Alina Szapocznikow, Natalia LL, and Maria Pinińska-Bereś, all of whom engaged with women's issues in their sculptures, photographs, and performances.[1] These artists were unique in their exploration of the politics surrounding the female body, consumerism, and sexuality. Alina Szapocznikow (1926–73) was a Polish sculptor known for her innovative sculptures combining her (and later, her son's) body and everyday objects, such as *Lampe & Bouche (Illuminated Lips)* (1966). Szapocznikow posthumously received international acclaim, but was quite well known within Poland prior to this success.[2] Natalia LL (Lach-Lachowicz), born in 1937, is known for her conceptual projects, photographs, and videos that deal with consumerism and sexuality, such as *Consumer Art* (1972), which documented the artist suggestively consuming a banana. Maria Pinińska-Bereś (1931–99) created three-dimensional works that engaged with issues of female sexuality, such as the 1972 work *Is a Woman a Human Being?*, which features the hollow torso of a woman bisected by a sign that asks, "Data Produkcji…Data Ważności…?" or "date of production…date of expiration?" In such works, Pinińska-Bereś questions not only women's reproductive cycles but also the long-term value that women have in society. Inspired by the feminist tendencies of these women artists, Jabłońska's work similarly engages with gender, notions of the domestic, and issues of female identity as it is related to the maternal. Early work by Jabłońska investigated the human figure but in abstracted form—for one of her early exhibitions she created a system of signs that described different emotions.[3]

In 1997, after giving birth to her son, Antek, the artist's work shifted to clearly engage issues of the artist-parent identity, its challenges and dilemmas. Jabłońska noted, "it was starting my own family that gave me an impulse to adopt a specific approach to art."[4] Confronted by her childcare obligations, time dedicated to art-making became restricted, confined.[5] Struggling to balance the two, Jabłońska took advantage of the short moments she had free—usually when her son was sleeping—to create small works on cardboard. The series, *When Antek Sleeps,* became one of her first works from after her son's birth. Consisting of small drawings created in pastel, paint, and pen, their subject matter can be roughly categorized into two major themes: family and domestic objects. The family theme is comprised of variations of the same figures—a man, woman, and child. Jabłońska illustrated them performing mundane activities like sleeping or sitting at a table. The second is comprised of domestic objects—she drew individual items such as radiators, televisions, and hot plates, which together with the images of the nuclear family, show how Jabłońska found a way to creatively process and take advantage of her new domestic role.[6] Jabłońska found inspiration from her everyday life. She proclaimed that both the "rewarding and tiring moments" spent with her child caused her to create these images.[7] Presented in a solo exhibition at Mógz in Bydgoszcz, she titled the exhibition, *The Polish Mother Presents No. 1, Home Stories: Pictures of the cycle* When Antek Sleeps (1998). This exhibition marks the first occasion in which the artist publicly proclaimed herself as the *matka polka*, or Polish Mother. The Polish Mother is a stereotype that constitutes an equally heralded and maligned identity for women in Poland, thus heightening the artistic risk Jabłońska undertook in naming herself as such and setting the stage for her public identity as an artist-parent.

Jabłońska negotiates the artist-parent identity in several ways. Her work, at times, seems to wholeheartedly or ironically embrace notions of motherhood (*Supermother*, 2001*)* and domesticity (*Through the Stomach to the Heart*, 1999–05 and the inter-related *Kitchen*, 2004–13) and at other times, appears to deny overt maternal imagery such as in *New Life* (*Nowe Zycie*, 2010). Yet as I will argue, each position can be related to a maternal subjectivity or modality that structures, informs, and compels the artist to create the work that she does. For this concept, I draw on the work of scholars who theorize motherhood as a critical position, not a biological condition. My argument may appear inherently biological as the artist did give birth to her child, but as discussed in the Introduction, the artist-parent identity may be inspired by biological reproduction, but it is not a precondition for it. To reiterate, the artists to which I attribute to this term are critically and conceptually engaged with the issues surrounding the politics of family, gender, and nationhood as it pertains to their specific circumstances. They reflect on their dual roles as artists and parents, sometimes unconsciously, and create works of art that provide plural interpretations, at least one of which pertains to gender roles and/or the family and domesticity.

From this perspective, Jabłońska's projects—particularly those discussed in this chapter (*Supermother, Through the Stomach to the Heart, Kitchen,* and *Helping*)—can be interpreted through multiple lenses and perspectives. I argue that there is a consistent thread between these projects that stems from Jabłońska's identity as a mother and an artist and her performance as an artist-mother. Multi-work projects like *Through the Stomach to the Heart* and *Helping* (2004–09) may not incorporate her son visually, but as suggested in this chapter, they are inspired by the mundane or everyday tasks of nurturing, giving, and teaching one's own child how to navigate through life. With this foundation, one can view Jabłońska's inclusion of her children (at exhibition events), her positioning of adults as children (as discussed in the project *Kitchen*), and her use of the homeless, unemployed, or under-employed (in *Through the Stomach to the Heart* and *Helping*) as participants in her art as key elements to her maternal artistic practice.

Jabłońska has admitted that her initial self-championing as a Polish Mother-artist has become limiting to larger understandings of her artistic practice, as critics and museums often request to include her *Supermother* series in their exhibitions, ignoring or omitting her more recent work.[8] Mindful of this pigeonholing, I begin this chapter by examining the *Supermother* series, but this is done, not to reinforce the project as definitive of Jabłońska's practice, but rather to generate a discussion around the status of women, the gender issues at work in Poland, and the historical burden women face even now in the post-communist era. These issues allow for a broader understanding of her other projects, such as the various iterations of the *Through the Stomach to the Heart* series, which comprises the heart of this chapter, and the series *Helping*. In the various performance and photographic elements that constitute the *Through the Stomach to the Heart* series, I argue that Jabłońska begins to approach art-making as a socially minded practice, which is reaffirmed in the last section that explores the series *Helping*. In the latter two series, Jabłońska's practice becomes more and more conceptual, and in line with artistic trends of the late 1990s and 2000s, but also remains tied to an ingrained maternal thinking.

Beyond the culturally specific historical and political issues that Jabłońska's art evokes, foundational questions regarding the artist-parent identity underline this chapter. Namely, is it possible for a woman artist to engage with issues of motherhood or the maternal when not directly representing her child? If so, what does this type of art or practice look like? Can parenthood function as a subjective mode of practice? And if it can, does the artist (and scholar) define such an identity or modality without restricting him or herself to biography and/or biology? This chapter explores these issues and attempts to articulate a way in which a parental (in this case maternal) subjectivity can be promoted without falling into retrograde concepts of women-artist-mothers. That is, the artist's oeuvre does not need to represent female sexuality nor biology. Works do not need to be tied to other aspects of the woman's body (though it may also be highlighted explicitly) and children are not necessarily represented in their work. The presence of these elements, as mentioned in the introduction, caused women artists' work to be labeled saccharine, kitschy, and not serious. Thus, this chapter attempts to tread a delicate balance between the revealing the personal material of the artist without, as Anna Chave noted in regard to minimalism in the 1960s, "corroborating invidious stereotypes of the narrowly confessional and autobiographical impulses underlying women's creative processes."[9] Through her art, Jabłońska negotiates the personal and domestic in relationship to public and critical notions of women in Poland.

Confronting Tradition: The Super—Polish—Mother?

In 2001, Jabłońska created a series of photographs titled *Supermatka* (in Polish) or *Supermother* after being inspired by her son dressing up as Zorro.[10] These images rose to great critical acclaim, traveled widely in international exhibitions, and even became part of a public art-billboard exhibition, which will be discussed later in this chapter. In each work, the artist, dressed as Superman, Batman, or Spider-Man, poses with her four-year-old son, Antek, on her lap.[11] Situated in the spaces of their small apartment in Bydgoszcz—namely, the hallway, kitchen, and living room—Jabłońska simultaneously addresses issues of maternity, domesticity, and popular culture.[12] There are several levels of meaning embedded in these images, ranging from the international and public to the very personal, familial, and private. On one level, these images can be interpreted as a series of playful theatrical acts recorded by the camera in the confines of the home. On another, they can be viewed as revealing (perhaps even critiquing) the gendered role of women in Poland and their relationship to both historic and contemporary heroes. The series clearly draws from the religious iconography of the Madonna and Child, however Jabłońska transforms the sacred into the profane by situating herself in the domestic spaces of contemporary Poland and by inserting the presence of comic book heroes.[13] This series, as I will argue, demonstrates Jabłońska's critical exploration of motherhood in a country that is caught between traditional values (seen as "East") and adventurous notions of democracy and capitalism (the "West"). By approaching these issues from a variety of cultural and historical perspectives, Jabłońska demonstrates the multiple demands mother-artists face in the twenty-first century.

Formally, there is slight variation among these images, and in how closely Jabłońska chooses to portray the superhero. All of the works are consistent in their formal or traditional positioning in the format of the Madonna and child, yet Antek's position on his mother's lap and both of their gazes vary. In each image, Jabłońska sits on a plain chair or stool. Antek rests on her lap and they both appear to either gaze in one of three directions—directly at the viewer, to the left, or to the right. Polish scholar Sebastian Cichocki notes Jabłońska's gaze as the Virgin varies from "stern" as an acknowledgment of the "sin and decay [that has] found a place to thrive on earth"; to "indifferent"; to "fearfully ordinary" as she appears like a "country girl with a tiny, skinny child."[14] Cichocki's assessment seems to refer more to the traditional images of the Virgin to impose those discernable elements, rather than by seeing them directly in Jabłońska's photographs. Jabłońska may appear stern or indifferent, but by no means can her superhero costume be interpreted as ordinary, nor should Antek be considered a particularly skinny child.

In one of the most widely reproduced images, Jabłońska and Antek are seated in their living room (Plate 2). Jabłońska's legs are spread open in what could be interpreted as a masculine pose, yet she warmly embraces her son who is kneeling on her lap and gazing into the distance. Jabłońska gently kisses her son and gazes into the opposite direction. Surrounding this traditional Madonna and Child pose are objects of everyday life. A torn blue cardboard box filled with toys, a boom box, books piled on the ground, a small lamp, and a candelabrum with red candles are positioned in what appears to be their everyday setting. On the wall behind them, framed photographs of a man and woman (possibly grandparents or great-grandparents and family homes); a drawing, possibly made by Antek himself; and a heart-shaped wall ornament. These elements hinge the mother and child into the secular space of the home and to a larger family structure. In a second version of this photograph, a vase of tulips has been placed just within the left edge of frame, and a television, a reminder of one of the primary means that foreign countries learn of American/Western ideas, sits in the corner. In this image, a book lies untouched and discarded on the floor, encapsulated in the shadow cast by the superhero's body, and a black cat peeks out from behind the red cape. The slight disarray in the home, along with the various placements of objects in each image, reveals that what the image documents is the living, breathing, and ever-changing space of the family and not the unchanging image of the Virgin and Child.

The format, or rather pose, of Jabłońska and Antek does draw distinct references to Renaissance-era religious paintings, such as those by Giotto or Leonardo whose paintings and frescos of the Virgin Mary and Child comprise many a Polish individual's religious and cultural memory, or even familiar Byzantine icons in which the image of Mary functioned as an intercessor for the devotee. But the primary difference between, say Giotto's *Ognissanti Madonna* (1310, tempera on wood, Galleria degli Uffizi), and one of Jabłońska's images, is not simply context. They are also distinct in the messages that they convey about the status of the Virgin, the roles that women should maintain, and the place of women in society. For instance: both Giotto's *Ognissanti Madonna* and Jabłońska's *Supermother* similarly confine the woman to interior or religious spaces, inspired by contemporary architectural practices, but Giotto's is relatively free of secular references. The additional figures in Giotto's work represent angels in attendance, resembling the architecture and filigree of early renaissance churches and make little reference to contemporary everyday life. This causes the work to be more iconic than depictions of the Virgin created by artists from the North.[15] Depictions of the Virgin, particularly in Italian art, often portrayed her seated in nature (such as in Leonardo's *Madonna of the Rocks*, 1483, oil on canvas, Musée du Louvre), enthroned or with a golden background (as an icon) to affirm her biological role as Christ's mother, her position as queen of heaven, or her ability to intercede for the devout.[16] Marian iconography provides many local and global meanings, as the image of Mary is powerful in a variety of cultural contexts and locations.[17]

Devotees of Catholicism have very particular, sacred relationships to the Virgin, which historically has caused tremendous outcries to artists' appropriation of her image. Consider, for example, Chris Ofili's *Holy Virgin Mary* (1986), which caused then New York City Mayor Rudy Giuliani (among others) to protest its display as a part of the *Sensation* exhibition at the Brooklyn Museum of Art in 1999; or Katharina Fritsch's florescent-yellow *Madonnenfigur* (1987), which she positioned in a Münster plaza between a department store and a church and scandalized the local population.[18] It is significant that Jabłońska's series has not caused such an outcry, even when photographs from *Supermother* were enlarged and amended to include words referring to domestic tasks—cooking, washing (dishes), and laundry—as part of the public art billboard exhibition, *Home Games*, in 2002.

The relationship between women and the Catholic icon of the Virgin Mary has a particular history in Poland, one that is relevant to the probable reading of these images there. Many scholars tie the myth of the Polish Mother to the figure of the Virgin Mary, who often was also known as the *Mater Dolorosa*, or mother of sorrows. In an insightful essay, historian Brian Porter traces the history of the Virgin as a national icon of Poland. The Marian cult, he writes, can be traced to the seventeenth century when King Jan Kazimierz crowned the Virgin as the Queen of Poland, simultaneously intensifying Poland's Catholic nationalism and women's burden to embody her virtues.[19] This ideal lasted for centuries and has been reaffirmed in more contemporary events.

In particular, when the Poles defeated the Bolsheviks in 1920, they attributed the victory to the intervention of the Virgin, who became a *hetmanka* or military leader. The *hetmanka* became publicly imagined as a "Joan of Arc figure, leading men into battle for God and Fatherland."[20] Over time, this ideology transformed or melded into the *matka polka* or Polish Mother stereotype, which originated in the eighteenth century, a time when Poland was partitioned and under control of various states.[21] This political situation led to a model of heroic womanhood that praised women for staying at home while the men went to war, and for serving her (Polish) nation by educating her children (particularly her sons) to have a patriotic spirit. By the nineteenth century, the ideals of the Polish Mother and the Virgin were seen as saviors of the nation, modeling proper behavior and upholding feminine virtues. Both models became synonymous with a more mature and skillful wife who took care of her men and represented nationalist ideals.[22] By the mid-twentieth century, men were deskilled and seen as individuals who needed to be cared for by women.[23] The disparity between the skillful stay-at-home wife and the worker-husband generated another gender relationship that sociologists Mira Marody and Anna Giza-Poleszczuk term the 'big child' (man) and 'brave victim' (woman).[24] Like the Virgin of Sorrows, the 'brave victim' identity encouraged women to be proud of sacrificing an advanced education and work status in exchange for an important domestic role that focused on the greater good of raising children. Similarly, notions of the 'brave victim' recognized women as "the real head of the family."[25] The 'brave victim,' like the Virgin and the Polish Mother, sacrifices personal desires and needs for the benefit of her son. Scholars have noted these stereotypes have been upheld through the post-socialist period. One of the most notable agents of this insistence is the Roman Church, which continues to represent women as mothers and vessels of the nation in their public campaigns.[26] But, as Elżbieta Ostrowksa keenly articulates, this iconography has also been transparent in Polish cinema, which in its attempts to reclaim a national identity after 1989 has reawakened collective memories and other national myths such as the Polish Mother.[27]

As Jabłońska appropriates the iconography of Mary in a contemporary setting, her performance of self-as-Madonna lies somewhere between two of the five approaches James Elkins outlines in his study of contemporary religious art, between conventional and art that is critical of religion. In his book, *On the Strange Place of Religion in Contemporary Art*, Elkins explains the hazardous position of religious art in relation to postmodern standards of high art.[28] Using case examples from students he encountered at the Art Institute of Chicago, Elkins defines conventional religious art as not typically accepted into the 'high art' category. This is because art that demonstrates the artist's contemplation of religious faith, perhaps even her second thoughts about it, and shows that the notion that the artist is "meditative and uncertain about both art and religion" has become integral to academic conceptions of postmodern art.[29]

In this vein, Jabłońska's series suggests a confrontation with Catholicism, but also can be perceived as a lauding of it. If Marian theology teaches that Mary was both a virgin and a mother, is she not more than human in her embodiment of the two contradictory ideals? And also, isn't to suggest that Mary knew that she was going to bring a child into the world who would be sacrificed for the greater good of the people, to claim that she performed the supreme superhero duty? On the other hand, the series can be read as one that is critical of religion, because it does conflate the gender identity of the Virgin and superhero. Elkins notes that this category of art is "not only art that criticizes religion, but art that ponders religion from a few steps outside it."[30] From this perspective, Jabłońska appropriates a religious figure (Mary) and infuses her with secular images that are sometimes lauded to a saint-like status: Superman, Batman, and Spider-Man are seen as heroes and saviors, much like Christ. Elkins warns that art that becomes too critical of religion becomes "too strident, too superficial" and I would argue that the images in Jabłońska's series are carefully constructed to fall between direct criticism of contemporary religion and religious devotion. Certainly, her decision to cast herself *as* the Madonna, rather than a third person, could encourage accusations of blasphemy or self-sanctification. The costume and context cause the work to shift between the extreme anti-religious connotations and gentler, but perhaps more subversive appropriations. But according to Cichocki, Jabłońska chose such references to "evoke among the believers a feeling of security, harmony, and remind them of the Love sent down from ... Heaven."[31] Suggesting a reification of religious values and sentiments in relation to the Virgin, Cichocki focuses on the aspects of Jabłońska's images that are similar to those of Italian Renaissance artists who emphasized the maternal relationship. For example, when the artist is dressed as Superman, she lovingly embraces her son, kisses his cheek, and suggests the loving relationship of the Virgin and Child. However, when posing as Spider-Man she leans or slouches back, supporting the sleeping boy and gazes knowingly through her mask at the viewer; one could speculate that Antek's closed eyes and relaxed position on Spider-Man references the child's knowledge of the sacrifice the superhero must make, but in all likelihood, he is tired of posing with his mother before the camera. Most importantly, the donning of superhero costumes, rather than the sweeping cloaks and garments traditionally seen in Virgin iconography, intones that this is not a divinely inspired love, but rather one that is gained through hard work, sweat, and heroic acts. Interestingly, when the artist dresses as Batman, she again unflinchingly confronts the viewer, distracting Antek's gaze with an orange wedge, possibly one cut from those on the counter behind them with the knife on the cutting board, ultimately revealing there is an aspect of masquerade and even trickery involved in being a *Supermother*.

To separate the sacred nature of the icon, Jabłońska's Virgin-Superhero is placed within the spaces of the contemporary Polish home, full of knickknacks, televisions, and contemporary conveniences. As Cichocki noted, the presence of Jabłońska's furniture and pets contribute to both the sense of security and concept of the domestic. He notes, "sometimes they're tamed, sometimes scary. And not just the pets, [the] furniture too. An old gas heater growls and purrs, mysterious scratching sounds come from the pipes, the computer crashes for no apparent reason—maybe to show its second mischievous nature."[32] The secular domestic items become a means to distance the *Supermother* from the strictly religious context.[33]

Jabłońska's reference to the Virgin and Child is not unique within contemporary art—in 2009–10, Jenny Saville created a series of large-scale drawings titled *Reproduction Drawings* in which she appropriated Leonardo da Vinci's cartoon *The Virgin and Child with St. Anne and John the Baptist* (ca. 1507–08). In the life-size drawing, *Reproduction Drawing I and III (After the Leonardo Cartoon)*, Saville drew, erased, and superimposed the image of the mother and child in order to "record the mother's patient efforts to hold the wriggling infant."[34] Saville's drawings capture the movement of the young Christ, cementing the notion of the Mother as a stable force, or rock, engaging traditional notions of motherhood.

Artists' relationship and references to the religious iconography of the Virgin and Child do not end with the British artist Saville. Polish artist, Katarzyna Górna similarly engaged in a series of religious works, titled *Madonnas* (1996–2001). These photographs similarly transpose the iconography of the Virgin to a contemporary context; however these images are not filled with the material culture of contemporary life. The three images that comprise the series depict an adolescent girl, a young woman with an infant, and an older mother with her adult child. In the first, the adolescent girl stands nude in an exaggerated *contrapposto*, covering her pudendum with her right hand. From her fingertips, one notices the streak of dark liquid that trickles down her left leg and onto her foot, revealing that she has entered womanhood—and thus has the potential to conceive. Set in the same empty room with a half-moon window, the second *Madonna* depicts a young woman seated with a young child. Breasts exposed and confidently confronting the viewer, this image in both the mother's and child's poses bear the most similarity to traditional images of the Virgin and Child, and Jabłońska's *Supermother*. The third image depicts a slightly older woman with a full-grown man on her lap—a clear reference to the Pietá (and Michelangelo's sculptural depiction of it), though scholar Magdalena Ujma suggests that it may also depict a woman and her lover—or even the 'big child'—as he is alive, head turned towards the viewer and positioned closely to her breasts.[35]

To return to Jabłońska's work, a comparison to her series and the second image of Górna's *Madonnas* is productive due to their similar use of the traditional Madonna iconography. Both the *Supermother* series and this image by Górna depict a seated woman with legs spread and a child resting on one thigh. Each artist stages the Madonna within an interior space, but the contents of each space are distinct. Górna's image refrains from the inclusion of extraneous elements. Other than the window behind the woman, which provides a view of the sky and clouds, it is unknown if the space they occupy is part of a studio, home, or business. Context is completely removed to reiterate the viewer's focus on the subject of the Madonna, her role in contemporary Catholic culture, and the broader effects it has on women. Górna's series was branded as a scandal by Polish media when it was included in the *Irreligia* exhibition at Atelier 340 in Brussels in 2001–02, primarily due to the *Madonnas'* eroticized nature—not only the Virgins' exposed breasts and perceived reference to a sexual relationship, but also the physical reference to menstrual blood caused a stir.[36] Due to the reasons mentioned above, reminders of the Virgin's human nature, and in particular, her sexuality defy notions of women as sacred vessels for divine men and threaten popular Catholic theology. Grzegorz Dziamski suggests that Górna's project "asks if the Christian narrative can co-exist with the feminist narrative? Can the Christian vision of a woman be reconciled with modern feminism?" Dziamski notes that this is a question of "great importance in modern Poland, a Catholic country, that has been ruled for centuries by Holy Mary, and where the father of the Catholic Church, Pope John Paul II is the highest moral authority."[37] While Dziamski may be overstating the dominance of the church, the role of the Virgin Mary and the presence of Catholicism are key questions for Jabłońska in this series. The message is similar but the contents surrounding the Madonna and child reveal Jabłońska's interest in questioning not only the ideology behind womanhood and femininity, but also tangible, consumption-based notions of motherhood—the elements of everyday life. Like Górna's project, Jabłońska attempts to humanize the Virgin through her context of things, but evades public outrage, for she does not overtly sexualize her. Rather, she elevates her to a super-reality, drawing on Polish concepts of the Virgin, her complex relationship to the Polish Mother, and the modern superhero.

The presence of things—the television, books on the floor and stacked on shelves, boom boxes, flowers, framed photographs and art works in the Superman living room image; or, the shoes stacked on shelves and discarded on the floor, coats hanging on hooks, photo albums, posters, a telephone, backpack and light fixtures in the Spider-Man hallway work; or the pots, pans, cups, cupboards, and pet food bowls, burners and serving platter in the kitchen images—they all connote the presence of an active family life (Figure 3.1). Nothing is omitted or disguised for the camera and viewer. It is all left in view, like an open book to reveal the intricate nature of art and parenthood. The home is never perfectly clean or tidy. Jabłońska humorously noted that she is afraid

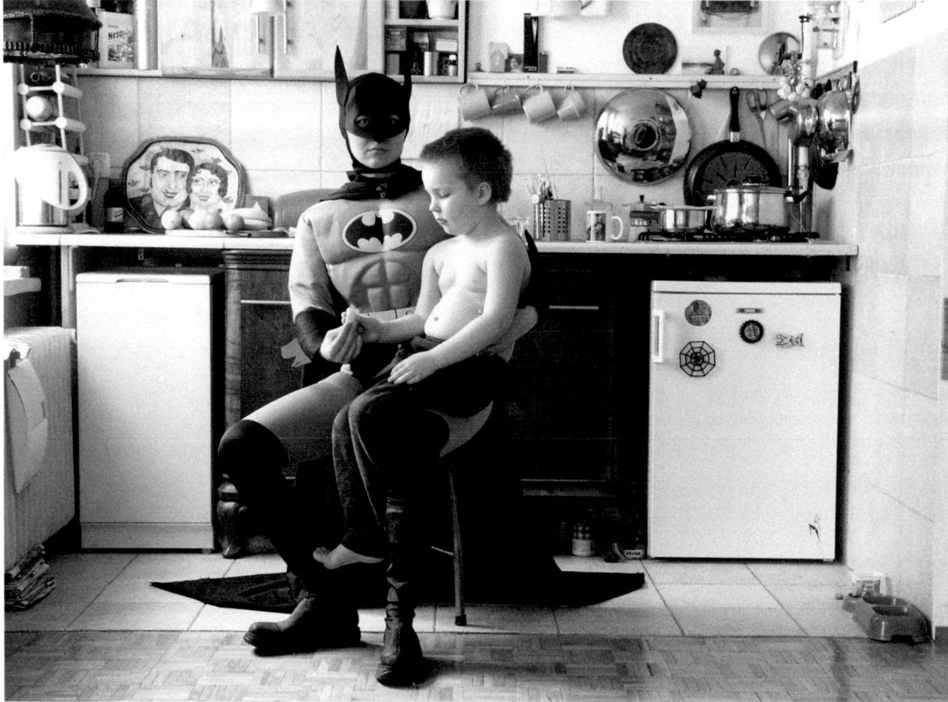

Figure 3.1 Elżbieta Jabłońska, *Supermother*, 2002. Photographic series. Courtesy the artist.

to look in the nooks and corners of her home, areas from where "aggressive objects" can attack—for example a vacuum cleaner pipe that falls out of the closet door, thus making it impossible for her not to do something with it, or the spaces underneath the radiator, where one can always find toy cars, nuts, paper or feathers that belong to their cat Mikolaj.[38] These elements reaffirm what Cichocki terms the 'super-realism' of the living world—the superhero must fight these and other challenges for the good of her child and her home.[39]

Thus, on one level, Jabłońska's *Supermother* series can be interpreted as a reification of these values—the superhero, supermother who sacrifices all personal needs for the betterment of her son. She does not clearly discredit such a role because she places herself in this position, employs her son, and poses within the confines of her own home. In addition, the lack of public opposition to her images, and the public's viewing of them in billboard form likely reproduced, without a full grasp of the irony of Jabłońska's project, the status of women as the "brave victim," Madonna, and Polish Mother. As sociologists Marody and Giza-Poleszczuk have written, "Today, women must choose between the old and the new—between roles that undoubtedly will take them in opposite directions."[40] The attempt to unite, occupy, or transform those roles harkens on the heroic and the ironic concepts of the superhero.

Batman, Spider-Man, and Superman are comic book superheroes who all share in their desire to help those in need, fighting villains and trying to make the world a better place. At various moments throughout American history, superheroes functioned as rallying symbols in the battle against, for example, the Nazis during World War II, the establishment in the 1960s, and other key social issues.[41] Their appeal spread as the communist era came to a close and the comic book, cartoons, and movies were more readily accessible. As Cichocki notes, "Batman, Spiderman, and Superman are good guys in funny outfits. They help the weak, they are absolutely reliable, they can appear in a number of places simultaneously, they never complain, they never hesitate on whose side to take."[42] Beyond sheer strength, each has special elements which contribute to their success: Batman has the financial prowess and childhood trauma of witnessing his parents' death which inspires his crime-fighting; Spider-Man has a genetic mutation which provides him agility and the ability to make spider webs; and Superman, who is an alien from another planet, can fly, has X-ray vision, and insurmountable strength—each of these powers are used for the protection of the innocents, to destroy and conquer the evil forces, and never do they use their powers for their own sake.[43] The enemies they fight include evil professors, drug-dealers, corrupt police officers, terrorists, and other mutants. But unlike these superheroes, the Supermother, as Izabela Kowalczyk explains, fights:

> Dirt, dust, filthy pots and pans, germs on the filthy floor, her son's stained T-shirts and dirty hands, milk split and burnt on the cooker. Supermother not only fights, but also saves (for instance, she saves her child from boredom, danger, filthy floor and toilet). … Although a supermother wages an everyday fight, nobody is aware of the effort she puts in running the house. She fights in an unnoticeable way, and the effects of her activity fade away so quickly that nobody even realizes how much she does.[44]

The Supermother's heroic actions are not those that are immediately recognizable. They are subtle, common, and contained within the domestic spaces of the home. In this series, Jabłońska asks the viewer to consider how important it is to have clean toilets, pots, pans, and clothing for one's existence. If a mother did not complete these tasks and her child had stained clothes and dirty hands, what would one think? She likely would not be considered a 'supermother' nor a good mother' but rather be given that contentious label of 'bad mother.' But whether a tidy home is the sign of a good or bad mother is not really the issue of this series. Rather it is the revelation that the process, challenge, and attempt to do such things is heroic. This causes the masking aspect of the superhero to be of particular interest—Superman, Batman, Spider-Man wear costumes and, except for Superman, wear masks to disguise their identities (impossibly, Clark Kent only needs to remove his glasses to become the alter ego, Superman). Because these are common men by day, heroes by night, a dualism is created through their masking. Jabłońska appropriates the mask but this element of her photographs raises questions of why the artist would or not show her face, gaze, expressions, and importantly, her true identity. Is it that she wanted to continue the mythology of the superhero and not expose her everyday identity, or that her personal identity does not matter, as long as the mother is garnering attention? In revealing the superhero nature of motherhood, Jabłońska effectively masks her own identity, suggesting that the multiple roles of the artist-wife-mother-artist are quite difficult to balance.

For Jabłońska, the Supermother identity is ironic. It is unattainable, with all of its expectations of women, mothers, and wives, but she does believe that the reconciliation of mother and artist is possible, yet difficult.[45] In a way, by photographing herself within the confines of the domestic, Jabłońska reaffirms the woman's place is within the home, but this is not because she believes this to be true. She does this because, culturally, the myth of the Polish Mother persists. Therefore, she dresses as a superhero so show just how challenging it is to achieve cultural change.

In the immediate post-communist era, women in Poland continued to be affected by expectations of maintaining the household, providing childcare, and work outside the home. It was hoped that the end of the Soviet era would socialize domestic duties, but as social historian Chris Corrin notes, "generally many women were still expected to look to their older female relatives for suitable child-care."[46] Therefore women in Poland, like many other countries, were and are doubly burdened with work and childcare, forcing them to become "superwomen." It is difficult to imagine that this level of meaning is not intended in Jabłońska's series. A superwoman, superhero, or supermother all require actions that exceed expectations. The superwoman must work, clean, and care for her child; the superhero must fight for the less fortunate and the supermother, well, in this case, it seems that her heroic task is to maintain the duties of the superwoman and continue her artistic practice. Or perhaps, the heroic deeds are really performed inside the space of the home.

When costumed as what can be called "Spidermother" or "Batmother," the artist's (hybrid and cross-gender) rendition of these superheroes raises the tasks of cooking, cleaning, scrubbing, and caring for her children and husband to the level of heroic duty. Jabłońska makes these domestic activities 'worthwhile' endeavors for women.[47] Ujma notes,

> This kind of Superman is not only heroic in significant crucial moments, but on a regular, everyday basis—in running the house, bringing up children, professional work, washing clothes, cooking, washing-up, clearing doing homework and playing with the child. What makes her a superhero is an attempt to reconcile the role of a mother, a wife, a cook, a maid, a friend, an employee and a satisfied woman at the same time.[48]

Drawing from this claim that the multiple tasks of primary caregiver make one a superhero, I would even suggest that Jabłońska promotes the tangible reality of motherhood as an artistic endeavor—she documents the excesses of life, the imperfections and the messy nature of parenting. This isn't predicated on the presence of the child, but is aided by it in this case. In this vein, Antek does not need to be visually included, as he is always present within the body of Jabłońska. To visualize the maternal does not specifically mean that one needs to represent the child.

But as the *Supermother* became displayed outdoors in 2002, the subtle critique was dominated by the scale and text on the images—cooking, washing (dishes), laundry (Figure 3.2). These terms could be seen as accusations or demands. Jabłońska noted that *Shrek*, the 2001 animated story released by Dreamworks Studios, inspired the phrases for the billboard. In the story, the prince is to choose a wife from three candidates, one of whom is Cinderella. Each of the potential wives is announced and described in sequence, as in a pageant. For Cinderella, the announcer proclaims: "And number three: Cinderella! A mentally disabled girl whose favorite hobbies are doing dishes, cleaning, and cooking."[49] Jabłońska, struck by the characterization that the enjoyment of domestic work by women signals a mental or social ineptitude, chose to superimpose those words on the images from *Supermother* that are situated in the

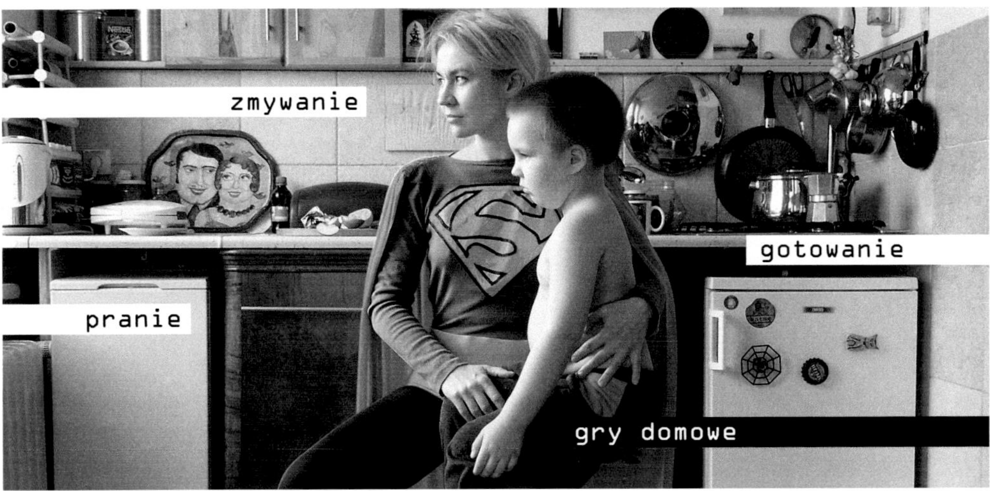

Figure 3.2 Elżbieta Jabłońska, *Supermother*, *Home Games* exhibition, 2002. AMS Outdoor Gallery, 400 billboards in Poland. Courtesy the artist.

kitchen. Placed over the washer, near the sink and above the stove, the words can be seen as labeling and defining women's and the Supermother's duties. As scholar Jolanta Ciesielska noted, the everyday Polish woman is expected to be more modern than her predecessors who thanklessly cooked and cleaned for their families.

So, as billboards, the *Supermother* series could be seen as advertisements aimed at viewers to "purchase an attractive commodity, to benefit from some services" or "cause a change in our attitude."[50] Considering that 'public space' as a term did not exist under communist rule, there was no space for non-propagandist messages. As Poland transitioned back to a parliamentary democracy in 1989, public spaces became areas for commodity and corporate advertisements, fueling the transformation of Poland into a consumer-driven society.

Thus, in 1998, when the Art Marketing Syndicate S.A. (AMS) started an "Outdoor Gallery" (Galeria Zewnetrzna) in which 400 billboards in major cities would be dedicated to the presentation of Polish artists.[51] It was a significant feat for the arts. Many of the early billboard projects were not overtly political, but did approach social issues. Jadwiga Sawicka's *Converting, Domesticating, Taming* (1998) confronted the changing cultural paradigms of the country and its acceptance of difference. While confrontational, Sawicka's work retained a certain level of ambiguity for viewers. Over time, the works selected by the Outdoor Gallery, such as those by Katarzyna Kozyra and Marek Sobczyk, were more direct and controversial. For example, Kozyra's work *Blood Ties* (1999) featured Kozyra and her handicapped sister nude, lying on a red crescent (Kozyra) or upside down on a red cross (Kozyra's sister). These images probed the systems of religion, government, and the history of the Solidarity movement in Poland, which caused great offense to some viewers.[52] Kozyra's work, in particular, was accused of Satanism by one Gdansk politician because of the woman's inverted position on the cross. For Marek Krajewski, one of the organizers of the project, the billboards provide a means of generating a public discourse, both positive and negative, as the Polish art world was "having difficulties clearly communicating with its audiences."[53] Thus, Jabłońska's participation in this outdoor exhibition provided an opportunity for the artist to challenge or test notions of maternal identity in Poland. Indeed, the ambiguity of the message contributes to the overall success of the work. If the viewer remained committed to notions of the Polish Mother, her presence on the billboard glorifies or increases the myth's popularity. To those that are struggling against it, the billboard heightens awareness of the inequity women continue to experience in their aims to become superwomen and/or supermothers.

In many ways, the images discussed above are those that have defined Jabłońska's career. Initially, she embraced the maternal persona. As previously mentioned, she staged many of her early exhibitions with the phrase, *"The Polish Mother Presents..."* (*Matka Polka prezentuje*) and even created her own set of stamps each with a different superhero emblem in the center (the Batman logo, a spider on a web, and the "S" of Superman). But what at first seemed like a fun artistic pseudonym has over time made her frustrated. Jabłońska notes that even when adopting the name Polish Mother she did not believe that she had much in common with the "stereotypical image of the Polish Mother who is usually believed to be an overprotective woman finding fulfillment only at home, usually surrounded by many children."[54] Yet she also acknowledges that events, such as the "Action Table" that served ice cream to children during her exhibition opening at the Zachęta National Gallery of Art, were inspired by conversations with her mother, who baked and cooked her entire life, and the Supermother's desire to be a "cool mother."[55] Even when turning away from the tangible and physical representation of herself and her son to a more socially based practice, Jabłońska continues to engage and be informed by a maternal subjectivity or modality.

Motherhood as Mode of Practice

Jabłońska gained critical acclaim for her work highlighting the experience of being a mother; she not only physically represented the mother in her art, but also deployed motherhood with a critical subjectivity that molded and defined her artistic actions. The artist's strong emphasis on the maternal has caused Magdalena Ujma to proclaim, "[Jabłońska] discovered her artistic way due to the experience of being a mother. ... It is her maternity that has given this particular shape to her artistic activity."[56] While Ujma tied artistic action to the experience of being a mother, Jabłońska's art—particularly the performance series *Through the Stomach to the Heart* and *Kitchen*, which features the consumption of food as the primary artistic act—extends beyond her biological status and posits a critical reflection of the cultural expectations of mothering and domesticity in Poland (Figure 3.3).

The artist's practice has several components. For actions in which the artist cooked for gallery attendees in a makeshift kitchen the title, *Through the Stomach to the Heart*, was used; in cooking performances utilizing a disproportionately sized kitchen counter and table, *Kitchen*; and for a series of photographs documenting artists and curators in their own kitchens, the title *Zasiedzenie*. Through these acts, Jabłońska transforms the domestic space and labors of the home into artistic endeavors, thus confronting misconceptions that the role of the female artist and mother, and the artist/curator and the everyday, are incompatible.[57] By focusing on the domestic space of the kitchen, Jabłońska transgresses the distance between art and life, as well as the space between the public institution and the private home.

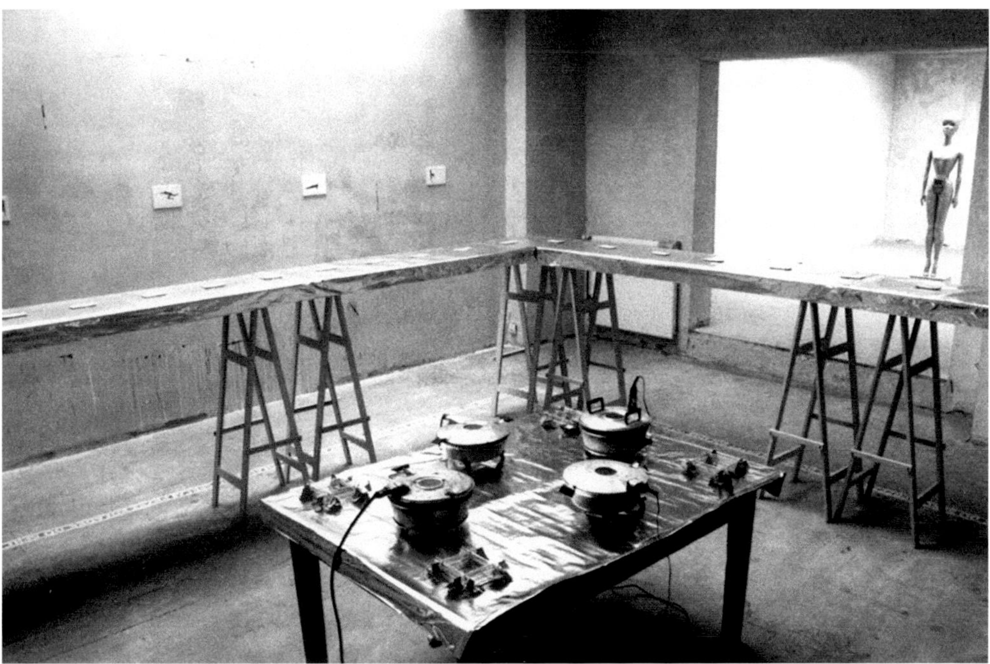

Figure 3.3 Elżbieta Jabłońska, *Through the Stomach to the Heart*, 1999–2005 Performance at the exhibition *Masquerades*, Inner Spaces Gallery, Poznan, 2001. Courtesy the artist.

By transforming the domestic spaces and labors of the home into artistic endeavors, Jabłońska appropriates the strategies of relational aesthetics and participatory art to confront the misconception that the roles of the female artist and mother are incompatible. Throughout the series, Jabłońska offers to care for others—acts that provide her a means to reconcile her roles as a mother and artist as dynamic and simultaneous, thus positing motherhood as a potential mode of artistic practice. In the performance projects of *Through the Stomach to the Heart* the artist prepares and cooks food for others to consume in the space of the museum or gallery. Her 'art' includes the very act of eating, yet by examining the documentary photographs one also sees an interest in the aesthetics of the kitchen. In some versions of the performance the kitchen is makeshift, with unfinished wooden supports and reflective polished metal (or tinfoil) countertops. In others, the preparation spaces appear to be an enlarged version of an IKEA-style kitchen counter and table.

The pristine white counter and table, though proportionally exaggerated, draw associations to the modernist white wall; the artist creates a neutral ground to highlight the preparation of food, its display, and its subsequent consumption (Plate 3). The distinction between the two kitchens is permanence: the makeshift metallic surfaces are temporary structures, while the white kitchen counter and table become objects of display for the exhibition's duration, acting as mementos of the action that had taken place and the food that was consumed. By erecting and displaying a kitchen in the space of the museum, Jabłońska transforms the traditional exhibition opening to emphasize the creation, presentation, and consumption of food as a social interaction and artistic action. Each of these events demonstrates various aspects of a maternal subjectivity, which here are defined as performing domestic acts of cooking and caring for others, positioning visitors in the role of children, and exposing the invisible labor connected with the consumption of meals.

Jabłońska appropriates the strategies of relational aesthetics and participatory art to confront the misconception that the roles of the female artist and mother are incompatible. By utilizing food as her medium, Jabłońska offers to care for others, acts that provide her a means to reconcile her roles as a mother and artist as dynamic and simultaneous, thus positing motherhood as a potential mode of artistic practice. In doing so, she simultaneously transforms the act of cooking into an experimental process, akin to Michel de Certeau and Luce Giard's conception of cooking in the practice of everyday life; it provides an opportunity for creativity and self-expression.[58] Sometimes using fresh fruits and vegetables, and at others, premade pastries and drinks, Jabłońska utilizes the contemporary items that the exhibition sponsors and curators were able to obtain, which reflects the culinary choices available in contemporary life.

The food commonly prepared by Jabłońska ranges from the modification (cutting, rolling, arranging) of simple or premade items to the extensive preparation of traditional Polish cuisine. Jabłońska culls her recipes from her mother and does not openly divulge the recipes themselves.[59] This causes somewhat of a problem for the art historian, not knowing exactly what the "art" was that was consumed; but the few documentary images that depict the artist cooking reveal, somewhat inadequately, the extent of her cooking—in at least one photograph leeks and green onions are prominently positioned near the potato the artist is cutting—all three vegetables are commonly used in Polish cuisine, such as soups, stews, and salads (Plate 4). In other documentary photographs, items for consumption are heating on hotplates. These images, in conjunction with those that document the public interacting with or surrounding the artist while she dices watermelon, reveal that Jabłońska's project contributes to the discourse of contemporary food-based art practice in a very particular way. When the project turns to other Polish artists and curators in their kitchens, Jabłońska documents twenty-three individuals in the mundane activities of cooking and cleaning. In each the curator or artist is seen directly from behind, or slightly from the left or right as he or she cooks, cleans, or patiently tends to the meal being prepared. This part of the series, a complement to the artist's own cooking actions, demonstrates her desire to convey the human and everyday aspects of artists' lives, and suggests that actions within the home can be artistic activities as well.

While Jabłońska cannot be considered an innovator in her actions, she does provide a new, family-centered interpretation of "food art." In the 1930s the Italian Futurist Filippo Tammaso Marinetti made a series of proposals that utilized food as the "raw material for art." These propositions became known as *The Futurist Cookbook*, which prescribed the abandonment of nineteenth-century notions of dining that consisted of "nourishing fare, gathered from the countryside and prepared at length with loving care" in adamant support of "low-calorie, high-tech cuisine" that was more appropriate for modern life.[60] In a sense, Jabłońska revives Marinetti's inquiry through her series. She utilizes the items that the exhibition sponsors and curators were able to obtain. Art historian Maria Poprzęcka writes of Jabłońska's *Kitchen* performances:

Everything is predictable. The only thing that remains uncertain is the food. …
You can make predictions on the basis of the list of sponsors: Blikle?—doughnuts.
Palikot?—liqueurs. Polmos?—vodka. But you can also ask yourself the question
with somewhat old-fashioned seriousness—will there be any chance for art to
exist in this social and snobbish tumult, in this general lack of concentration and
attention? … Or is art only a pretext to organize a fashionable get-together combined with consumption?[61]

As Poprzęcka notes, Jabłońska is not so much concerned with high-tech as she is about
considering what contemporary cuisine and dining entail. Food consumption practices
in Poland (and in the Czech Republic), Joe Smith and Petr Jehlička argue, provide
expressions of "identity, tradition, community and family relations," but consumers are not steadfastly traditional or solely interested in Western products.[62] Rather
Smith and Jehlička note that during socialism, "national food traditions and newly
adapted practices helped to mark out and defend an independent cultural space that
was beyond the realm of an otherwise all-pervasive state."[63] The modern consumers,
like Jabłońska, utilize products in an ongoing negotiation between modernity and tradition; namely by using what can be acquired at any given moment including prepared
and pre-packaged items as well as fresh items from the country. Jabłońska is interested
in how identity is constructed, and how the consumption of food at an art opening
might create social interaction among strangers that might change that notion of self
and family. This is her primary interest in the series, and as such, the documentary
images that display the artist rolling slices of deli meat, slicing kielbasa, or cutting vegetables, are only fragments that aid one's understanding of how the artist transforms
the labor of the home into artistic endeavors in the space of the gallery.

In considering these projects, I contend that Jabłońska embraces a "maternal subjectivity" that does not necessitate her own physical representation. In this sense, I
draw upon Ruddick's theory of maternal thinking, because of its focus on the diurnal
activities—namely, thinking in regard to raising and educating one's children rather
than the biological or sociological aspects of motherhood.[64] Ruddick's argument that
the work of mothering "demands that mothers think" posits motherhood in terms of
critical action, rather than essentialism or biological function, thus offering a way to
read Jabłońska's work as one of cautious critique, or what she terms, quoting Luis
Buñuel, a "gentle perversion."[65]

For these performances, Jabłońska's "gentle perversion" entails the slight adjust-
ment of the traditional practice of the "art opening." Jabłońska's transposition of
domestic cooking to the public spaces of the gallery arose from her desire to have
contact with her audience. She wanted to "observe them and try to help them," and
determined that cooking was a means to connect with others in a more meaningful
way. Using the language of maternity, Jabłońska stated, "out of this need [to interact
with others] and my willingness to help, the first action was born," and thus she began
feeding visitors during exhibition openings as her artistic practice.[66] Such statements
by the artist have caused critics and scholars to superficially confuse her role as a
mother and her relationship to the art world, causing some to interpret her work as
purely feminist and tied solely to her biology, much to the artist's dissatisfaction. By
reading her actions through a maternal subjectivity, the artist does not represent the
bodily aspects of motherhood but uses the lived condition of it (daily chores, pleasure, frustrations, and thoughts) to inform her identity and particular position as an

artist.[67] And in *Kitchen*, which has been staged in the major European cities of Berlin, Kraków, Paris, Regensburg, and Wilno, Jabłońska "perverts" the notion of women being natural within such a space. She not only removes the kitchen from the domain of the domestic and places it into the space of what can be considered public—the art museum and gallery—but also, having raised the cabinet, table, and counter height, makes the action of cooking awkward and somewhat precarious (the artist must stand on a block to safely reach the counter).[68] Similarly, in documenting and exhibiting photographs of curators and artists in the kitchen, Jabłońska suggests that these cultural workers are not natural or unnatural within these spaces—they too reveal a certain awkward relationship to the kitchen and the stereotypes the space suggests.

Jabłońska's choice of title for the series provides a compelling layer of meaning for the acts that take place in performances. *Przez żołądek do serca*, or *Through the Stomach to the Heart*, references the proverb, which applies in Poland as much as it does in English-speaking cultures: "the way to a man's heart is through his stomach." This sentiment also has a particular meaning in Poland, as it is often passed down from mothers to their daughters—or alternatively, by media outlets. The statement champions the merits of "home cooking" and the power women have to sway men's affections if they cook well. Such proverbs reaffirm women's place within society—to the private spaces of the home and the kitchen—and subsumes them under the patriarchal system of the family. This is a point of contention for Jabłońska. Such sayings evoke the notion of the Polish mother—the stereotypical mother who cooks for the whole family, looks after the children, and encourages everyone to eat. This mother, according to Jabłońska, "is a busy body in the kitchen, while the others are having a good time."[69] Polish scholars assert that the "symbolic meaning" of the Polish mother is still alive, as "women are still expected to sacrifice their personal aspirations," in favor of supporting their husband's careers and their children's needs above all else.[70] Haunted by this stereotype, the items prepared by Jabłońska are not those created for her pleasurable consumption. Both the artist and the documentary evidence from the performances confirm that she does not partake in the eating.[71] Instead, Jabłońska prepares the food, invites the audience to consume the items, and then stands back from her creation to observe the consumption. She then cleans up after them.[72] Nothing perishable is left for display, thus emphasizing the preparation of food, its consumption, and the considerable time taken to clean up functions as the artistic act.

Much like Mierle Laderman Ukeles's transfer of the domestic tasks of cleaning in her performances *Hartford Wash* (1973–74) at the Wadsworth Atheneum, critics have noted that the transfer of such "typical and obvious" actions of the housewife to the confines of the gallery "robs them of their supposed naturalness."[73] While Ukeles had this intention as part of her project, hoping to unearth the structures of power and art related to the care of objects, this does not hold true in Jabłońska's case. To consider the kitchen as an oasis on the one hand suggests a positive and productive space of creativity, somewhat akin to concepts of the artist's studio, while on the other reinforces notions of the woman's space being the kitchen. To this end, Jabłońska's project is somewhat ambiguous. The artist is clear to distance herself from the prototypical housewife. She has stated that the kitchen is not her realm, noting, "it is a special place in the home where we like spending time together, having tea, but tea is sometimes the only thing available in our kitchen. … The kitchen is my mother's realm and this is what my works are about."[74] Such a statement denies the act of cooking as a normal action for women, and reveals that the actions staged within the gallery really are *performances* for the artist, not simply a *transfer* of her domestic actions to the space of the institution. Thus, the artist reveals that the series is a performance and exploration, if not a complete denial, of the notion that she embodies the Polish mother. Perhaps out of a "maternal guilt" or simply from the perspective that the role is increasingly absurd, she performs the stereotype for the public because that is what they expect a mother to do—care for, and feed, others. Jabłońska also employs the kitchen with considerations of how the space is occupied. She notes, "kitchens have always been places of conversations and meetings, it was always kitchens that were the most interesting and fun, frankly a kitchen is a small paradise of a sort. Far from the rooms and offices [which are solitary and quiet]."[75]

However, the artist engages these notions with tinges of irony, such as changing the scale of her kitchen to make both her and the audience embody the child reaching for what they cannot see on the counter, or by labeling each item with its caloric value. In the former, the large scale of the kitchen table, on the one hand, may be perceived to counteract the pedagogical practices advocated by Maria Montessori, who encouraged the creation of a "prepared environment" in the home, such as a smaller table where the child could dine. However, on the other, it could be viewed as a return to the sensorial exercises and the discovery that the child experiences in the home.[76] By applying Montessori's idea of the training of the senses to Jabłońska's *Kitchen*, one can determine that not only the sense of touch is evoked (through one's limited scope of the food placed on the table), but also the sense of smell.[77] The recognition of smells, as Montessori determined, deserved special attention as it enabled the child's selection of different types of foods, determined nutritional life, and functioned as the origin of taste.[78]

In two versions of the performance held at the Sculpture Center in New York and the Inner Spaces Festival in Poznán, Jabłońska labeled each food item she prepared with flags denoting their caloric content and the activity required to burn it off—for example, one slice of cheese equals forty six calories, which the flag informs takes "ten minutes of vigorous marching to burn off," or one serving of carrot equals twenty-eight calories, which takes "thirty-two minutes of love-making to burn off."[79] By acknowledging the nutritional value of each item in terms of gendered action—marching as masculine, militaristic, and ordered; love-making as feminine, seductive, and spontaneous—Jabłońska could be suggesting that people choose between love and war as they consume, or it could serve as a reference to the multiple demands on mothers to be thin and attractive, but also to be full-figured and nurturing (Figure 3.4).

By considering standards of beauty, Kowalczyk's essay "The Ambivalent Beauty" perhaps can provide more insight to the contrasting associations of food with love and war. Kowalczyk notes that during socialist rule, women of the lower classes of society were seen as healthy, sensual, and connected with nature, while social realist works presented women as "powerful, muscular, and 'male,' [meaning that they are] capable of working hard and physically."[80] Essentially, one can see these notions of women as the distinctions between mothers and workers, with no consideration of standards of beauty. A woman's value was placed in her ability to bear children or labor in the factory or farm. Under socialism, sociologist Anna Titkow has argued, Polish women's entry into the workforce "amounted to the *loss of a chance* for fundamental changes in the essential social and cultural identity of Polish women, the *loss of a chance* for

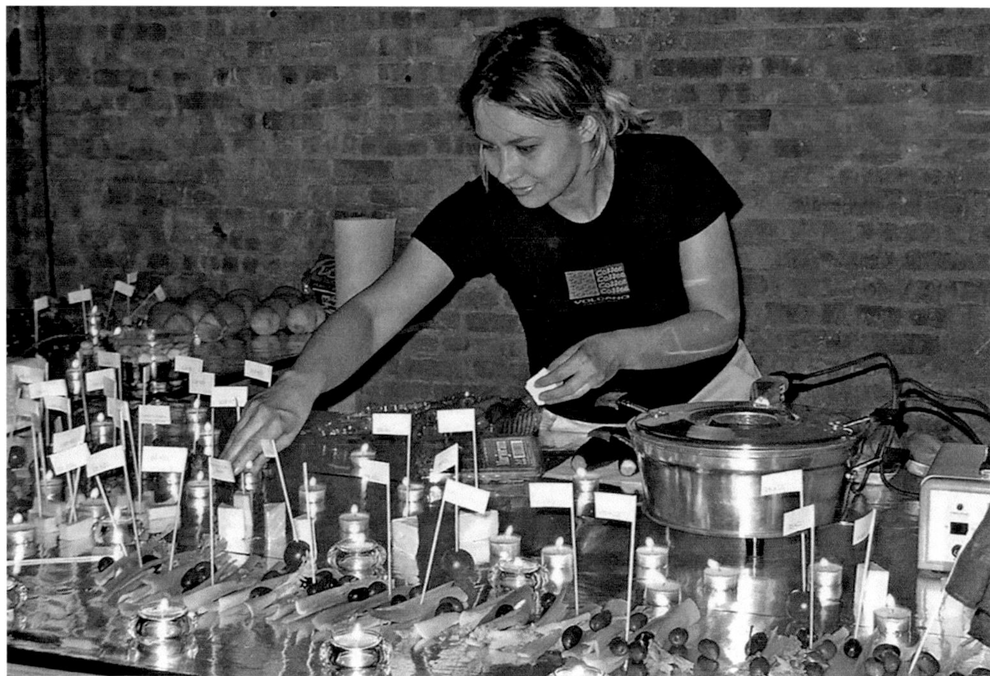

Figure 3.4 Elżbieta Jabłońska, *Through the Stomach to the Heart*, 1999–2005. Performance at exhibition *Architectures of Gender*, SculptureCenter, Long Island City, New York, 2003. Courtesy the artist.

full and permanent conversion from sex identity to gender identity."[81] Therefore, in the post-socialist era, the change in government, the workforce, and the availability of foodstuffs and other items created ambivalence in notions of womanhood.

As Kowalczyk argues, however, as "woman is freed from [the] reproductive task [of the traditional Polish Mother] by consumer culture," this very same culture "creates unattainable patterns of appearance and behavior (an eternally beautiful, young, attractive woman, perfectly able to reconcile the demands of private and professional life)."[82] Thus women as supermothers are still caught in a perpetual battle between traditional or socialist notions of femaleness, and contemporary (or democratic, capitalist) valuation of youth and attractiveness. The consumption of food becomes inextricably linked to politics, gender roles, and standards of beauty. If the ideal consumer of Jabłońska's food is a woman, the woman is directed to choose between an intimate encounter that might put her on a trajectory toward motherhood, or a vehement denial of it through militaristic exercise (that is, if she follows Jabłońska's instruction). This is significant as Poland banned abortion in 1993, and a majority of its population is pro-life.[83] Ashley Weeks Cart, on the other hand, interprets this duality not as a choice but as a reflection of the multiple duties leveled on women and considers the work primarily from the standpoint of a consumer who is already a mother. For Cart, the flags with the caloric value suggest the culturally imposed requirements of the "modern woman and mother to maintain a physically fit, healthy, slender figure." This, in

Cart's opinion, suggests that Jabłońska refers to a double burden that requires mothers to serve and care for others "while remaining desirable and attractive objects."[84] While this notion is certainly true, Jabłońska has never limited her food to women only, nor does she consume any of the items herself. She enacts the caring mother, who is concerned about other's nutritious and balanced consumption and the choices that they may make. Though not often mentioned, for men the choice in their consumption of calories is also between love and war, which have different, yet similar, notions of fatherhood, masculinity, and fitness.

Sebastian Cichocki offers yet another reading of these actions. Continuing to name Jabłońska a supermother, he writes:

> What is important to a supermother? Cooking is important. Wonderful things happen in the kitchen: peeling vegetables, counting calories, boiling rice and pasta, cracking nuts, portioning herbs, smelling, slurping …, and pilfering for something delicious around the pots and pans. Motherhood is important. With all the mess, lack of sleep, and the stupidest questions (How old is the youngest artist? Who rules the cosmos? Why is the color black sad?) Jabłońska once recapped her art in one sentence: *if you have a family, one with a mom, a dad, and a child, you'll know what it's about.*[85]

In this statement, Cichocki unites the action of cooking, counting calories, and art-making as universal questions of the family. No matter if you are a husband, wife, or child consuming Jabłońska's selection of cheeses or vegetables, you understand that caring, counting, and questioning life is something familiar, common, and perhaps, innate to the structure of the family. A mother (whether your own or not) is there to guide you.

In placing the creation of food items and their consumption as the primary artistic act, Jabłońska recalls the food-based work of Fluxus artists, such as Alison Knowles, who similarly brought food inside the space of the museum in works like *Make a Salad* (1962). Performed at the Institute of Contemporary Art, London, Knowles's proposition, as she termed it, included musical scores by Mozart before and after the preparation of the salad, and included the aid of assistants who swiftly and rhythmically chopped vegetables for the salad.[86] Restaged several times in recent years, Knowles's project is similar to Jabłońska's in the provision of food to an audience.[87] Nevertheless, the use of assistants and the musicality of Knowles's performance distinguish the project as one of shared labor, rather than the individual and silent (as in there is no musical accompaniment) labor of Jabłońska's *Kitchen*. Jabłońska's burden is isolated and individual, while Knowles's shared and communal. Both encouraged the meeting of individuals through the act of consumption, and as women artists, this transposition of the gendered act of food preparation from the private to public space asserts female creativity and the creation of food as an artistic act.

Similar notions of food and art were explored by Daniel Spoerri, who in 1968 opened Restaurant Spoerri on Burgplatz in Düsseldorf after years of integrating foodstuffs, kitchen appliances, cooking, and eating into his artistic practice. In 1963, Spoerri began preparing meals and inviting guests to eat an intricate meal that was served to them by an art critic. This format made gallery visitors the true consumers of the art, literally, and the art critics as the "intermediaries between the products of the artist and the general public."[88] Spoerri would photograph the remains and debris of the meal as a *tableaux-pièges* or *Trap Pictures*. This methodology is somewhat akin to a later work by Jabłońska, titled *Accidental Pleasure* (2005–06), in which she photographed and documented the leftovers or remnants of her family's daily meals that become trapped in the kitchen sink sieve when washing dishes.[89] For Jabłońska, the series revealed a beauty in the debris of eating, and was complete when she recorded 365, or one year, of photographs. The idea of capturing the aftermath of a dinner, for Spoerri, inspired more reconsiderations of the day-to-day necessity of eating. According to Renate Buschmann, "Spoerri discovered the act of eating as a focal point that brought societal and cultural significances to light."[90] In 1970, fueled by the success of Restaurant Spoerri, the artist began Eat Art Gallery where he continued to explore how food, while being vital to life, can radically change established traditions.[91] To show individuals how this existed, Spoerri hosted *Eat Art Banquets* where meals were "artistically fashioned dinners," sometimes providing inedible "food" that would draw attention to notions of nutrition, poverty, or the relationships among guests. The difference between Spoerri's Eat Art practices and Jabłońska lies primarily in the ultimate intentions of their cooking. The literature on Spoerri rarely discusses paternalistic or familial notions of cooking, but rather considers it in terms of the individual—the poor man, the professional chef, critic, and artist. While both reconfigure the relationship between art and spectator, for Jabłońska the act of cooking figures an important part of the work as the connections to gender, domesticity, and notions of the Polish mother are critical for the overall conceptual thrust of the project. In these performances, one author recounts,

> everything must work perfectly: the food looks lovely, and it is served in a sophisticated way, just like the dishes shown in cookery books. After she prepares the food and invites others to help themselves, she always just stays in the background. She never leaves art objects, apart from the leftovers.[92]

To clarify, Jabłońska's art object is the food to be consumed, but she does not leave it in the gallery to act as an art object either. In essence, Jabłońska brings the dinner party atmosphere, with the proper culturally constructed notions of dinner party etiquette, to the gallery, in order to encourage her guests to meet, mingle, and enjoy themselves. Once the party is over, whatever is perishable is removed, and the *Kitchen* becomes the only object of permanent display.

Food culture, particularly in Eastern European countries, is marked by the circumstances of politics. Many individuals who were born before 1989 recall the scarcity of available products, and the prohibition of prepackaged items from the West that made one's relationship to the food that was available, particularly important. After 1989, Polish shoppers gained access to both Western items and those found only in particular regions of Poland, deeply altering their food consumption and nutrition.[93] In addition, fast food chains McDonald's, Burger King, Kentucky Fried Chicken, and Pizza Hut opened their doors and were popular establishments for the younger generation.[94] In recent years, cuisine in Poland has become more international in scope as well as more health conscious with television shows highlighting both innovative cuisine and calorie consciousness.[95] At the same time, considering caloric value in relationship to war, Jabłońska ties the food item to its historical context. Could it be that a simple piece of cheese is available because of the militaristic intervention of socialist rule?

Ultimately, the projects *Through the Stomach to the Heart* and *Kitchen* have the purpose of feeding others and creating a problematic situation, a meeting, or an interaction among strangers. Outside of the major urban center of Warsaw, this is particularly important, as food maintains its central role in the family and eating out occurs on special occasions only.[96] Thus, it is not particularly surprising that in Jabłońska's performance staged in Łódź (filmed and later presented as the work, *Meeting*, 2004) was not well received even if she herself finds exhibition openings akin to holidays or special occasions.[97] Jabłońska invited 140 dismissed workers from a local textile factory in Łódź to an elegant banquet at the Poznański Palace in the hope of generating direct contact with this group of people.[98] Known as the "Polish Manchester," "a woman's city," and "a dark city," the textile production dominated Łódź's industry but went into severe decline in the 1990s.[99] Most of its workers were women and with a population of two million, it has one of the country's highest unemployment rates. In addition, by mid-1991, it was estimated that 100 nursery schools had been closed down, doubly burdening the female population.[100] So Jabłońska's invitation aimed to reach those women who, unemployed in "a woman's city," she believed deserved some recognition. The site of the banquet, however, could have been one of the deterring elements. The Poznański Palace is known as one of the most magnificent homes of Izrael Kalman Poznański, the owner of the major textile factory in Łódź in the nineteenth century. This setting may have caused mixed reactions due to class disparities and/or the nostalgia of the bygone productive textile era. According to the artist, only one-third of the invited people attended the meal, and most of them the management, not her ideal recipient. Her targets were the female laborers, but they largely refused the invitation.[101]

While this reveals the nature of the refused or unacknowledged gift, it also reflects the cultural intimacy of food consumption—meals are times where families convene. The invitation to a public meal prepared by Jabłońska was not interpreted as one where the Polish Mother was feeding her family. It was rather seen as a threat. As Miwon Kwon has written, "the refusal of a gift functions as a rejection of both the giver's superiority and his or her invitation to solidarity," therefore making the act of giving always laden with the risk of humiliation and a "breach in the social relations involved with gift-giving."[102] Thus, Jabłońska's act of kindness, or giving, was encountered with skepticism, denial, and for those who attended, embarrassment.[103] They were not prepared to reciprocate her gift and affirm her solidarity with blue-collar work, particularly at a site formerly owned by the wealthy owner of a textile factory. It can be argued that Jabłońska's maternal act was organized for an inappropriate setting—inviting guests to a public museum, rather than a lavish historical home, which would have been less threatening. The artist noted, "I wondered why they had not come, what had caused their resistance. Maybe they did not have proper shoes to put on? Maybe my offer seemed to be out of this world for them?"[104] It could also reflect that maternal subjectivity is not always "right" or "correct" and that sometimes, the desire to help others, even if from deriving from a good place, is not always what others want.[105] Her attempt to give praise to invisible labor was more successful in the work *83 Waiters and a Helper* (2006) (Figure 3.5). For this project, Jabłońska installed a large and domineering cabinet in the space of the Atlas Sztuki Gallery and hired eighty-three waiters to serve wine while the artist read a long list thanking over 100 people involved in the presentation of her work.[106] This

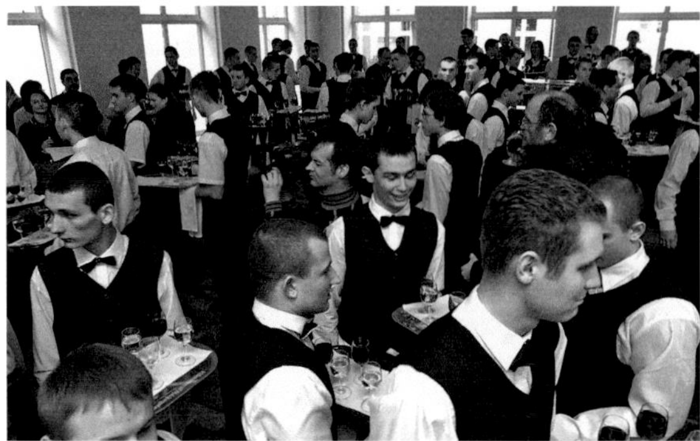

Figure 3.5 Elżbieta Jabłońska, *83 Waiters and a Helper*, 2006. Atlas Sztuki, Łódź, Poland. Courtesy the artist.

action, in addition to *Meeting*, draws on class disparities and makes visible those who are typically ignored by society and do not typically take a primary role in art events. The presence of the well-dressed waiters interrupted conversations, made the space cramped and caused the art patrons to acknowledge these young men's and women's presence. This coupled with the list of individuals who are not always publicly thanked in the undertaking and execution of an exhibition again reveal Jabłońska's desire to make others care.

With the notion that the performance should encourage a meeting, Jabłońska similarly aligns herself with contemporaries such as Julita Wójcik. Wójcik's *Peeling Potatoes* performance at the Zachęta National Gallery of Art in Warsaw just a few years earlier is somewhat similar in terms of public interaction. In 2001, Wójcik donned an apron, sat on a stool in the gallery, spoke with viewers, and peeled fifty kilograms of potatoes. Sometimes, visitors (including men, women, and children) would squat on the ground and peel potatoes with her.[107] Anda Rottenberg noted that this event aroused significant criticism. The work was discussed in a manner Rottenberg believed "that only a criminal deed of exceptional cruelty could arouse."[108] Mostly, however, critics questioned the act of peeling potatoes as an art form and if it was a form that should be supported by taxpayer money. Recounting the controversy, Karol Sienkiewicz wrote,

> Defenders of the "status quo" protested that potatoes belong at home, in the kitchen, by the sink, over a bucket of parings. When brought to the gallery, which is regarded as a temple, a place endowed with a unique power of sanctifying, it endows the objects the rank of a "piece of art" (i.e. relics), the activity became taboo. Potatoes and art (sacred, national) do not go hand in hand.[109]

Likewise, Gabriela Świtek noted that the performance came on the heels of the 2000 Zachęta exhibition of the controversial Maurizio Cattelan installation, *The Ninth Hour* (1999), in which Cattelan depicted the beloved Polish pope John Paul II struck by a meteorite in the midst of the gallery. Wójcik's performance created the "logical sequence: saber-meteorite-potatoes" that journalists and critics found threatening to their values, culture, and notions of art. Iza Kowalczyk's comments on this work in her essay on Polish feminism gets to the heart of the Wójcik scandal. She writes:

> It's a girl playing, and a willful girl at that: in the time of feminism, she assumes the part of a decent housewife peeling potatoes (2001), and what's more significant, the event takes place at Zachęta—an institution dedicated to preserving our national heritage. But can one categorize peeling potatoes as belonging to national heritage? Thereby the event, apart from containing irony, acquired a critical, if not outright feminist dimension.[110]

If Wójcik's performance deliberately and critically questions the place of women in Polish national heritage, so does Jabłońska's. Her projects, however, have not struck the same level of outrage because, one, critics and visitors are now likely more accustomed to the integrative performances of contemporary artists; and, two, Jabłońska does not simply prepare vegetables; she cooks them and offers them for consumption, thus fulfilling the expectations of the audience and the culinary process.

In doing so, Jabłońska engages with the current discourse on relational aesthetics and participatory art, both of which have been notably debated and theorized by Nicholas Bourriaud, Claire Bishop, and Grant Kester. In the 1990s, Bourriaud proclaimed the existence of a relational art, that is, "an art taking as its theoretical horizon the realm of human interactions and its social context, rather than the assertion of an independent and *private* symbolic space."[111] The Thai, New York-based artist Rirkrit Tiravanija may be considered one of the most prominent artists operating in a relational mode. In projects like *Untitled (Free)*, 1992, Tiravanija moved the offices and packing and shipping areas of the 303 Gallery in New York to the public areas, and set up a makeshift kitchen, tables, and chairs for eating in the back room. Cooking Thai curry vegetables for anyone who entered during the show's duration, Tiravanija gave the food to anyone who wanted it, and provided a place to eat.[112] Through this action, "being together" became a central theme, thus emphasizing the crucial connective role of the gallery-goer or participant.[113] This emphasis on free food and the interaction of people has caused scholars to draw on Jacques Rancière and his notions of democratic art. For Rancière, democratic art is the result of emancipation, and what he theorizes as the "distribution of the sensible."[114] In terms of emancipation, Rancière argues that art becomes emancipated and emancipatory when the artist knows that they cannot make others share their views, and when the object "renounces the authority of the imposed message, the target audience, and the univocal mode of explicating the world," or "it stops *wanting* to emancipate us."[115] Rancière's notion of the "distribution of the sensible" is that the distribution of the objects, affects, pleasure, and pains that are apprehended by the senses structures how an individual may perceive, think, and act. The distribution of the sensible divides, or partitions (to use Rancière's term), the world and people. It works on two fronts: it "separates and excludes" but it also allows participation through sensory experience.[116] But in terms of the aesthetic regime, we must consider the complicated relationship between art and life, or rather the ever-increasing blur between what is and is not art.[117] For Jabłońska's project, the merging of the artist, Polish mother, housewife, and hostess denotes a redistribution of the sensible, a "recomposition of the landscape of the visible, a recomposition of the relationship between doing, making, being, seeing, and saying."[118] This emancipated form of art, that is, not necessarily food art, but art that eliminates the gap between both the institution and the social space, and the artist and the viewer, enables a direct exchange between the artist and the individual, which is key to Jabłońska's project.[119]

Like Tiravanija, Jabłońska seeks to create a situation, a relationship among "lots of people."[120] These artists are similar in their desire to give, which as Pierre Bourdieu has argued, is determined by the *habitus*, the internalization of collective practices that organize society.[121] The act of giving food aids the artists' negotiation with society, but it is similarly rooted within each artist's cultural background. As Jabłońska interrogates the Polish mother stereotype, Tiravanija's work is often linked to his memories of his grandmother's restaurant in Thailand.[122] While linked to the experiences of women, the reenactments, if one chooses to call them such, are quite different. Tiravanija's cooking enables an open dialogue, while Jabłońska's encourages the visualization of the unpaid labor of the mother. As Marek Krajewski has noted, "the artist feasts her guests like the typical housewife does, but at the same time does so as an artist for whose sake viewers have come to the gallery. ... It is only here that she can serve others and be celebrated at the same time."[123] Thus Jabłońska's cooking in the gallery is a means to *simultaneously recognize the values of domestic and artistic action that has been historically erased or omitted.*

As a woman, it is imperative that Jabłońska does not continually cook for her audience; to do so would be to perpetuate the myth of the Polish mother and eliminate her artistic identity. Jabłońska has very deliberately stated that these performances contain "very little or even nothing" of herself.[124] To demonstrate this, she clearly limits the scope of her meal: it will take place at a certain date, in a certain place, and in a certain absurdist way—enlarging both the volume and scale of her cooking. She simultaneously performs and confronts the motherly role of domestic cook and host, and makes a private labor public.

As the artist makes the work of the housewife/hostess visible, she simultaneously brings forth the notion of the consumption of food as a private affair, but one that can be extremely public—a spectacle to be observed and in which to participate.[125] Regarding the entire series, she notes, "I gave public to an ordinary, everyday activity—eating. It was food that replaced lofty ideas included in the works of art. If wine and snacks are so essential, why consume them secretly as in Buñuel's film [*The Phantom of Liberty* (1974)]?" This statement evokes the infamous scene from *The Phantom of Liberty* where the private act of defecation is made public (guests sit on toilets around a table, smoking and discussing important issues) and the consumption of food is made private: guests must excuse themselves to eat in a "dining room" that resembles a water closet.[126] Jabłońska draws upon this reversal in her authorization of food within the space of the gallery. On this, she claims she "decided ... to give official permission for secret consumption," suggesting that while food is typically not permitted within the space of the gallery, it is often snuck in.[127] Therefore, the artist's series not only perverts understandings of gender stereotypes, but also the proper behavior within an art institution.[128] Indeed, scholar Deborah R. Geis has argued that "the public space of performance allows women artists to interrogate the boundaries between the private and the public ... [and where] entering the territory of public space through food can be a transgressive or defiant act."[129] Jabłońska, as the mother-artist, sanctions the forbidden act.[130]

The artist deliberately attempts to transform the standard exhibition to awaken one's recognition of the everyday—from burdens of the Polish mother, the disparity with the traditions of the art world, to the viewer's consumption of food. She aims to expose the invisible work of the mother, but also the domestic duties of the artist and curator. Jabłońska's series *Through the Stomach to the Heart* insists on revealing the structure of the everyday aspect of cooking, serving, and laboring for others. She takes the social structure of a woman cooking for her family, makes it an artistic act, and visualizes a labor that should be celebrated, praised, and thanked. By paying attention to these invisible roles, Jabłońska's photographs of curators and artists destroy the notion of a romantic artist and stereotypes that may be ingrained about the living spaces of the artists and curators.

Paraphrasing an interview with the artist, Jabłońska noted that artists are trained to be resourceful, to act as their own curators, managers, and leaders. They should be current and attend exhibition openings, lest they be forgotten.[131] Interestingly, requirements of the artist that Jabłońska details do not include taking care of one's family, cooking, or eating. These essential elements of life are what become stripped away from the notion of the artist and curator and perhaps it is through the visual image that she is able to reinsert this human element into notions of the artist. It is significant that these kitchens are just as unremarkable as those that Jabłońska placed in the gallery. They are small, ordinary spaces with burners, sinks, and sometimes ovens; most are crammed with kitchen utensils, pots, pans, dishes, and drinkware. They all document a single worker, who is often represented by the work that they create—art, exhibitions, or writing—but rarely are they praised or documented within the domestic for the labor performed there (Plate 5).

The domestic, though frequently the topic of public political debate, is often regarded as a private and personal space. Typically, one must be invited into it or exist as a part of it as a family. Therefore, it is not surprising that these individuals seem to be documented almost in secret. The rear-view of the individual positions the viewer as a voyeur, peeking into the lives of the mythic artist and the heralded curator. In most of the images, one has the sense that the person is in the midst of a solitary activity, which plays into the myth of their lonely artistic existence, but also reveals their individual labor for others. Food, as Jabłońska has reiterated throughout this series, is a means of generating openness and dialogue by providing direct contact. Similarly, kitchens are spaces of activity, debate, and dialogue—particularly during dinner parties. So what initially seems like a secretive activity can also be seen as one that encourages a relationship between the artist and the viewer. The viewer effectively becomes the guest in the artist's home, providing a chance for both to explore the relationship between art and life.

But Jabłońska does not stop at the photograph or its chance of display in the gallery. She incorporated these images into at least one edition of her *Kitchen* performance by printing them on napkins that were folded and made available during the action. Visitors were able to use one of these napkins to wipe their hands and protect their clothing, and likewise be confronted with the image of an artist or curator in the act of cooking. By creating functional art objects, Jabłońska further combines the artist and quotidian in the space of the gallery.

Although Jabłońska's desire to cook and care for others can be understood in light of theories of relational aesthetics and food-focused art, it is important to note that the artist has not claimed to be in conversation or even inspired by these ideas. Her projects can be distinguished from the food-based practice of Spoerri, Knowles, Wojcík, and Tiravanija due to her emphasis on the maternal associations of food. By using the maternal as a subjective, critical position from which to interrogate the presumed disparities of the Polish mother and those of the institution of art, Jabłońska employs a maternal mode of artistic practice. She simultaneously *performs* the roles of the *mother* and the *artist* through her perversion and distortion of the private spaces of cooking. Jabłońska reveals that their traditionally assumed opposition is absurd. She asserts that the institutions of motherhood and eating, like the systems of display and dispersion of art in galleries, are structured on social assumptions and pressures that are no longer desirable and need to change to accommodate what is valuable in both sets of activities: the act of caring for others.

Care: Helping Oneself and Others

As Jabłońska asserts a maternal mode of art making that emphasizes the connections between motherhood, art, and everyday life, the series *Helping* demonstrates Jabłońska's continued interest in people beyond the spaces and structures of the museum and gallery. Rather than providing a simple one-time meal, *Helping* constitutes a series of actions that are aimed at providing people unexpected pleasure, income, rest, and relaxation. These are elements that have the possibility of affecting the individual beyond a single meal. Indeed, aspects of *Helping* appeared in the *Through the Stomach to the Heart* series. As a part of her 2003 *Kitchen* installation at the Neuer Berliner Kunstverein, Jabłońska included announcements for "a young, energetic Polish woman" looking for a job on dishtowels that hung from her enlarged cupboards. This advertisement struck Jabłońska because Germany, and in particular, the city of Berlin, has a large community of Polish people who began to migrate there at the beginning of the 1990s. To compound the migration issue, Jabłońska found that there were many illegal Polish women living there who worked as housekeepers. She wanted to hire a woman, illegally, to work in her kitchen, to further explore the relationship between unseen and undocumented labor, but she was unable to do so. "It didn't work," she noted, so instead, she placed the advertisement on dishtowels that were easily read while hanging on the cupboards of her *Kitchen*. Since she was not able to physically bring an illegal worker to *Kitchen*, she chose to use this subtle reminder to acknowledge her existence.

This gentle perversion by Jabłońska similarly reveals broader cultural issues of domestic workers and globalization. Will Hutton, in a conversation with Anthony Giddens on the topic of globalization, notes: "… the growth in personal household services is the result of the emergence of two-earner households who have to buy in service because the woman is no longer at home."[132] Sociologist Helma Lutz promptly argues that Hutton's notion reaffirms the antiquated concept that "'the woman' is a housewife and a natural provider of services at home" where "care work and housework are not considered 'work' in the *real sense*, but as *lovework* (Arbeit aus Liebe) which is performed as a part of the natural female role."[133] As discussed previously, confronting cultural definitions of womanhood is certainly part of Jabłońska's artistic investigation, and it becomes even more tangible here with her dishtowels. The individuals who provide "personal household services" are predominantly migrant women, and in 2000 it was estimated that there were 2.4 million of these types of workers in Germany, many of whom work semi-legally or illegally.

In Berlin, Lutz explains, Polish women take advantage of the German–Polish agreement and the proximity of their home country to enter Germany without visas, work for two months, and return home. Five or six women will share an apartment, clean for several households, and pass work to relatives and acquaintances.[134] While Polish workers were the highest paid domestic servants in the 1990s, ethnic hierarchies and racist stereotypes determine the actual amount of remuneration received. In addition, there are the many problems that domestic workers encounter, sociologists Bridget Anderson and Annie Phizacklea report. In their study, *Migrant Domestic Workers: A European Perspective* (1997), Anderson and Phizacklea found that domestics are often unpaid for hours worked; have a low income (less than minimum wage); are denied wages; have employers refuse to arrange their legal status, or by whom they are sexually harassed, and are pressured to do additional work.[135] Jabłońska's simple translation of a woman seeking work does not overtly refer to this larger and much deeper social inequity, but her reference to it would be apparent to Berliners. The issue of domestic workers was of growing interest and topic of discussion at the time, and Helma Lutz was conducting the first larger study on "new domestics" in Germany.[136] The themes of acknowledging invisible labor and providing aid, whether tangible or psychological, are similarly present in the previous series discussed in this chapter; however they become the dominant elements of the *Helping* series.

This series is significant for Jabłońska's artist-parent identity because it has both a caring aspect directed toward others and one that has some "therapeutic influence" for herself. While the desire to care for others is not exclusively a maternal or parental coda, it is one that is often characterized as 'motherly' or 'parental.' Similarly, the act of caregiving by a non-parent can assume sentiments of closeness, intimacy, and the familial. Jabłońska has confessed that this series has, "helped [her] survive some difficult moments in [her] life," providing a release from the throes of family life but without sacrificing the maternal modality.[137] For example, the project *Help Yourself* (2003), held in a gallery in Ustka (on the Northern Coast of Poland), provided several days of seaside recreation for a group of artists, critics, and curators. This project, where she asked others to take a vacation (some of whom still recall that it was the only vacation they had taken in years), was significant because Jabłońska realized, "in my reality, where I am constantly involved in a difficult process of creating my own codes, I can handle everyday problems more easily and I am able to come up with more creative solutions."[138] By providing an opportunity for others, Jabłońska was able to imagine, arrange, and manage everyday aspects of life for those who had such solutions escape them.

To return to Jabłońska's *Kitchen* project in Berlin, her desire to utilize an illegal worker draws a connection to another contemporary artist, Santiago Sierra. Best known for the work *250 cm Line Tattooed on Six Paid People* (1999), Sierra continually exposes in his work the capitalist system and the value attributed to the laboring body. Over the years he has not only paid menial workers to be permanently tattooed with a line on their backs, but he has also paid individuals to masturbate, crouch in cardboard boxes, and have their hair dyed blonde in order to identify their presence (in Venice, Italy during the Fifty-third Venice Biennale). As Sierra's actions are considered to "unmask power relations that keep workers invisible under capitalism," Jabłońska's *Helping* actions are similar, yet they are more clearly tied to the post-socialist environment of Poland and do not have permanent, and perhaps damaging, effects on the person's body.[139]

Unlike the *Through the Stomach to the Heart* series, most of the actions that comprise *Helping* were staged within the borders of Poland and they are generally geared specifically toward helping Polish people. Only one of her helping actions took place outside of Poland, and this was for the Biennale in Prague in 2005. This action, unlike the others that resulted in some type of visual display for the public, consisted of providing aid to other artists participating in the Biennale. Jabłońska hired three men to wear special uniforms and help the artists with the installation of their projects. Artists found these men with the help of a map that Jabłońska provided.[140] Here, one can argue, Jabłońska demonstrates care for her colleagues, or the family of artists who have been joined together under the auspices of an exhibition. The other projects for the *A Woman Has a Soul*, *Women's Day*, and *Awakening* exhibitions are clearly focused on the "family" of Polish people.

For example, in the 2003 exhibition *A Woman Has a Soul* in Łódź (a city, as previously mentioned, with a high unemployment rate), Jabłońska hired a woman to embroider the text of an advertisement she saw posted on a wall while making her preparations for the exhibition. The advertisement was written by a woman—a single mother—who was seeking employment. After calling the number listed and getting no answer, Jabłońska decided that she would help another unemployed woman. Paying her with the funds she received for participating in the exhibition, Jabłońska hired her to embroider the advertisement and display it as her contribution to the exhibition. In this project, Jabłońska returns to the myth of the Polish Mother, asking the viewer to remember the sacrifices she makes to ensure the future of her child(ren). The woman in the advertisement publicly announces her single-ness, her role as a mother, and opens herself up to the interpretation that she is currently unable to support her child. By acknowledging herself as a mother, she also panders to readers' notion of the 'brave victim' and attempts to appeal to their sense of humanity. But Jabłońska expands the context of this message and makes it much more specifically about the employment situation in Łódź. Jabłońska sought out an unemployed textile worker to stitch the message. Embroidery typically falls under the domestic, but in Łódź it was the job of a trained individual during the textile boom, therefore the medium and the message become intertwined.

While the job was a one-time-only opportunity, Jabłońska sees the *Helping* series as her attempt to "handle the unsolvable problem of social helplessness," and draw attention to certain social problems. By offering a woman some money in exchange for a personal item, perhaps the woman will be propelled to market her services for financial gain. Jabłońska acknowledges that it is "not [her] job to solve these problems" as she is an artist and not a social activist, but there is an element of hope that raising awareness through art will help others come up with solutions.

In contrast, Claire Bishop asserts that artists that utilize other people's bodies (such as Santiago Sierra) know "that there is no such thing as a free meal: everything and everyone has a price. His work can be seen as a grim meditation on the social and political conditions that permit disparities in people's 'prices' to emerge."[141] She notes that Sierra's collaborators are asked to do things that "are invariably useless, physically demanding, and on occasion leave permanent scars."[142] But his goal in asking these individuals to participate in his work, Bishop argues, is not to create an empathic response in the viewer, but rather to generate a "pointed racial and economic non-identification: 'This is not me.'"[143] Sierra's work does, however, provide a shockingly apt metaphor for the actual damages that menial workers are routinely expected to suffer, and an effective, if questionably justified, aspect of his work. In contrast, Jabłońska attempts to preserve the individuals' integrity and never performs or requests permanent changes on their bodies. While she typically pays individuals for their work, her actions are more consistently *maternal* and nurturing in practice. For example, Jabłońska's project with the homeless *Helping* (2004) for the *Women's Day* exhibition in Kraków didn't take any portraits of the individuals, allowing them to retain their integrity and only photographing their hands as they created origami tulips. With a previous group of homeless individuals living at a railway station, she asked that they write down their private wishes.[144] Jabłońska took these wishes and printed them on the pieces of paper that the next group of homeless men would fold into tulips. Much of the text regarded having a job, home, wealth, and the desire to "return to normal" printed on them. These flowers were then presented to women the homeless men met on the street as Women's Day presents on March 8.[145] This choice was made with the purpose of "motivating and stimulating" but the overall message suggests that individuals, including the creators, receivers, and witnesses of this action, should realize there are more important things than art.

But not all of Jabłońska's *Helping* actions involve financial remuneration. In 2001 Jabłońska gave away small bags with snacks in the town center of Bytom, exploring the boundaries of art. The project *The Line of Art* questioned the boundaries of art practice, but more importantly provided individuals with gifts of food. She also carried out actions where gallery visitors were able to take any and all clothing they needed or wanted. But on St. Nicholas's Day in 1999 and in 2008, Jabłońska tied religious tradition to her artistic giving.

St. Nicholas' Day, celebrated on December 6, is distinct in Central and Eastern European countries. In most Catholic regions that celebrate the holiday, St. Nick visits the homes of children and provides them gifts (often, candy and other small items) or a punishment (variably, a lump of coal or the threat of a beating with a rod). Known as *Mikołaj* in Poland, St. Nicholas' presence and its celebration is different there because often an angel and a devil will join him, to balance the forces of good and evil. For Jabłońska's first version of the project, performed for the exhibition *Package* at Club Mózg, Bydgoszcz, she simply wrapped a variety of packages, placed them in the club and allowed individuals to take the gift. Jabłońska performs the role of the angel or St. Nicholas by giving helpful or positive gifts, and removes the presence of the devil: there was no threat of someone receiving the rod. Similarly, for the exhibition *Awakening* in Swiecie upon the River Vistula in 2008, Jabłońska gave away traditional gifts such as socks, scarves, gloves, calendars, books, pictures, mugs, candles, and candies.[146] By moving further outside of the institutional structure of "art," Jabłońska removes herself from the confines of the gallery space and demonstrates that she is not solely concerned about exploiting economic or gender inequities. She prefers to "enter an interaction with her recipients, make them feel important, appreciated, noticed and free from everyday reality." Jabłońska realizes that she has been "Supermother for a long time and now [she doesn't] want to function as superhelp," but she continually returns to the theme of helping others. She does this by bringing people together, cooking for them, and helping them because she believes "life itself is art" and "art makes happy."[147]

Like *Through the Stomach to the Heart*, Jabłońska's helping actions are predicated on a relationship between the giver and receiver. The individual must take and accept her gifts (of candy, food, clothing) in order to complete the relationship and the art. As Maurice Godelier wrote, the giving cycle does create solidarity through the act of sharing or giving, but it also creates superiority because, "the one who receives the gift and accepts it places himself in the debt of the one who has given it, thereby becoming indebted to the giver and to a certain extent becoming his 'dependent,' at least for as long as he has not 'given back' what he was given."[148] The creation of this relationship seems to suggest yet another mode of maternal action that is tied to the Polish Mother. To give selflessly to others, including and especially strangers, is a way that the Polish Mother can demonstrate her care for the nation and her desire to see it succeed. As Kowalczyk notes, "The Polish Mother was responsible for the continuity of faith, language, and culture" when Poland lost its independence in 1795, and it can be argued that the Polish Mother once again functions in this mode as Poland attempts to grow as an independent and successful capitalist country as a part of the European Union.

Jabłońska's statement regarding not wanting to be "superhelp" recognizes the degree to which Supermothers are needed to generate a sense of community, family, and garner prosperity. There is a critical need to bring awareness to social issues, and not to simply reiterate or expose social disparities as Santiago Sierra's work often does. Like the series *Through the Stomach to the Heart*, Jabłońska's *Helping* actions are meant to bring people together, encourage a meeting and an exchange for the betterment of the people. Jabłońska's actions, according to Krajewski are not to:

> demonstrate that being a wife, a mother, a teacher, a friend or the good Samaritan is more important than art-making, but rather to highlight the consciousness that it is but one of many roles that, while helping us adapt to reality, fulfill the expectations of others [to be] treated like normal persons, make it difficult for us to notice that those are but roles and there exists something far more fundamental: the experience of oneself as a person, contact with others not mediated by roles, perception of reality free of the viewpoint imposed by it.[149]

Krajewski argues that Jabłońska's art is less about roles, whether a mother or not, and is simply about people and direct contact among individuals. Jabłońska's actions revolve around aspects of everyday life, but one should not disregard the role that maternity has had in generating her particular artistic discourse. Jabłońska approaches the subject of people with a specific intention to help, reveal, enable and provide. These are intentions that are rigorously and intellectually conceived by a woman, who employs maternity as a lens through which to view the world.

Care as Artistic Practice

Elżbieta Jabłońska approaches her artistic practice from her heart and her head, meaning that there is a loving and caring element to the work as much as there is a critical, conceptual one. This chapter has highlighted three important series of works—*Supermother*, *Through the Stomach to the Heart*, and *Helping*—series that clearly demonstrate this dual focus. However, I choose to term this focus not as "heart and mind" but as a *maternal subjectivity*. While Jabłońska may embrace or strongly rebel from some of the characteristics of maternity, her work is always in relation to it. Even in 2007, when her rejection became physically manifest in a performance where she admired, and then destroyed, her out-of-scale kitchen with a sledgehammer (Plate 6), Jabłońska revealed and affirmed the contemporary stereotypes regarding women in the space of the kitchen and her own misgivings about being a mother-artist. But yet, as Ujma notes, she just exploits the image of a mother and involves it in her art. She develops her concept of being an artist on the basis of features that maternity is normally associated with. The artist plays the role of a mother, and maternity becomes her way to create art: through care, helping, and also upbringing.[150]

Ujma views Jabłońska's art not as part of a sentimental or biologically-based practice, but as a maternal sensibility and a chosen artistic identity. Jabłońska's art making functions as a means to explore the issues of maternal identity and care.

Even in works that seem to have little to do with motherhood, Jabłońska sometimes attributes personal meaning that suggests otherwise. For the work, *New Life* (*Nowe Zycie*), 2010, a neon sign illuminating those same words is not one that was custom-made by the artist (Figure 3.6). Rather, it is a 1970s-era sign that stood atop an abandoned communist-era building, which was part of a PGR (*Państwowe Gospodasrtwo Rolne*), a collective farm run by the state in the village of Trzeciewiec, near Bydgoszcz. The work clearly draws on the heritage of the People's Republic of Poland (Polska Rzeczpospolita or PRL), which is frequently characterized as a ghost that "coexists with the new modernization/Westernization narratives, crucially influencing the post-Communist transition period and its hybrid peculiarities."[151] Indeed, artists like Jabłońska who were born in the 1970s (and 1960s) have crossed two worlds: the PRL and democratic Poland.[152] Thus, the ghost of the PRL holds a

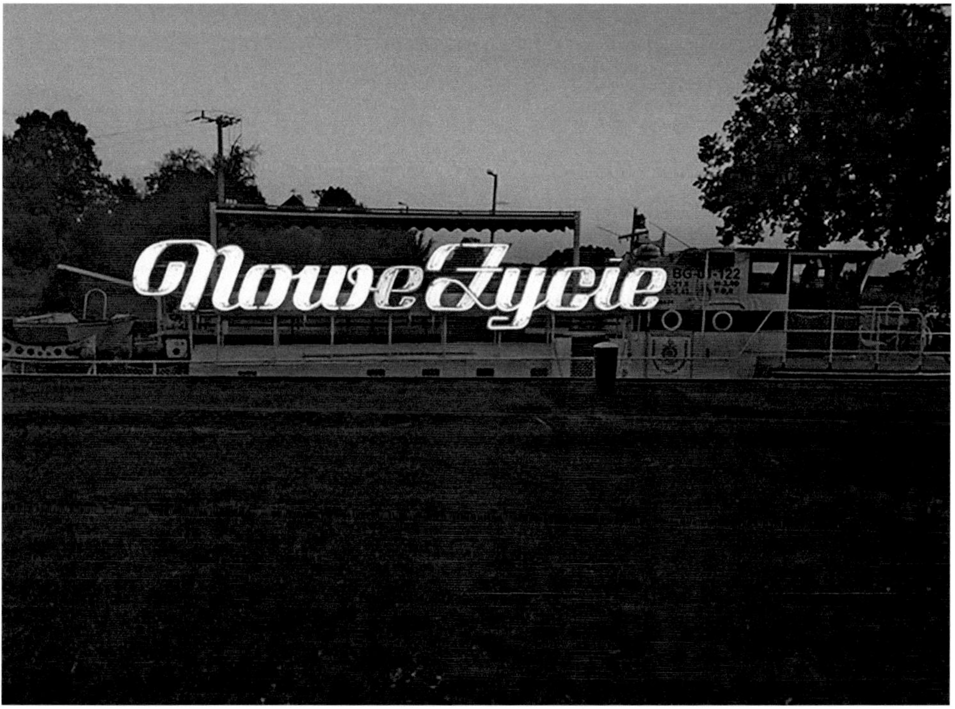

Figure 3.6 Elżbieta Jabłońska, *New Life*, 2010. Neon. Collection Nomus Nowe Muzeum Sztuki, Gdansk. Courtesy the artist.

place in the media, is the topic of scholarly debates, and part of the day-to-day life of the Polish people. At the time *New Life* was erected, it stood for the prosperity and the shared role that each member of the community would have in creating a better life. It has been documented that these former state farm settlements, in the post-communist era, are spaces of poverty and lack of opportunity.[153] For Jabłońska, this failed promise on the part of the PRL does not mean lack of hope. For example, in transferring the location of the sign to the exterior of the Gallery Arsenal in Poznań while it was undergoing renovations, it positively suggested the chances one has to start again or begin anew. The artist suggests that an individual can "start a new life every morning," and choose their fate—a positive message in the midst of the economic woes and a high unemployment rate.[154] But in addition, the sign has personal meaning for the artist—it represents the birth of her second child, her entry into a new phase of motherhood, and perhaps, the start of a new phase of her work.[155] Like all of Jabłońska's oeuvre, *New Life* has deeply political, social, and personal meaning. One simply has to decide which of those meanings speaks to them the most, and be receptive to the message.

Even as Jabłońska's artistic production has become more and more distanced from the visualization of traditional representations of motherhood, her work remains fundamentally tied to it through a maternal thinking, care, and action. Whether performing the role of Supermother, Superwoman, or Polish Mother, Jabłońska articulates her artist-parent identity in relationship to the personal, political, and cultural circumstances she experiences as an artist in Poland and attempts to expose those issues to society at large. While much of her work has only been seen or experienced by the Polish people, her messages have the ability to connect to individuals living, working, and parenting beyond the confines of Poland.

Notes

1 Jabłońska indicated that works by Szapocznikow and Pinińska-Bereś were particularly influential. Elżbieta Jabłońska interview with the author, January 24, 2011, Torun, Poland. For more information on these influential artists, see Elena Filipovic, et al., *Alina Szapocznikow: Sculpture Undone, 1955–1972* (New York: Museum of Modern Art and Warsaw: Muzeum Sztuki Nowoczesnej w Warsawie, 2011); Natalia LL, *Natalia LL: Teksty* (Bielsko-Biało: Galeria Bielska-BWA, 2004); Bożena Gajewska and Jerzy Hanusek, *Maria Pinińska-Bereś: 1931–1999* (Kraków: Galeria Sztuki Współczesnej Bunkier Sztuki, 1999).

2 Critical interest in Szapocznikow's work rose around 2010. The Museum of Modern Art, in conjunction with WIELS Contemporary Art Centre, Brussels and the Museum of Modern Art, Warsaw, hosted a major retrospective of her work in 2012–13.

3 Elżbieta Jabłońska, "Gentle Perversity—That is My Ideal: Elżbieta Jabłońska Speaks with Emilia Iwanciw," in *Elżbieta Jabłońska: (Un)usually Successful,* ed. Magdalena Ujma (Olsztyn: BWA Galeria Sztuki w Osztynie, 2011), 63.

4 Ibid.

5 For a discussion of women artists' difficulty in finding time for their art (and the repercussions of this choice) see the second chapter.

6 The artist was not able to locate these works for inclusion in this chapter. Descriptions of the work are provided in Elżbieta Jabłońska, "Home Stories," *Elżbieta Jabłońska: (Un)usually Successful,* 70–71.

7 Ibid., 70.

8 Jabłońska, conversation with author, Toruń, Poland, January 24, 2011.

9 Anna Chave, "Minimalism and Biography," *The Art Bulletin* 82 no. 1 (March 2000): 154.

10 Adam Mazur, "Supermatki gry domowe," (Supermother's home game), Foto Tapeta (May–June 2002), http://fototapeta.art.pl/2002/ejb.php.

11 Jabłońska chooses to embody male superheroes, as opposed to heroines like Wonder Woman, because she wants to portray the heroes that her son admires.

12 Jabłońska stages her photos in two different locations in the living room, in one set the viewer gazes toward the interior wall and in the other, toward a door that is likely the main entry to the home.

13 Thanks to the acceptance of American television, film, and comic books, Polish audiences would readily identify these superheroes and see them as men who fight evil and defend the weak, as men who are outside the law but do not violate the freedom of citizens.

14 Sebastian Cickocki, *Sztuka domowa: cała prawda o planecie X*, trans. Ewa Kanigowska-Gedroyc (Katowice: Górnośląskie Centrum Kultury, 2002), np.

15 Representations of the Virgin in domestic settings were more common in the Netherlands, for instance, where contemporary earthly items were imbued with religious significance.

16 Theologian Edward Schillebeeckx noted that during the Second Vatican Council (1962–65), there were different, contrasting ideas of Mary. On the one hand, Mary was considered to be a sister, "an eminent and model member of the church's community of faith," but in terms of Christological Mariology, she was "mother of the church." See Edward Schillebeeckx, *Mary: Yesterday, Today, Tomorrow* (New York: Crossroad, 1993), 12–15.

17 See C. Notermans, "Local and Global Icons of Mary: An Ethnographic Study of a Powerful Symbol," *Anthropos* 103 no. 2 (2008): 471–81; Jaroslav Pelikan, *Mary Through the Centuries: Her Place in the History of Culture* (New Haven: Yale University Press, 1996); or, Melissa R. Katz and Robert A. Orsi, *Divine Mirrors: The Virgin Mary in the Visual Arts* (New York: Oxford University Press, 2001).

18 For more information on the responses to Ofili's work, see Donald Cosentino, "Hip-Hop Assemblage: The Chris Ofili Affair," *African Arts* 33 no. 1 (Spring 2000): 40–51, +95–96; and, Coco Fusco, "Captain Shit and Other Allegories of Black Stardom: The Work of Chris Ofili," *NKA: Journal of Contemporary African Art* 10 (Spring/Summer 1999): 40–45. For more about Fritsch, see Jessica Morgan, "From Out There to Down Here," *Parkett* 87 (2010): 34–39.

19 Brian Porter, "*Hetmanka* and Mother: Representing the Virgin Mary in Modern Poland," *Contemporary European History* 14 no. 2 (2005): 152, doi: 10.1017/S0960777305002298.

20 Porter, "*Hetmanka* and Mother," 157.

21 Hanna Bulawka, "The Myth of the Polish Mother (PM)," in "Locating the Female Identity in the Polish Media: A Feminist Critical Discourse Study" (PhD diss., University of Birmingham, 2011). Section on the PM provided courtesy of the author, 2012.

22 Porter, "*Hetmanka* and Mother," 160.

23 This concept arose as women gained new educational and work opportunities and as economic conditions required both spouses to work outside the home. Women's magazines from the 1970s feature several articles that recount women's tactics to increase their husbands' drive to become educated, find better jobs, and increase the amount of financial support they could provide. See Mira Marody and Anna Giza-Poleszczuk, "Changing Images of Identity in Poland: From the Self-Sacrificing to the Self-Investing Woman?," in *Reproducing Gender: Politics, Publics, and Everyday Life After* Socialism, eds. Susan Gal and Gail Kligman (Princeton: Princeton University Press, 2000), 160–62.

24 Ibid., 163.

25 Marody and Giza-Poleszczuk note that the "brave victim/big child" relationship positively helped couples focus on their children and family but also caused gender structures within the marriage to remain stagnant. See Ibid., 163–65; see also, Peggy Watson, "Eastern Europe's Silent Revolution: Gender," *Sociology* 3 (August 1993): 471–87.

26 Bulawka, "The Myth of the Polish Mother (PM)"; and Marody and Giza-Poleszczuk, "Changing Images of Identity in Poland," 166.

27 Elżbieta Ostrowska, "Filmic Representations of the Myth of the Polish Mother," in *Women in Polish Cinema*, eds., Ewa Mazierska and Elżbieta Ostrowska (New York: Berghahn Books, 2006), 49.

28 Elkins rigidly defines 'art' in very rigid art market or institutional terms which enables him to make the claims that he does. James Elkins, *On the Strange Place of Religion in Contemporary Art* (New York: Routledge, 2004), 37.
29 Ibid., 47.
30 Ibid., 65.
31 Cichocki, *Sztuka domowa*, np.
32 Ibid.
33 Though, one might argue that Jabłońska could be drawing inspiration from Northern Renaissance artists such as the Master of Flemalle who, in works like *The Merode Altarpiece* (ca. 1427, oil on wood, Metropolitan Museum of Art), portrayed the Virgin in contemporary fifteenth-century spaces laden with religious symbolism.
34 "Jenny Saville: *Reproduction Drawings*," Gagosian Gallery, Press Release, April 6, 2010.
35 Magdalena Ujma, "Katarzyna Górna" in *Katarzyna Górna*, ed. Program Art Gallery (Warsaw: Program Art Gallery, 2006), www.artprogram.pl/ARTISTS/GORNA/OBRAZY/katalog.pdf (site discontinued). In her catalog essay for Górna's retrospective exhibition, Anna Smolak similarly suggests that the man in this image is "self-content" and "cuddling her breasts." See Anna Smolak, *Happy Birthday: Katarzyna Górna 1994–2004* (Kraków: Galeria Sztuki; Bunkier Sztuki, 2004), 28.
36 Smolak, *Happy Birthday*, 30.
37 Grzegorz Dziamski, "Virgins, Mothers, Wives," in *Katarzyna Górna*, np.
38 Cichocki, "Three Heroes in the Kitchen," in *Elżbieta Jabłońska: Supermatka*, VIII.
39 Ibid., IV.
40 Marody and Giza-Poleszczuk, "Changing Images of Identity in Poland," 166.
41 Superman first appeared in 1938. Wonder Woman, in particular, functioned as a rallying symbol in the battle against Nazi forces. According to Marc DiPaolo, she was also inspiring to feminists of the 1960s and 1970s. Spider-Man was a favorite of the anti-establishment. See Marc DiPaolo, *War, Politics, and Superheroes: Ethics and Propaganda in Comics and Film* (Jefferson, NC: McFarland & Co, 2011), 8, 29.
42 Cichocki, "Three Heroes," III.
43 As DiPaolo explains, the creation of Batman has been slightly altered between the 1988 comic book and the film, *Batman Begins* (2005). In both, Bruce Wayne witnesses his parents' mugging and death in an alley after attending the cinema. In the comic book, *Batman: Year One*, the family watched a revival of the Tyrone Power film *The Mark of Zorro*. After his parents' murder, Bruce decides that because Zorro did not intervene to save them, he would become a hero like Zorro. See DiPaolo, *War, Politics, and Superheroes*, 55.
44 Izabela Kowalczyk quoted in "Who Wouldn't Like to Have a Supermother?" in *Elżbieta Jabłońska: (Un)usually Successful*, 73.
45 Izabela Kowalczyk, "Iza Kowalczyk rozmawia z Elą Jabłońską: Supermenka w krainie codzienności," *Artmix, sztuka feminism kultura wizualna*, February 16, 2011, http://free.art.pl/artmix (site discontinued).
46 Chris Corrin, ed., *Superwomen and the Double Burden: Women's Experience of Change in Central and Eastern Europe and the Former Soviet Union* (Toronto: Second Story Press, 1992), 8.
47 Magdalena Ujma, "A Child to be Proud Of," nd., Elżbieta Jabłońska archive, Bydgoszcz, Poland.
48 Ujma, "Who Wouldn't Like to Have a Supermother?" in *Elżbieta Jabłońska: (Un)usually Successful*, 72.
49 Cichocki, *Sztuka domowa*, np.
50 Jolanta Ciesielska, Między Naturą a kulturą (Bielsko-Biała: Galeria Bielska BWA, 2002), 55.
51 Aneta Szylak, "Have Billboards Changed the Meaning of Public Space in Poland?" *M/E/A/N/I/N/G Online* 1 (July 2005), http://writing.upenn.edu/epc/meaning/01/anetaszylak.html.
52 Ibid.
53 Ibid.
54 At this exhibition, Jabłońska covered the gallery floors with hollow plastic balls, akin to those placed in ball pits at children's amusement centers in conjunction with the over-life size prints of the *Supermother* series. For the exhibition's stop in Bydgoczsz, over 800

people attended, many of them children, and Jabłońska offered not only ice cream, but other 'unhealthy snacks' which included chips, Coca-Cola, chewy candies, and chewing gum cigarettes. Jabłońska quoted in Izabela Kowalczyk, "Iza Kowalczyck rozmawia z Elą Jabłońską."

55 Mazur, "Supermatki gry domowe."

56 Magdalena Ujma, "Breaking the Kitchen into Pieces," in *Elżbieta Jabłońska: (Un)usually Successful*, 85.

57 For more on the notion of the "everyday," see Henri Lefebvre's *Critique of Everyday Life*, trans. John Moore; preface by Michael Trebitsch (London: Verso, 1991); Michel de Certeau, *The Practice of Everyday Life*, trans. Steven F. Rendall (Berkeley: University of California Press, 1984). In terms of art and the everyday, Stephen Johnstone's edited volume, *The Everyday: Documents of Contemporary Art* (London: Whitechapel Gallery; Cambridge, MA: MIT Press, 2008), introduces key issues related to the subject.

58 See Michel de Certeau, Luce Giard, and Pierre Mayol, *The Practice of Everyday Life, Volume 2: Living & Cooking*, trans. Timothy J. Tomasik (Minneapolis: University of Minnesota Press, 1998), and Michel de Certeau and Luce Giard, "The Nourishing Arts," in *Food and Culture: A Reader*, 2nd ed., ed. Carole Counihan and Penny Van Esterick (New York: Routledge, 2008), 67–77.

59 Rirkrit Tiravanija has published a collection of his recipes. See Rirkrit Tiravanija, *Rirkrit Tiravanija: Cook Book* (Bangkok: River Books, 2010).

60 Lesley Chamberlain, introduction to *The Futurist Cookbook*, by Filippo Tommaso Marinetti, trans. Suzanne Brill (San Francisco: Bedford Arts, 1989), 7.

61 Translation by the author. See Maria Poprzęcka, "Czy będzie jedzenie? (Will There Be Food?), in *Arteon—magazyn o sztuce* 72 no. 4 (April 2006): 3, http://goo.gl/P9UEw0.

62 Joe Smith and Petr Jehlička, "Stories Around Food, Politics and Change in Poland and the Czech Republic," *Transactions of the Institute of British Geographers* 32 no. 3 (September 2007): 404.

63 Ibid., 402.

64 Ruddick, *Maternal Thinking*, 24.

65 Jabłońska quoted in *Elżbieta Jabłońska: (Un)usually Successful*, 66. The artist claimed inspiration from Buñuel's late-career film, *Phantom of Liberty* (1974), which as one of Buñuel's most "free-form" films, alludes to the filmmaker's own personal life. It, one can argue, acts as a source of inspiration for Jabłońska's transposition of cooking in the home to the public spaces of the gallery. It is necessary to note that Jabłońska's comments regarding the work have also been ever evolving, due to what she views as the pigeonholing of her work.

66 Jabłońska, interview with Katarzyna Bielas, "Duży Format," *Gazety Wyborczej*, January 2, 2006, 8, cited in Jabłońska, *Elżbieta Jabłońska: (Un)usually Successful*, 74.

67 Ulrike Sieglohr discusses the potentiality of maternal subjectivity in her study, *Focus on the Maternal: Female Subjectivity and Images of Motherhood* (London: Scarlet Press, 1998). At the time of her writing, Sieglohr found maternal subjectivity "marginal and repressed." This study is proof of a visible change within the institution of art.

68 Deborah R. Geis has argued that the space of the kitchen continues to exist as the realm of the "private, a realm most often associated with the female," which women artists are able to make public through performance. See Deborah R. Geis, "Feeding the Audience: Food, Feminism, and Performance Art," in *Eating Culture*, ed. Ron Scapp and Brian Seitz (Albany: State University of New York Press, 1998), 222.

69 Jabłońska, *Elżbieta Jabłońska: (Un)usually Successful*, 75.

70 Justyna Włodarczyk, ed., *Gender Issues 2009: Gender Equality Discourse in Times of Transformation 1989–2009 The Czech Republic, Poland, Slovakia and Ukraine* (Warszawa: Heinrich Böll Stiftung, 2009), 105.

71 Ben Kinmont, for example, invited gallery attendees to call and schedule a mutually convenient time to come over for breakfast as part of his work *Waffles for an Opening*, 1991. While he did not clearly explain what would happen when the guest would arrive, Kinmont would cook his guest(s) and himself waffles, which they would consume while discussing the relationship of art and food. See Laura Trippi, "Untitled Artists' Projects by Janine Antoni, Ben Kinmont, Rirkrit Tiravanija," in *Eating Culture*, 134–35.

72 Preparing the food in what has been termed by critics as "a sophisticated way, just like the dishes shown in cook books." See "The Whole Trick Is to Meet Well," in *Elżbieta Jabłońska: (Un)usually Successful*, 73.
73 A part of Mierle Laderman Ukeles's *Maintenance Art Performances, Hartford Wash* highlighted, transferred, and transformed the power structures related to the maintenance of art museums (washing, dusting, mopping, etc.) from the custodial staff to that of the conservator/curator all the while highlighting female subjectivity.
74 Translation by author. Elżbieta Jabłońska quoted in Izabela Kowalczyk, "Iza Kowalczyck rozmawia z Elą Jabłońską: Supermenka w krainie codzienności," *Artmix, sztuka feminism kultura wizualna*, http://goo.gl/sK2Fq3.
75 Sebastian Cichocki, *Sztuka domowa: cała prawda o planecie X* (Home Games: The Whole Truth about Planet X) (Katowice: Górnośląskie Centrum Kultury, 2002), np.
76 Elizabeth Hainstock, "Montessori in the Home," in *Montessori: Her Method and the Movement: What You Need to Know*, ed. R. C. Orem (New York: Putnam, 1974), 130.
77 Maria Montessori, *The Discovery of the Child*, trans. M. Joseph Costelloe, SJ (Notre Dame, IN: Fides Publishers, 1967), 124.
78 Ibid., 129.
79 Aneta Szylak, *Architectures of Gender: Contemporary Women's Art in Poland* (Long Island City: Sculpture Center, 2003), 6.
80 Kowalczyk, "The Ambivalent Beauty," in *Gender Check: Femininity and Masculine in the Art of Eastern Europe* (Cologne: Walther König, 2009), 39.
81 Italics in the original. Anna Titkow, "Political Change in Poland: Cause, Modifier, or Barrier to Gender Equity?" in *Gender Politics and Post-Communism*, eds. Nanette Funk and Magda Mueller (New York: Routledge, 1993), 253.
82 Kowalczyk, "The Ambivalent Beauty," 42.
83 Poland banned abortion in 1993, except in instances when abortion saves the life of the woman, the pregnancy is the result of rape, or the fetus is malformed. This ruling emphasized family values and traditional roles for women.
84 Ashley Weeks Cart, "(M)Other Work: Feminist Maternal Performance Art" (MA thesis, University of Southern California, 2010), 41.
85 Cichocki quoted in Charlotta Kotík, "Post-Totalitarian Art: Eastern and Central Europe," in *Global Feminisms: New Directions in Contemporary Art*, eds. Maura Reilly and Linda Nochlin (New York: Brooklyn Museum of Art, 2007), 153.
86 Julia Robinson, "The Sculpture of Indeterminacy: Alison Knowles's Beans and Variations," *Art Journal* 63 no. 4 (Winter 2004): 97.
87 Knowles's project was re-performed at the Baltimore Museum of Art in 2003, the Wexner Museum in 2004, and the Tate Modern in 2008 as a part of *The Long Weekend: States of Flux*.
88 Renate Buschmann, "Evocation of Pleasure and Disgust. Daniel Spoerri and the Establishment of Eat Art," in *Eating the Universe*, ed. Sylvette Babin, (Köln: Dumont, 2009), 237. On Spoerri, also see Margherita D'Ayala Valva's essay in this volume.
89 This first word from the series title, *Przypadkowa Przyjemność*, translates as accidental or casual and it has been translated as both *Casual Pleasure* on the artist's website and *Accidental Pleasure* in the exhibition catalog, *Elżbieta Jabłońska: (Un)usually Successful*. For consistency, I employ "accidental" as the translated title.
90 Buschmann, "Evocation of Pleasure and Disgust," 237.
91 Spoerri's press release for the gallery in Buschmann, "Evocation of Pleasure and Disgust," 238.
92 "The Whole Trick Is to Meet Well," *Elżbieta Jabłońska: (Un)usually Successful*, 73.
93 Michal Sznajder and Benjamin Senauer, "The Changing Polish Food Consumer," Working Papers 14306, The Food Industry Center, (St. Paul: University of Minnesota, 1998), 11. doi:10.22004/ag.econ.14306
94 Ibid., 13.
95 A recent article in the *New York Times'* "Dining & Wine" section explains that there has been a food revolution in Poland where restaurateurs like Magda Gessler are teaching other restaurants to use butter instead of margarine and that Polish cuisine is not just "simple food like fat kielbasa and pierogi." See Ginanne Brownell, "Warsaw's Restaurant

Guru Moves Past Traditional Polish Cuisine," *New York Times*, January 6, 2012, http://www.nytimes.com/2012/01/07/dining/07iht-magda07.html?pagewanted=all.

96 See Brownell, "Warsaw's Restaurant Guru." Warsaw is Poland's largest city with a population of over 1.5 million. Krakow and Łódź are the second and third largest cities, respectively, with populations around 750,000.

97 In an interview with Tomasz Załuski, Jabłońska noted that the "opening day of an exhibition is a distinctive type of holiday and this holiday is my inspiration." Translation by author. See "Zależy mi znalezieniu małej szczeliny, która powoduje chwilowy zwrot akcji, wprowadza zamęt, a czasem zadziwia z Elżbietą Jabłońską rozmawia Tomas Załuski,"*Arteon—magazyn o sztuce* 72 no. 4 (April 2006), http://www.atlassztuki.pl/pdf/jablonska3.pdf.

98 Jabłońska, "Gentle Perversity—That Is My Ideal," 68.

99 Craig Young and Sylwia Kaczmarek, "Changing the Perception of the Post-Socialist City: Place Promotion and Imagery in Łódź, Poland," *The Geographical Journal* 165 no. 2, The Changing Meaning of Place in Post-Socialist Eastern Europe: Commodification, Perception and Environment (July 1999): 185.

100 See Titkow, "Political Change in Poland: Cause, Modifier, or Barrier to Gender Equity?," 254.

101 Jabłońska, *(Un)usually Successful*, 74.

102 Miwon Kwon, "Exchange Rate: On Obligation and Reciprocity in Some Art of the 1960s and After," in *The 'Do-It-Yourself' Artwork: Participation from Fluxus to New Media*, ed. Anna Dezeuze (Manchester, UK: Manchester University Press, 2010), 235.

103 Jabłońska filmed this event for the film *Meeting*, thus putting those who did attend at further unease with the situation.

104 Jabłońska, interview with Katarzyna Bielas, "Duży Format," (January 2, 2006), 8, reprinted in *Elżbieta Jabłońska: (Un)Usually Successful*, 74.

105 Perhaps such a grand gesture was not the kind of help out-of-work workers needed, and thus Jabłońska's "helping" was akin to Marie-Antoinette's infamous statement "let them eat cake."

106 The Poznański Palace is acclaimed as one of the most magnificent homes of Izrael Kalman Poznański, the owner of the major textile factory in Łódź in the 19th century.

107 See Julitą Wójick rozmawia Małgorzata Lisiewicz, "Obieranie ziemniaków" (Peeling Potatoes), *Magazyn Sztuki* 26 (2001), http://goo.gl/1eVkqo.

108 Anda Rottenberg, "Biały Mazur," in *Biały Mazur*, ed. Alexander Tolnay (Berlin and Warsaw: Neuer Berliner Kunstverein, 2004), np.

109 Karol Sienkiewicz, "Julita Wójcik: Peeling Potatoes," Culture.pl, March 2011, edited and translated by Sylwia Wojda, July 2011, http://goo.gl/TRoJcv.

110 Iza Kowalczyk, "From Feminist Interventions to Post-Feminism," in *Biały Mazur*, np.

111 Bourriaud's definition upends the aesthetic, cultural, and political goals of modern art. He uses the phrase "relational art" exclusively for a group of artists included in his exhibition *Traffic*, 1996, at the CAPC Musée d'art Contemporain de Bordeaux. The term has since been applied to Liam Gillick, Rirkrit Tiravanija, Phillippe Parreno, Pierre Huyghe, Carsten Höller, Christine Hill, Vanessa Beecroft, Maurizio Cattelan, and Jorge Pardo. Bourriaud's term and definition of the movement has been the subject of much criticism, notably by Claire Bishop and Grant Kester. See Nicholas Bourriaud, *Relational Aesthetics* (Dijon: Les Presses du Reel, 2002), 14. Italics in original text. For criticisms of this argument, see Claire Bishop, *Artificial Hells: Participatory Art and the Politics of Spectatorship* (New York: Verso, 2012), and Grant Kester, *The One and the Many: Contemporary Collaborative Art in a Global Context* (Durham, NC: Duke University Press, 2011).

112 Janet Kraynak, "Rirkrit Tiravanija's Liability," in *The 'Do-It-Yourself' Artwork*, 166.

113 Bourriaud, *Relational Aesthetics*, 15.

114 Jacques Rancière, *The Politics of Aesthetics*, trans. and intro. Gabriel Rockhill (New York: Continuum, 2004), 7–45.

115 Rancière in conversation with Fulvia Carnevale and John Kelsey, "Art of the Possible: An Interview with Jacques Rancière," *Artforum International* 45 no. 7 (March 2007): 258.

116 Jacques Rancière, *Dissensus: On Politics and Aesthetics*, ed. and trans. Steven Corcoran (New York: Continuum, 2010), 36.

117 The blur between art and life is also a subject of interest in Claire Bishop's work. In her study, *Artificial Hells: Participatory Art and the Politics of Spectatorship*, she discusses Rancière's notion of the aesthetic regime in relation to how it may apply to participatory art that does not clearly fit into conventional or traditional notions of attractiveness or beauty. See Bishop, *Artificial Hells*, 26–30.

118 Ibid., 45.

119 Democratic, or emancipatory, art is the crux of Jacques Rancière's *The Politics of Aesthetics*, and his text, "The Emancipated Spectator," *Artforum International* 45 no. 7 (March 2007): 271–80.

120 Claire Bishop, "Anatagonism and Relational Aesthetics," in *The "Do-It-Yourself" Artwork*, 259.

121 Pierre Bourdieu, *The Logic of Practice*, trans. Richard Nice (Stanford: Stanford University Press, 1990), 45–46.

122 Kraynak, "Rirkrit Tiravanija's Liability," 175.

123 Marek Krajewski, "Distanced Towards One's Role: On Ela Jabłońska's Art," nd, courtesy Elżbieta Jabłońska Archive, Bydgoszcz, Poland, 2011.

124 Elżbieta Jabłońska quoted in Emilia Iwanciw, "Gentle Perversity—That Is My Ideal," *Elżbieta Jabłońska: (Un)usually Successful*, 68.

125 The public consumption of food is an interesting avenue for further development. On the one hand, food is celebrated and consumed publicly at restaurants and eating contests; on the other, it is considered inappropriate in certain volumes and places.

126 Spoerri similarly reversed the consumption of food in the film *Resurrection* (1968). Co-created with Tony Morgan, *Resurrection* recounts the digestive process from the end result (excrement), to consumption (food), to source (animal, in this case, cow).

127 Jabłońska quoted in *Elżbieta Jabłońska: (Un)usually Successful*, 66. In recent years, museums themselves have begun to rent out their galleries in the evenings for private events, both personal and corporate, often in the form of celebratory dinners and fundraisers. It is not clear that this has been occurring in Polish institutions. Regardless, it is rare for museums to sanction food in their galleries during their open public hours.

128 Critiques of the institution of art are not unfamiliar in the history of art; one may recall Piero Manzoni's *Merda d'Artista*, 1961, in which the artist canned his own excrement (labeled as "Freshly preserved, produced, and tinned in May 1961," and sold by weight based on the current price of gold) as a criticism of the value placed on the creator's body in the art world. See Gerard Silk, "Myths and Meanings in Manzoni's *Merda d'Artista*," *Art Journal* 52 no. 3, Scatological Art (Autumn 1993): 65–75; and Jacopo Galimberti, "The Intellectual and the Fool: Piero Manzoni between the Milanese Art Scene and the Land of Cockaigne," *Oxford Art Journal* 35 no. 1 (2012): 76–93. Sharon Hecker also discusses this piece in her essay for this volume.

129 Geis, "Feeding the Audience," 222.

130 Of course, some museums now willingly rent space in rooms hung with art to corporations and individuals who can afford serving a large party, and Jabłońska herself has been "sanctioned" by the museum.

131 Jabłońska, "Gentle Perversity—That Is My Ideal," in *Elżbieta Jabłońska: (Un)usually Successful*, 67.

132 Will Hutton quoted in Helma Lutz, "At Your Service Madam! The Globalization of Domestic Service," *Feminist Review* 70 (2002): 90.

133 Ibid.

134 Ibid., 91.

135 Bridget Anderson and Annie Phizacklea, *Migrant Domestic Workers: A European Perspective*. Report to the Equal Opportunities Unit, DGV, Commission of European Communities, May 1997 (University of Leicester, 1997), referred to in Lutz, "At Your Service Madam!," 92.

136 Ibid., 102.

137 Jabłońska, "Gentle Perversity—That is My Ideal," *Elżbieta Jabłońska: (Un)Usually Successful*, 68.

138 Ibid.

139 Teresa Margolles, "Santiago Sierra," *BOMB* 86 (Winter 2004), http://bombmagazine.org/articles/santiago-sierra.
140 "Helping," *Elżbieta Jabłońska: (Un)Usually Successful*, 77.
141 Bishop, "Antagonism and Relational Aesthetics," 267.
142 Ibid., 268.
143 Ibid., 274.
144 Jabłońska, "Helping," *Elżbieta Jabłońska: (Un)Usually Successful*, 77.
145 Krajewski, "Distanced towards One's Role. On Ela Jabłońska's Art."
146 "Giving Away," in *Elżbieta Jabłońska: (Un)Usually Successful*, 76.
147 Jabłońska quoted in "Helping," *Elżbieta Jabłońska: (Un)Usually Successful*, 76.
148 Maurice Godelier, *The Enigma of the Gift*, trans. Nora Scott (Chicago: University of Chicago Press, 1999), 12.
149 Krajewski, "Distanced towards One's Role. On Ela Jabłońska's Art."
150 Ujma, "Breaking the Kitchen into Pieces," 85
151 Andrzej Szczerski, "Why the PRL Now? Translations of Memory in Contemporary Polish Art," *Third Text* 23 no. 1 (2009): 85.
152 David Crowley, Zofia Machnicka and Andrzej Szczerski, "The Power of Fantasy," in *The Power of Fantasy: Modern and Contemporary Art from Poland* (New York: Prestel, 2011), 23.
153 They, in conjunction with old industrial cities, are the two major areas of Poland where unemployment, lack of education and lack of opportunity persist. See Elżbieta Tarkowska, "Poverty and Education Risk of 'Inheritance' of Poverty in the Former State Farms in Poland," *Polish Sociological Review* no. 138 (2002): 203–15.
154 Jabłońska quoted in "Found Words," in *Elżbieta Jabłońska: (Un)Usually Successful*, 82.
155 Jabłońska, conversation with the author, Toruń, Poland, January 24, 2011.

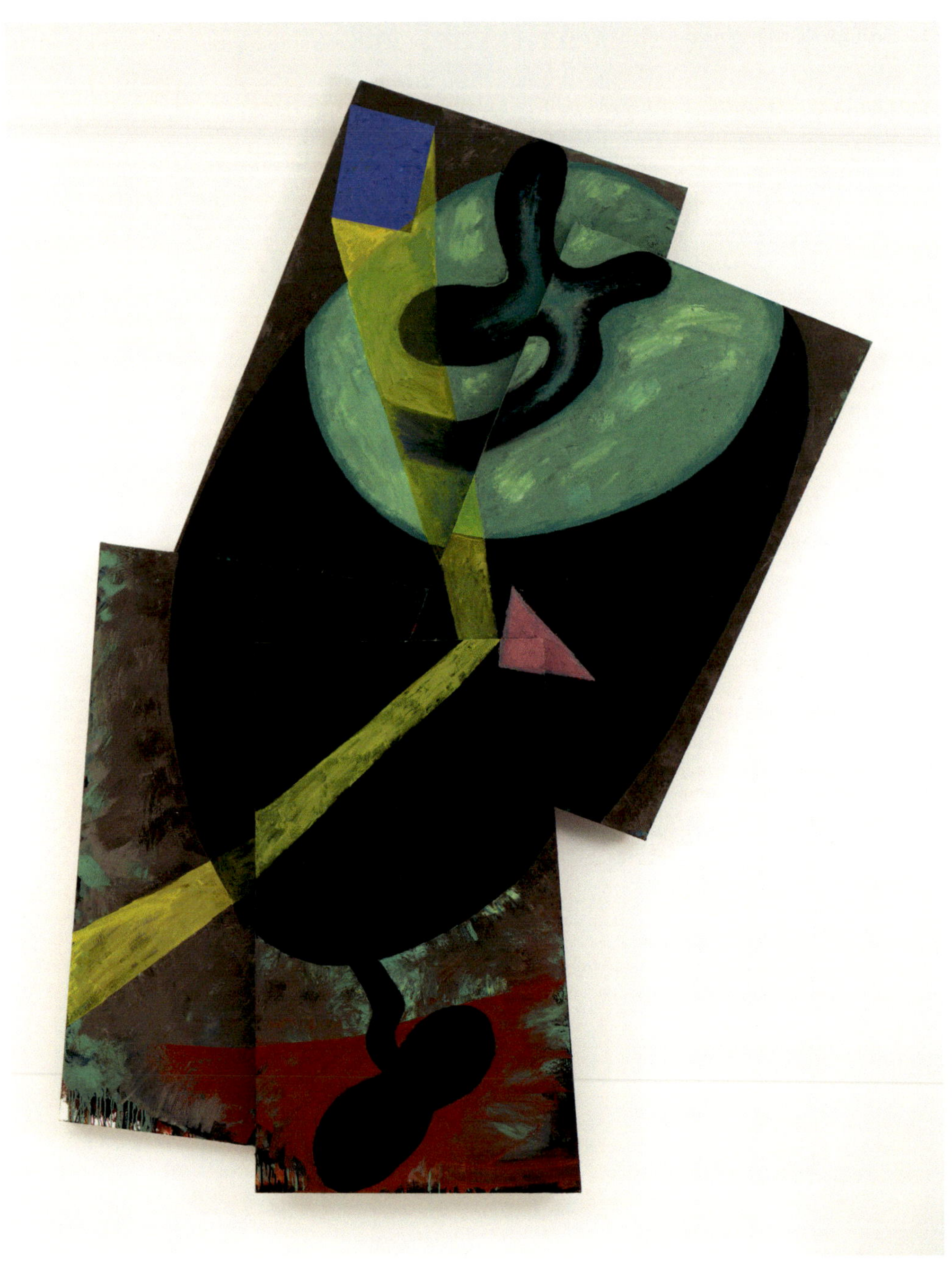

Plate 1 Elizabeth Murray, *Beam*, November 1982. Oil on canvas, four panels. 9' 2" × 6' 3 7/8" × 3 7/8." Collection Museum of Modern Art, New York. © 2019 The Murray-Holman Family Trust / Artists Rights Society (ARS), New York.

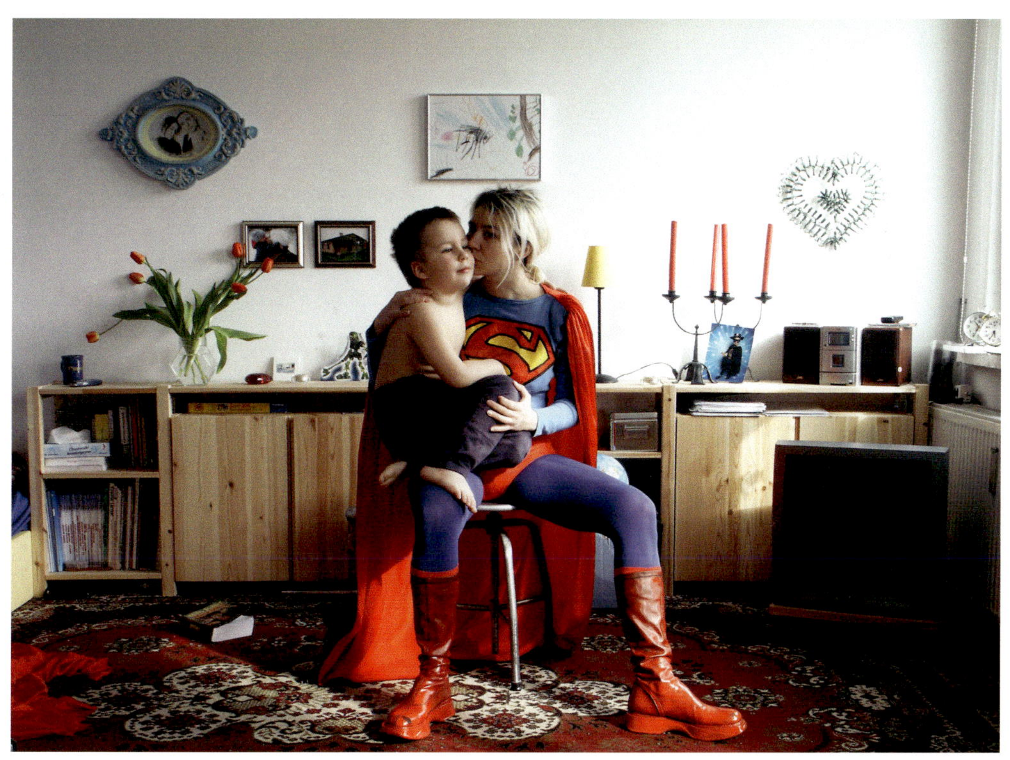

Plate 2 Elżbieta Jabłońska, *Supermother*, 2002. Photographic series. Courtesy the artist.

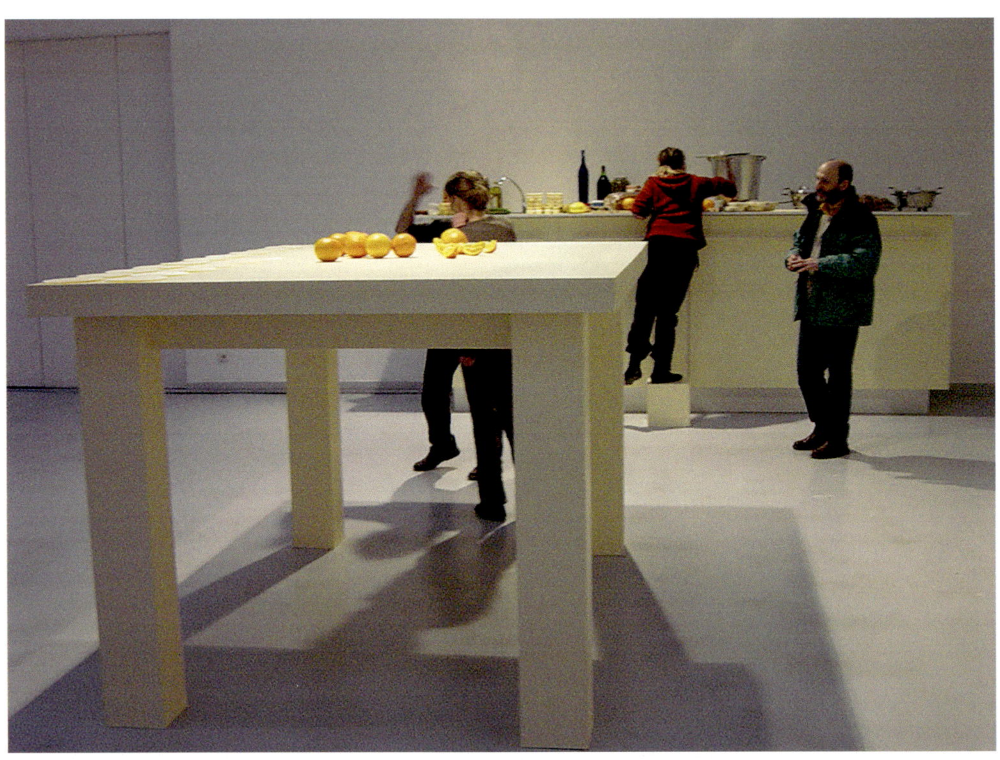

Plate 3 Elżbieta Jabłońska, *Kitchen,* 2004, from *Through the Stomach to the Heart,* 1999–2005. Performance at exhibition, "Under the White-and-Red Flag," CAC Wilno, Lithuana. Courtesy the artist.

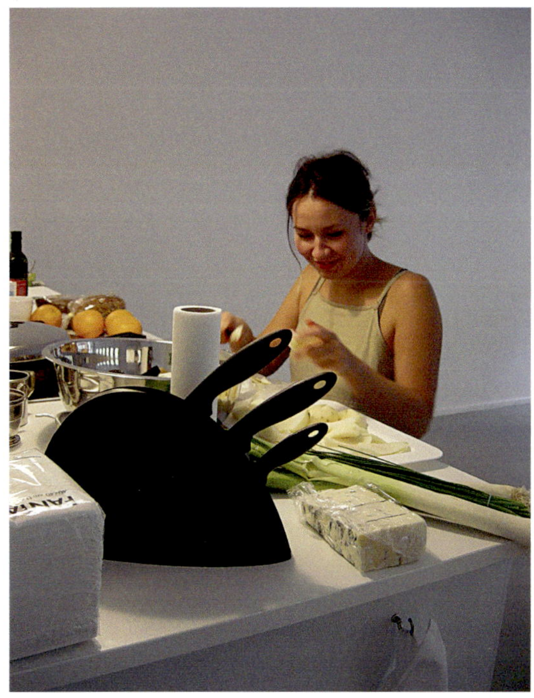

Plate 4 Elżbieta Jabłońska, *Kitchen*, 2003, from *Through the Stomach to the Heart*, 1999–2005. Performance at exhibition, "Biały Mazur," NBK, Neuer Berliner Kunstverein, Berlin, Germany. Courtesy the artist.

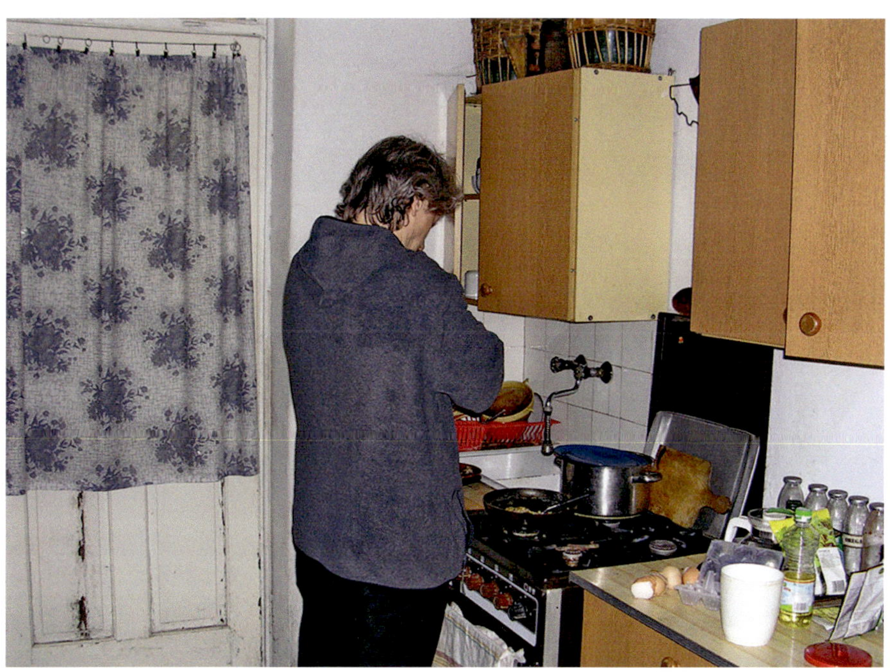

Plate 5 Elżbieta Jabłońska, *Untitled*, from *Zasiedzenie*, 2004, photograph. Courtesy the artist.

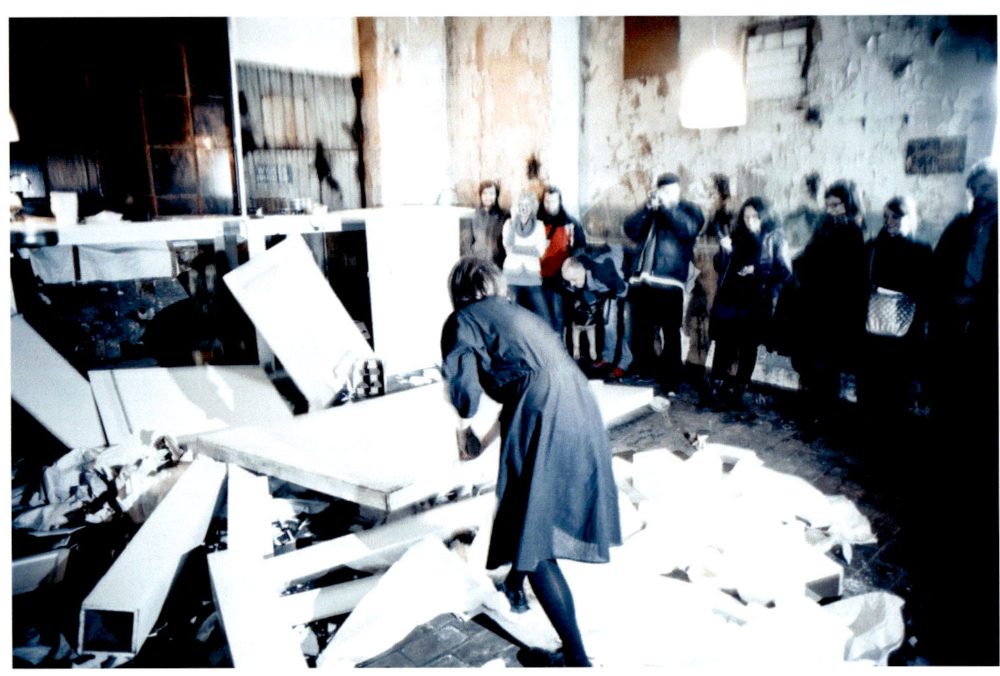

Plate 6 Elżbieta Jabłońska, *Kitchen*, 2007. Performance. Courtesy the artist.

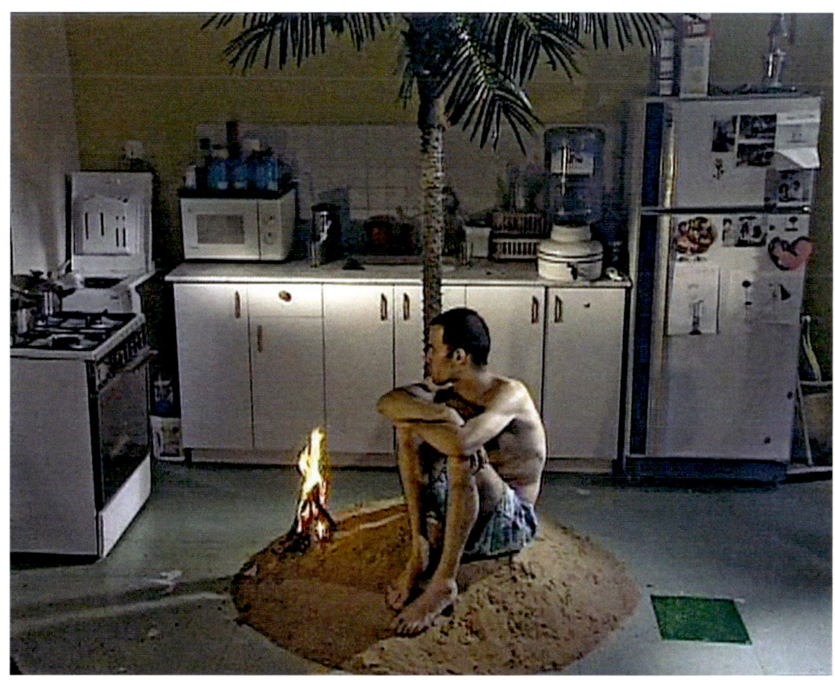

Plate 7 Guy Ben-Ner, still from *Berkeley's Island*, 1999. Single channel video with sound, 15 minutes. Courtesy the artist.

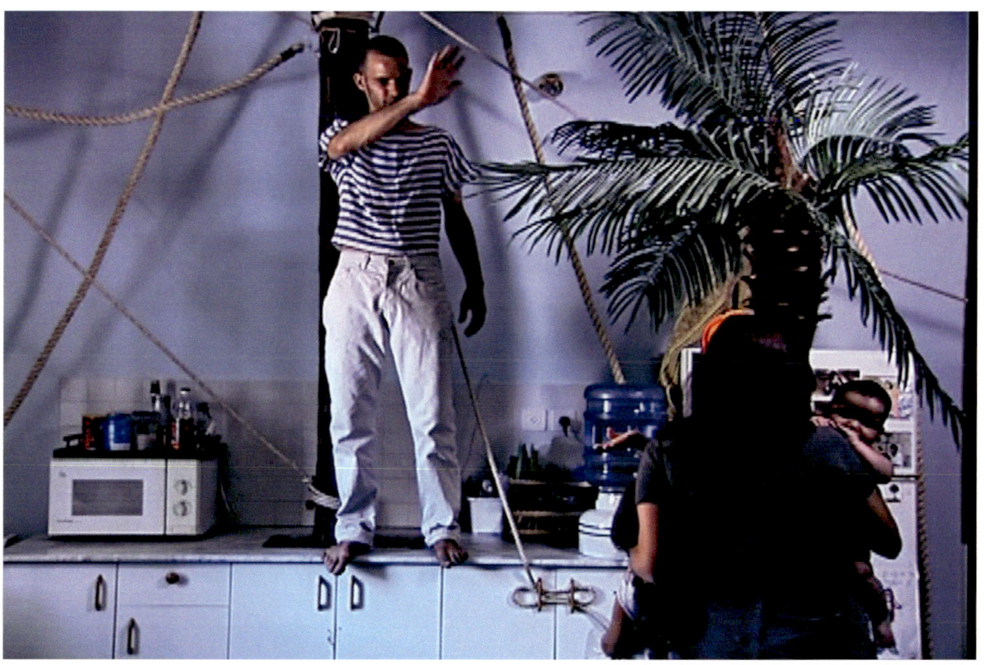

Plate 8 Guy Ben-Ner, still from *Moby Dick*, 2000. Single channel video, 12 minutes, 35 seconds. Courtesy the artist.

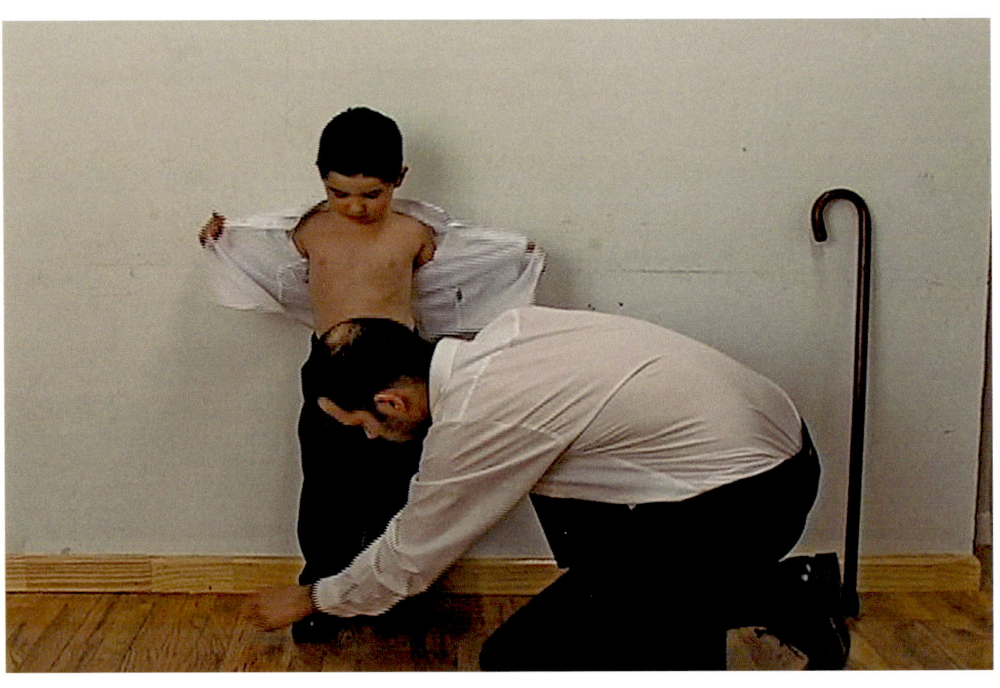

Plate 9 Guy Ben-Ner, still from *Wild Boy*, 2004. Single channel video, 17 minutes. Courtesy the artist.

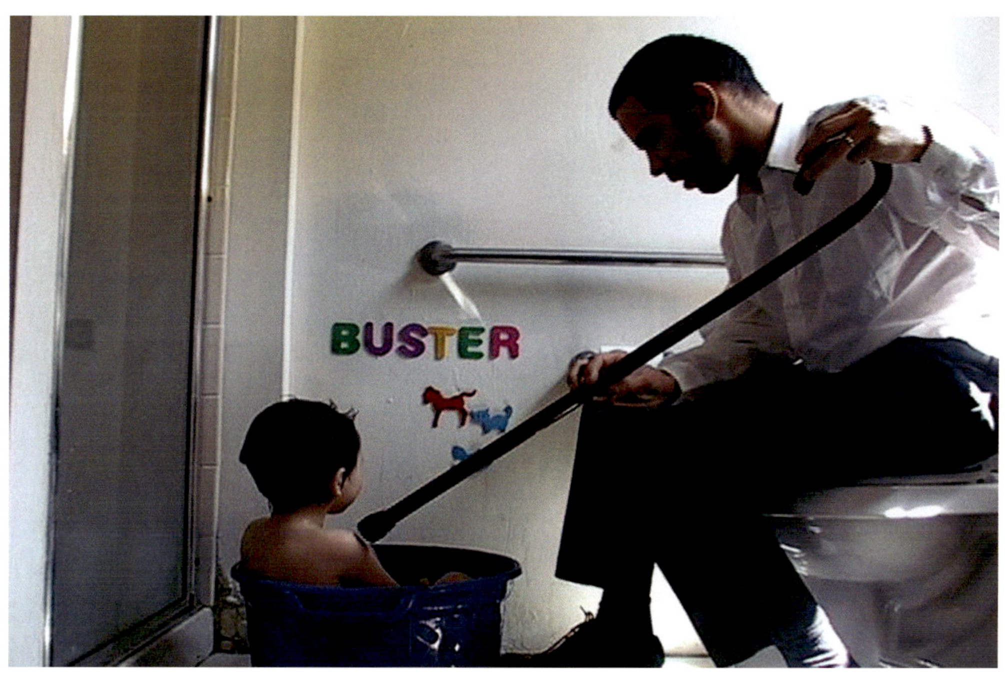

Plate 10 Guy Ben-Ner, still from *Wild Boy*, 2004. Single channel video, 17 minutes. Courtesy the artist.

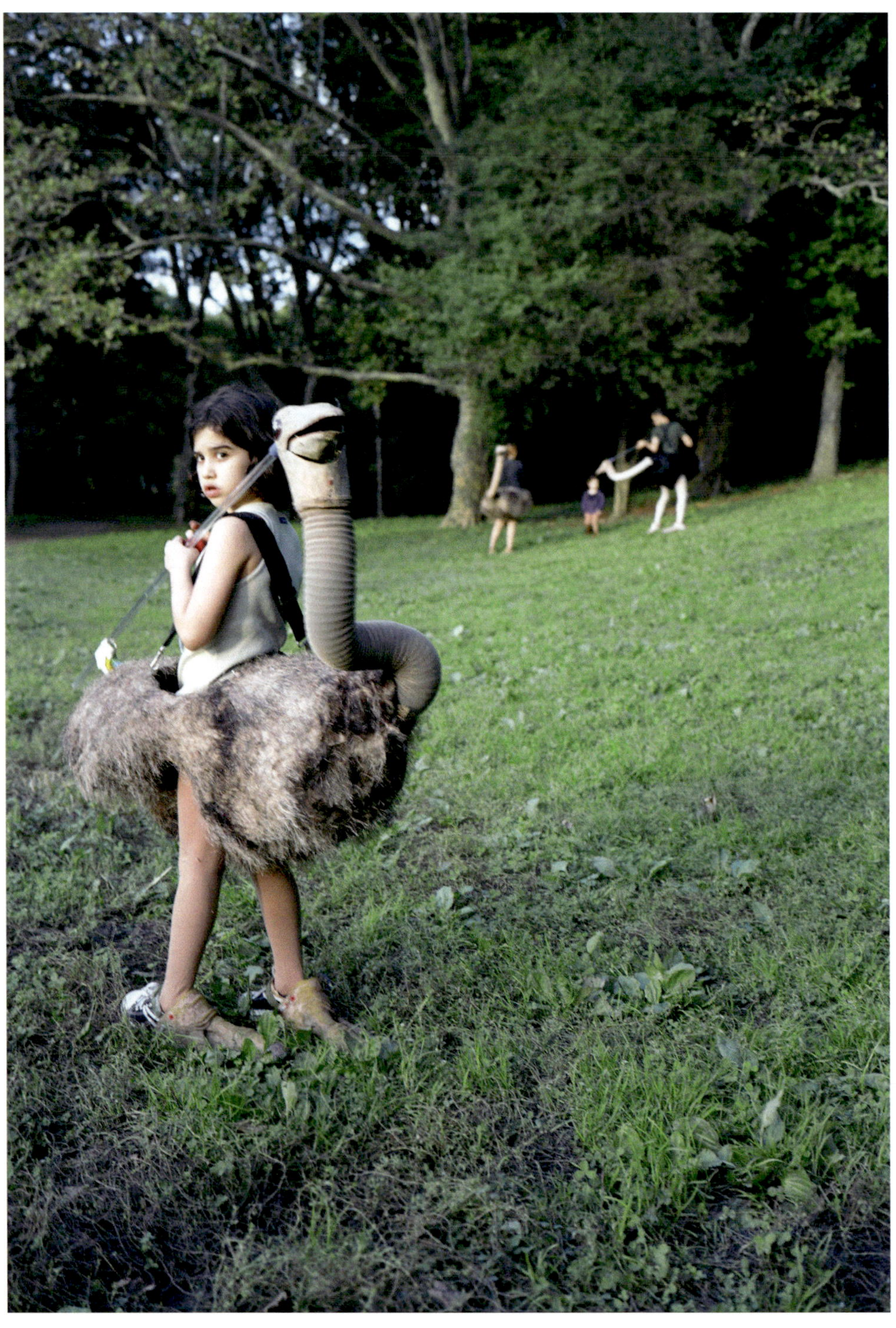

Plate 11 Guy Ben-Ner, still from *Elia: A Story of an Ostrich Chick*, 2003. Single channel video with sound, 17 minutes. Courtesy the artist.

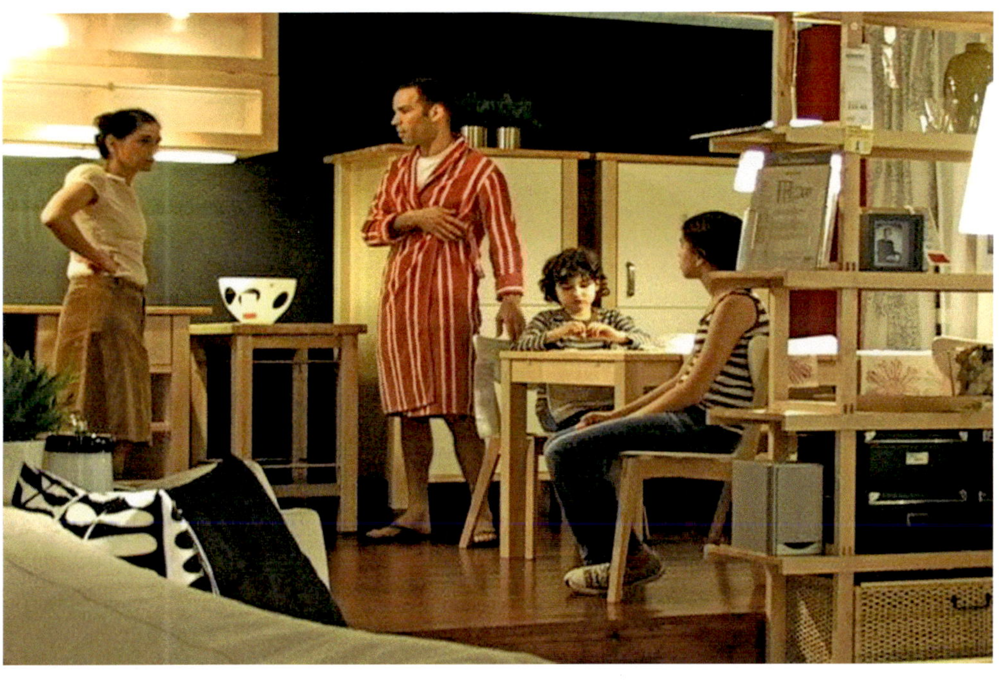

Plate 12 Guy Ben-Ner, still from *Stealing Beauty*, 2007. Single channel video with sound, 17 minutes 40 seconds. Courtesy the artist.

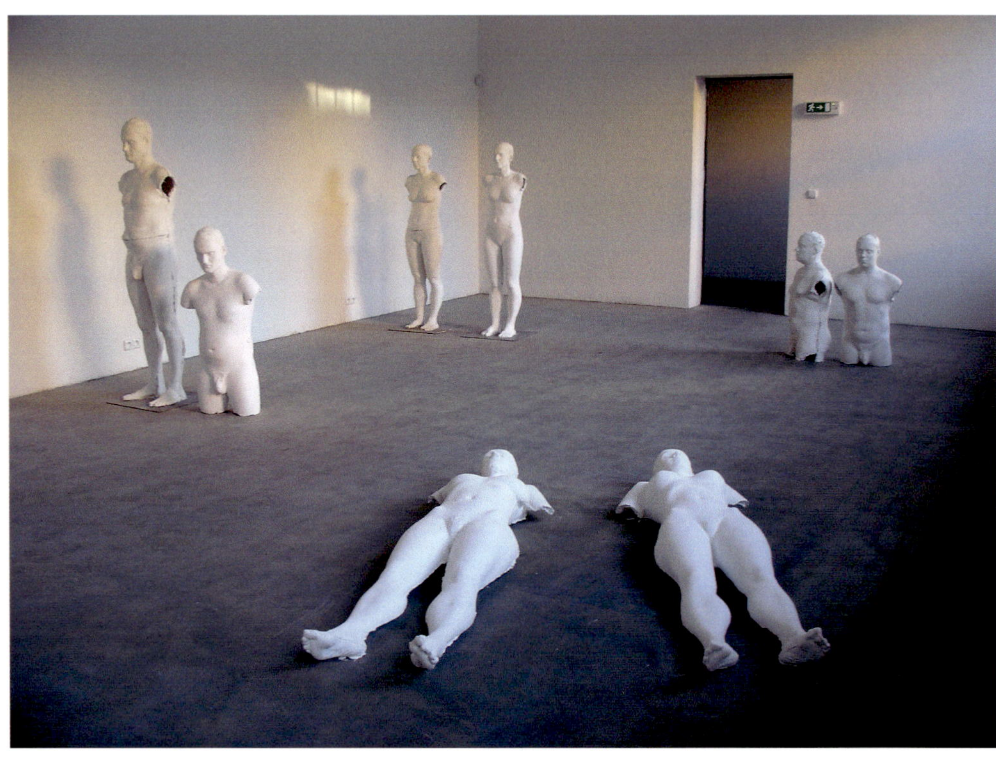

Plate 13 Mothers and Fathers, *What Would We Be Without Children?*, 2007. Plaster casts of the artists' bodies. Installation at C2C Gallery, Prague. Courtesy the artists.

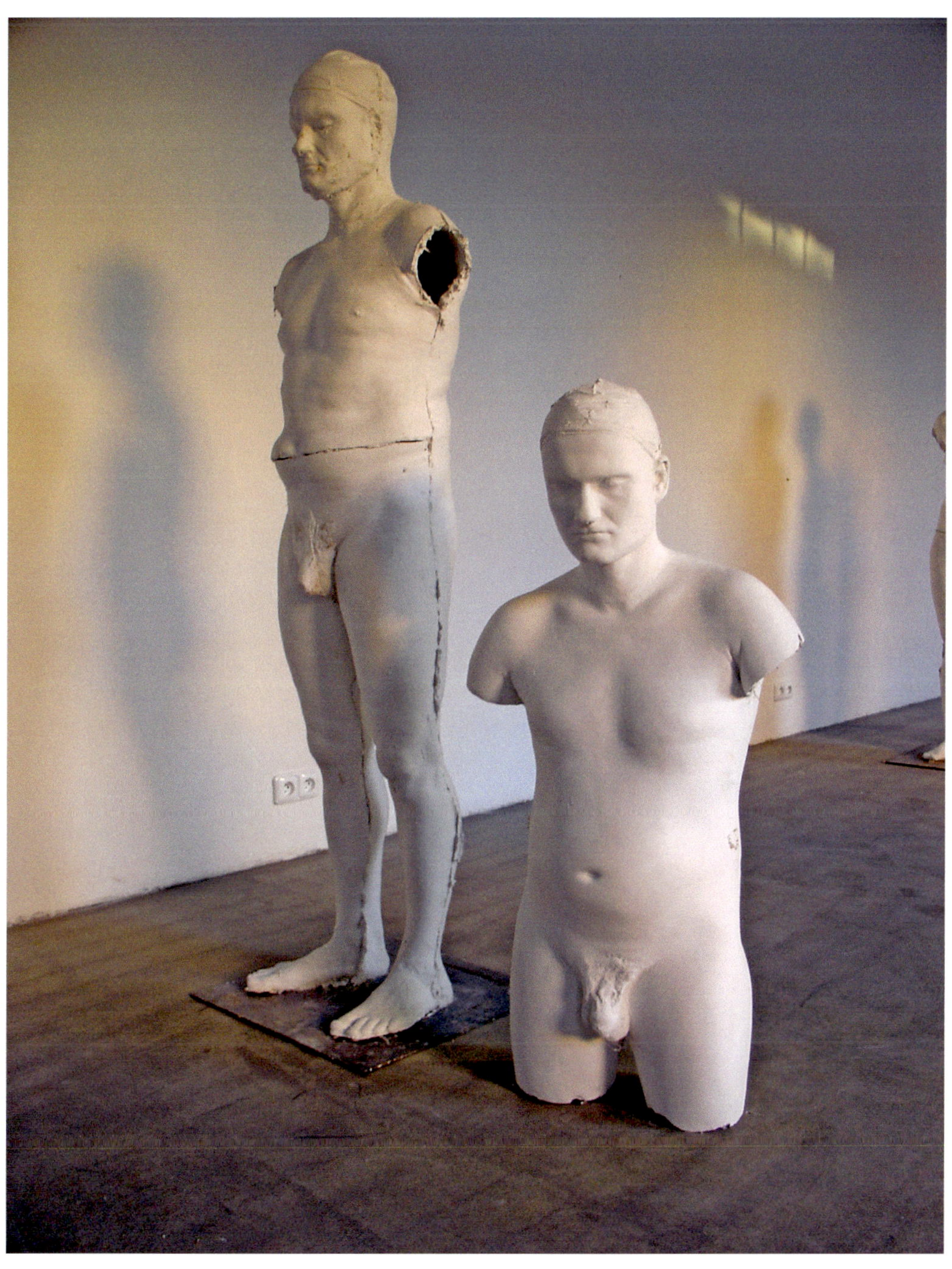

Plate 14 Mothers and Fathers, detail, *What Would We Be Without Children?*, 2007. Plaster casts of the artists' bodies. Installation at C2C Gallery, Prague.. Courtesy the artists.

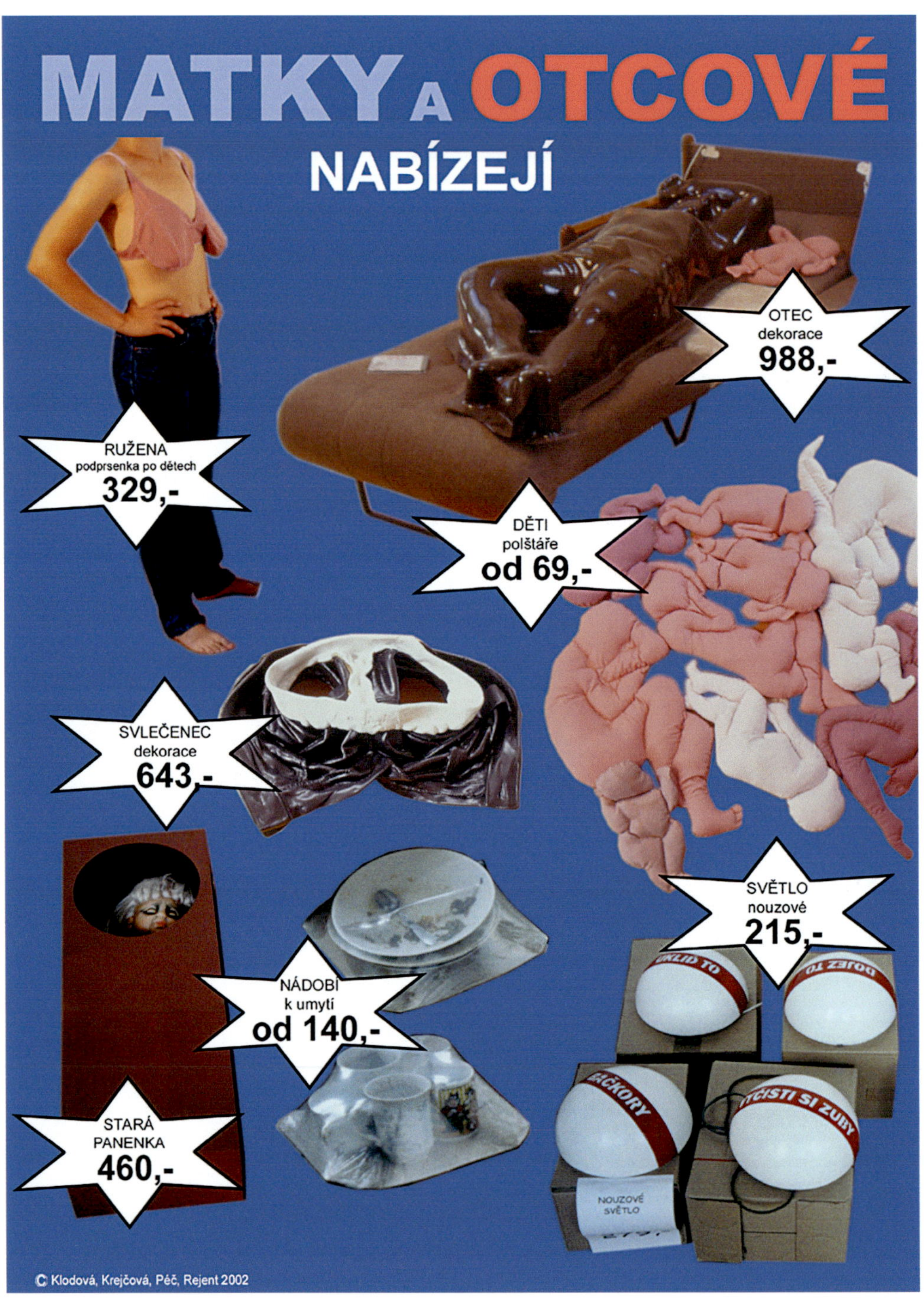

Plate 15 Mothers and Fathers, *Mothers and Fathers Offer*, 2002. Exhibition poster. Courtesy the artists.

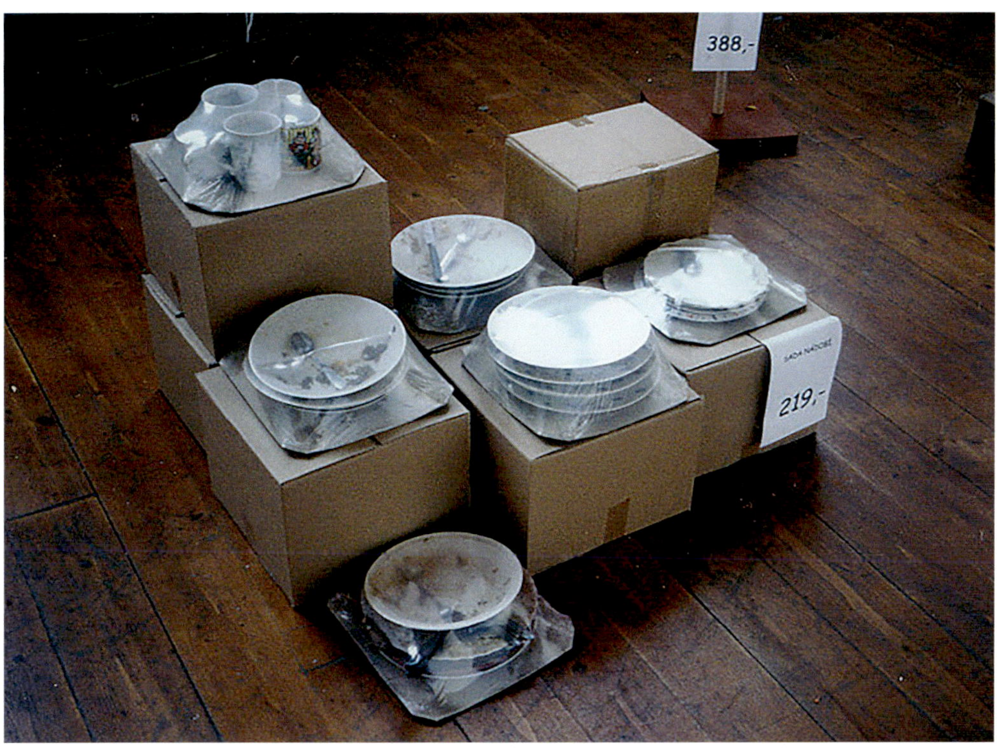

Plate 16 Mothers and Fathers, *Dishes (to Wash)* from *Mothers and Fathers Offer*, 2002. Shrink-wrapped porcelain dishes. Courtesy the artists.

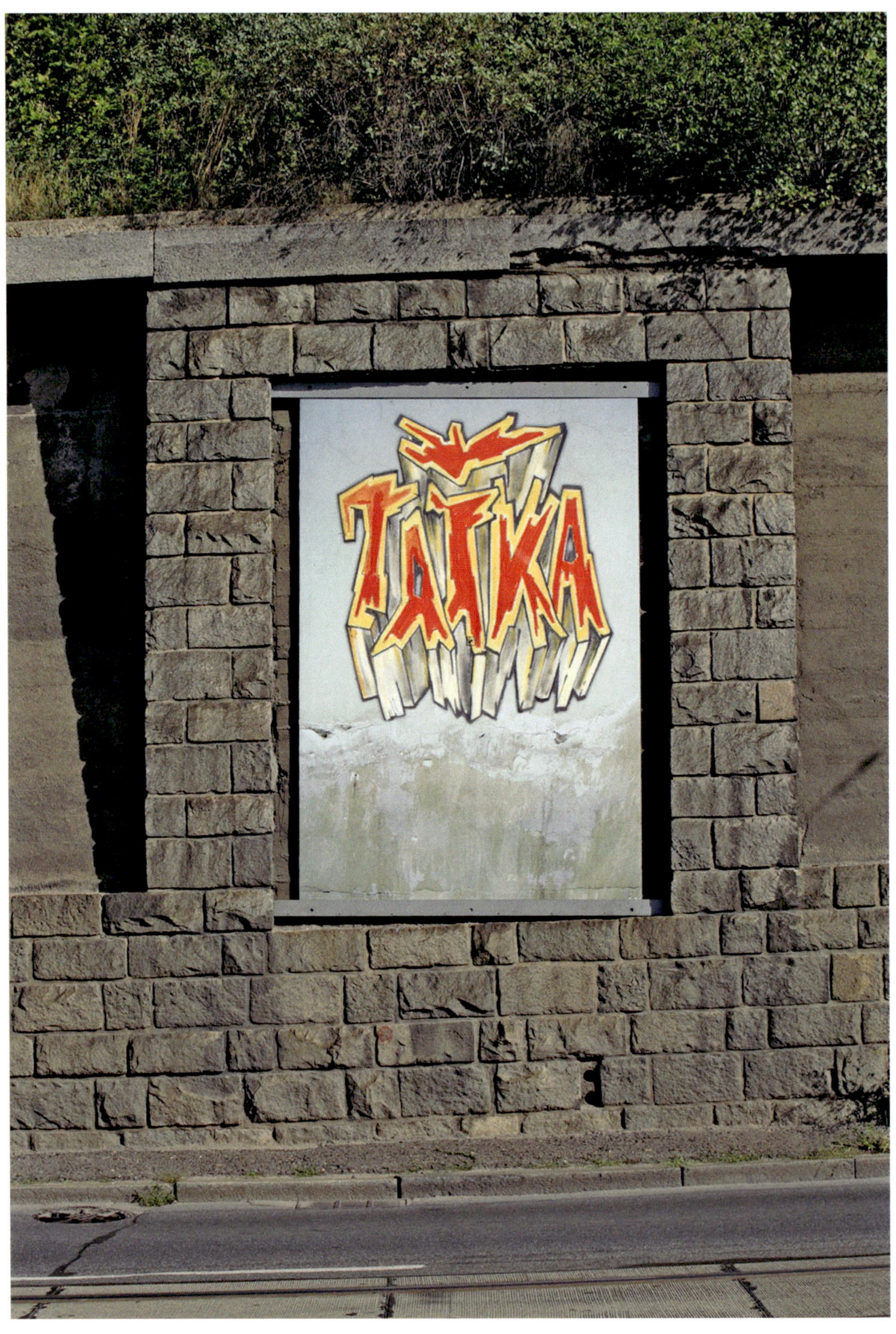

Plate 17 Mothers and Fathers, *Father from Family Art Crimes*, 2006, digital print. *ArtWall* public art installation, Prague, CZ. Courtesy the artists.

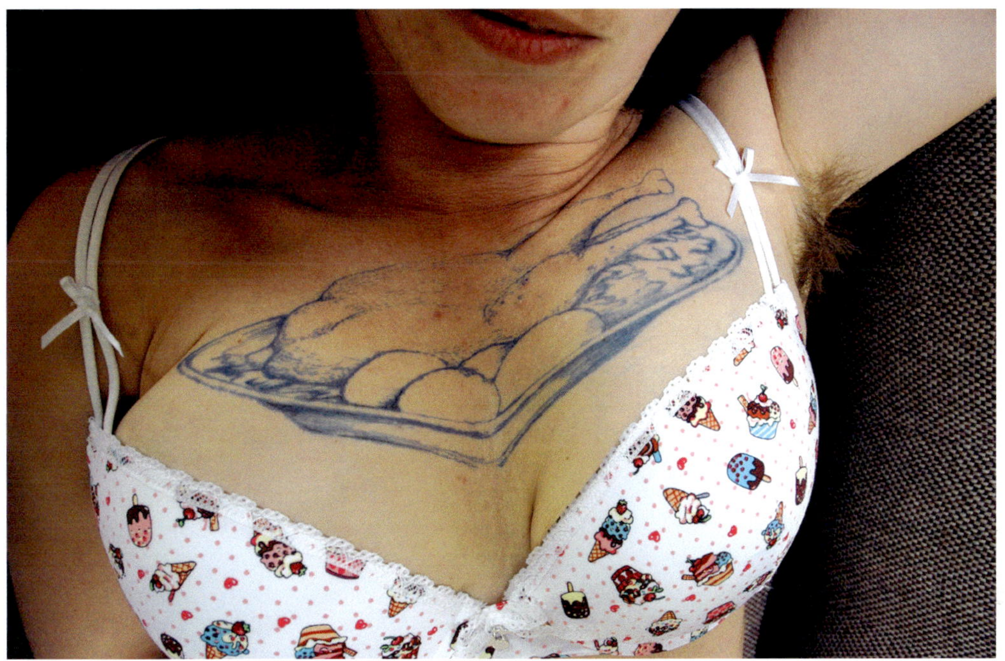

Plate 18 Mothers and Fathers, *Duck* from *Bared!*, 2009, photographic project for *Fotograf* magazine. Courtesy the artists.

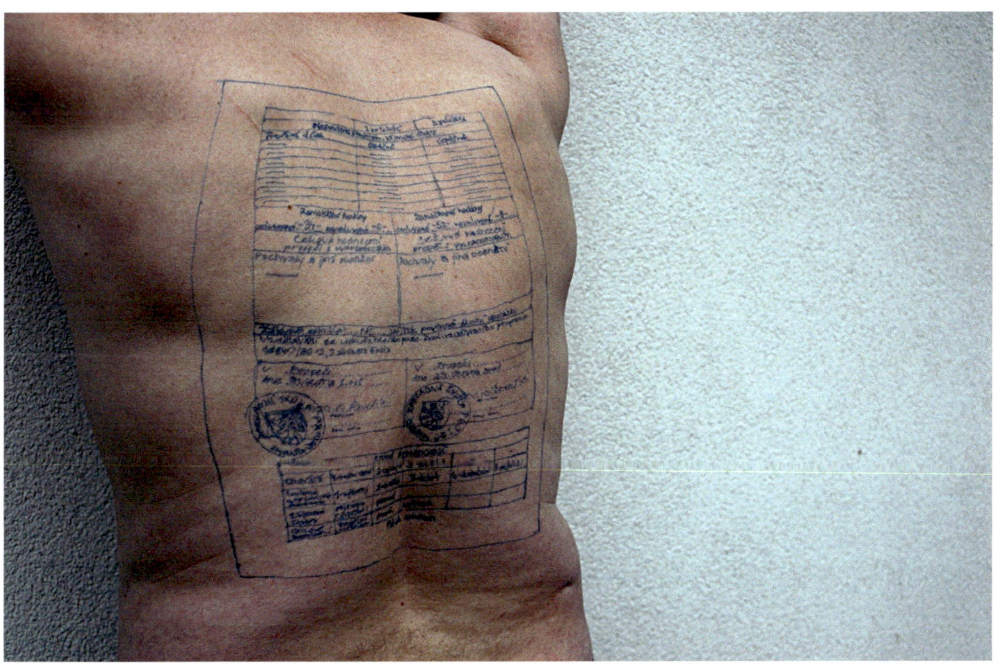

Plate 19 Mothers and Fathers, *Report Card (back)*, from *Bared!*, 2009, photographic project for *Fotograf* magazine. Courtesy the artists.

4 Articulating the Artist-Father

Guy Ben-Ner

While feminist scholars frequently cite the disparity of maternal expectations from reality, their arguments frequently presume or rather, ignore, that the paternal role is just as fraught. For example, when Simone de Beauvoir penned her influential text, *The Second Sex*, her goal was not to explore the role of the father or men, but rather to articulate the history, experience, and life of women. Nevertheless, the instances wherein she mentions fathers are telling of the persistent cultural perceptions or mis-perceptions of fatherhood. In one pertinent passage, Beauvoir asserts the image a young girl has of her father: He is mysterious, communicates for the family, is all-powerful, and that, "he is God."[1] Such sentiments reiterate a particular vision of ideal fatherhood and masculinity that men can never achieve. They reference the structural, symbolic position of the father that exists in fantasy, rather than truly reflecting the lived realities of fathers. Beauvoir acknowledges the sovereignty of the father but the implications of what this may mean for male identity did not concern her. Recent studies and cultural shifts have shown that such sentiments reiterate a particular vision of ideal fatherhood and masculinity that men can never achieve. Attention to the structural, symbolic position of the father reveals that it largely exists in fantasy, rather than truly reflecting the lived realities of fathers. Recent scholars of masculin-ity and fatherhood, who witnessed the effects of women's liberation—particularly, the greater presence of women in the workforce and the growth of the stay-at-home dad—turn to a variety of literary, psychological, and theoretical sources to understand how the concept of fatherhood has created social, cultural, and individual turmoil for men who choose not to conform to the stereotype of the omnipresent, judging, and breadwinning image of the father. Men who do not conform to the fatherly ideal of the 'primary breadwinner'—often articulated in popular cinema and television—are seen as weak, inadequate, 'losers,' and *not real men*. Scholars in the various fields of cinema, sociology, and culture, such as Stella Bruzzi, Andrea Doucet, and Jeremy Adam Smith, articulate the various conflicts men encounter due to the stereotypical notions of fatherhood.[2] Some of these constructs are due to theories of the father articulated by Freud, who believed that men were more advanced than women, and thus were more responsible for his child's successful entry into society.[3] While this view has been largely discounted, the primacy of the father in psychosocial development has remained ingrained in popular belief.

To this end, Guy Ben-Ner has created a body of work exploring his relationship to fatherhood, masculinity, and identity. In videos created between 1999 and 2005, Ben-Ner negotiates his role as an artist, father, and a man, thus articulating the artist-parent identity. In his videos, Ben-Ner exclusively employs his children, Elia and Amir, as his primary actors. He educates and guides them through their roles—both on screen and off, but he also mimics their actions and equally participates in the playful aspects of theater. I begin by discussing *Berkeley's Island* (1999), a work that reveals the young artist's struggle to find self. Through his use of tricks, the deliberate inclusion of his daughter, and narrative of self-discovery, this video demonstrates the crisis of masculinity and artistic identity that Ben-Ner experiences as he explores his new artist-parent identity. In the next section, I argue that Ben-Ner visually embraces this artist-parent identity, fully exploring the possibilities of an artistic fatherhood as seen in his video, *Moby Dick* (2001). This work, which features the artist and his daughter almost exclusively, highlights play as a medium of not only fantasy, but of education, and familial bonding. The third section of this chapter explores the father–son relationship as seen through Ben-Ner's 2004 work, *Wild Child*. Drawing on the complicated history of father–son relationships, Ben-Ner questions the complicated role of fathers in nineteenth century theories of education and explores how these notions have persisted. Lastly, I investigate Ben-Ner's work, *Elia: A Story of an Ostrich Chick* (2003) and the stigma of the 'male mother.' *Elia* features the entire family dressed in ostrich costumes, traces the growth of Ben-Ner's eldest child, and simultaneously examines Ben-Ner's role as the nurturer of the family. In sum, these videos suggest a privileging of nurture over nature, dispel the notion that men can't mother, and reflect the changing nature of parenting, artistic identity, and the father–child relationship.

Setting the Stage: Art, Education, and the Space of the Home

Ben-Ner's decision to explore his relationship to his children came as a result of a particular set of circumstances. In the mid-90s, Ben-Ner was enrolled at the Hamidrasha Art College in Ramat Hasharon, Israel to study painting and sculpture.[4] In 1994 his daughter Elia was born. When he graduated in 1997, Ben-Ner made two radical moves: He embarked upon a career as a video-based artist and he moved his studio to the home in order to be near his daughter. Both reflect the politics of circumstance. The first reflects artistic ambition: Video art was a field that was ripe for development and experimentation in the relatively non-existent Israeli scene. According to Sergio Edelsztein, video art, both in courses and artistic experimentation, all but disappeared in Israel in the 1980s, which may be due to the country being embroiled in the Lebanon War in 1981 and the Palestinian Intifada in 1987.[5] These events propelled artistic culture toward one of politicization, demonstration, and criticism—and thereby privileging photography and painting.[6] However, those who did explore time-based media as a mode of artistic inquiry, Yair Garbuz, Raffi Lavie, Michal Na'aman, Tamar Getter—all Ben-Ner's teachers—brought or referred to early video artists' performances in the classroom.[7] This set of cultural factors may, indeed, explain why many of Ben-Ner's references to other artists within his work date to, or before, the 1970s. And perhaps the political realities of Israel, and the country's constant state of turmoil, may help explain why Ben-Ner chose to explore the self and the family. According to Octavio Zaya, "tragic and extraordinary are the realities in which the contemporary art produced in Israel—or by Israeli artists undergoing the conditions and vicissitudes of artistic practice in a country in a constant state of emergency—is inspired and debated, where it is found and lost, that transcend and ignore it."[8] That is, artists either deliberately engage with the quagmire of politics and its repercussions, or avoid it completely. For the most part, Ben-Ner avoids direct references to the political state, but one can argue that the enclosed world of the kitchen (where a majority of his videos are set) is a rejection or refusal of the politics of land, nature, and therefore the state of Israel.

By 1998, video art in Israel could be viewed at key galleries and locations, especially the Tel Aviv Cinematheque, a place Ben-Ner frequented. At the galleries, Ben-Ner viewed a series of body-related actions by Boaz Arad and Dana Zonshein, Aya & Gal, and Hilla Lulu Lin. Of the more important works Ben-Ner saw, according to Edelsztein, were those from Matthew Barney's *Cremaster Cycle*, which were screened at the Center for Contemporary Art in December 1998.[9] By this time, Barney would have completed number four (1994), one (1995), and five (1997), each of which deals with metaphors of the universe and biological reproduction.[10]

The second circumstance of Ben-Ner's move to the home was a matter of much more practical concerns: With a young child, the Ben-Ner family had limited financial resources, thus making a studio rental quite taxing. However, that is not to relegate the choice to solely financial terms.[11] Ben-Ner had a strong desire to be a good father, so his choice to work from home was, according to the artist, "a type of compromise" between being a "bad father away from home a lot, and being a good father staying at home and making concessions."[12] Clearly, Ben-Ner associated "good fathers" as those men who are available to spend time with their children. This choice is in cadence with a larger cultural shift of men who have reacted positively to feminism. Jeremy Adam Smith, author of *The Daddy Shift: How Stay-at-Home Dads, Breadwinning Moms and Shared Parenting are Transforming the American Family*, points to the growing trend of men desiring to stay at home with the kids.[13] This and other studies conducted on the rise of fathering in international contexts support the view that men are more actively choosing to stay at home and take an active role in the primary care of his children.[14]

As an artist whose practice was based in the home, Ben-Ner reiterated the circumstances that several women artists experienced and still experience today: As they moved their studios into the domestic space and worked on their art projects while their children were sleeping or in school, they were perceived by critics and fellow artists as 'giving up' or being a 'dilettante.' However, the home studio provided artists a creative outlet, a means of creating art without neglecting their children and thus being—or being labeled—a 'bad mother.' Elżbieta Jabłońska, as discussed previously, commented in an interview that she had to quickly adapt her art to reflect her circumstances. She began making drawings of her son in the space of the kitchen while he slept. The products of these sittings were small drawings that could be completed quickly. Seen largely as sentimental, these works were her only creative means between feedings, changing diapers, cleaning, and cooking. When Antek grew older, sustaining the artistic and home balance caused the artist to posit herself as a *Supermatka*, or supermother, with her son as the saved or savior—as they assume the pose of the Madonna and Child.

Like Jabłońska, Ben-Ner adapted his practice by adopting video, a medium that can be started and stopped as needed and most importantly, edited later. However, there is difficulty in having a four-year-old in the home and attempting to pursue independent artistic projects. There will inevitably be moments when the child will distract or outright impede the artist from his work. Thus, by the very nature of working while at home, Ben-Ner's camera captured more than scripted storylines. For example, in the introductory scene of *Berkeley's Island*, the camera pans over Elia building a fortress out of oversized building blocks—likely an attempt to keep the child occupied for the duration of the scene. Later, in the same work, we observe Elia playing in the sand of the kitchen island, walking in front of the camera, and being chastised by Ben-Ner for moving the camera from its focused position—all moments which appear to be unscripted. In *Moby Dick,* the viewer observes a short clip of an infant Amir in his baby swing, someone coming home with the groceries, and several moments in which Elia is clearly playing and having fun with her father. In *Elia: A Story of an Ostrich Chick,* a young Amir notably breaks character and removes his costume. All of these clips reveal the complicated circumstances of raising children while working at home and their inclusion marks Ben-Ner's interest in exploring, nay highlighting, this aspect of artist-parent life.

The Space of the Home

Ben-Ner's choice to use the kitchen for most films visualizes the domestic in a loaded manner. For *Berkeley's Island,* despite the pun on actual 'kitchen islands,' Ben-Ner's storyboard notes the transformation of the 'island' to the 'I-Land," and thus it becomes a space for self-inquiry, akin to the studio. In *Moby Dick,* the kitchen becomes a site of fantasy, a ship, and a place for play. The kitchen, however, still largely functions as the gendered space of the woman. It is a space that became the site of politics in 1959 thanks to the "Kitchen Debate" between Vice President Richard Nixon and Soviet Premier Nikita Khrushchev, in which the two leaders discussed the modern household innovations of the Americans.[15] In response, women artists highlighted the kitchen within their work. These works were alternately read by critics as kitschy—for example Joan Brown's *Noel in the Kitchen* (1964) in which Brown's son Noel is depicted semi-nude in a 'funky' kitchen with a wobbly stack of pots and pans and two dogs; or critical, such as in Martha Rosler's *Semiotics of the Kitchen* (1975), in which Rosler critiques the stereotypes of the 'domestic goddess,' cooking shows, and gendered space by violently animating the tools of kitchen from A through Z. Rosler's exploration of the kitchen provides a unique correlation to Ben-Ner, as both artists restructure the space to explore identity and function. Rosler's use of the kitchen rests on a critique of female gender roles, whereas Ben-Ner employs it as a space for action, creation, and play.

Visualizations of the kitchen are often transformed into avant-garde strategies when undertaken by male artists. For example, Andy Warhol and Claes Oldenburg were praised for their pillaging of domestic and commercially available items under what became the Pop Art movement. As such, the kitchen-inspired items sold in *The Store* by Oldenburg or the Campbell Soup cans of Warhol appropriate items generally considered to belong to the female domestic sphere, yet when placed in the male artists' oeuvre, they were heralded as critiques or engagements with consumption practices.[16] But as Cécile Whiting contends, not all male artists' appropriations of the domestic reinvigorated the space as an avant-garde subject. Whiting argues that Tom Wesselmann's interiors "only partially disrupted cultural hierarchies" because they were often interpreted as white, middle-class, and feminine and therefore only partially distanced from images that would have been seen in women's magazines like *Good Housekeeping.*[17] Thus, as an artist limited to the household *and* tasked with the care of his daughter, Ben-Ner's choice of setting seems to some degree reinforce the kitchen as a feminine space and to allow interpretations of Ben-Ner assuming the primary domestic role in the home. Perhaps to counter this feminization of the space, and assert it as Ben-Ner's domestic-artistic domain, there is only one instance where an adult female appears within the kitchen, thus suggesting the artist's natural occupation in the role and space.

Disrupted Narratives: Fatherhood, Masculinity, and Domesticity

The artist stated that becoming a father at a "young age and trying to understand what he was doing as an artist" caused a forced situation in which he had to make a "moral choice."[18] This acknowledgment of his artistic immaturity parallels what can be seen in Ben-Ner's early works at home—they utilize what one might consider, a 'boyish' subject—namely, his penis. The interest in one's member evokes a line from the infamous child development guru, Dr. Benjamin Spock, who suggested that men may be anxious about their new roles as fathers but are simultaneously "proud of [their] virility."[19] Ben-Ner's short videos, *Karaoke* (1997), *Untitled (Rolling Pin)* (1998), *Untitled (Forked)* (1998), as well as two untitled photographs from 1998 record the artist's preoccupation with his bodily member and the tricks he can make it do. For example, in *Untitled (Rolling Pin)*, Ben-Ner approaches the kitchen table, places his penis on it, flattens it using a rolling pin (the penis becomes replaced with a pliable putty), and cuts out a crescent moon and the star—the moon symbolic of the Islam, and the star of David from Judaism.[20] In other untitled photographs Ben-Ner documents his performance of household tasks—hanging laundry and washing dishes—with a visible erection. In these images he confronts the stereotype of the domestic as rendering the male impotent. Read together with *Untitled (Rolling Pin)*, these photographs evoke contradictory notions of masculinity being eroded by domesticity and being reinforced, causing arousal.

By 1999, Ben-Ner expanded his creative oeuvre by creating, filming, and starring in what is largely considered his first major work, *Berkeley's Island* (Plate 7).[21] A loose adaptation of Daniel Defoe's classic adventure novel, *Robinson Crusoe* (1719), *Berkeley's Island* parallels many of the themes and narrative aspects of Defoe's novel, but also makes significant departures—at least six scenes in the fifteen minute video include or visualize the artist's daughter, Elia; and three of those seem to have no narrative purpose—they visualize the seemingly unscripted interactions of Ben-Ner with his daughter. In these scenes, Ben-Ner abandons his character and visibly enacts a fatherly role. It is these scenes, in addition to at least five that can be best described as variations of slapstick that reveal the artist's struggle to define the self as artist and father in the domestic context. It is these 'bloopers' in Ben-Ner's video that parallel the non-narrative structure of Defoe's story, enable the artist to deconstruct notions of the home movie, and acknowledge his negotiation of the artist-parent identity.

Berkeley's Island takes place in the domestic confines of the artist's kitchen. Starring as Robinson Crusoe, Ben-Ner defies his father at the age of eighteen, gets aboard a ship that succumbs to a raging storm, and becomes the sole survivor. Ben-Ner awakens to find himself alone on a remote island with the ship's helm on top of him. He removes the helm to reveal his burnt stomach, visually referencing Dennis Oppenheim's 1970 work, *Reading Position for Second Degree Burn*. This was a project in which Oppenheim explored the body as a captive surface that can be changed by the sun in terms of color and sensation—two notions that, as Ben-Ner's video draws to a close, are revealed as greatly important to the work's meaning.[22] Ben-Ner draws on Oppenheim's notion that the body becomes a canvas, a site that becomes colored and sensitized through prolonged exposure—a solipsistic view that is similarly reinforced in the work's opening frame, which quotes a line from Jean-Paul Sartre's biography of playwright Jean Genet, *Saint Genet: Actor and Martyr*: "To the child who steals and child who masturbates, to exist is *to be seen by adults* and since these secret activities take place in solitude, *they do not exist.*"[23] Sartre, writing on the ethics of childhood existence (in relation to the writer Jean Genet), builds on the view that to exist is to "belong to someone" but it also allows us to reject aspects that others do not see, or ignore—such as theft and masturbation—as a means of proclaiming one's saintliness.[24] Rather than hide these aspects of oneself, Ben-Ner exults in them, places them in full view of the conscientious viewer, ultimately denying a god- or saint-like status of the father.

This particular strategy places Ben-Ner's work within the postmodernist paradigm and a contemporary culture of confession.[25] Initially, the film reads as a somewhat comedic—the helm sunburn is a humorous indicator that the castaway was unconscious and spent many hours in the sun, but it also sets the tone of the film—it is lighthearted, yet melancholy once the viewer realizes that he is "stuck" on a man-made kitchen island—a clear metaphor for the isolation of domesticity. The reference to Oppenheim appeals to the sophisticated and savvy art viewer, yet the work also recalls the mundane activities of the artists in the studio in the 1970s that the less astute viewer can infer. But as Ben-Ner evokes the existentialist theorists Sartre and George Berkeley, to whom the video's title refers, he pushes the work into philosophical discourse. Thus, *Berkeley's Island* conveys a palimpsest of meanings, allowing for readings of Ben-Ner, fatherhood, and masculinity beyond the traditional visual sign of fatherhood—a man and his child. And while the surface-value of these references provide one interpretation, a thoughtful investigation of the outliers to the story reveals yet another.

As the reader becomes exposed to the man's inner thoughts, actions, excitements, and absurdities in the text of *Robinson Crusoe*, it is through the use of voice-over that Ben-Ner is able to narrate the tale of his shipwreck and his subsequent life on the island in the form of a travel diary. Beginning with the date, reflecting on how long he has been on the island, and what he has experienced and learned of himself, Ben-Ner follows the basic narrative, though improvises contemporary replacements for the finer details. We learn of how he discovered that animal fat can be used for lamps—Ben-Ner uses the refrigerator light; and how he taught his parrot to speak—Ben-Ner's cat stands in as the parrot, climbing on the single palm tree on his makeshift island. With the inclusion of these scenes, *Berkeley's Island* seems like a true adaptation of the story of the castaway and his mostly solitary adventures. However, deciding on whether or not to call either a 'true' narrative is complicated. Literary scholars debate the actual narrative quality of Defoe's book, as there are several loose ends, rambling and random moments within the text that undermine the traditional narrative structure where all scenes advance the plot in some way, or reveal clues about the characters.[26] Coupled with the fact that contemporary audiences viewed Defoe's text as a nonfiction novel, we might begin to understand how Ben-Ner's adaptation of the text is not merely a fictional recreation, but rather a way to investigate the self and his relatively new place in the realm of fatherhood or as the stay-at-home dad. For example, in a scene where Elia and Ben-Ner are seated on the island, Ben-Ner appears to be between takes as he has put on a collared shirt (he is usually bare-chested during the narrative moments) and Elia has her beach toys out—she is raking, patting, and generally just *playing* in the sand as if she were on a real beach. A verbal exchange occurs between daughter and father—this is a real conversation—not the voice-over narration heard in the rest of the film. Elia tells Ben-Ner that she will "flatten it" for her father, that is, she will smooth out the areas of the island that she is currently tilling with her rake, making his island less of a unified spherical form. Ben-Ner, however, tells her "no." In response, Elia exclaims "Daddy!," to which Ben-Ner gives in, warning her that "if [he] doesn't like it, [he] will change it back." Elia proceeds to tap her plastic rake into the sand as Ben-Ner gets up and attempts to light a cigarette on the stove. As he moves across the island, Elia exclaims that he is "ruining" her design in the sand and that she will ruin his (island or movie) in return. Then Elia runs off giggling and the viewer senses that she has run behind the camera. In turn, Ben-Ner smiles yet demands, "Elia, don't move it." He repeats the statement again more sternly, while Elia pans the camera up to the ceiling where she reveals that a mirror has been positioned directly above the island and single palm tree (Figure 4.1). In itself, this sequence has no purpose. It seems to merely document the interaction between father and daughter, and perhaps, the novelty of the child having a sand island to play with inside the home. In his review of Ben-Ner's first comprehensive exhibition in Tel Aviv, critic Nuit Banai asserts that the "invasiveness of [the] home appliances is aggravated by the incursion of Elia who walks in and out of the frame." Banai continues, stating Elia "completely disregarding her father's project, moves the camera."[27] Banai's interpretation of the scene seems to

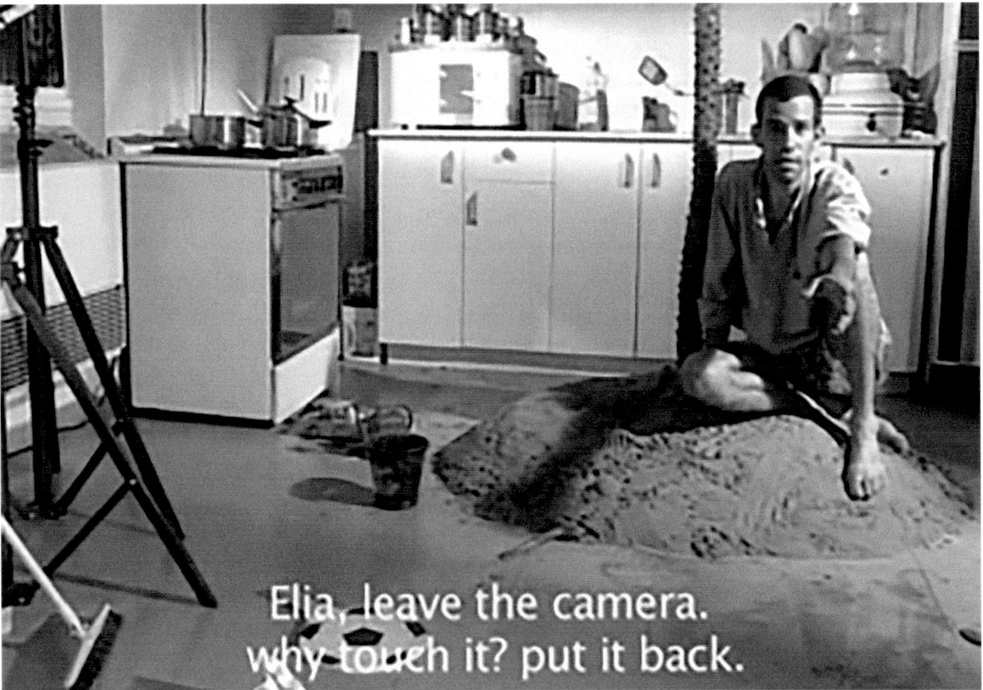

Figure 4.1 Guy Ben-Ner, still from *Berkeley's Island*, 1999. Single channel video with sound, 15 minutes. Courtesy the artist.

critique the movie's setting, suggesting perhaps her frustration in watching the scene in an impartially disguised kitchen and Elia's interruptions. This statement disregards some of the more nuanced meanings behind Elia's action, as Banai does not connect Elia's movement of the camera to the staging of the next scene. She does note that the "dialogue reveals the conflict between the humdrum constraints of a shared domestic sphere and the artist's desire to fabricate his own separate aesthetic environment" yet one can consider the aesthetic quality of the work akin to the home movie.[28]

The home movie, as film scholar Patricia Zimmermann has argued, has often been defined as a product of amateurs and dismissed as a nostalgic memento of the past, or as an "insignificant byproduct of consumer technology."[29] However, as Susan Stewart has demonstrated, nostalgia is important to the construction of self and community. In a sense, the inclusion of the scenes of Elia is a way of collecting her image, her actions, her presence, capturing her childhood, and proving her existence under the guise of aesthetics—something that artist-parents are wont to do.[30] This seems particularly true as the film was conceived to be about a domesticated castaway, and not about Elia, though she becomes part of the artist's larger construction of self. Elia's actions during this filmed non-narrative moment have been purposefully placed before a sequence that begins with the image of Ben-Ner reflected through the ceiling mirror, thus casting Elia in a positive light—she assisted her father in the production of the work and did not hinder it. Sure enough, it is important to note that Ben-Ner's interest in conveying narrative stories through the video both allowed for and necessitated that the entire family participate in his art—they were the actors immediately available to him. In an interview, Ben-Ner stated that video "became the best way of handling the situation I found myself in. It meant the whole family could get involved because with movie-making there is always a lot to do. It also allowed me to give them instant feedback."[31] Such a statement implies the possible 'directing' of such a scene—that is, Elia may have observed her father move the camera toward the ceiling in preparation for the next scene and Elia decided to copy his actions when she ran behind the camera. Elia's engagement in *Berkeley's Island* quickly advances into works which involve her prominently—notably, *Moby Dick* (2000) and *Elia: A Story of an Ostrich Chick* (2003).

Perhaps aware of the saccharine associations artists have historically garnered for including their children in their work, Ben-Ner interjects scenes in *Berkeley's Island* to demonstrate his masculinity. One such scene includes the artist/castaway digging a hole and then humping it as we are told that he has been "testing the island's limits" which "has maddened" his mind. In another, the viewer sees a man, who one assumes is Ben-Ner, rubbing his genitals against a mirror (the head remains beyond the frame of the camera), which then creates an illusion of the body bouncing in the air through the mirror. The last words of the narrator (before this passage) note that "contact with the world [has become] unbearable," yet all he does is touch things. This commentary suggests that the truly unbearable aspect of the island is the absence of sexual activity, of touching another person. To reinforce this, a sequence of objects flash across the screen—a pen, toothbrush, perfume bottle—all with feminine attributes, most prominently breasts and hips. These images and scenes of self-pleasure could suggest sexual delusion and desire experienced through prolonged isolation, or alternatively, Ben-Ner's fear of everything becoming feminine, including his self. Freud suggested that dreams were ways of fulfilling one's wishes, and thus we may interpret this as Ben-Ner's assertion of his masculine desire, or as a sign of his fear of becoming feminine. Though not necessarily accepting or employing such views, Freud's study of sexuality seems to be a recurring reference, as we see Ben-Ner use a copy of Freud's *Analysis of a Phobia in a Five-Year-Old Boy* (1909) as a set prop in the later work, *Wild Boy* (2004).

What is notable, despite the psycho-sexual and gendered associations tied to the space of the kitchen, is that this is a site that becomes a studio, a place for introspective inquiry as much as creative fantasy and experimentation with materials and actions. It would encompass and transform into the remote island (for Ben-Ner) and sandbox (for Elia) in *Berkeley's Island*, the whaling ship in *Moby Dick*, and the natural landscape in *Wild Boy*. One imagines that the Ben-Ner family lived *around* the island in their kitchen, much like they would later live with an artificial hill from *Wild Boy*, and the camera equipment that would likely be continuously placed within plain view, at least during the months, weeks, or days of filming. The process of creating these films, Edelsztein notes, must have been "long, tedious, and quite hard for the children, as they lack the discipline needed for repetitive shots," and thus possibly creating a surreal world for the children where reality and fantasy are intertwined.[32] Thus, life and art for Ben-Ner were invariably intermixed, reiterating what Bruce Nauman once said about artists' actions, particularly those that contain "passion, concentration, and practice," and whether mundane or creative, are art.[33]

While the kitchen remains the primary setting for the narrative to unfold, important secondary events of *Berkeley's Island* take place elsewhere. That is, in other spaces of the home, notably the laundry room, which may or may not be a space within the kitchen, bath, bedroom, or a space unto itself. One scene reinforces the sexual frustration of the castaway as it is introduced in a sequence dated to July 2. The voice-over narration informs the viewer that he's "learned to use what the island supplie[d] [him] with" and cuts to a fifteen-second clip of the artist's penis resting on a washing machine in its spin cycle. Resting on uneven ground, the machine rocks back and forth, and seems to vibrate. A glass of water and a green ball accentuate the motion of the machine. One might expect that such a moment would cause arousal, however the penis remains flaccid, suggesting that domestic chores have emasculated the man or stifled his libido. Conversely, the island could serve as a metaphor for domestic life, which forces one to think creatively, make the most out of each opportunity—perhaps one can relate this scene to Ben-Ner finding ways of making it physically, artistically, and intellectually stimulating.

This creative pleasure reaches new boundaries when the narrator informs viewers that he has taught his parrot how to talk and exclaims that it is nice to have "someone to call me by my name." On this cue, the viewer is confronted with a one-minute excerpt from an early film by Ben-Ner titled, *Karaoke* (1997). In this clip, viewers are confronted with a close up of a man's crotch. He unzips his trousers and pulls out his penis, which is adorned with two paper eyes to create a face. Using his thumb and forefingers, the man moves the urethra of his penis to 'lip-synch' Connie Francis' 1959 song, "Lipstick on Your Collar."[34] The lyrics tell the tale of male infidelity, the act of getting caught, and irresponsibility—and suggest the ultimate rebellion from the 'good father' stereotype. Thus, Ben-Ner assumes an irreverent, non-domestic masculinity through what is assumed to be *his* exposed genitals.

Additionally, as the finale to *Berkeley's Island*, Ben-Ner demonstrates the 'special skill' that he acquired on the island. The film cuts to another early video by the artist, *Untitled (Forked)* (1997), in which a man enters a sparsely adorned room, removes a fork with the two bent central prongs from his shirt pocket, and holds the twisted fork to his penis. He begins to urinate, simultaneously extinguishing the flames in the terracotta pots on each side of him. Once finished expelling his urine, he returns the fork back to his shirt pocket—as if it were a pen— and concludes the event. Critic Jon Davies interprets this 'penis trick' as a method to make fun of the "supposedly castrating effects of domesticity on dads," and as such, Ben-Ner's combination of childish, masturbatory scenes with the successful result of ejaculatory emissions (a child) is unique.[35] As Davies notes, "If Ben-Ner is a reluctant family man, we could argue that sex with someone other than himself is what got him into this mess to begin with."[36]

Putting aside familial references, one may consider Duchamp's *The Bride Stripped Bare by her Bachelors, Even (The Large Glass)* (1915–23) and Vito Acconci's *Seedbed* performance from January 1972 as similar moments of, or references to, ejaculatory emissions, yet they each reject any acknowledgment of the final potentially biological product of the seed. The artists thus seem to prefer to omit any traces of the reproductive possibility—the child—in favor of what seems to be shorter-term and more directly 'artistic' or professional metaphors. Perhaps, Duchamp and Acconci were more interested in entering their own personal concerns, rather than integrating this with aspects of the family. Regardless, David Hopkins speaks of these works in terms referencing the potential for growth, and celebrating in the "ejaculatory iconography celebrated by men" which was largely contested by the first wave of feminist artists.[37]

Ultimately, why Ben-Ner chooses to include these seemingly irrelevant shots in the film can perhaps be explained by the film's title, *Berkeley's Island,* a reference to the eighteenth-century philosopher George Berkeley and his theory of vision. For Berkeley, the object is perceived through vision and by touch, and by no other means. Berkeley rejected Albertian geometry as the means to perceive depth and culminates his theory with the proposition, *esse est percipi*—existence is perception. As Ann Gibson and Lucia Palmer interpreted the phrase, Berkeley "makes perception itself the primary creative act."[38] Applying this idea to *Berkeley's Island,* one can read the work as one related to perception and existence—isolated on an island in an unremarkable kitchen, Ben-Ner needs to visualize his existence, his masculinity, and his daughter, so the viewer can perceive *him,* know him to be alive, as an artist and as a father, or rather, as an artist-parent. This notion can illuminate why, before cutting to the clip of *Untitled (Forked),* Ben-Ner states,

> One thing is for certain, while I've been living on the island I gained abilities, and as ridiculous as they may seem, they are mine. Creating an identity—building a self; and it is through these abilities that I want you to remember me. You understand? What you are about to see right now belongs to me, being the only one capable of performing it.[39]

Ben-Ner desires to be perceived, to be remembered for his unique talents and qualities as a man, father, and artist. He wants to be championed for his heroic feats, his isolation, and his decision to create an "I-Land" in the home, rather than in a distant studio. Likewise, Defoe's Robinson Crusoe needed to be perceived—called by his name—and thus, there is a symbiotic relationship between the two. Ben-Ner's early reference to Oppenheim similarly draws on this idea—in both, the body becomes a canvas that needs to be exposed in order to be perceived through color and to gain sensitivity.

By recording the symbols of masculinity (his body and penis) and fatherhood (Elia) through the video camera's lens, Ben-Ner reveals his sensitivity to and struggle against social stereotypes in order to define his identity as a man, an artist, and a father. Thus, what seem at first to be flubs and loose ends in Ben-Ner, turn into retrospectively true accounts of his struggle to reconcile the social, ideal, and practical as he assumes the artist-parent identity. Indeed, Sergio Edelsztein asserts that these short scenes "are not an integral part of it, but rather interpret, broaden or reinforce the main narrative."[40] The main narrative embodies not the storyline of *Robinson Crusoe*, but the successful negotiation and articulation of Ben-Ner's artist-father identity. In fact, the scenes inserted between those that mark Crusoe's loneliness and isolation are not intended to draw sympathy from the viewer. Helena Winston writes, "As is implied by … those unedited moments in *Berkeley's Island*, Ben-Ner consciously chooses to reveal to the viewer the artifice of the situation, and humorously undercuts any self-pity or pathos-inflected sentiment that might otherwise take hold."[41] This reading reaffirms that those uncut moments reveal the process of filmmaking, the artifice of the situation, and ultimately posit *Berkeley's Island* as a home movie-like visualization of Ben-Ner's transition to an artist-parent.

Playing "Moby Dick": Ishmael and the Great White Beast of Parenting

Ben-Ner's next major work, *Moby Dick*, features a more elaborate role and relationship with Elia, and reveals a father–daughter relationship based on play. For both *Berkeley's Island* and *Moby Dick*, Ben-Ner claims that he did not return to the original texts, but rather worked from his memory of the stories, and knew them "like everyone else does."[42] As such, the novels *Robinson Crusoe* and *Moby-Dick* are known, at least cursorily, in the Western cultural consciousness, yet they are more frequently satirized, adapted, and referred to within popular culture.[43] It is the latter that Ben-Ner's video draws upon as it incorporates the genre of silent film, slapstick, and vaudeville. He employs aspects of these cinematic forefathers to not only recount the tale of Ahab, Ishmael, Pip, Queequeg, and the whale, but also to explore the intersection of nation, family, and faith. These elements make Ben-Ner's version of the story, originally written by Herman Melville, less about one man's search for the thing that eludes him than the way that Ben-Ner desires to raise and educate his children. What better way can one educate than through instructive play? In *Moby Dick*, Ben-Ner creates an engaging allegory about fatherhood, the Jewish faith, and the nation of Israel.

In recreating the tale of Ishmael, Ahab, and his search for Moby Dick, Ben-Ner appropriates the most basic elements. The film begins with clips of Elia and Ben-Ner facing the camera, smiling and laughing, with the intertitle, "Call me Ishmael," inserted in between the shots. Elia and Ben-Ner are twinned, both with nude torsos and missing their upper central incisors (Ben-Ner obscures his with a dark tape or paper); however, in the next sequence, Elia, is dressed in an oversized shirt and vest with her hair in pigtails and donning a mustache. She appears seated in the kitchen sink, which is now transformed into a bar at The Spouter Inn, in New Bedford Bay, where Ishmael (played by Ben-Ner) enters. The two converse as Elia, playing the role of the barkeep, pours him a drink, which Ishmael imbibes. Attracted to a black and white linocut of a whale, the conversation turns to whaling. Someone enters the kitchen bar, denoted by the text, "Hi You," fearful of the approaching visitor, Ishmael draws a gun while the barkeep takes a bottle and breaks it over his head, rendering him unconscious.

Still located within the space of the kitchen, in the next scene the space has been transformed into the whaler on which Ishmael finds himself. A mast becomes positioned in the sink and is surrounded by plates, reminding of the space's continued domestic function. Ropes are tied and placed diagonally to suggest the system of supports and levies for the sails and other necessary whaling instruments. In accordance with this transformation of the kitchen, the freezer section of the refrigerator becomes a food depot, as we observe Ben-Ner's friend and colleague, the artist Boaz Arad, hauling in a water jug, bags of frozen vegetables, half a watermelon, and a large bottle of Coca-Cola. These modern conveniences mark, expose, and reinforce the artifice of the entire scene and its place between art and life. That is, the items are likely actual items on the family's grocery list and will be consumed; it was merely the putting away of the items that became incorporated into the film. Similarly, when Ishmael is done storing the items, he closes the freezer door to reveal a series of family photos adorning its exterior. The lower portion, the camera later reveals, displays child-like drawings of a fish, a mermaid, and a third image, likely to be Elia's own art contribution to the ship's décor—a sentimental reminder that this artistic space also functions as a domestic space.

As the ship is stocked and readied, the artist's family appears next to a palm tree that glides across the kitchen—Nava, turned away from the camera, holds Amir in her arms, as she and Elia wave goodbye, sending off Ishmael, the aimless wanderer (Plate 8). In the subsequent scenes, Ishmael introduces the members of the ship's crew: Pip, Queequeg, and Ahab.[44] Pip (Elia's new role in the video), appears standing on the kitchen counter, eating a snack out of a paper cup with a spoon, while the other characters, Queequeg, the harpooner and cannibal, and Ahab, are portrayed by the artist in various guises. A series of non-narrative sequences follow, explicating the "cabin fever" experienced by the crewmembers. Once Ahab appears on the deck (kitchen counter) the narrative resumes. Ahab offers a gold coin to the first to locate the whale and nails it on the mast for all to behold. Another series of non-narrative sequences aboard depict the antics of Pip and Ishmael, which is followed by Pip spotting the whale—Ahab gives her the prize and she immediately bites into it to reveal it is a chocolate coin in a gold wrapper—Hanukkah gelt. As will be discussed below, within this sequence, Ben-Ner weaves in a real-life object that aids children's religious learning.

The vignettes that follow highlight the business of whaling, including the rendering of whale fat into oil (Ishmael stands on the kitchen counter with a large wooden spoon, stirring the contents of a very large stock pot cooking on the stove) and the presence of carcass eaters (sharks) in the sea surrounding the ship. Here, only the fins of the predators are shown as they glide around the kitchen floor.[45] This scene cuts to Elia in the bath, where the viewer observes Ben-Ner's hand lathering up her hair, cuts back to the predators in the kitchen, and then jumps to the shower, revealing Elia's hair has been coiffed into a shark fin. The scene returns to the kitchen, where the camera, low and close to the ground, reveals that the viewer has become the predator—for watching the scene of Elia in the shower, or perhaps, for thinking that she was a "carcass eater" as well. Verging close to the border of exploitation and, to some, pedophilia, Ben-Ner's quickly changing camera angles suggest a trepidation and uncertainty with both the desire to record his child's actions, fear of her existence (as an "alien creature" or a savage), and caution in producing something that might be seen as pornographic.[46] On this, Chris Jenks has argued that in the postmodern world, childhood has come to represent security and stability in a world where relationships are, more often than

not, insecure and unstable, and thus dramatic societal responses to child abuse become
a means to preserve childhood, child–parent relationships, and create stability in a
volatile world.[47] Ben-Ner does not directly refer to such concepts yet alludes to them
by positioning the camera at a high angle (the jumpiness of the frame suggests that
he uses a hand-held camera as opposed to one stationed on a tripod) and framing of
Elia's body. She turns away from Ben-Ner, does not look into the camera, and is barely
contained within the lower right corner of the frame. This approach reveals that this
is a moment of everyday life, Elia is not pretending to be Pip, nor is Ben-Ner Ishmael,
Ahab, or Queequeg. He is merely a dad and giving his daughter a bath. The next
scenes seem to 'punish' him for such a depiction. In his role of Ahab, he stands on the
deck with his amputated leg supported by a series of inadequate substitutes, a stack
of glasses, a pitcher, a ladle (which he must hold to his stump), all before Ahab locates
his prize, and spots the whale.

A series of quick scenes demonstrates the whale's movement. A stream of water
bursts from the sea floor (in the kitchen), from a duplicated kitchen counter, and then
again in the living room (another part of the sea). Ishmael lowers the boats; Queequeg
throws his harpoon and then takes a boat with Pip away from the whaler.[48] Ahab
similarly throws his harpoon, gets in his boat, and pulls the camera to him, suggesting that he has pulled in the beast. A text screen declares "the end," but the addition
of an ellipsis to the text denies its proclamation. The next scene shows Ahab on top
of the duplicate kitchen counter, repeatedly stabbing into it, suggesting that he has
taken his vengeance on Moby Dick, yet a blast of water spurts forth, blinds him, and
he succumbs to the belly of the whale. The film cuts to the sequence of the shark fins
again, with the camera again taking a predatory role—suggesting that the viewer has
devoured and consumed the image Ben-Ner and Elia. While literally referring to the
events in Melville's story, reading the scene from the perspective of the artist–parent
offers another meaning.

With the whale, in its embodiment as a non-functional kitchen counter and placed
within another domestic setting—the living room—Ben-Ner suggests that trying to
contain, capture, and defeat domesticity is futile. Once a parent, one or both of the
parents will become restricted to the space of the home, and possibly even be figuratively swallowed by it. The ambiguous relationship Ben-Ner demonstrated between
masculinity and the home in *Berkeley's Island* has evolved into an ungendered conflict
between allowing domesticity to rule one's life and fighting to transform it to one that
allows functional things, like the kitchen, to become non-functional. Ben-Ner continues this exploration in his next film, *House Hold* (2001), in which he becomes trapped
underneath his newly born son's, Amir's, crib and he must go at great lengths to
escape, including biting off his own finger, peeling off a toenail, plucking armpit hair,
and stealing a carrot from his son in order to fashion tools for his escape. In this film,
unlike in *Moby Dick*, the family remains nearby, but oblivious to Ben-Ner's entrapment, thus Ben-Ner clearly references his sense of isolation and feelings of imprison-
ment due to his identity as a parent.[49]

As in *Berkeley's Island, Moby Dick* concludes with a final "trick." Dressed in the
same white shirt, black pant uniform of the earlier works, the scene cuts to a face-off
between Ben-Ner and Boaz Arad, who holds an obviously fake Persian scimitar. Two
men appear and carry Ben-Ner to the white wall and turn him to face the camera.
Arad swings the sword, slicing Ben-Ner into half, where rather than dying, his legs run

off (Elia becomes his legs, evident as she peeks out over the edge of the pant legs), and the upper portion of Ben-Ner is placed on the ground. Ben-Ner manages to get his legs to come back to him, where he pieces himself together and is whole once again. This finale, unlike the one of his own creation in *Berkeley's Island*, recreates Georges Méliès 1904 trick from *The Terrible Turkish Executioner*. By referencing Méliès, Ben-Ner creates what André Gaudreault has termed a *"fantastic action"* where "impossible events occur all by themselves without the presence of some mediating deus ex machina that would have caused or 'justified' them."[50] Interestingly, if Ben-Ner employed this scene as homage to Méliès, the following quote by Méliès may prove enlightening:

> In these sorts of films, the importance lies in the ingenuity and unexpected nature of the tricks, in the picturesqueness of the sets, in the artistic positioning of the dramatis personae, and also in the invention of the star-turn and the finale. Contrary to the way things are usually done, my procedure for constructing these sorts of works consisted of inventing the details before the whole thing, a *whole* that is nothing other than 'the script.'[51]

In essence, what Méliès reveals about his films—that their primary subject revolves around the tricks, actions, and cinematic devices he invented, rather than a narrative—parallels what one observes within *Moby Dick*. The importance of Ben-Ner's film exists in the positioning of the dramatis personae—himself and Elia; the tricks and cinematic actions they perform; and the artistic, literary, and historical references that he can include. Closely investigating the tricks performed by Elia and Ben-Ner together and those Ben-Ner creates on his own reveals the extent of preparation, coaching, and teaching needed to complete the work.

True to the genre of silent cinema, gestures, actions, and dialogue are exaggerated to convey the interaction between the two characters. Elia's actions are closely guided and directed. Her speech, to make sure that the audience understands that she is the one who is speaking, is clearly a series of "blah, blah, blahs," which can be clearly discerned in her close-ups. Clearly enunciated actions and communication that is culturally coded are key in silent cinema, as they ensure that viewers will understand the films' meaning. George Wead, using the analogy of a child to discuss the technique of silent films, writes,

> It is more obvious with a child that the culture does not control *what* he says. He may be a genius, like Mozart, who is perfecting his piano technique while other children stumble over two-syllable words. Still, he can choose to communicate only in *ways* the culture understands, which are the only ways it can teach.[52]

Thus, Ben-Ner's casting of Elia as Pip (a minor character in Melville's novel), requires a clear decisive direction to communicate clearly to the viewer. The minor role of Pip, who is now a major character in Ben-Ner's rendition, allows Ben-Ner more room to improvise and invent the actions Elia will make before the camera. As the artist stated, "I wanted to stage an adventure in the home: to turn the inside into an outside, to create a fantasy, and to find the minimum number of lures needed in order to set the fantasy going."[53] Together, they enact a series of playful actions that either evoke or refer to vaudevillian acts of Charlie Chaplin.

The early indication of slapstick occurs under the guise of communicating the tedium of daily life on the whaler; Ben-Ner, as Ishmael, and Elia, as Pip, enact a series of actions where they exit the cupboards and refrigerator (which has been emptied of its contents) as if they were the crew's sleeping quarters. To communicate that these spaces were the sleeping quarters, Ben-Ner needed to only show the scene once, but he repeats the action five times, with each rendition revealing Pip and Ishmael hiding in different quarters. In the first, Pip exits the refrigerator and Ishmael the nearest cabinet; in the second, Pip hides in the fridge and Ishmael crouches in the smaller left-hand side cabinet; in the third, they reverse the formation of the first; in the fourth, Ishmael hides within the larger right cabinet and Pip in the smaller left; and lastly, they both emerge from the refrigerator. In each repeated instance, the mundane becomes more absurd, establishing the hilarity and the boredom of life on the ship and suggesting the boredom of being at home.

These actions are clearly playful. Each time Elia stretches out of her 'sleeping quarter' she appears smiling, happy, and overall enjoying herself. This repeated action is clearly an act of play, a form of the game of hide and seek, yet placed within the kitchen and with no one, other than the camera, doing the seeking. Even Ben-Ner seems to be enjoying himself. In each scene, as he exits his cabin and stretches, he looks for Elia. In the beginning, this is possibly to make sure that she plays her respective part, but subsequently he too smiles and laughs as he sees how much fun she is having. This interaction suggests a bond has formed between father and daughter, which as Stella Bruzzi has noted, is an uncommon subject in terms of film, as most paternal films focus on the father–son relationship.[54] Indeed, Elia is cast in the role of a boy, which suggests a subversion of the ideal father–son relationship. Davies considers this gender confusion ironic, stating, "beyond the irony of having a little girl inhabit a man's world of adventure and hard living on the high seas, the tape is marked by Ben-Ner being on the receiving end of a barrage of exaggerated, often punishing pratfalls, both of his own devising and at the hands of Elia."[55] Davies suggests that there is a punishment for asking his daughter to play the role of a male, but that the pretend-play of Elia and Ben-Ner does not revolve around myths and stereotypes of men wanting sons, which pepper cultural conceptions of fatherhood. Rather Ben-Ner reveals the possibility of establishing a powerful parent–child relationship, regardless of the child's sex.

The subsequent scene reveals Ishmael and Pip seated across from each other at a table in the kitchen (Figure 4.2). The entire space rocks back and forth, implying the violent waves crashing against the whaler, and causes the plate of food to slide from one side to the other, forcing the crewmates to share the same plate. Quoting, at least initially, a scene from Charlie Chaplin's 1917 film, *The Immigrant*, the scene of Ishmael and Pip sharing a plate of food quickly dissolves to one where Ben-Ner and Elia are sharing a humorous family meal. Ben-Ner begins visibly laughing, so much that his entire body is shaking while he tries to remain in character. It seems, perhaps that Elia broke her character by climbing on top of the table after losing her spoon with the plate, in order to reach the food. Interestingly, *Moby Dick* shares more similarities than the dining room scene of *The Immigrant*. Like *Moby Dick*, Chaplin's film partially takes place on a ship; it actually begins with a view of a ship filled with several immigrants huddled together suffering the effects of the sea. The pronounced pitch of the ship reinforces the immigrants' sickness, which sets the stage for the dinner scene that Ben-Ner quotes. At the call for dinner, Chaplin, playing the role of the

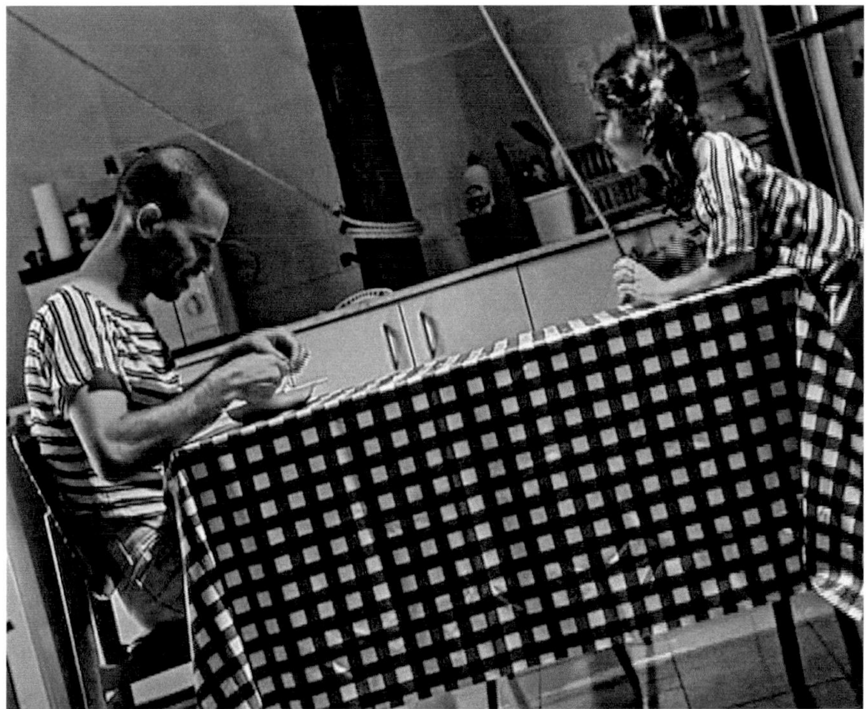

Figure 4.2 Guy Ben-Ner, still from *Moby Dick*, 2000. Single channel video, 12 minutes, 35 seconds. Courtesy the artist.

Tramp, takes a seat on the right side of a long table, unintentionally sharing a bowl of food with the man seated across from him because of the sway of the boat.

Despite the humorous meal in *The Immigrant*, the story quickly develops to be one about companionship, which is also paralleled in Ben-Ner's *Moby Dick*. In *The Immigrant*, the Tramp meets a woman on the ship, played by Edna Purviance, with whom he falls in love.[56] The affection that becomes a major part of Chaplin's comedy similarly plays an important role within Ben-Ner's film. The laughter and enjoyment witnessed between Ishmael and Pip, Ben-Ner and Elia, father and daughter appear to be of true affection and love. With this scene and the one prior, father and daughter have reached a relationship that supports the notion that they have become a dyad, learning and growing from each other in unison. Indeed, Ben-Ner noted that the film collapsed a "private family story into a cultural fantasy," and relating it to a family photo album, said the two are similar because "it is very private but it looks the same everywhere, because it is culturally dictated in many ways."[57] As noted above, cultural cues allow viewers to not only interpret the father–daughter relationship, but also understand the events and jokes of slapstick and silent cinema.

Tom Gunning argues that the presence of slapstick in Ben-Ner's works is a response to the condition of video art being exhibited in spaces where audiences are in transit, "coming and going without necessarily watching the entire tape or getting the whole story, needing brief bits of self-contained attention-drawing attractions."[58] While this may be partially true, it is clear that the broader context of his intentions and references that Ben-Ner's "bits" are carefully selected to imbue deeper meaning about the artist and convey how he departs from expected social roles, particularly those of fatherhood, masculinity, and morality.

Like the portions of Melville's novel that are unrelated to the plot's development and instead recount aspects of the whaling process, manufacture, and sale of goods, the many scenes of slapstick in Ben-Ner's film reveal little about the narrative of *Moby Dick*, yet convey much about the playful and active fantasy life of a child. As nurtured by the father, the support of a child's imagination is a critical part of a child's social and intellectual development, and a key tool in the understanding of complex social interactions.[59] Sociologist Amal Treacher discusses the importance of studying children's imaginings as she notes, "it has become commonplace to theorize childhood and children as sites of social construction."[60] In fact, Treacher's research reveals how children's imaginings, narratives, and play are integral to a child's development of their sense of self.[61] Indeed, the father–daughter scenes of vaudeville clearly illustrate how important the interactions between Ben-Ner and Elia are to understanding Elia's role as an actor in her father's movie and the reality of it. While many of the scenes of fun were clearly scripted to some degree, the outright joy, happiness, and laughter of Elia and Ben-Ner suggest that many of the scenes turned into moments of play and fantasy.

Fantasy, according to D.W. Winnicott, serves two purposes: one is a way of remembering or conceiving the past, while the other aids the child's understanding of her present reality.[62] The active fantasy life suggested in the non-narrative scenes of *Moby Dick* allows Elia to take part in the creation of her own reality and involve herself in the world enclosed within the space of her family's apartment. Yet, it is clear that she has fun doing so. In a sequence following the introduction of Queequeg, Ishmael conveys his "fear of sleeping with a cannibal"; the camera is positioned at an angle to view into the bedroom, where the viewer observes a man sleeping with his shoes on. Elia, notably *not* Pip—her hair is loose and she wears a pair of white, rose-patterned pants, not the striped shirt and loose pants of Pip—enters the bedroom, seemingly unaware of the camera, pulls away the bed sheet to reveal Ben-Ner (or Ishmael) has been sleeping with his hands in his boots to surprise any potential assailants. In this action, Ben-Ner clearly quotes Charles Chaplin's action in his 1925 film, *The Gold Rush*, where he sleeps in this position to keep an eye on his cannibalistic cabin-mate, Big Jim. In Ben-Ner's film, Elia reveals the farce, but claims no affiliation to the cannibal in *The Gold Rush*, an issue which will be discussed in more detail below. Rather, she runs out of the room—mouth wide in screams of laughter—suggesting that this scene was one of true fun, laughter, and play.

By playing, Gunning asserts that Ben-Ner sees his children "not simply as alien creatures, but as participants in fantasies he shares with them."[63] Gunning continues,

> his work captures something fundamental about a child's imagination, yet he never sentimentalizes childhood, choosing instead to reveal the truly serious role that playing constitutes for children. Play provides the means of acculturation in human society, helping children to adapt to the world of adults.[64]

Gunning interprets the work as one that conveys childhood imagination, but it is Ben-Ner's imagination that drives the play—as a father, Ben-Ner has the freedom to create a visual fantasy that educates his children and fulfills his drive as an artist to make. The sociologist Chris Jenks further articulates the idea that the child learns the world of adults through fantasy. Jenks notes the following about the postmodern child:

> The child in the setting of what are now conceptualized as postmodern cultural configurations has become the site or the relocation of discourses concerning stability, integration and the social bond. The child is now envisioned as a form of 'nostalgia,' a longing for times past, not as 'futurity.' Children are now seen not so much as a 'promise' but as primary and unequivocal sources of love, but also as partners in the most fundamental, unchosen, unnegotiated form of relationship.[65]

In other words, Jenks argues that children reflect parents' own memories and thus become symbols of the parents when they were young, not individuals in their own right. Ben-Ner's on-camera relationship with Elia, particularly in *Moby Dick*, perhaps reveals his nostalgia for childhood, yet without exhibiting saccharine or gendered sentimentality. Elia does not play the role of a little princess, but the role of Pip, the deck boy who rambunctiously entertains and torments Ishmael.

Interestingly, curator Tali Tamir places such interest in childhood in the larger cultural context of Israel. Tamir asserts, "The Israeli man wishes to reclaim his private hallucinatory world, his childhood and his frailness. He rises against the soldier entity transplanted into his existentialist definition and presents a critical stance toward the Zionist masculine ethos."[66] If Tamir claims that Israeli men lost their youth or grew up 'too fast,' her statement then casts Ben-Ner's enactment of a fantasy or adventure novel with his child as a form of reclaiming this loss. Tamir does not make this a broad statement about Ben-Ner, but by limiting her implicit claim to the latter's interest in fantasy, childhood, stereotypes of masculinity, and fatherhood I would suggest that his work may serve as a very prominent and powerful critical voice of the Israeli male identity.

As in *Berkeley's Island*, Ben-Ner adeptly couples the more serious issues he raises with scenes of lighthearted fun, and vice versa. As Ben-Ner and Elia have their fun, the narrative transitions to a series of solitary scenes of Ahab, standing and subsequently falling, due to the sway of the ship (and leaving the wooden peg on the deck). In another scene, Elia runs up and takes Ahab's wooden leg away. Two short slapstick scenes featuring Ben-Ner follow these abuses by Elia. The first features the artist in a space, empty except for a ladder propped against the wall. As Ben-Ner climbs the ladder, all the planks split in half, making him fall. The second shot reveals the artist in the same space, but this time there is a rope strung across the room, which he cuts with scissors, causing a heavy bag to fall on his head. These sequences refer to a series of slapstick actions performed by Buster Keaton in *One Week* (1920). In *One Week*, newlyweds Buster and Sybil receive a build it yourself in-one-week house and a plot of land, which becomes the site of Buster's antics.[67] Just as the building of the domestic home becomes a place of parody and jokes in Keaton's film, Ben-Ner's enactment of the 'man-as-builder' role becomes dismantled and serves as a form of punishment.[68] The artist's reference to these social expectations of men and fathers to make repairs in the home draws interesting questions of the fairness of such stereotypes, and whether, as the primary at-home parent, Ben-Ner can fulfill such a role. These aforementioned sequences suggest that his attempts have failed, as nothing is constructed at the end.[69]

Ben-Ner's references to *The Immigrant*, and, in an earlier scene, to *The Gold Rush*, demonstrate his knowledge of cinematic history. In *The Immigrant*, Chaplin, in the role of the Tramp, procures some money and enters a restaurant to satiate his hunger. As the Tramp receives his plate of beans, he begins to eat them one by one, but his hunger overpowers him and begins shoveling the beans into his mouth. Hunger was a recurrent theme within Chaplin's skits, and Ben-Ner draws on yet another Chaplin film to reveal the hallucinations starvation can incur. In the scenes that follow Ishmael's declaration of fear of sleeping with a cannibal (which occurs earlier in the film with the introduction of Queequeg), the action returns to the kitchen where one observes Ishmael gloomily seated at the kitchen table and Pip near the stove. Pip walks toward the kitchen table, where she transforms into a chicken—shocking Ishmael, who places his index finger on his open mouth in awe. Transforming back to Pip, Elia turns back toward the stove, lifts the lid of a pan to inspect the progress of their meal. There is no actual food in the pan, but one recognizes the lifting of a lid and peering into it as a sign of food preparation. The camera returns its focus on Ishmael who continues his bewildered expression, places his finger on his lips, and exclaims again, when Elia turns into a chicken that is preparing their meal. This sequence recalls the joke of Chaplin's 1925 film, *The Gold Rush*, in which Chaplin, playing the part of the Lone Prospector, appears as a chicken to his fellow gold prospector, Big Jim, who becomes delirious in his hunger and similarly places his finger in his mouth.

Like Chaplin's hallucination of the bird, Elia flaps her wings and sits down at the table before transforming back into Pip. The conflation of Pip, Elia, and the chicken suggests not only that Ben-Ner conceives of his child as something threatening to be devoured—akin to Cronus who devoured his children because he feared the child that would overthrow him—but also that he has become delirious in his confinement to the home. Indeed, the hallucination in *The Gold Rush* occurs because of Chaplin and his fellow prospector's forced confinement in a cabin due to a snowstorm. Their 'cabin fever' escalates to the point of near cannibalism and only ceases once the character of the fugitive returns with the bounty he stole. Ben-Ner however does not merely reference or recreate the two iconic scenes from *The Gold Rush* (the bed scene and the kitchen), he transposes the narrative events in order to highlight the sentiments of Ishmael. In Chaplin's skit, the Prospector changes his sleeping position after Big Jim imagines him to be a chicken, and only after Big Jim decides that he is going to eat him regardless of whether he is a chicken or not. In this reversal, Ben-Ner clearly reveals that Elia is not a man-eater; rather it is he who is the cannibal.

Ben-Ner seamlessly integrates these scenes of homage to Keaton and Chaplin with references to body art performances of the 1960s and 1970s. According to Edelsztein, the slapstick in Ben-Ner's work becomes "akin to a mirror image, a parody of body art."[70] In fact, Ben-Ner introduces art historical references before introducing the slapstick scenes. Both appear with the introduction of Queequeg, who is named a "good hearted harpooner" in the intertext and as represented by Ben-Ner, shirtless, wearing swim trunks, and with his chest hair shaved into a heart shape. On the one hand, this heart shape acts as a literal visualization—a heart on the chest to indicate he has a good heart, but it also points to the history of hair-related body performances. Edelsztein claims Ben-Ner's action is in allegiance with Vito Acconci's *Openings* (1970), however this relationship seems tenuous at best.[71] In *Openings*, Acconci plucks hair with his fingers from around his navel, noting that he was "opening up" part of his body, exposing the navel and transforming it to a vagina.[72] The deliberate sexual reference and scopophilic gaze of the camera is not shared by Ben-Ner's body hair. Furthermore, the viewer does not witness Ben-Ner's process of removal; the heart shape is physically posited as part of Queequeg's person, not something that he must suffer or endure. Ben-Ner's performance seems more akin to a PG-13 version of Acconci's X-rated work. Edelsztein also notes Geoff Hendricks's performance *Body/Hair* (1971), in which Hendricks shaved his entire body from the neck down. This performance, like Acconci's, was staged for an audience and was documented in process. Ben-Ner only reveals the aftereffects and does not create a series of relics out of the removed hair as Hendricks did in his action.[73]

When Ben-Ner's video introduces the cannibal, Queequeg, the artist appears with multicolored plastic clothespins adorning his body, a clear reference to Natsuyuki Nakaniski's 1963 performance at the Fifteenth Yomiuri Independent Exhibition.[74] Queequeg appears with two rows of pins placed along his torso, one aligned with his navel and the other midway between the navel and his chest, another semi-circle between and including his nipples, along his arms and two placed near his clavicle. This arrangement, intended to evoke the tattoos that adorn Queequeg's body in Melville's novel, occupies a space between the absurd and the artistic body performance. Clearly the clips are uncomfortable. Ben-Ner's body bears red markings indicating the places where the clips were adhered but did not remain, suggesting their discomfort; yet the choice of donning multicolor clips, rather than choosing the sameness of the more classic unpainted wooden ones, suggests the action as a farce brought on by domestic boredom.

When Nakaniski staged his action, he sought to eliminate the boundary between art and life, and to respond to the narrow criteria of "what is art" issued by the Tokyo Metropolitan Art Museum. The Museum's standards refused works that: "involve loud, unpleasant sounds, that smell bad, that decompose, that are dangerous or potentially toxic, that are installed either directly on the floor or hung from the ceiling."[75] In rebellion from these restrictions, Nakaniski created his work *Clothespins Assert Churning Action* (1963), which included hundreds of tin clothespins attached to pieces of canvas, underwear, and clothing that were hung on the wall and piled on the floor. The artist, in affinity with his work, also clipped the pins to his face and body. Nakaniski co-founded the Hi Red Center in Tokyo, staging actions with Jiro Takamatsu and Genpei Akasegawa using "'society as material, as a canvas' so that the action would be viewed not as a 'work of art' but as a disruptive element within the fabric of everyday life."[76] Similarly, Ben-Ner's action can be read as a disruptive element of everyday domestic life, perhaps critiquing the notion that parents cannot make sophisticated art.

Edelsztein claims the basic difference between body art and slapstick lies in the perception of the pain inflicted on oneself. Body art "demonstrates the artist's strength and commitment to the visualization of his/her idea" while slapstick causes others to "laugh at the farcical situations of indignity, practical jokes or self-inflicted physical mishaps" because there is no clear communication of pain.[77] Slapstick is "akin to a mirror image, a parody of body art" in Edelsztein's view, and thus one can interpret Ben-Ner's partial appropriation of body art by artists like Nakanishi, Acconci, and Oppenheim as mirror images to body art or slapstick with an artistic heritage because he does not perform these actions before a live audience or endure the pain associated with each for very long.[78] Indeed, the original recording of Hendrick's performance is eight hours long, Acconci's performance endures for fourteen minutes, and Oppenheim's took five hours of exposure—Ben-Ner's performances last a few seconds, or are faked with body paint or self-tanning lotion, which ultimately reveals that they are superficial references, not necessarily evidence of a deep commitment to communicating the artist's original idea. Perhaps it is enough for Ben-Ner to refer to a sunburn without experiencing the pain of it. His short performances do, however, suggest that the body action Ben-Ner truly undertakes is that of *parenting*.

Parenting, while not a unique action, can be considered a long-term performance—lasting at least eighteen years, if not for life—affecting the parental body in unforeseeable ways; causing stress, anxiety, sleeplessness, or as the expression goes, 'making one go gray.' In this sense, Ben-Ner's series of videos with his children, which span nearly a decade, can be considered documents of this life-long performance. Ben-Ner turns to slapstick, early cinema, and early body art to pay homage to his cinematic forefathers and help his children learn about the adult world, all the while having fun and constructing links with filmic, conceptual, and body art. He incorporates some of the specific elements of these modes of art, and repurposes them to serve his and his family's needs.

Therefore, the works become sites where one's life-long performance as a parent cannot be devoid of context. And as such, references to one's national and religious identity are particularly fraught. Artists who do so have often been derided as sensationalists, taking advantage of personal and national convictions for nothing but shock value and personal gain.[79] But as mentioned previously, Ben-Ner is cautious to not make overt political references to the settlements, Palestine, or Zionist politics, which have been the subject of great debate and political turmoil. But that does not mean that Ben-Ner's spaces are devoid of political or cultural heritage. Instead, as Gunning notes, Ben-Ner reinforces that our homes are not just places for survival and quotidian needs but also "spaces that shelter the essential functions of make-believe and that provide the basis of literature, religion, and rituals—in short, human culture."[80] Ben-Ner's *Moby Dick* transforms the interior landscape from functional space into a fantasyland. Alternately, in the context of *Wild Boy*, Aim Dueul Lusky suggests that the kitchen "turns into nowhere … the [child] then turns into the father's father, the homeless' landlord."[81] In this denial of exterior land, Ben-Ner does not abandon all national and local ties. The kitchen (and apartment as a whole) may partially deny the exterior, mundane world, but it does exist in a place—Tel Aviv and the State of Israel.[82] Drawing on Ben-Ner's somewhat sarcastic self-identification as an "Eternal Jew," Ben-Ner's adaptation partially transforms Melville's novel to a Jewish and Israeli context.[83] As noted in the introduction to this chapter, Ben-Ner does not overtly reference the politics of Israel in his films, though it can often be inferred and drawn out through small signs and references within the story. In Ben-Ner's *Moby Dick*, the relationship to Judaism is deepened through the story of *Moby-Dick* itself. In terms of the novel, parallels exist between Ahab and the crew of the Pequod—as both Ishmael and literary scholars perceived the ship as its own functioning world.[84] On one level, this reiterates Ben-Ner's solitary exploration from *Berkeley's Island*, suggesting that *Moby Dick* is a continuation of his investigation of the isolated stay-at-home artist-parent, yet recording his thoughts and deeds in a much more nuanced and coded way.[85] As Ahab, Ben-Ner could be seen as enacting the ideal, aloof, and domineering father, while as Ishmael, he becomes the more accessible, fun, and loving father. But more relevantly, Ishmael, the major character portrayed by Ben-Ner, brings forth the larger religiously charged and politically turbulent context of Israel.

In Genesis 16:12, Ishmael is proclaimed to be "a wild ass of a man" where "his hand shall be against every man, and every man's hand against him" and "he shall dwell in the face of all his brethren." He is the illegitimate child of Abraham and his maidservant, Hagar, conceived because Abraham's own wife, Sarah, was barren and Abraham needed heirs to inherit the land. Both Hagar and Ishmael are exiled into the desert because of Sarah's (Abraham's wife) jealousy, causing the name to connote otherness and exile.[86] In Melville's rendition, Ishmael conveys this exile by informing the reader that he feels alienated from human society and thus decides to join Ahab on the Pequod. An influential early critic of the book believed that this creative imagining of Ishmael "gave [Melville] the power to find the lost past of America, the unfound present, and make a myth of *Moby-Dick*, for a people of Ishmaels."[87] Ben-Ner's rendition evokes both references, yet with one distinct difference—he is tricked onto the ship. Elia, in the guise of the barkeep, hits Ishmael over the head, knocks him out in order to place him on the whaler. He is essentially tricked into his isolated state, as if the bottle that knocks him in the head is the unexpected news of his wife's pregnancy and his impending role as father. In the next scene, Ishmael, dressed in the crew's uniform, busily makes preparations for his unexpected life at sea. The lack of choice Ben-Ner allows Ishmael in his rendition, suggests that exile is not always by choice, as in Melville's story, rather it becomes something that is determined by external factors out of one's control, for example, being born in Israel, being raised in the Jewish faith, or becoming a parent.

In an interview, Ben-Ner claimed an affiliation to the identity of the "Eternal Jew" seeking emancipation and the promised land, the land of "milk and honey," in which he can raise his family.[88] Though the term arose out of Christian legend concerning the Jewish man who taunted Jesus and was then condemned to wander the earth until the Second Coming, the term became associated with the fate of the entire Jewish people.[89] In this respect, the notion that the ship is a world unto itself (in Melville) can suggest that the kitchen, the home in Tel Aviv, can be a suitable place to grow and raise a family as well. In this vein, even the stocked and filled refrigerator can be read to symbolize the fertility and plenty of the Holy Land—the areas of Jerusalem and Israel. This land, as recounted near the end of the Book of Joshua in the Hebrew Bible, was distributed to the tribes of Israelites, fulfilling Yahweh's promise to Abraham. The Book of Joshua tends to be regarded as theological model, one that instills the notion that moral uprightness will deliver prosperity. This model is not emphasized to correct Elia's behavior, but rather in as a means to bring morality to Ben-Ner, who in many scenes, as discussed above, is seen punishing himself.

The system of punishment and rewards can be inferred in another moment of *Moby Dick* as well. As the coin Ahab mounted, (and possibly even those scattered around in *Berkeley's Island*) revealed itself to be a chocolate coin given in the tradition of Hanukkah gelt, Ben-Ner evokes yet another tie to the Jewish faith, Israeli history, and children's upbringing. The tradition of giving "gelt" is often considered to have begun in the Middle Ages, yet some have dated the tradition to date as far back as 142 BCE, when Simon the Maccabee brought independence to Judea. King Antiochus VII, according to Maccabees 15:6, declared that Simon could make his own coinage for his country, thus minting the first coins of the Jewish people. In 70 CE, however, when the Romans destroyed the Second Temple, the production of Jewish coinage ended. The lack of readily available coins made the gelt a precious gift, which was then expanded to children. Children would receive the gelt because it emphasized the importance of the study of the Torah and Jewish education. Present-day gifting of the gelt has transformed into a game played with a Dreidel. When parents play Dreidel with their children, they participate in the religious education of their children.

The Hanukkah gelt used in Ben-Ner's film is a unique piece, as most candy manufacturers use the prominent image of the menorah on the coin; this one, rather, has a ship on it between two towers, a symbol reminiscent of the outdated Israeli tender, the one agora coin.[90] The coin itself was based on the design of a coin from Herod Archaelaus's reign (4 BCE–6 CE) depicting a ship's prow, wreath, and his abbreviated name. The Bank of Israel adopted the ship emblem, naming it an ancient galley and thus connecting the modern currency to Jewish history. Compared to the chocolate coin, there are several similarities. Both coins depict a galley with several oars protruding from the ship, yet instead of the name "Israel" in Hebrew, Arabic, and English, the chocolate coin offers the phrase, "Made in Israel," noting its origin in the Holy Land.

The parallel between the action within Ben-Ner's video and Melville's text is striking, yet distinct. Ahab offers the same reward within Melville's text; however it is clear that the gold ounce acted solely as incentive for locating the whale, and nothing else. For Elia, the coin has a triple meaning. She receives it as Pip for spotting the whale, as Elia for participating in her father's movie, and lastly, as a young Jewish girl receiving Hanukkah gelt.

In many ways, Ben-Ner and Elia's enactment of the story teaches the six-year-old Elia not only the plot of the Melville classic, but also about religious identity and the history of slapstick—all in a "teaching by doing" fashion (as articulated by Jean Piaget) that transforms the kitchen as a space for play.[91] For this, and for his subsequent films with his children (his son Amir is born in 2000), Ben-Ner embraces the genre of vaudeville as a model. Noting that vaudeville allowed him to achieve what he desired, that is, "to erase the space between work and home. It was a way that kids could work. They were part of the structure, as essential as adults."[92] Thus *Moby Dick* largely incorporates Elia as a variety of characters, from the barkeep that tricks Ishmael aboard the ship, to Pip, the deck boy and his tormentor, both on and off the ship. Amir notably even appears for a few seconds, swinging in a chair in cadence with The Spouter Inn sign above him. Elia's incorporation within the movie acts not only as Ben-Ner's way of teaching her tangible things about play and her larger cultural context, but also as a means to mold her into a person who can interact with others in complex ways.

On Father–Son Relationships, Education, and *Wild Boy*

By 2004, Guy Ben-Ner fully embraced his role as a father and as an artist, as he completed at least two major projects with his daughter—*Moby Dick* (2000) and *Elia: Story of an Ostrich Chick* (2003). A new challenge arose when Elia went to school and his wife, Nava, went back to work—Ben-Ner was jobless and studio-less, so he had to stay at home to care for his son, Amir.[93] Yet, unlike the previous work, which revealed a visual crisis of masculinity, domesticity, and identity, Ben-Ner created *Wild Boy* (2004), a seventeen-minute video that captures and traces the development of the father–son dyad and thereby, the process by which the ideal father educates his son, morally and intellectually. The concept of fathering that is based on moral and intellectual education derives from Enlightenment thinkers such as Jean-Jacques Rousseau, and is largely reiterated in popular cinema from the 1950s to the present.

Film historian Stella Bruzzi investigates the variety of fathers depicted in blockbuster Hollywood films, noting that the 1950s had a tendency to cast the father in Oedipal terms, while films of 1960s and 1970s, such as *To Kill a Mockingbird* and *The Sound of Music*, reinvented the patriarch to "ensure his longevity."[94] Ben-Ner absorbs this paternal ideology in both subject and medium, and much like the methods he used in *Moby Dick*, he simultaneously confronts it through the insertion of slapstick and play.

Like in *Berkeley's Island* and *Moby Dick*, Ben-Ner draws on an array of cinematic references, but instead of drawing principally on literature, *Wild Child* is loosely based on François Truffaut's 1970 film *L'Enfant sauvage*, or *The Wild Child*. In addition, Ben-Ner culls other famous father–son dyads in art and film, such as in Dennis Oppenheim's *Transfer Drawing Series* and Buster Keaton's films with his father Joe, intertwining them with concepts of the ideal nature of fatherhood and patriarchy. Ben-Ner's film draws on various models from the 1970s, which acknowledge earlier ideas and sources, ultimately conflating past and present modes of parenting and father–child relationships. By using such complicated references, but structuring the film's actors—himself and his son, Amir (tellingly named Buster in the film)—largely on mimicry, Ben-Ner reveals the complicated nature of "new fatherhood," which demands a larger nurturing role of the father. Thus, what began as systematic lessons in language and morality, ends up revealing the dynamics of the father–son relationship, one in which the father may even learn something from the son.[95]

In addition to the father–child relationship, Ben-Ner chose to draw from Truffaut's film, using the same title, as well as appropriating the same basic narrative. Ben-Ner recounts and adapts the pedagogical strategies undertaken by Dr. Jean Itard, who in *L'Enfant sauvage* is played by Truffaut, and appears in *Wild Boy* as Ben-Ner. Both men assume the role of father-educator to the boy found in the "wild"—Victor in *L'Enfant sauvage*, portrayed by Jean-Pierre Cargol, and Buster, enacted by Amir, in *Wild Boy*. Based on the true story of a wild child named Victor of Aveyron, who was discovered in a forest near St. Sernin in 1798, Victor became the subject of both medical and educational experimentation for enlightenment thinkers who found the appearance of wild or feral children as the ideal opportunity to test theories of the "noble savage,"—an understanding of human development that was similarly perceived to be evident in children.[96] The timing of Victor's entry into the social world of France coincided with the rise in the study of morality, ethics, education, and simply, man. Victor was taken to an institute for the deaf to be examined by Roch-Ambroise Cucurron Sicard, who participated in a group called the Society of Observers of Man, and who believed that by educating and studying the boy, he would find the evidence needed to support an empiricist theory of knowledge.[97] Truffaut read Itard's *Mémoire et Rapport sur Victor de l'Aveyron*; therefore he was quite familiar with the events and co-wrote the screenplay with Jean Gruault.[98]

The subject of Truffaut's thoughts over five years, *L'Enfant sauvage* is historically based in the early nineteenth century and filmed in black and white. Considering the story in the contexts of legends like Romulus and Remus, Mowgli (from Rudyard Kipling's *The Jungle Book*), and Tarzan, Truffaut distinguishes *L'Enfant sauvage* from the others because, the story he claimed was "absolutely authentic."[99] The story of Truffaut's Victor and Itard does not constitute a fictional story, but rather a series of interactions that lasted over several years, until the boy was nineteen years old.[100] The attempt for authenticity made the casting for the role of Victor difficult, as the child would need to use solely bodily motions and facial expressions to communicate.

After auditioning hundreds of children, Jean-Pierre Cargol was cast for the role, in part because he had the gymnastic ability and strength to portray a child who has no language. Truffaut considered the role to be too difficult for a child to play without a competent lead, so much so that Truffaut chose to cast himself as Itard, so he could "control and shape the performance of Jean-Pierre Cargol as the boy."[101] This careful directing of the child is paralleled within Ben-Ner's version, where in an interview with Stephanie Smith, he stated:

> I was interested in Truffaut as a director who worked quite a lot with children long before I made *Wild Boy*. In this case I knew the source before setting to work with it. In his *Wild Child*, Truffaut cast himself as Doctor Itard. That made me realize that he was not really talking about taming a wild boy, but rather about a director who tames a child actor. That is why he dedicates the movie to Jean-Pierre Léaud, his first child actor. That spoke to me. More than anything, I felt it was an account of a guilty man regarding his early sins: telling truth through fiction. But for me, to use a source I need it to connect to many things in which I am interested, not just one.[102]

While Ben-Ner did not have to "cast" the child, in identifying with the autobiographical nature of Truffaut's films he draws upon the guilt of using children in his work, and the effect it could have on the developing child. Film scholar Patrick E. White regards Truffaut's dedication of *Wild Boy* to Jean-Pierre Léaud (the first child actor Truffaut cast for a series of autobiographical films) as "recognition that just as Itard plays a complicated role as the teacher to the wild boy, Truffaut's role in the early life of Léaud, giving him language, and indeed self-consciousness, is fraught with joy and anxiety."[103] Ben-Ner, like Truffaut, provides his son Amir language, joy, and perhaps not directly, anxiety. More than imbuing an affect or behavior, Ben-Ner's training or directing of Amir suggests *his* anxiety to raise a child who can civilly and morally interact within society—to be a future father and communicate with the world. As such, the introductory scenes of *Wild Boy* reveal the "directing" of Amir. While the screen is still blank, Ben-Ner's voice-over in Hebrew, subtitled in English on the screen, communicates the directorial process:

> One minute. The camera doesn't see you.
> Amir: I can't do it again
> One last time
> Watch out, you're falling
> Get in the frame
> OK, I'm counting to three---Don't look at the camera.
> When I reach three you should step outside.
> One, Two
> No, no, no, no wait till we reach "three"
> Get in the frame
> You're outside. Go to your right.
> Nice. Are you ready?
> Don't look at the camera.
> Amir: Yes
> One, two, three[104]

This introductory dialogue communicates the frustration and exhaustion the child actor experiences, and the convincing that the director must do to get the scene he desires—which is not unlike the experiences of a parent trying the convince the child to eat, behave, or perform an activity undesired by the child. In an interview, Truffaut recounted a similar experience with Jean-Pierre Cargol, noting that he complained while shooting the film and was particularly embarrassed to film the scenes where he was naked, forcing Truffaut to remove all women from the set.[105] Except for one short scene where Elia dances in the kitchen, no women are ever presented in *Wild Boy*, the film solely depicts the interactions between father and son, whether both are on screen or not. After the introductory dialogue, the camera subsequently cuts to the artist's kitchen, where an artificial hill has been created out of plywood, two-by-fours, and artificial turf, thus beginning the tale of the savage child (Figure 4.3). The camera follows the boy's movements around the natural environment, replete with two rabbits and two songbirds—domesticated animals that can be read as analogous to the conception of children as wild beings that become civilized through education. There is no conversation, no sounds except for the ambient noise of the space and the dripping of water in the kitchen sink. All speech is mimed by Ben-Ner, articulated only by interjecting black frames with typed text—just like the intertitles of silent film.[106]

The wild boy, we learn, is discovered "in the woods, twenty miles east of the town of R." As in Truffaut's film, Ben-Ner inspects the child's teeth, cuts off his long curly hair, and bathes him. However, Ben-Ner's film is not set in the nineteenth century—in *Wild Boy*, Amir is placed in a large blue bucket and washed with the modern convenience of Johnson and Johnson baby shampoo. Ben-Ner, taking the role of the father and the educator, determines that the boy doesn't talk and never smiles—two traits that Itard also noted in Victor—and names the wild boy Buster. This is Ben-Ner's homage to Buster Keaton and his films with his father Joe from the 1920s and 1930s. Buster was known as the "silent comedian who never smiled," and thus Ben-Ner's naming of the wild child evokes relationships to both Truffaut's film and the famous vaudeville and silent film star.[107] For the majority of the film, Ben-Ner teaches Buster proper behavior—how to stand up on two legs (rather than crawl on all fours), dress himself, eat with a spoon, and problem solve—all actions in which a parent assists his child.

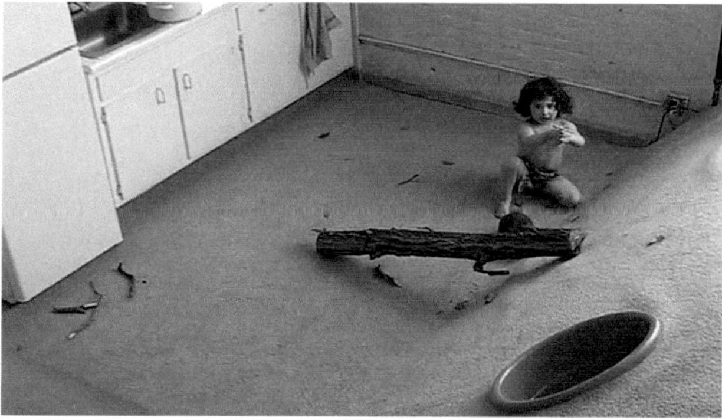

Figure 4.3 Guy Ben-Ner, still from *Wild Boy*, 2004. Single channel video, 17 minutes. Courtesy the artist.

While these actions mirror the events depicted in *L'Enfant sauvage*, they also become intertwined with the daily life of Ben-Ner and Amir, further blurring the relationship between art and life that was begun in *Berkeley's Island*. *Wild Boy* occupies a precarious position between art film and home movie, as he actually records major firsts in the child's life. Ben-Ner revealed in a 2011 interview that the film recorded Amir's first haircut, the first time he put on a shirt on his own, and his first English word—notable events in a child's life (Plate 9).[108]

The tasks and tests Itard gave Victor to complete determined his capacity for critical thinking and social interaction. Both films show the doctor and boy walking "outside," that is, in *Wild Boy*, the artificial landscape within the home. This, the voice-over informs us, functions as "a great joy for the young Buster, who always longs for fresh air," reiterating the sentiment expressed in Truffaut's film, as Itard took Victor to the countryside to enjoy nature as a reward for his dedication to learning the alphabet. The parallels between the films continue: Itard uses mimicry to teach Victor how to use a spoon, as does Ben-Ner; as Itard teaches the relationship between word and symbol to Victor in *L'Enfant sauvage*, Ben-Ner teaches Buster the family structure—dog, boy, mother, father—notably a patriarchal one (Plate 10). In this hierarchy, Ben-Ner identifies himself as the father, yet Buster humorously replaces the mother with a rabbit—who he calls "mother." This moment marks Amir's first English word and the transition from "savage" to "civilized," as the acquisition of language was the key faculty that distinguished humans from animals for Enlightenment thinkers. This becomes the turning point for the father–son, doctor–patient relationship and is commemorated by the sudden soundtrack of The Doors' debut single, "Break on Through (To The Other Side)" (1967)—an anthem that suggests that knowledge has been transmitted and, importantly, received, and that the barrier between father and son has been broken; a bond has formed between the two.[109]

This bond becomes elaborated through mimicry as the film and song continue. In Truffaut's film, Itard taught Victor to mimic the various sounds of a drum, exploiting his hearing faculty to determine that he could, indeed hear. This lesson is repeated in Ben-Ner's film; however in lieu of a drum, Ben-Ner and Buster beat pots and water bottles. Buster notably mimics the actions, not the sounds; the viewer does not hear the actual beating of the "instruments" but rather The Doors' song.[110] However, the fact that Buster (Amir) copies Ben-Ner's actions, or vice versa, suggests that the lesson is more about perception than actual transfer of knowledge—banging on the plastic drums seem to be the equivalent of teaching someone to play the 'air guitar'—no actual musical knowledge has been transmitted, rather the impression of it has. Similarly, two additional scenes reinforce the importance of public perception of the father–son relation in terms of education—one, a scene where Buster is seen writing and the other, when he is reading.

The writing sequence is particularly poignant, as it is in Truffaut's film. To teach Victor how to write, Itard begins by having Victor copy a line on the chalkboard. This rudimentary skill, in which the child learns how to hold a tool for writing, is skipped in Ben-Ner's rendition, as Buster writes a full sentence with his childlike handwriting on the wall while Ben-Ner imparts the desired statement by writing on the child's back. In this scene, Ben-Ner departs from Truffaut's scene of the child imitating the teacher, and rather chooses to quote part of Dennis Oppenheim's *2-Stage Transfer Drawing (Advancing to a Past State)*, 1971. This important work by Oppenheim shows Oppenheim drawing on his son's back and his son, Erik, using his sensory knowledge to mimic the image on the wall (Figure 4.4). This work not only explores the transfer of information from one to another nonverbally, but it also suggests the possibility of genetically transmitting creativity. Oppenheim claimed:

> My activity stimulates a kinetic response from his sensory system. I am, therefore, drawing through him. … Because Erik is my offspring and we share similar biological ingredients, his back (as surface) can be seen as an immature version of my own. In a sense, I make contact with a past state.[111]

Thus for Oppenheim, drawing on his son's back is akin to drawing on his own youthful skin and teaching himself art at an early age. Indeed, Oppenheim operates as an appropriate reference, as his work is an early video-art example of father–son artistic collaboration.[112] Ben-Ner teaches his son not only how to perceive touch, but also the proper behavior of young boys. Rather than the abstract line Itard draws on the chalkboard, or the geometric pattern Oppenheim draws on Erik, Ben-Ner writes, "I promise to be a good boy," on Buster's back which he, in turn, writes on the white wall. Through genetics and creativity, Buster transcribes a phrase that is akin to one a

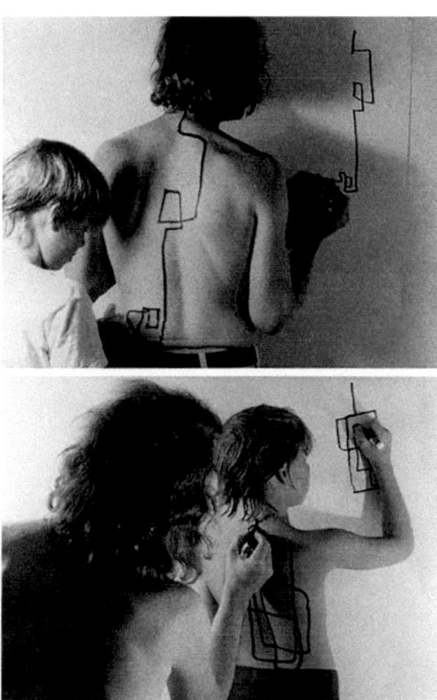

Figure 4.4 Dennis Oppenheim, *2-Stage Transfer Drawing. (Advancing to a Future State)*, 1971. Boise, Idaho. Erik to Dennis Oppenheim As Erik runs a marker along my back, I attempt to duplicate the movement on the wall. His activity stimulates a kinetic response from my sensory system. He is, therefore, drawing through me. Sensory retardation or disorientation makes up the discrepancy between the two drawings, and could be seen as elements that are activated during this procedure. Because Erik is my offspring, and we share similar biological ingredients, my back (as surface) can be seen as a mature version of his own … in a sense, he contacts a future state. *2-Stage Transfer Drawing. (Returning to a Past State)*, 1971. Boise, Idaho. Dennis to Erik Oppenheim. As I run a marker along Erik's back, he attempts to duplicate the movement on the wall. My activity stimulates a kinetic response from his memory system. I am, therefore, drawing through him. Sensory retardation or disorientation makes up the discrepancy between the two drawings, and could be seen as elements that are activated during this procedure. Because Erik is my offspring, and we share similar biological ingredients, his back (as surface) can be seen as an immature version of my own … in a sense, I make contact with a past state. Copyright Dennis Oppenheim Estate.

child must repeatedly write on a chalkboard or in their notebook as a punishment for misbehavior. This transfer of information is not only sensory and genetic; it also offers a model of paternal behavior and modeling that a father is 'supposed' to transfer to his son.

The notion of fathers being the models of ideal behavior is noted in Freud, who placed the father at the pinnacle of the family and, according to at least one scholar, "thought of the father as the guide who, departing from a still amorphous child, constructed a social being."[113] Freud, in fact, provides a key reference to the meanings explored by Ben-Ner as the father of Amir and the doctor who teaches Buster how to exist in civilization. Not long after cleaning and naming the wild boy "Buster," we find that Buster still eats on the floor without using his hands. Like Itard, who wished to test the intellectual capacity of the child, Ben-Ner begins to drill into the kitchen table, where the words, "A puzzle box; a tool used to measure animal intelligence; a closed box with a pedal inside. Pressing the pedal will open the box," flash across the screen (Figure 4.5). To create this puzzle box, Ben-Ner creates a pedal by loading a spring inside of a book—but not any book, the viewer clearly reads the title, *II – "Analysis of a Phobia in a Five-Year-Old-Boy," 1909*, thus revealing the volume to be one of Freud's studies. In fact, "Analysis …" is widely known as the case of 'Little Hans,' a young boy whose behavior was observed by his father and reported to Freud.[114]

While 'Little Hans' was the subject of the study, child development specialist John Munder Ross notes that much of the phobia Hans' father reported to Freud stemmed from the father's failure to educate him on the reproductive process and the role of

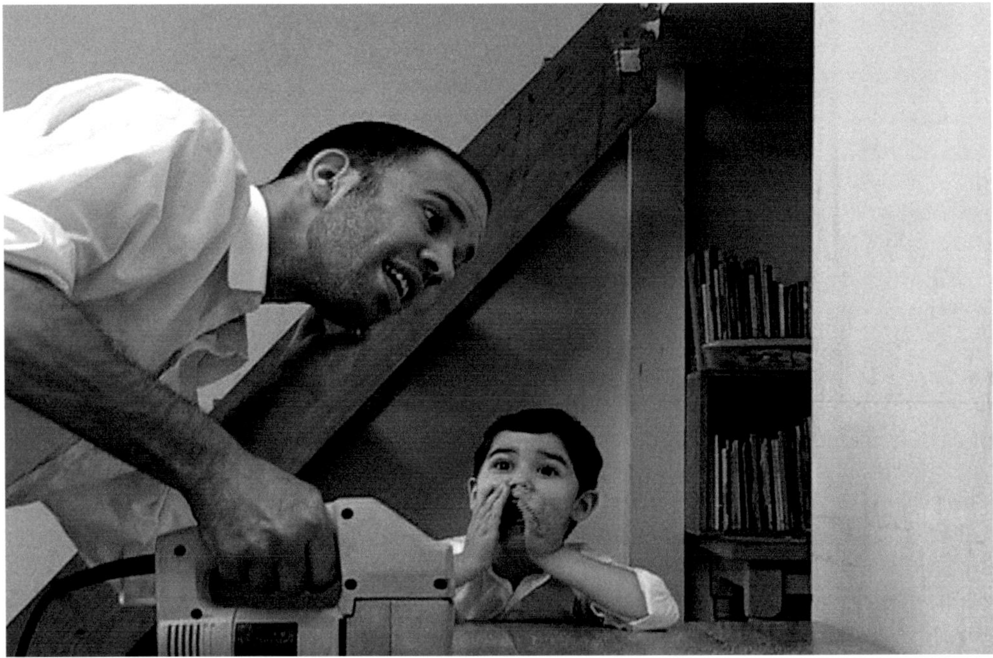

Figure 4.5 Guy Ben-Ner, still from *Wild Boy*, 2004. Single channel video, 17 minutes. Courtesy the artist.

paternity.[115] Ross argues that the "father then became all too present—forceful, intrusive, and stimulating to a fault," which ultimately suggests that the case may reveal more about the father, Max Graf, than about 'little Hans.'[116] On this, Ross notes "[we learn about] *his* [Max's] wish to mother the child better than his wife; *his* ambivalence to deferring to and later rebelling against the father figure in the person of Freud; *his* uncertainty about ceding his own paternal authority to his son."[117] Like Graf, Ben-Ner's method of educating and studying 'Buster' reveals more about *his* identity, as a father and man, than about the intellectual capacity of the child. Even so, in contemporary society the misbehavior of boys is largely attributed to the failure of the father, above all else, and Ben-Ner's appropriation of the book, and his utilization of it as an object with use-value, a pedal, suggests the "closing of the chapter" on that part of his inquiry. Buster must push the book closed in order to open the puzzle box, which he accomplishes in record time (Ben-Ner sits back with a pen, pad of paper, and large clock to record the task) allowing Ben-Ner to move past his paternal uncertainty.

In the scene where Ben-Ner exposes Buster to reading, the refrigerator has been transformed to contain a large format version of *Aesop's Fables*—notable for its moralizing tales of proper behavior. Ben-Ner opens the refrigerator door to the pages of the stories of the "Fox and the Crow" and "The Crab and its Mother." Buster appears to read the tale of "The Crab and its Mother," in which the mother asks the crab why it walks one-sided, as it would be more direct to go straight forward, wherein the crab asks his mother to model this walk. The mother cannot, and thus the tale teaches that parents can project behaviors for their children, but are unable to do the same. This perhaps suggests that Ben-Ner will not actually be able to guide his child to any greater moral behavior. This was an idea that, once again, was noted in Rousseau, who found reasoning with children, a mode of parenting asserted by John Locke that was "most in vogue" at the time of his writing, as outrageous, as he claimed, "if children understood reason, they would not need to be raised."[118] In addition, Rousseau argued that the very action, of teaching children fables, is wasted. He believed that fables can instruct men, but "the naked truth has to be told to children."[119] In *Emile*, he dissected the fable of the "Fox and the Crow," in which the Fox cheats a Crow out of a piece of cheese through deception and flattery—a tale that Ben-Ner will notably broach in 2008 in his work *Second Nature*.[120] In the context of *Wild Boy*, however, it is worthwhile to return to Rousseau on the subject. He proclaimed: "I ask whether it is necessary to teach six-year-old children that there are men who flatter and lie for profit," and in the end, concluded: "it is a horrible lesson for childhood."[121] Buster (Amir) is no older than four, thus proving the lesson somewhat moot—as according to some child development sources, a four-year-old child has developed an understanding of justice and care, and knows the difference between morals and social rules; however, this is not understood in relation to the self, though a child's capacity for abstract reasoning is growing.[122] While Ben-Ner may attempt to teach these moral lessons to his son, they are beyond the grasp of his cognitive capacity and identity formation at this stage of life.

To return to the notion that Buster (Amir) may in fact be teaching his father, or that Ben-Ner is miming the actions of his son, one might consider Jacques Rancière's *The Ignorant Schoolmaster*, a text written about Louis Jacotot's theories of education and learning, which Jacotot began to articulate as early as 1818, well before Rousseau developed his theories of education in *Emile* and the original 'wild boy,' Victor of Aveyron, and other 'wild children' were discovered and studied for their primal nature and untainted minds. Jacotot was an exiled schoolmaster who fled Paris during the Restoration, took up residence in Brussels in 1818, and was tasked to teach Flemish students without knowing any Flemish, nor the students knowing any French. What Jacotot learned, according to Rancière, was that the students were able to learn French on their own, thus diminishing the role of the teacher who "explicates."[123] From this discovery "he proclaimed that one could teach what one didn't know, and that a poor ignorant father could, if he was emancipated, conduct the education of his children, without the aid of any master explicator," merely by asking the proper questions.[124] Jacotot believed that all men were of equal intelligence, a notion that was tested later by the studies of feral children; however, for Rancière, it erases, at least in part, the notion of paternal failure. This is important in relation to the parent identity of Ben-Ner. The father needs to be neither wealthy nor the breadwinner in order to ensure one's intellectual upbringing. But rather, he must exhibit an interest in his son's actions. This interest creates a family unit that for Rancière generates a "new consciousness, of an overtaking of the self that extends each person's 'own affair' to the point where it is part and parcel of the common reason enjoyed by all."[125] In other words, the family becomes equally involved in the educational process that removes selfishness. Ben-Ner does not necessarily exhibit Jacotot's pedagogical practice per se, but the reference can be inferred. If one is acquainted with Jacotot's principles, the fact that his roles as artist, father, doctor who observes, and educator are inexplicably intertwined and negotiated within the film in moments of leading and following Amir, Ben-Ner functions as the "ignorant schoolmaster" to some degree.

Regardless of the variation between the teacher and learner (and regardless of whether Ben-Ner actually knew of Jacotot's assertions or Rancière's references to them), Ben-Ner educates Buster. He transfers knowledge to him by showing him proper hygiene, dress, and behavior—and how to be a good boy. He also entertains him by showing him the possibilities of cinema. In a wonderful mise-en-scène, Ben-Ner creates a flip book of Louis Lumière's famous film, an "icon of cinema's birth," *L'Arrivée d'un Train à la Cioat* from 1895, which wows Buster. A close-up of Amir's reaction reveals his wonderment and refers to the myth that early French audiences ran out of the theater for fear that the train was going to hit them.[126] This scene counteracts Buster's previous sentiment, "'Life Sucks,'" and pays homage to the father of the moving picture—Louis Lumière. In deconstructing the myth of *L'Arrivée d'un Train*, scholar Martin Loiperdinger notes that the people waiting at the platform of the train station were in fact staged to await the train and included several family members who were instructed not to look at the camera and follow a general set of instructions. There was, however, one exception, a child. Loiperdinger notes, "this child keeps looking into the camera, though not in a particularly curious or even alienated manner," and evokes another parallel between Ben-Ner's film to this early work.[127] Amir gazes in the camera on a few occasions, his wide-eyed expression confronting the viewer with a frankness and natural demeanor that demonstrates his comfort before the camera. This directness has caused at least one critic to dismiss the work as "unbearably cute and sentimental"—a statement similar to those attributed to works by women who represented their children.[128] While Gunning disagrees with this critic, he claims, "a superficial experience of Ben-Ner's work may dismiss playfulness the same way that adults tend to dismiss children and their games as immature and silly," and argues that such ideas regarding parents and children, men and childcare in particular, reiterate the gendered constructions of the family, and the restrictive term "Mr. Mom," as if a man who nurtures his children is betraying his nature as a man.[129] This notion of "Mr. Mom" is further developed in the next section as it becomes a key theme of the work *Elia: A Story of an Ostrich Chick*.

The 'Male Mother': Nature, Nurture, and the Search for Home

Becoming or enacting 'mother' is one of the major subtexts of Ben-Ner's 2003 film, *Elia: A Story of an Ostrich Chick*. Though preceding *Wild Boy* in creation, *Elia* departs significantly from the model established in his other films. Created while Ben-Ner pursued his Masters of Fine Arts at Columbia University, the twenty-two-minute film is set, not in the domestic space of the home, but outdoors, in New York's Riverside Park (Plate 11). This change, like most of Ben-Ner's work, occurred due to circumstance. The Ben-Ner family lived in housing provided by Columbia University and did not have a lot of space; in an interview, Ben-Ner claimed that his New York apartment was simply too small to film in.[130] The film, however, is one of Ben-Ner's most successful and widely exhibited. Dressed in homemade ostrich costumes, the entire family takes part in a whimsical nature documentary that focuses on the elder sibling, Elia. While some argue that this film aims to convey the family structure from the perspective of Elia, I contend that Ben-Ner continues to reflect on his family as a whole and his role as the 'male mother.'[131] As I will show, Ben-Ner's transition from the kitchen studio to the man-made park reveals a complicated relationship to the documentary tradition, the father's responsibility to lead and nurture, and most importantly, to find a location for his family to thrive. These elements reveal a larger exploration of the father as auteur of the family, in regard to more than just one of his children or the abstract idea of the domestic, and the burdens of this role.

The story of Elia begins with the voice-over narration by Carson Grant.[132] He informs the viewer about the family of ostriches depicted on the screen wandering through the forest. They are a family who left their natural habitat in search for "sacred feeding ground." There is a baby brother, who is "irresistible, annoying," and most importantly, "still used to getting whatever he wants." The father ostrich, who is described as having the provider function, is the 'male mother' to the chicks. And there is the mother who, always in the rear, watches and protects her young. The narrator informs us that the family left a larger flock where Elia had peers to play with. Now she only has the family; she tries to play with her father, but he had more important things to do, so she wanders away from the family, and sees butterflies.

Meanwhile, the father courts his mate by fluffing his feathers and dancing—preening—yet the mother protects her young son. Elia returns to taunt her brother—she wants to be alone with her mother. The father ostrich, annoyed with Elia's actions, ultimately brings her joy, because all she wanted was his attention. Elia, however, becomes separated from the family and finds it almost impossible to survive alone. She searches for food, but is unsuccessful. Eventually she hears her father's loud snoring and she finds her way back to the family. Overall, the tone and content of the narration evoke the nature documentaries created by Walt Disney from 1947–60, which Ben-Ner watched and enjoyed as a child.[133] These documentaries, released as part of Disney's *True-Life Adventures* series, depicted the everyday lives of animals in what was believed to be their natural surroundings. The writer and director James Algar (1912–98) was praised for his ability to imbue nature and living things with a "human touch."[134]

The anthropomorphism of animals in nature documentaries follows what Jan-Christopher Horak has termed "the classic documentary aesthetic."[135] Such films were popular because they were seen as "an expansion of human vision, a means of entering into a world that was invisible to the human eye, an extension of the physical body of the subject, allowing for the creation of pleasure by bringing animals in their natural habitat closer to humans through the act of visualization in moving image media."[136] Algar's work for Disney was key in propagating this notion of expanding human vision. For example, in *The Living Desert* (1953), the opening scenes create a vision of a barren landscape that, beyond the human eye, teems with an abundance of animal life. To illustrate this idea, the film depicts a series of "docu-dramas"—turtles mating, a tarantula family, etc. Perhaps what is most deceiving is the notion that all the action takes place there and that there is no human life within the vicinity. As Horak notes, *The Living Desert* is carefully edited to create a "synthetic [story] out of heterogeneous filmed material," which was filmed by cameramen who spent many months in the desert, waiting for the desired animal behavior to occur. These films, as Steve Baker has described, resulted in the reduction of animals into stereotypes and mere images—the so-called *Disneyfication* of animal life.[137] In the 1980s it was revealed that Disney in fact staged some of its *True-Life Adventure* films and even promoted myths about the animals it featured, such as the lemming mass suicides.[138]

The hiding, and later revealing, of artifice is not lost on Ben-Ner who deliberately exposes the constructed-ness of his animals. His family's costumes are constructed from objects that are clearly consumer conveniences—mop handles and vacuum hoses in combination with papier-mâché. When the butterflies appear to Elia, they are clearly hung from wires, exposing their constructed nature. Importantly, the ostriches face the opposite direction of the actors and the actors must hold up the long neck and heads of the ostriches with mop handles. There is a certain 'DIY' playfulness in this creation; not bound to the confines of the home, the family has the space to explore the imagination and play. In fact, Ben-Ner has explained that he had to follow and mimic his children, as Amir would not follow him, and thus the film is played in reverse to create the desired ostrich-movement.[139] This change becomes visible in the film when a minor element, such as a leaf, floats upwards, or Amir seems to glide up a slope.[140]

In revealing the artifice of the wildlife film, Ben-Ner's films as a whole can also be read in terms of the broadly defined documentary, which reveals yet another set of constructs. Dai Vaughan explores some of the nuances and tropes evinced by the documentary in his collection of essays, *For Documentary*, in which Vaughan notes that there are certain assumptions related to the genre that become pronounced through its distribution. For example, Vaughan suggests that scenes of someone speaking holds more validity than someone listening; if someone acknowledges the camera, they are aware of the ultimate audience; and that the action recorded would happen if the camera were absent.[141] Although not often speaking directly to the camera, Ben-Ner's conversation with Elia in *Berkeley's Island* and with Amir in *Wild Boy*, close-up scenes of himself and the children looking directly in the camera and both the scripted and the non-scripted actions recorded by the camera, all intone a real or documentary aesthetic. However, these points mean little without consideration of the ultimate audience, which brings into consideration how the director should end the film—should he or she tie up all the loose ends or leave it open-ended and allow possible negative audience responses?[142] In essence, Ben-Ner does both in *Elia*; he resolves her isolation from the family; however, he leaves the search for the sacred feeding ground unresolved.

As in his other films, Ben-Ner makes no attempt to hide the artifice of his documentary, nor the natural world. The park in which they filmed is artificial in itself—Riverside Park was designed in 1875 by Frederick Law Olmsted, the co-designer of Central and Prospect Parks in New York, and was modified over twenty-five years to create a space "with grand, tree-lined boulevards, combined with an English-style rustic park with informally arranged trees and shrubs, contrasting natural enclosures, and open vistas."[143] The park, like the family of actors, is partly tamed, or alternately, partially wild. Why Ben-Ner approached his subject in a way that can be related to wildlife documentaries is also a subject of interest. If part of the drive to create animal documentaries, as Horak suggests, is to "'save' wildlife for a virtual world," then one might consider Ben-Ner's works as his attempt to virtually preserve his family.[144] This may be particularly true for the work *Elia*. In this video, he casts his entire family as animals and documents them as a way of 'saving' childhood, the family structure as it is right then, before it changes, and in doing so, projects an ideology of the family.

Notably, animal documentaries are always informed by ideology. Cynthia Chris argues that wildlife films "are sites of both purposeful ideological work and unconscious elaboration of beliefs so normalized as common sense—about nature, animals, race, gender, sexuality, economic and political formations."[145] More specifically, the Disney nature films, according to Scott MacDonald, had a tendency to promote a certain vision of not only "family life and gender, but a deep complacency about the history of Manifest Destiny and modern middle-class life."[146] Indeed, Ben-Ner was aware of these ideological constructions when conceiving of *Elia*. To paraphrase Ben-Ner, in documentary films animal behavior was presented to suggest that the "hierarchical structures of the civilized world" had been copied from nature and were thus justified to be the way they were.[147] Ben-Ner's version, however, reveals its structure, thus inverting the hierarchy to allow deeper readings of sibling rivalry and the structure of the modern family.

As such, ostriches provide an interesting model for the struggle between domesticated and wild, civilized and savage. Ostriches were the subjects of nature documentaries as early as 1901, when Siegmund Lubin and the motion picture company, American Biograph, documented ostriches on a farm in Pasadena in a film titled, *Ostrich Farm at Pasadena* (1901). The film was created to generate an interest in ostrich meat, as they were domesticated animals by the mid-nineteenth century.[148] Thus, even in the embrace of a natural or wild subject, one finds that it has already been tamed.[149] Ben-Ner chose ostriches for his family because they are one of the few species in which the father is the primary caregiver. Identified by their glossy black feathers and white wings, male ostriches are territorial males that share childcare duties with the dominant or 'alpha' hen. However, as Ben-Ner found, the ostrich was not considered a father, but a 'male mother' in science books, which he said, "testifies to our language's inability to cope with gender switches. They would rather put their own gender at stake than threaten the big 'Father' word."[150] Drawing on the continual denial of fathering within popular culture and science, the narrator, almost ironically, identifies Ben-Ner as the "male mother."

This gendered understanding of primary caregiving can be attributed to both the *Disneyfication* of wildlife films and middle-class ideals of the nuclear family. Even though the Ben-Ners were in many ways the prototypical nuclear family, Ben-Ner's films exhibit his constant negotiation with gender expectations and mothering. On this subject, one may again turn to the notions of mothering articulated by Ruddick.

In *Maternal Thinking*, Ruddick concentrates on the quotidian activity of thinking and its relationship to education and childcare. With the basic premise that mothering requires thinking above all else, this perspective allows anyone committed to parenthood to parent, and thus contrasting greatly from early debates whether men could mother.[151] Thus, in Ruddick's definition, maternal thinking is genderless work that shapes and educates the parent as much as it does the child, making cognitive development mutually beneficial.[152] In this context, Ben-Ner's *Wild Boy* offers a glimpse at his maternal thinking, as he demonstrates the reciprocal education that one has while raising a child, and what one can learn by looking at life to see what it offers, while *Elia* embraces the ideal fully. In *Wild Boy*, Ben-Ner modeled behavior for his son to imitate (this is actually revealed in a split-screen sequence that shows Buster and Ben-Ner, in and out of the character of Itard, making identical gestures), but in *Elia*, both children are aped by Ben-Ner, rather than vice versa. This choice functioned as a means to manage the unpredictable children, but also to visualize the idea that, "one becomes the mother of the other and can change the other."[153]

The film itself demonstrates the unpredictable situation of the mother, regardless of the gender of who does the "mothering." In what can be considered a familial power struggle recorded for artistic purposes, the focus on Elia's jealousy of Amir, the younger sibling who steals the attention of both mother and father, demonstrates the agency she has in her representation and within the family—she received attention for negative actions toward her sibling within the script, causing the primary caregiver to keep a watchful eye on her.[154] On the other hand, there is Amir, who draws the viewer's attention not only in his antagonistic role, but also because he seems unable to remain in character. Several scenes show Amir partially in costume—he often dons the ostrich tights and claws but not the ostrich body (Figure 4.6). These elements reveal the inability to manage or even demand consistent performances from children. This, however, does not indicate Ben-Ner's failure to mother, as some might proclaim; rather it seems that the artist uses and includes such moments to reveal the truth, as unseemly it may appear, of parenthood in general. Scholars have noted the parenting styles of men are indistinguishable from those of women; men and women encounter the same situations of parenting and react to them similarly.[155]

The truth of parenting for Ben-Ner is the dependence on his children—for his art but also his livelihood. He claimed that they were aware of it as his works provide a space for open dialogue, stating "I can tell my kids things that they might not know: the burdens of having a family, how I feel about them. My children know I'm dependent on them. The relationship is double-sided. Parents are usually dependent on their children, but the kids are not generally aware of it."[156] Ben-Ner frequently referred to the plight of the stay-at-home father, the struggle he has to establish a masculine identity while still being an attentive and nurturing father. Ben-Ner requires his children to be present in his work but they also require him to make the work so he can 'make a living' and that they can survive.[157]

Thus, through his works, Ben-Ner fulfills the three criteria, or 'maternal demands' outlined in Ruddick's text—to protect one's children, to ensure their growth, and assure their social acceptability.[158] Andrea Doucet, however, considers the fulfillment of these criteria as not mothering, but the "reconfiguring of fathering and masculinities."[159] Whether considered mothering or fathering, Ben-Ner asserts a strong parental voice and presence within his films, one that cannot be easily dismissed.

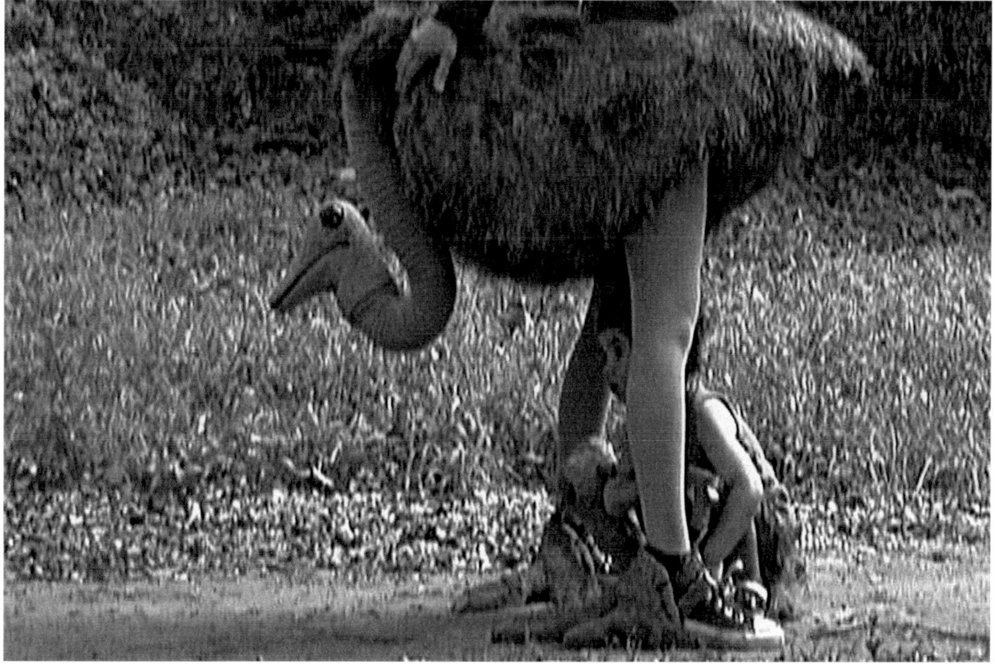

Figure 4.6 Guy Ben-Ner, still from *Elia: A Story of an Ostrich Chick*, 2003. Single channel video with sound, 17 minutes. Courtesy the artist.

The Survival of the Artist-Father

When looking at *Elia* in comparison to the body of works discussed in this chapter, survival, or the notion of surviving, is one of the many consistent threads. On the most basic of levels, *Berkeley's Island*, *Moby Dick*, and *Wild Boy* are stories about survivors, their encounter with cataclysmic events, and the struggle to exist. Likewise, *Elia* is built on the premise of a family that is in migration, seeking a sacred ground, and documents both the wanderings and individual plight of Elia. If one returns to the idea that the film functions as a documentary of the family in a foreign place (New York, as opposed to Tel Aviv), film scholar Dai Vaughan's interpretation of documentaries can illuminate its purpose. Vaughan asserts that the documentary film makes two claims: "on the one hand, to present us images referring unashamedly to their sources; on the other, to articulate a statement of which those sources will be the object," thus allowing for multiple interpretations to be associated with the same image.[160] Ben-Ner's use of voice-over narration and dramatic music (composed by Mariano Weinstein) places the story in the genre of wildlife films (as discussed above); however the content of the narration reveals the reality of the family migration, thus conflating truth and fiction.[161] Moreover, as filmmaker Jill Godmilow suggests, traditional documentaries exploit certain perspectives in order to "feel better" about oneself and make the viewer believe they are compassionate.[162] In a sense, Ben-Ner does just this. He asks the viewer to sympathize with not only Elia's plight, but also with that of the ostrich family as a whole that is seeking a permanent place to settle, which is also akin to the displacement of the Jewish people.

Ben-Ner admits that the reference to Judaism was not intentional. Boaz Arad was the first to point out the film's relationship to Israel and Judaism as it is one of migration, immigration, and the search for 'home.'[163] Ideas of 'finding home' have been significantly investigated within contemporary art and literature, particularly within the political history of Israel and the Israeli settlements. The Israeli settlements on the West Bank, along with those on the Gaza Strip and Golan Heights, have been sites of perpetual conflict since their establishment in the late 1960s.[164] Occupied primarily by Jewish settlers, these settlements spurred the Six Day War in 1967 and the ongoing Palestinian–Israeli conflicts, causing some settlers' displacement or worse, death.

This conflict is somewhat of a footnote in Ben-Ner's larger oeuvre, but he has jested that the family longed to leave Israel for "a year or two" as he, "longed for some boredom."[165] Clearly jesting, Ben-Ner elaborated that he desired "political boredom. But really, it was my wife who wanted to leave, not me."[166] Leaving Israel meant going to New York City, where Ben-Ner studied at Columbia University, lived in Columbia's housing, then Queens, and then the Brooklyn neighborhood of Bushwick. In the transition from Israel to New York City, Ben-Ner began to refer to himself as the "Eternal Jew," who is forever wandering to find better living conditions.[167] Thus, when viewing *Elia*, one can see the parallel to Judaism that Arad noticed. As a responsible father, he leads his family through Riverside Park to find a place that will nourish them and become their home. Interestingly, New York did not become that home; the family moved back to Tel Aviv and when Ben-Ner received a Deutscher Akademischer Austauschdienst (DAAD) award, they moved to Berlin. The two works conceived there, *I'd Give It to You If I Could But I Borrowed It* and *Stealing Beauty*, both created in 2007, demonstrate a transition from his investigation of fatherhood and identity to a larger analysis and critique of the family that began in *Elia* as it is conceived culturally and intellectually (Plate 12). Notably, in *Stealing Beauty*, which is filmed using the display sets in IKEA stores in Israel, Germany, and the United States, Elia reads from Frederick Engels' *The Origin of the Family, Private Property and the State* (1884) and in the finale, the children chant the manifesto, "Children of the world unite! Steal from the state! Steal from your parents! Steal your inheritance!"[168] (Figure 4.7) These works with his significantly older children reveal a changed family dynamic; they would be the last works the family would make together for some time.[169]

Interestingly, with his relocation to New York, Ben-Ner began to receive critical attention in the art world, gaining representation through Postmasters and being selected by Israel to represent them in the Fifty-first Venice Biennale. In his opinion, the move and recognition from a non-Israeli community motivated Israel to select him as the representative artist for the Biennale, stating, "Maybe I'm wrong, but I feel that it is natural for any place that is off-center—it needs confirmation from the center."[170] For the Biennale, Ben-Ner created *Treehouse Kit* (2005), the first major work that did not include his children—they appear only as a family photo. However, in it he not only revisited the adventures of *Robinson Crusoe*, but also "an Israeli settler," and "extol[led] the inventiveness of the individual in the face of hardship. He [was] a nomad seeking refuge, one that he himself create[d] out of his own environment."[171] As would later be revealed, Ben-Ner could build a career on his children, but would be unable to sustain it.

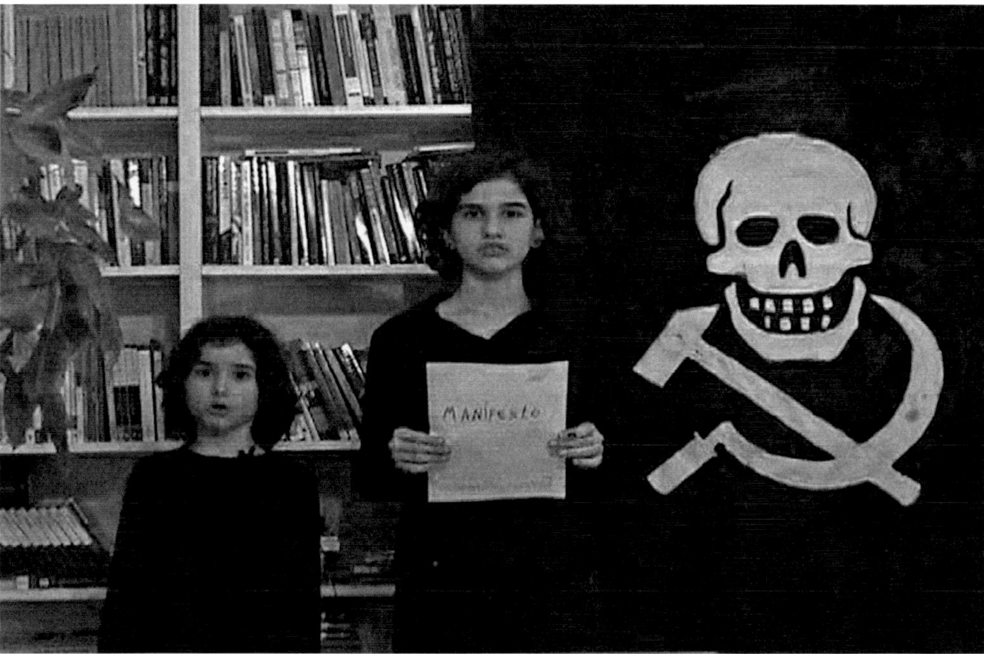

Figure 4.7 Guy Ben-Ner, still from *Stealing Beauty*, 2007. Single channel video with sound, 17 minutes 40 seconds. Courtesy the artist.

In as much as the works discussed in this chapter record the development and growth of the interpersonal relationships and the many firsts of a child's life, Guy Ben-Ner's videos function on the level of the home movie or documentary. They record a personal vision of Ben-Ner's and his children's reality. Whether the children remember it or not, they will have this visual document to aid their recollections. Wittgenstein proclaimed in *Tractatus Logico-Philosophicus*, "the picture is a model of reality."[172] Péter Forgács elaborated on this idea in the context of the home movie stating, "the act of mimesis seems to signify 'I exist' or, rather, 'I represent myself here for immortality.' This imitation of ourselves is an authentic 'copy' of the original, since the actor and the role are identical."[173] To this effect, Ben-Ner's miming of his children (or his children miming him) in his films reiterates the notion of immortality through both the recording of the image and through genetics. Like Oppenheim's *Transfer Series*, a present, future, and past of the artist's actions and interactions are memorialized. However, in his annexation of other artists' works and films, Ben-Ner feels no obligation toward fidelity.[174] Instead, he "uses them to tell [his] private tale, a tale that is unable to escape cultural limits." Continuing, Ben-Ner asserts, "I do not use myself to retell these narratives, I use them to tell myself. My obligation is to Guy Ben-Ner." Notably, his duty is not to *Moby-Dick*, *Robinson Crusoe*, *L'Enfant sauvage*, or any other artist's work that he, to some degree, has appropriated and recreated.[175]

However, Ben-Ner's use of his family in his work caused him sometimes to be proclaimed as the perpetuator of child exploitation, or worse, child abuse. In his interview with Alanna Heis, Dennis Oppenheim similarly made such a statement when speaking of the work *Color Application for Chandra*, where the artist asked Chandra to memorize and repeat the names of colors. Oppenheim admitted the work was, "child abuse, yes, but in the context of Conceptual Art, and I use that term loosely, I was teaching and implanting something onto a mind."[176] As noted previously, Ben-Ner made the choice to work at home, yet he did not let the criticism escape his attention. In fact, he claims that the scenes of "comic comeuppance"—for example, the moments where Elia slams the refrigerator door on Ben-Ner's behind or steals his peg-leg in *Moby Dick*—are in fact to punish him for exploiting his children for his art. Likewise, at the end of *Wild Boy*, Ben-Ner appears in a wheelchair in a subway car, using his son's legs as if the deformity were his own (Amir hides underneath the chair) to generate empathy from the other riders and procure enough money to finish his movie and 'get out of trouble.' In regard to this scene, Ben-Ner notes, "this shot is actually a remark I make regarding the whole movie: Yes, I use my children to attract attention. Funny enough *Moby Dick* also ends with my daughter functioning as my legs. Both endings are foot notes."[177] Ben-Ner seems to consider these actions, on some level, to absolve him of his guilt, noting, "After I 'beat myself'—or 'get punished' in the slapstick scenes, I can do whatever I want." Edelsztein ultimately views these scenes as creating a "tension between masochistic and sadistic acts, between gratification and punishment that also call the dynamics of Vito Acconci's works to mind."[178] While the relationship to Acconci's body art is certainly prevalent, the significant aspect of Ben-Ner's statement is the ongoing conflict he has, as an artist-parent, in incorporating his children in his art. His desire to be a 'good father' caused him to move his studio to the home, but it also complicated his relationship between work and home, art and life. His works, thus, not only reference the dynamics of the parent–child relationship, but also the ongoing guilt parents have regarding the decisions and choices they make and what, if any, repercussions they may have for the parent and child.

Ben-Ner's critical success using the space of the kitchen and his children may ultimately convey a privileging of the male appropriation of the feminine, rather than a positioning within it. This is an important point to consider, as Martha Schwendener has noted.[179] Ben-Ner's gender identity, like it or not, positions his role as artist who uses his children differently than if he were a woman, as scholars continue to debate whether feminism has truly created an unbiased art world. In 2007, Jerry Saltz wrote in *New York Magazine*, "It has become bitterly clear that MoMA's stubborn unwillingness to integrate more women into these galleries is not only a failure of the imagination and a moral emergency; it amounts to apartheid."[180] While the Museum's permanent collection rotation may still be in question, in 2010 the Museum mounted a major retrospective of Marina Abramović, *The Artist is Present*, where the artist staged a performance incorporating the artist and museumgoers for the duration of the exhibition. This exhibition, in Carrie Lambert-Beatty's view, placed the woman artist as a "saint or celebrity," noting that the "cultural forms evoked by this scene are either grandiose (the pope) or absurd (shopping-mall Santa)," and ultimately positioned Abramović as a "woman artist" to be ogled rather than simply an "artist."[181] While many, including the artist, do not share Lambert-Beatty's sentiment, a documentary by Lynn Hershman Leeson, *!Women Art Revolution*, reveals that many museumgoers know little, if anything, about women artists.[182] This suggests that male artists are continuing to be favored both within the art institution and the public eye, even if unconsciously.[183] For Ben-Ner to use the kitchen and his children, and for the most part, be heralded for it, suggests that his sex has enabled his critical success. Critic Karen Rosenberg even proclaimed Ben-Ner as "one enviably cool father," a far cry from the "bad mother" label that is often given to female artists who depict their children, and I have yet to discover a woman artist to be proclaimed in the pages of *Artforum*, as an "enviably cool mother."[184]

While Ben-Ner may be a "cool" dad, reviews of his work have not been universally positive. Critic Karen Wilkin, in her review of *Greater New York, 2005* at P.S. 1, Queens, New York, characterized Ben-Ner's *Elia* as uneven. She proclaims it "repetitious, a little ponderous, and ... too long," but with "moments of pure inspiration."[185] She, however, outright pans *Moby Dick*, as "childish and dull."[186] Regardless, most critical responses to Ben-Ner's work have been positive. For example, Jerry Saltz writes, "while trying to make art and be a loving father, Ben-Ner creates androgynous and empathetic psychic sparks. He recombines ideas of masculinity in ways that few male artists have."[187] More often than not, critics proclaim his works enjoyable to watch for his integration of family, self, and art.[188]

To conclude, Ben-Ner's series of films featuring his family are so loaded with historical, educational, artistic, and cinematic references that, despite my reading of his works within the artist-parent paradigm, they are simply too pluralistic to nail down with one reading, or viewing for that matter. Saltz aptly characterizes the appeal of Ben-Ner's work. He notes, "What makes Ben-Ner's art stand out is that he puts these ideas together so well, continually cannibalizing the culture and objects he encounters, trying to make these things work for his art and his family."[189] Ben-Ner's films are evidence of much more than an artist-parent identity.

Ben-Ner's negotiation of masculinity, fatherhood, motherhood, education, and artistic identity in *Berkeley's Island*, *Moby Dick*, *Wild Boy*, and *Elia: A Story of An Ostrich Chick* are full of references to other genres and ideas that exist within past and present social, cultural, and artistic realms. Ben-Ner embraces postmodernist strategy where nothing is "off limits," visually engaging with understandings of new fathering and what it means to raise a family. He investigates his own transition from a young artist to an artist-parent, embracing his relationship with his children. And, he uses the history of cinema, slapstick, vaudeville, and art to educate them about the world in which they live. The variety of sources, references, and quotations similarly reveals just how complicated and varied parenting in the new millennium can be, especially for an artist-parent.

Notes

1 Simone de Beauvoir, *The Second Sex*, trans. Constance Borde and Sheila Malovany-Chevaillier. Introduction by Judith Thurman (1949; repr. New York: Vintage Books, 2011), 301.

2 On the subject of men in cinema, see Stella Bruzzi, *Bringing Up Daddy: Fatherhood and Masculinity in Post-War Hollywood* (London: British Film Institute, 2005). On the subject of fathers not being "real men," see Andrea Doucet, *Do Men Mother? Fathering, Care, and Domestic Responsibility* (Toronto: Toronto University Press, 2006); Jeremy Adam Smith, *The Daddy Shift: How Stay-at-Home Dads, Breadwinning Moms and Shared Parenting Are Transforming the American Family* (Boston: Beacon Press, 2009). In these two texts, Doucet and Smith use interviews with parents to explore the phenomena of male parenting, though they have varying goals. Doucet approaches her subjects with a theoretical

approach, based on Ruddick's "demands of mothering," while Smith investigates the reasons why there is an increasing number of men who choose to stay at home.

3 Freud addressed the Oedipal complex in several of his texts including *The Interpretation of Dreams* (1909), *A Special Type of Object Choice Made by Men* (1910), and *Totem and Taboo* (1913).

4 This is noted in the catalog for Eva Atlan's 2008 exhibition, *Access to Israel*. Eva Atlan, ed., *Access to Israel 1: Israeli Contemporary Art* (Köln: Walther König, 2008), 85.

5 Sergio Edelsztein, "Guy Ben-Ner: Self-Portrait as a Family Man," *Self-Portrait as a Family Man* (Tel Aviv: Hakibbutz Hameuchad Publishing House, 2005), 19.

6 It would be remiss to make a sweeping statement such as "video art" did not exist. It certainly did not have a visible presence within the Israeli context, and its concurrent disappearance and the advent of Israel's "Operation Peace for Galilee" campaign marked the societal transition toward military service, rather than creativity. See Sarit Shapria's essay, "Some Notes on the History, Context and Non-Context of Israeli Art," 17–23 in *Access to Israel*.

7 Edelsztein, *Self-Portrait*, 19.

8 Octavio Zaya, "Inside-Out: Disillusioning Uncertainties: Between an End and a Beginning, Between Anxiety and Speculation," in *Del Revés: Artistas contemporáneos de Israel, (Inside-Out: Contemporary Artists from Israel)* (Vigo: Museo de Arte Contemporánea de Vigo, 2006), 124.

9 Edelsztein, *Self-Portrait*, 81 no. 1.

10 The *Cremaster* cycle is alternately heralded as a major work of art (or avant-garde film), on par with Louis Buñuel and Salvator Dali's *Un Chien Andalou* (1929) or as horrible, vapid tedium. See Jonathan Jones, "The Myth-Maker," *The Guardian*, October 16, 2002, http://guardian.co.uk/film/2002/oct/16/artsfeatures/print for a positive review; J. Hoberman, "Cults of Personality," *The Village Voice*, March 11, 2003, http://www.villagevoice.com/2003-03-11/film/cults-of-personality/ for a negative one.

11 Edelsztein notes that Israeli artists prior to the 1980s worked in the home, "in small studios or closed balconies," began renting public bomb shelters as studios in the eighties, and by the nineties, renting a studio was common practice. Edelsztein, *Self-Portrait*, 81 no. 2.

12 Guy Ben-Ner quoted from an unpublished interview with Boaz Arad, referenced in Edelsztein, *Self Portrait*, 20.

13 Jeremy Adam Smith has coined this change in male domestic responsibility as the "Daddy Shift." Smith attributes the shift to both reactions to feminism and the greater mobility of families today causing them to be distanced from family members who could assist with childcare.

14 Most notably, Sweden proclaims to have the most progressive laws regarding parental leave, instituting paternity leave as early as 1974; both parents can take as many as 390 paid leave days up to their child's eighth birthday. Sweden's progressive parental rights had resurgence in the news in 2010. See Katrin Bennhold, "In Sweden, the Men Can Have it All," *New York Times*, June 9, 2010. Even so, Luigi Zoja suggests that the primary care of children still remains at the hands of women and cites that men only care for children one-quarter of the time. See Luigi Zoja, *The Father: Historical, Psychological and Cultural Perspectives*, trans. Henry Martin (Philadelphia: Brunner-Routledge, 2001), 249.

15 This event, of course, was of the utmost importance to American and Russian audiences, and likely had little direct relationship to Israeli gender politics. However, if one considers the effects of American consumer ideology on a global scale, and gender relationships within Israel, the "Kitchen debate" casts a significant political lens on this work. On a similar note, men in the kitchen are not usually presented within video art, nor are they typically seen within the space of the kitchen, doing domestic tasks, such as cooking, within film.

16 Lucy Lippard, "Household Images in Art," *The Pink Glass Swan: Selected Feminist Essays on Art* (New York: The New Press, 1995), 62.

17 Cécile Whiting, *A Taste for Pop: Pop Art, Gender and Consumer Culture* (Cambridge: Cambridge University Press, 1997), 65–68.

18 sitegallery, "Guy Ben-Ner Interview," YouTube Video, 6:56, March 10, 2011, http://youtu.be/MSbz9G-qRqs.

19 Spock notes, "a man can be a warm father and a real man at the same time." Spock, *Baby and Child Care*, 29.

20 This reference is noted in Edelsztein, *Self-Portrait*, 22.

21 Edelsztein notes that *Untitled (Rolling Pin)* "breaks with the single-shot approach of the two earlier videos, being an interesting first attempt at making a 'movie.'" In it, Ben-Ner alternates the camera angle from frontal and lateral, effectively moving the camera ninety degrees, which Edelsztein notes is an "atypical" and unsuccessful strategy in filmmaking. Consult Edelsztein, *Self-Portrait*, 25.

22 See Alanna Heiss, *And the Mind Grew Fingers: Dennis Oppenheim: Selected Works 1967–90* (New York: Harry N. Abrams, 1992), 62.

23 Emphasis in original text. Sartre develops this idea in order to explain the later actions of Genet, namely the theft he commits, and partially attributes such to an upbringing that emphasizes saintliness. As such, the translator notes that Sartre's title, in French, alludes to St. Genestus, a third-century Roman martyr and patron saint of actors. Jean-Paul Sartre, *Saint Genet: Actor and Martyr* (New York: New American Library, 1971), 15.

24 This explanation is developed in Peter Caws, *Sartre* (New York: Routledge, 2008), 64.

25 The notion of the "culture of confession" is epitomized by popular talk shows and by artists, such as John Borofsky, Sophie Calle, Tracy Emin, and Mike Kelly, who express personal pain, anguish, and emotion in their art. For a particularly informative view of Sophie Calle's "confessional art," see Shirley Ann Jordan, "Exhibiting Pain: Sophie Calle's *Douleur Exquise*," *French Studies* LXI no. 2 (2007): 196–208.

26 On the uses of narrative within Defoe, see Michael M. Boardman, *Defoe and the Uses of Narrative* (New Brunswick: Rutgers University Press, 1983), 5–10.

27 Nuit Banai, "Guy Ben-Ner: Tel Aviv," *Art Papers* 30 no. 4 (July/August 2006): 71.

28 Ibid.

29 Patricia R. Zimmermann, "The Home Movie: Excavations, Artifacts, Minings," in *Mining the Home Movie: Excavations in Histories and Memories*, eds. Karen L Ishizuka, Patricia Zimmermann (Berkeley: University of California Press, 2008), 1. In another work, *Reel Families*, Zimmermann recounts how the rise in home movies coincided with the discourse of the nuclear family and consumption. See Zimmermann, *Reel Families: A Social History of Amateur Film* (Bloomington: Indiana University Press, 1995).

30 Stewart defines the collection on the substitution of aesthetic value for use value, which in turn mediates the collector's relationship with the world. This idea is paralleled to kinship systems where the child becomes a way for the parent to interact with the world, though retaining the child's use-value. See Susan Stewart, *On Longing: Narratives of the Miniature, The Gigantic, The Souvenir, The Collection* (Durham: Duke University Press, 1993), 151–52.

31 Ben-Ner quoted in Rachel Spence, "The Art of Guy Ben-Ner," *Jewish Quarterly* 52, no. 2 (Summer 2005), 26.

32 Edelsztein connects Ben-Ner's process with that of Joe and Buster Keaton, noting that since Ben-Ner was born after the 1960s' parent revolution, "his parental relationship with Elia, his daughter is much more complex and conscious than, for instance, that of Joe Keaton and his young son Buster." Edelsztein, *Self-Portrait*, 40. I hesitate to draw out Edelsztein's conclusion as we have the benefit of perspective when discussing Keaton, and there has been a growing body of criticism and rejection of perceived parent–child relationships from the perspective of the child, once an adult. See, for example, Musa Mayer, *Night Studio*; the series of articles surrounding the availability of the film *Growing* by Larry Rivers, which features his naked teenage daughters: Marlon Bishop, "Larry Rivers: Right or Wrong" *WNYC Culture*, July 23, 2010; and, Kate Taylor, "Artist's Daughter Wants Videos Back" *New York Times*, July 7, 2010. Similarly, the documentaries *Alice Neel* and *The Kids Grow Up* reveal the complicated relationship between parent and child, namely the child's perception of the parent, as they mature. See Andrew Neel, *Alice Neel*, SeeThink, 2007; and Doug Block, *The Kids Grow Up*, HBO Documentary, 2009.

33 Tom Gunning draws the connection between Nauman and Ben-Ner when discussing Ben-Ner's photographs of domestic work; however, I believe it is fair to claim that there is a sense of artistic living that takes precedence when considering the staging of the kitchen

could and would require the entire family to live with the art. Gunning, "The Videos of Guy Ben-Ner," in *Self-Portrait*, 25.

34 Edelsztein notes that there are two versions of this early work, a looped version and a linear one. The former lasts for the entire duration of the song, concludes with Ben-Ner returning his penis inside his pants, and was exhibited at the Julie M. Gallery, Tel Aviv; the latter is shorter and fades out at the end. In *Berkeley's Island* the shorter version is used. See Edelsztein, *Self-Portrait*, 82 no. 4.

35 Jon Davies, "Family Romance: IKEA Sets the Stage for Israeli Artist Guy Ben-Ner's Household Politics," *C Magazine* no. 96 (Winter 2008): 11.

36 Ibid., 10.

37 Consult David Hopkins, *Dada's Boys: Masculinity after Duchamp* (New Haven and London: Yale University Press, 2007), 125; and particularly the chapter titled "Between Men," 109–35.

38 Ann Gibson and Lucia Palmer, "George Berkeley's Visual Language and the New England Portrait Tradition," *The Centennial Review* 31 no. 2 (Spring 1987): 144.

39 Quote from Guy Ben-Ner, *Berkeley's Island*, 1999

40 Edelsztein, *Self-Portrait*, 30.

41 Helena Winston, "Guy Ben-Ner: Postmasters" *ArtUS* no. 14 (July/September 2006): 46.

42 Ben-Ner quoted in Stephanie Smith, "Interview: Guy Ben-Ner and Stephanie Smith," Adaptation, University of Chicago, 2008, https://smartmuseum.uchicago.edu/adaptation/artists/ben-ner/interview/index.html.

43 Interestingly, there were several adaptations of Moby Dick in the late 1990s through 2000. See Robert K. Wallace, "Ben-Ner's *Moby Dick* and Melville's Mechanism of Projection," *Leviathan: A Journal of Melville Studies* 9 no. 1 (March 2007): 43–59.

44 Quotations refer to the text presented within the film, not Melville's text.

45 These fins appear to be captured using stop-motion, evoking the style and techniques of the surrealist filmmaker, Jan Švankmajer.

46 In his essay, Gunning suggests that Ben-Ner may have at some point perceived his children as "alien creatures." Tom Gunning, "Lost in Play: Adapting the Zone of Imagination in the Works of Guy Ben-Ner," Smart Museum of Art, Chicago: University of Chicago, 2008. https://smartmuseum.uchicago.edu/adaptation/2008/03/31/lost-in-play-adapting-the-zone -of-imagination-in-the-works-of-guy-ben-ner/

47 See Chris Jenks, "The Postmodern Child," in *Children in Families: Research and Policy*, eds. Julia Brannen and Margaret O'Brien (Washington, DC: Falmer Press, 1996), 13–25.

48 Notably, in Melville's original text, Queequeg dies, Pip becomes lost at sea, and Ishmael uses Queequeg's casket as a flotation device, becoming the only survivor.

49 This work, shown at the 2005 Venice Biennale, is discussed in Edelsztein and Davies, has been released in the Video Data Bank Collection, *Radical Closure* (2010). It, for unknown reasons, was omitted from Ben-Ner's MASSMoCA exhibition *Thursday the 12th* (2009). See Edelsztein, *Self-Portrait*, 49–55 and Davies, "Family Romance," 11.

50 André Gaudreault, "Theatricality, Narrativity, and Trickality: Reevaluating the Cinema of Geroges Méliès," in *Fantastic Voyages of the Cinematic Imagination: Georges Méliès's Trip to the Moon*, ed. Matthew Solomon (Albany: State University of New York Press, 2011), 36.

51 Méliès quoted in Gaudreault, "Theatricality, Narrativity, and Trickality," 36.

52 George Wead, *Buster Keaton and the Dynamics of Visual Wit* (New York: Arno Press, 1976), 6.

53 Ben-Ner quoted in Smith, "Interview."

54 Bruzzi, *Bringing Up Daddy*, xv.

55 Davies, "Family Romance," 12.

56 They part ways when they arrive in New York, yet meet again at a restaurant where Charlie tries to woo her and find a means to pay for their meal. The film ends with Charlie and Edna before the marriage license office, where he kisses her and tries to convince her to marry him, finally picking her up and taking her into the office. This was Chaplin's eleventh film in his series of twelve comedies contracted by Mutual Film Corporation between 1916 and 1917. Charlie Chaplin, *The Immigrant*, 1917, Mutual Film Corporation, 20 minutes. See Davin Anthony Orgeron and Marsha Gabrielle Orgeron, "Eating Their

Words: Consuming Class á la Chaplin and Keaton," *College Literature* 28 no. 1 (Winter 2001): 88–89.

57 Ben-Ner quoted in Smith, "Interview."

58 Tom Gunning, "Lost in Play."

59 In doing so, Ben-Ner recalls Keaton's own incorporation of fantasy. Keaton is quoted in Tom Dardis' biography of the actor as stating, "I used to daydream an awful lot in pictures. I could get carried away and visualize all the fairylands in the world. Dream sequences … I guess it was just my natural way of working." See Tom Dardis, *Keaton: The Man Who Wouldn't Lie Down* (New York: Scribners, 1979), 130.

60 Amal Treacher, "Children's Imaginings and Narratives: Inhabiting Complexity," *Feminist Review* 82, no. 1, Everyday Struggling (2006): 99.

61 Ibid. Similarly, see Pamela May, *Child Development in Practice: Responsive Teaching and Learning from Birth to Five* (New York: Routledge, 2011). May examines play as an effective tool for emotional, behavioral, cognitive, intellectual, social, and language development.

62 See D.W. Winnicott, *Dreaming, Fantasying, and Living in Playing and Reality* (London: Routledge, 1996).

63 Gunning, "Lost in Play."

64 Ibid.

65 Jenks, "The Postmodern Child," 19.

66 Tali Tamir, "12 Observations About Israeli Art," in Zaya, *Del Revés*, 135.

67 *One Week*, directed by Edward F. Cline and Buster Keaton (Metro Pictures, 1920), 19 minutes.

68 Notably, Ben-Ner is not the only artist to refer to *One Week*. Notably, Steve McQueen references Keaton in *Deadpan*, 1997 (4 min). The artist stands still outside of a house as the wall falls down and around him, as he is saved by the fortuitously positioned window, just as Keaton is in *One Week*.

69 Later, in *Wild Boy*, Ben-Ner teaches Amir how to use a table-saw. Together, they saw the seat and back of a chair out of the kitchen table, thus repurposing the object and teaching Amir how to fulfill his role as a man.

70 Edelsztein, *Self-Portrait*, 38.

71 Ibid., 40.

72 Amelia Jones, *Body Art/Performing the Subject* (Minneapolis: University of Minnesota Press, 1998), 108.

73 Hendricks' performance was well documented with an eight-hour video, written notes of his thoughts, and a reliquary of twenty labeled jars of hair. See C. Carr, "The Generation Gap: Three Performers and a Waterbed," *The Village Voice*, July 11, 2000, http://www.villagevoice.com/2000-07-11/news/the-generation-gap/1/.

74 On Nakanishi's performance see William Marotti, "Political Aesthetic: Activism, Everyday Life, and Art's Object in 1960s' Japan," *Inter-Asia Cultural Studies* 7 no. 4 (2006): 612; and Alexandra Munroe, *Japanese Art After 1945: Scream Against the Sky* (New York: Harry N. Abrams, 1996).

75 Charles Merewether, "Disjunctive Modernity: The Practice of Artistic Experimentation in Postwar Japan," in *Art, Anti-Art, Non-Art: Experimentations in The Public Sphere in Postwar Japan, 1950–1970*, eds. Charles Merewether and Rika Iezumi Hiro (Los Angeles: Getty Research Institute, 2007), 18–19.

76 Ibid., 19.

77 Edelsztein, *Self-Portrait*, 38.

78 The art of "reperformance" gained much interest in 2010 due to a series of exhibitions in New York. Considered a "year of performance," the Guggenheim staged an exhibition of Tino Sehgal's works, *This Progress* and *Kiss*, which required interpreters to interact with visitors (in the former) and lay in the floor of the rotunda kissing (in the latter), while the Museum of Modern Art presented a survey of Marina Abramović's performance work, re-performed by other young performance artists who were trained by the artist to endure the work's physical demands. Abramović, notably restaged six performances from the 1960s, five of those by other artists, in 2005 at the Guggenheim. Titled *Seven Easy Pieces*, Abramović studied the artist's works and performed each for a duration of seven hours.

Consult: Erika Fischer-Lichte, Sandra Umathum, Marina Abramović, *Marina Abramović: Seven Easy Pieces* (Milan: Charta, 2007); Caroline A. Jones, "Staged Presence," *Artforum International* 48 no. 9 (May 2010): 214–19; and, Jerry Saltz, "How I Made an Artwork Cry," *New York Magazine*, February 7, 2010, http://nymag.com/arts/art/reviews/63638.

79 Consider, for example, Andres Serrano's *Piss Christ* (1987), Chris Ofili's *Holy Virgin Mary* (1996), the entire controversy surrounding the 1997 exhibition *Sensation: Young British Artists from the Saatchi Collection*, and the controversy over the 2011 Lacoste Elysée Prize nominee, Larissa Sansour, who Lacoste wanted excluded from consideration for being "too pro-Palestinian." See: Hrag Vartanian, "Does Lacoste Hate Palestinians?" Hyperallergic: Sensitive to Art & its Discontents, posted December 21, 2011, http://hyp erallergic.com/43463/does-lacoste-hate-palestinians/; Arsalan Mohammad, "Artist Larissa Sansour Speaks Out About Her Ejection From the Lacoste Art Prize for Being "Too Pro-Palestinian," Artinfo: International Edition, December 21, 2011, http://www.artinfo.com/ news/story/754484/artist-larissa-sansour-speaks-out-about-her-ejection-from-the-lacoste -art-prize-for-being-too-pro-palestinian. On *Sensation*, see Lawrence Rothfield, *Unsettling 'Sensation': Arts Policy Lessons from the Brooklyn Museum of Art Controversy* (New Brunswick: Rutgers University Press, 2001). On Serrano, consult Peggy Phelan, "Serrano, Mapplethorpe, the NEA, and You: "Money Talks," October 1989," *TDR* 34 no. 1 (Spring 1990): 4–15.

80 Gunning, "Lost in Play."

81 Aim Dueul Lusky, "Guy Ben-Ner" in *Del Revés*, 28.

82 While recording his works, with the exception of *Elia: A Story of An Ostrich Chick*, Ben-Ner and his family lived in Tel Aviv.

83 Octavio Zaya has cautioned against promoting the "deceitful idea" of Israel as a Jewish State, "where Jews are the majority," which is not the meaning intended here. My assertion is that Ben-Ner, in identifying as a practitioner of the Jewish faith, associates Israel with its Jewish population. Zaya, *Del Revés*, 125.

84 It might be useful to note that Michel Foucault thought of boats as the "heterotopia *par execellence*," meaning that it is the ideal vessel that is a "place without a place" and "exists by itself" to act a space of illusion, fantasy, and imagination. One can argue that all of Ben-Ner's films function as heterotopias, in other words, as spaces of imagination, that are neither home nor studio nor public however this would negate the tangible inversions present within his work. For more on heterotopias, see Michel Foucault, "Of Other Spaces," trans. Jay Miskowiec, *Diacritics* 16 no. 1 (Spring 1986): 27.

85 In a feature published on Ben-Ner in *ArtAsiaPacific*, HG Masters claims that in *Berkeley's Island*, "Ben-Ner asserts that although he is at home, apart from the outside world, he still exists; his work as an artist and a father is documented, serving as a testament to his labors. Like keeping a diary, capturing oneself on the camera is a way of making one's thoughts and deeds visible to oneself and, eventually, others." HG Masters, "Solitary Refinement: Guy Ben-Ner" *ArtAsiaPacific* no. 66 (Nov/Dec 2009), http://artasiapacific.com/Magazine/ 66/SolitaryRefinementGuyBenNer.

86 The pair is not only expelled when Ishmael is a child, but again when he was older. On this occasion, Hagar, not wishing to witness the death of her son, sent him away and prayed to God–wherein God proclaimed she should take his hand, as he would "make him a great nation." Upon opening her eyes, Hagar saw a well, which saved both of their lives. See Genesis 21:18–19.

87 Charles Oslon, *Call Me Ishmael* (New York, 1947) quoted in Tony Tanner, Introduction to *Moby-Dick*, by Herman Melville (Oxford: Oxford University Press, 1998), viii.

88 Reference to the "Eternal Jew" is found in Atlan, *Access to Israel*, 85. To the perception of Israel as the land of "milk and honey," see "Guy Ben-Ner Interview."

89 This became known as "The Jewish Question" due to German historian Bruno Bauer's book *Die Judenfrage*, 1843. See also, Alex Bain, *The Jewish Question: Biography of a World Problem*, trans. Harry Zohn (New York: Herzl Press, 1990), 155-56.

90 The Bank of Israel ceased to produce and accept the coin as of April 1, 1991.

91 See Jean Piaget, *Play, Dreams, and Imitation in Childhood*, trans. C. Gattegno and F.M. Hodgson (London: Routledge, 1999).

92 Ben-Ner quoted in Spence, "The Art of Guy Ben-Ner."

93 Edelsztein, *Self-Portrait*, 58.
94 See Bruzzi, *Bringing Up Daddy*, 79.
95 In his review of Ben-Ner's oeuvre, Jon Davies suggests that Ben-Ner mimics his children's actions more than they mimic his. See Jon Davies, "Family Romance: IKEA Sets the Stage for Israeli Artist Guy Ben-Ner's Household Politics," *C Magazine* no. 96 (Winter 2008): 12.
96 See Jean-Jacques Rousseau, *Emile or On Education*, 1762, Introduction, trans. Allan Bloom (New York: Basic Books, 1979).
97 For more on the Society of Observers of Man, consult Harlan Lane, *The Wild Boy of Aveyron* (New York: Meredith Press, 1976).
98 Truffaut co-wrote the screenplay with Jean Gruault, adapting Jean Itard's novel *Mémoires et rapport sur Victor de l'Aveyron*, 1801 and 1806.
99 Claude Veillot, "Truffaut's Tenderness Tames His Wolf Boy," *L'Express*, August 18, 1969; reprinted in Ronald Bergan, ed. *François Truffaut: Interviews* (Jackson: University Press of Mississippi, 2008), 53.
100 The boy was estimated to be about twelve years old when discovered. He lived under Itard's care until the age of nineteen, learned to read and write approximately sixty words, and died at the age of forty in Paris living under the care of one of Itard's friends. This is mentioned in Derek Malcolm, "A Wild Boy Civilized" *Guardian*, November 19, 1970; reprinted in Bergan, *François Truffaut: Interviews*, 76.
101 Ronald Bergan in introduction to *François Truffaut: Interviews*, xix.
102 Guy Ben-Ner quoted in Smith, "Interview."
103 Truffaut cast Léaud as Antoine Doinel in the 1959 film, *Les Quatre cents coups*, a character who was based on Truffaut's own childhood. Truffaut and Léaud proceeded to work on an entire series of films that trace Doinel's development and growth as a man. Patrick E. White, "Portrait of the Artist as a Young Boy: François Truffaut, Antoine Doinel, and the Wild Child," in *Where the Boys Are: Cinemas of Masculinity and Youth*, eds. Murray Pomerance and Frances Gateward (Detroit: Wayne State University Press, 2005), 226.
104 Opening lines, *Wild Boy*, 2004.
105 François Truffaut quoted in Derek Malcolm, "A Wild Boy Civilized" *Guardian*, November 19, 1970; reprinted in Bergan, *François Truffaut: Interviews*, 76.
106 This changes dramatically toward the end of the film when Ben-Ner believes Buster has acquired language, and The Doors' song, "Break on Through (to the Other Side)" (1967), plays to the penultimate sequence of the film.
107 Keaton's parents, Joe and Myra, were vaudeville performers who incorporated Buster into their act from as young as three years, throwing him across the stage and into audiences. By the time Keaton was twenty-one, his father was an alcoholic and the family act had dissolved. When Keaton became a star in his own right, writing, directing, and starring in his own silent films, he found minor roles for his father. See Judith Sanders and Daniel Lieberfeld, "Dreaming in Pictures: The Childhood Origins of Buster Keaton's Creativity," *Film Quarterly* 47 no. 4 (Summer 1994): 14–28, and Buster Keaton, *My Wonderful World of Slapstick* (London: George Allen & Unwin, 1960).
108 "Guy Ben-Ner Interview."
109 Ben-Ner also describes the film in terms of "silent cinema as a wild child being tamed by language and sound." See Smith, "Interview."
110 When Buster Keaton began to appear onstage with his parents, he also mimicked his father's every move. Sanders and Lieberfeld, "Dreaming in Pictures," 16.
111 Oppenheim quoted in *Dennis Oppenheim: Retrospective-Works 1967–77* (Montreal: Musée d'art contemporain, 1978), 62.
112 Oppenheim used Erik in at least three versions of the *Transfer Drawing* series—*A Feedback Situation*, where Oppenheim drew on Erik's back while Erik simultaneously drew on Oppenheim's, thus confusing who is actually doing to creative thinking; and the *2-Stage Transfer Drawings, Advancing to a Past State* where Oppenheim draws on Erik's back; and the last, *Advancing to a Future State* where Erik draws on Oppenheim's. Oppenheim also incorporated his daughter, Chandra, in a work called *Color Application for Chandra*, 1971, in which he asked Chandra to memorize colors and then teach them to a parrot. Oppenheim perceived this as akin to painting and particularly, "Painting on Chandra's

memory." See Dennis Oppenheim interview with Heiss, *And the Mind Grew Fingers*, 21–33, 154; also, *Dennis Oppenheim: Retrospective-Works 1967–77*, 62. Additionally, Oppenheim did not conform to the isolated artist persona, as scholars have noted that he "lived a conventional life—a wife, children, one couch or more, a dining room." Heiss, *And the Mind Grew Fingers*, 5.

113 Zoja, *The Father*, 245.
114 This case ultimately led to Freud's development of infantile sexuality. See Sigmund Freud, "Analyses of a Phobia of a Five-Year-Old-Boy," 1909, reprinted in *The 'Wolfman' and Other Cases* (New York: Penguin Books, 2003), 1–122.
115 See, in particular chapter six, "The Riddle of Little Hans," in John Munder Ross, *What Men Want: Mothers, Fathers, and Manhood* (Cambridge: Harvard University Press, 1994), 129–45.
116 Ross, *What Men Want*, 143.
117 Ibid., 145
118 Rousseau, *Emile*, 89.
119 Ibid., 112.
120 This work notably tries to stage the fable of the fox and crow, employing a trained fox and crow and their trainers. Ben-Ner has the trainers direct the animals to capture the piece of cheese, but also has the trainers read lines from Samuel Beckett's *Waiting for Godot*, which premiered in 1953.
121 Rousseau, *Emile*, 115.
122 Tina Malti, Monika Keller, Michaela Gummerum and Marlis Buchmann, "Children's Moral Motivation, Sympathy, and Prosocial Behavior," *Child Development* 80 no. 2 (March/April 2009): 443. See also, Pamela May, *Child Development in Practice: Responsive Teaching and Learning from Birth to Five* (London; New York: Routledge, 2011), 16–25.
123 Jacques Rancière, *The Ignorant Schoolmaster: Five Lessons in Intellectual Emancipation*, trans. and introduction, Kristin Ross (Stanford: Stanford University Press, 1991), 1–6.
124 Ibid., 18.
125 Ibid., 38.
126 Martin Loiperdinger carefully deconstructs this myth of the film. See Martin Loiperdinger, "Lumière's Arrival of the Train: Cinema's Founding Myth," *Moving Image* 4 no. 1 (Spring 2004): 89–118.
127 Ibid., 109–10.
128 Gunning, "Lost in Play."
129 See Anna Gavanas, "The Fatherhood Responsibility Movement: The Centrality of Marriage, Work, and Male Sexuality in Reconstructions of Masculinity and Fatherhood," in *Making Men into Fathers: Men, Masculinities, and the Social Politics of Fatherhood*, ed. Barbara Hobson (Cambridge: Cambridge University Press, 2002), 213–42.
130 See: Atlan, *Access to Israel*, 85; and Martha Schwendener, "Family Guy: The Domestic Fantasies of Guy Ben-Ner," *Tablet Magazine*, April 16, 2008, http://www.tabletmag.com/arts-and-culture/732/family-guy/.
131 Altan, *Access to Israel*, 15.
132 Carson Grant is an environmentally conscious artist and actor based in New York.
133 Atlan, *Access to Israel*, 85.
134 Algar notably wrote and directed: *The Living Desert* (1953), *The Vanishing Prairie* (1954), *The African Lion* (1955), and *Jungle Cat* (1959). See Atlan, *Access to Israel*, 85.
135 Jan-Christopher Horak, "Wildlife Documentaries: From Classical Forms to Reality TV," *Film History* 18 no. 4, Documentary before Verité (2006): 459.
136 Ibid.
137 Steve Baker, *Picturing the Beast: Animals, Identity and Representation* (Urbana: University of Illinois Press, 2001), 175.
138 David Mikkelson, "Did Disney Fake Lemming Deaths for the Nature Documentary 'White Wilderness'?" February 27, 1996, https://www.snopes.com/fact-check/white-wilderness/.
139 Atlan, *Access to Israel*, 85.
140 Ibid.
141 Dai Vaughan, *For Documentary: Twelve Essays* (Berkeley: University of California Press, 1999), 11–12.

142 Ibid., 25–26.
143 "Riverside Park," City of New York Parks & Recreation, http://www.nycgovparks.org/par ks/riversidepark/history.
144 Horak, "Wildlife Documentaries," 460.
145 Cynthia Chris, *Watching Wildlife* (Minneapolis: University of Minnesota Press, 2006), xix.
146 Scott MacDonald, "Up Close and Political: Three Short Ruminations on Ideology in the Nature Film," *Film Quarterly* 59 no. 3 (Spring 2006): 7.
147 Atlan, *Access to Israel*, 85.
148 Ostriches were hunted to near-extinction in the eighteenth century for their feathers (used in women's wear). See Horak, "Wildlife Documentaries," 462 and 474 note 17.
149 While mostly found in zoos and on farms, some ostriches do live in nature preserves in central and southern Africa.
150 Spence, "The Art of Guy Ben-Ner."
151 See O'Reilly, "'I Envision a Future in Which Maternal Thinkers are Respected and Self-Respecting'," 296; and Risman, "Can Men 'Mother'?," 85–102.
152 This idea is summarized in William Grimes, "Sara Ruddick Dies at 76; Pondered the Nature of Mothering," *New York Times*, March 22, 2011.
153 Ben-Ner statement in "Guy Ben-Ner Interview."
154 Notably, Freud attributed Little Hans' phobia to stem from the birth of his younger sister.
155 Much of this debate centers on whether this should be termed "mothering" or if there is an alternate way to discuss such actions. Barbara Risman, *Gender Vertigo: American Families in Transition* (New Haven: Yale University Press, 1998), 70.
156 Schwendener, "Family Guy."
157 Being married at twenty-four and becoming a family not long after caused Ben-Ner and Nava to take on a series of jobs to support the family. Those jobs, according to Schwendener, included Nava working as a nanny and Ben-Ner as a waiter. Schwendener, "Family Guy."
158 Ruddick, *Maternal Thinking*, 17.
159 Doucet, *Do Men Mother?*, 210.
160 Vaughan, *For Documentary*, 30.
161 Sounds, according to MacDonald, are used in the *True-Life Adventure* films to create a cinematic mood that contributes to the animal narrative. MacDonald, "Up Close and Political," 8.
162 Jill Godmilow and Ann-Louise Shapiro, "How Real is Reality in Documentary Film?" *History and Theory* 36 no. 4, Theme Issue 36: Producing the Past: Making Histories Inside and Outside the Academy (December 1997): 82–85.
163 Schwendener, "Family Guy."
164 See Gershom Gorenberg, *The Accidental Empire: Israel and the Birth of the Settlements, 1967–1977* (New York: Times Books, 2006), 7–71.
165 Schwendener, "Family Guy."
166 Ibid.
167 However, Ben-Ner was not raised in a devout household. His exposure to Judaism was experienced mostly through school and holidays, and he embraces this at least on a superficial level. See Atlan, *Access to Israel*, 85; and Schwendener, "Family Guy."
168 Guy Ben-Ner, *Stealing Beauty*, 2007, single channel video, color with sound, DVD, 17:40 min; *I'd Give It to You If I Could But I Borrowed It*, 2007, single channel video, color with sound, DVD, 12:00 minutes; installation with bicycle powered reel.
169 Ben-Ner divorced in 2008. In his interview, Ben-Ner notes that in some way, one can read the work as being about the end of their relationship. See "Guy Ben-Ner Interview." Ben-Ner remarried, fathered another child, and in 2013 created, *Soundtrack* (2013), an 11:00 minute drama starring his new family, staged in his Tel Aviv kitchen, and set to the soundtrack of Steven Spielberg's *War of the Worlds* (2005).
170 Schwendener, "Family Guy."
171 Winston, "Guy Ben-Ner," 46.
172 Ludwig Wittgenstein, *Tractatus Logico-Philosophicus* (New York: Harcourt, Brace, 1922), 2.12.
173 Wittgenstein quoted in Péter Forgács, "Wittgenstein Tractatus: Personal Reflections on Home Movies," in *Mining the Home Movie*, 52.

174 Here I use the term 'annexation' as opposed to appropriation in accordance to how Rodney Graham described his artistic technique. Schwendener has cited that Graham, a Canadian artist, is a big inspiration for Ben-Ner. Schwendener, "Family Guy."
175 Ben-Ner quoted in Smith, "Interview."
176 Oppenheim quoted in Heiss, *And the Mind Grew Fingers*, 154.
177 Ben-Ner quoted in Smith, "Interview."
178 Edelsztein, *Self-Portrait*, 49.
179 In her *Artforum* review of Ben-Ner's show at Postmasters in 2008, Martha Schwendener writes, "A stickier question is how all this might play out were the artist a woman. ([Sally] Mann got saddled by some critics with the Bad Mother tag.) Ben-Ner doesn't have to answer this, although he does confront gender relations obliquely in *Stealing Beauty*, with Amir asking, 'Can I inherit Mommy when you're done with her?' (To which Elia replies, 'That's Freudian.')." Martha Schwendener, "Guy Ben-Ner: Postmasters," *Artforum International* 46 no. 8 (April 2008): 369.
180 Jerry Saltz, "Where Are All the Women?" *New York Magazine*, November 18, 2007.
181 Carrie Lambert-Beatty, "Against Performance Art," *Artforum International* 48 no. 9 (May 2010): 212. Lambert-Beatty articulated the second half of this idea at the "Thinking Performance" symposium at the Solomon R. Guggenheim Museum, New York, June 18, 2010.
182 For this documentary, the film crew asked people outside of the Whitney Museum and the San Francisco Museum of Modern Art (in 2008 and 2009, respectively) to name three female artists, which many could not. Chloe Veltman, "When Female Artists Were Storming the Gates," *New York Times,* April 15, 2011, National edition.
183 It should be noted that the string of major feminist exhibitions, *Global Feminisms* (2007), *WACK: Art and the Feminist Revolution* (2007–09), and *Elles@centrepompidou* (2009) garnered a renewed interest in the history of feminism and women artists, yet continue to remain relegated within the dominant discourse.
184 Karen Rosenberg, "Guy Ben-Ner: Postmasters," *Artforum International* 42 no. 9 (April 2005): 189.
185 Karen Wilkin, "Not-So-Great New York 2005," *The New Criterion* 23 no. 9 (May 2005): 47.
186 Wilkin, "Not-So-Great," 47.
187 Jerry Saltz, "Artist in Residence: When Guy Ben-Ner Goes to Ikea, He's Not There for the Meatballs," *New York Magazine*, January 31, 2008, http://nymag.com/arts/art/reviews/43567.
188 Carly Berwick, "Guy Ben-Ner," *ARTnews* 105 no. 9 (October 2006): 176.
189 Saltz, "Artist in Residence."

5 A Collective Artist-Parent Identity
Mothers and Fathers

In 1993, Emma Amos asserted that there is still "plenty of time for boredom and a feeling of isolation" when raising children.[1] The isolation that parents experience, while not unusual, has only recently become a subject of interest in childrearing journals, books, and magazines.[2] It is commonly noted among parents that a change occurs in one's social circles when one becomes a parent. First, they become separated from their non-parent friends due to their new child-rearing responsibilities. Artists, like Amos, have acknowledged this as a double bind; parental duties often isolate individuals from society, and artistic practice is often considered in terms of one's individual process of making. And as parents of young children, artists were thought to have no visible place in the gallery, museum, or studio, and frequently childcare prevents parent-artists' participation in such spaces. This is a problem experienced by artists in many nations besides the United States where Amos resides. For example, in Ireland, a 2017 study by The Mothership Project (a network of artist-parents) found that 83% of respondents were both caregivers and artists, and 76% turned down opportunities due to lack of childcare.[3] Attempting to capitalize on the difficultly of being an artist and parent, the artist collective, Matky a Otcové, Czech for 'Mothers and Fathers,' provided a new solidarity for the artists who comprised it. In 2001, the Czech artists: Lenka Klodová, Lucie (Krecjová) Nepasická,[4] Martin Péč, and Marek Rejent (two women and two men) participated in an exhibition in Prague that centered on the family.[5] Each member of the group, having at least two children of his or her own, found solace in the mutual experience as an artist-parent. They were all interested in art and the family, and deciding that they worked well together, the group Mothers and Fathers was formed.

To become a member, the artists decided that one had to be a parent and be interested in creating works reflective of the complex nature of being both an artist *and* a parent. Artists who were interested in these issues, but did not have a child, were turned away.[6] The members of Mothers and Fathers found that when artists who requested to join actually *had* children, they claimed to have no time due to the demands of child care. The group thus remained with the original four members. According to their self-produced documentation, they assembled to:

> Create exhibitions, actions and projects emanat[ing] from common experiences of battle or harmony between art and family. We want to be inspir[ed] by the most fundamental human relations, by the most profane household activities, by the strongest human feelings and also by connections between society and family.[7]

Mothers and Fathers have staged exhibitions of their multi-media works, musical performances, and public projects attempting to expose the conflicted nature of parenting and artistic identity. Their projects aim to reify the importance of the familial structure to the Czech public and to make them consider it anew. However, their very existence as an artist-group of parents challenges both the nature of the artist and the parent in contemporary Czech culture. They draw upon popular culture, art history, and the issues relevant to their specific context of living in a former Soviet territory to assert the importance of collaborative work. This is a complex notion given the communist history of the Czech Republic and the artists' experiences. The first part of this chapter situates the art-social group (as they define themselves) in relation to other artistic collaborations of the postmodern period, roughly 1960 to the present.[8] By exploring the nature of collaborations and collectives in the post-WWII period, one will better understand the formation of the group and how social and art history affected their status as a collective. Defining the nature of the collective, I then discuss the implications of Mothers and Fathers as a group (as opposed to an individual) identity. As a group, the artists are mobilized to explore their identities as artist-parents. Next, I turn to three major exhibition projects created and organized by the group that conveys their social, cultural and political concerns as artist-parents. In doing so, I show that Mothers and Fathers creates a socially, as well as personally, inspired art that reveals as much about the socio-political context of the family, parenting, and gender relations in the Czech Republic as it does about the nature of parenting for cultural workers beyond the country's borders.

Collaborations and Collectives: A Brief Social and Art History

Collaboration between artists is nothing new, nor is it unique to contemporary practice. Various scholars have asserted the prevalence of group activity via essays, for example on the guild-system in the Renaissance, as well as through exhibitions, such as *Collaborations: Artists Working Together*, which was organized by the Ruth & Harold D. Uris Center for Education at the Metropolitan Museum of Art in 1983, and *Team Spirit*, curated by Susan Sollins and Nina Castelli Sundell, and shown in various locations across the United States from 1990 to 1992.[9] These exhibitions considered collaborations of all variety: including Greek Vases created through the joint efforts of potters and painters, twentieth-century prints visualized through the "spontaneous expression" of a visual artist and writer coming together (*Collaborations*), and avant-garde and contemporary collective and collaborative enterprises (*Team Spirit*).[10] Artists who considered themselves Dadaists and Surrealists often came together for their whimsical performances, jointly developed collage techniques (John Heartfield and George Grosz), or to access the unconscious through the exercise of *corps exquis*. After World War II, the acclaim given to the isolated, individual artist grew, but this did not prevent groups from forming. CoBrA, for example, was a collaboration of artists and poets in the three cities of Copenhagen, Brussels, and Amsterdam in 1948. Artist partnerships grew in the 1960s and 1970s, with Gilbert & George, Bernd and Hilla Becher, Marina Abramović and Ulay, and Jeanne-Claude and Christo, serving as successful examples of the possibilities of collaboration. The conceptual movement of the 1970s and the social and political threats of the 1980s caused artists to form collectives such as Art & Language, Collective Actions, Colab, the Guerrilla Girls, and Gran Fury, which treated the collaborative art making environment in a different manner by allowing a more fluid membership. By the 1990s, artists such as the London-based group BANK found the act of collaboration to have expressive potential and rejected the allure of the artist as an individual. These affiliations set the stage for a group like Mothers and Fathers in the 2000s.

Scholars such as Charles Green, Robert Hobbs, Grant H. Kester, David Shapiro, and Reva Wolf have recounted the importance of collaborative activities as a means of dynamic production and social exchange, yet despite their championing of the collaborative, the formation of a group of artists who works together under one identity challenges the notion of the singular artist.[11] As such, the artists who comprise the group identity "Mothers and Fathers" create works alternatively attributed to the group and those individually recognized by each artist. They do this to provide autonomy to each individual member but also to collaborate in the contemporary period, which is significant, for as Green asserts, "collaboration is a special and obvious case of the manipulation of the figure of the artist, for at the very least collaboration involves a deliberately chosen alteration of artistic identity from individual to composite subjectivity."[12] However, this alteration, like identity, remains unfixed. The works created by Mothers and Fathers, such as *Bread (Chleba)* (2008), to some degree reject the notion of the individual creator, in order to create a universalist work that can address the condition of the parent (Figure 5.1).[13] The work, a large-scale soft sculpture taking the form of a half sandwich, refers to a child's lunch made by a parent—one that is cheap, and in their words, undesirable and largely tasteless. In the process Mothers and Fathers assumes a composite subjectivity that speaks as the parent. Yet, other projects like *What Would We Be Without Children? (Co Bychom Byli Bez Děti?)* (2007), that are carefully crafted on the actual body of each artist, do not lend themselves to group autonomy. So, what can we make of the artists who comprise this art-social group and what do we make of their activities in terms of the artist-parent identity?

In many ways, the solo artist remains highly celebrated, romanticized, and mythologized by art historians and the public alike. Proof of this may be found in the history of winners of the MacArthur "Genius Award," the Turner Prize, the Hugo Boss Prize, and the Golden Lion. These are some of the most prestigious honors awarded to living artists and looking closely at the honor roll one sees that the tendency to award the individual clearly remains. On the other hand, feminism has to attempt to dismantle

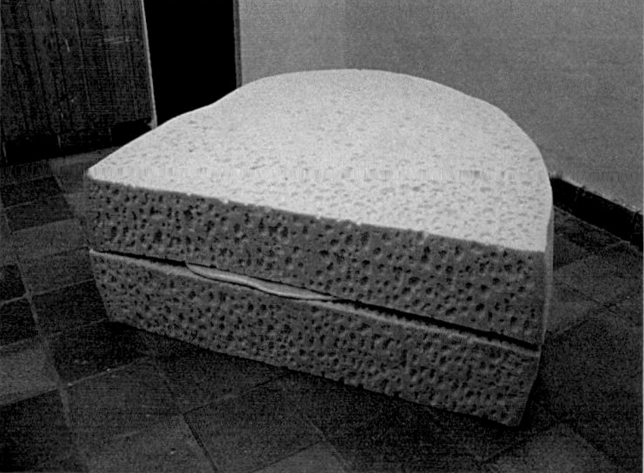

Figure 5.1 Mothers and Fathers, *Bread*, 2008, foam. Courtesy the artists.

the notion that the individual artist is male and perhaps as a reflection of this, Hugo Boss has awarded a little over one-third of its prizes to women; the Turner award has in recent years included more women on its short list and awarded six women artists since 2010. Notably, in 2015 the British collective Assemble received the award. If anything, these statistics reveal that the international art world as a whole still disproportionately values the male and individual creator, strongly suggesting that the choice to collaborate and create under a new name posits a risk to the very function of the artist and the artist's economic sustainability (i.e. the ability to provide for one's family). Ellen Mara De Wachter addresses this fact in her collection of artist interviews, *Co-Art: Artists on Creative Collaboration*, and points to the influence of politics of the Cold War as affecting artists' ability to collaborate.[14] Thus, Mothers and Fathers made critical choices when forming the mixed gender group, though they likely had no foresight of what those choices might mean for their role in the art world. Nevertheless, the fact that they set themselves apart in their formation as a mixed gender group, with a unique name, purpose, and process of art making surely has helped them survive as individuals and as a group.

The decision to join as two men and two women marks the collaboration, Mothers and Fathers, in a very specific way. The group is not a duo of related members, such as Jake and Dinos Chapman, the Starn Twins, or Jane and Louise Wilson, who draw upon blood relations, as well as choice, in their actions. The members of Mothers and Fathers draw upon a biological relationship, but not particularly to each other. Thus, the fact of their genders cannot be the root or even the sole subject of their combined work. If the Starn twins (even though they assert that their collaboration came naturally to them) or Jane and Louise Wilson dissolved their artistic partnership, familial bonds would remain.[15] This does not hold true for Mothers and Fathers. None of the members is related to any other; nor are they married or in an intimate relationship with each other.

Thus, neither represents a type of common collaboration, the couple.[16] Artist couples perhaps generate the most skepticism in the art world. Kristen Jones recounted the questions dealers and collectors asked of her and her partner Andrew Ginzel: "If I buy this piece, and they [Jones and Ginzel] stopped working together, whose piece would I have?" Jones further recounts, "It's almost as if working together is a recognition of the fact that we're mortals and that the identity of the individual who creates the work is not as important as what the work does for you," suggesting, very pessimistically, that the only reason collectors and dealers bought works was for the financial gain.[17] A work attributed to two artists no longer working together fundamentally has been seen to throw the authorship of the object into hiatus, or more optimistically, adds an asterisk behind the artists' names, with the explanatory "these artists no longer work together" statement.

The question of authorship in collaborations is a complicated one. For years, Ed Kienholz collaborated with his wife Nancy Reddin Kienholz, but only in 1981 did it become public that his works from 1972 on were co-authored with his wife. Their works have since become re-attributed to name both artists.[18] The same holds true for Christo, who in 1994, publicly acknowledged his wife Jeanne-Claude as a collaborator in their large-scale environmental projects.[19] When the works were attributed to solely Christo, however, Green asserts that the nomenclature was a "corporation, a trademark idea, and copyright ownership," as well as to the authorship of the individual, Christo Javacheff.[20] Green attributes the public revision of authorship to historical and political changes, such as the feminist movement, which allowed for greater women's presence and acceptance as artists in their own right.[21]

However, while artistic partners or duos deal with two voices, artist groups must incorporate several. In the 1970s, groups such as Collective Actions formed in Moscow, staging actions in open spaces to subvert the officially sanctioned Socialist Realist art. Their anonymity and ephemeral practices allowed them a greater sense of freedom and rebellion against the Soviet government and allowed a large variety of artists to engage with the group.[22] In this group, as with Art & Language in the United Kingdom and the United States, the title of the collective specifically references their artistic practice or mode of inquiry. It is important to note that even though both of these collectives erase individual identity, historical records are kept of the individuals who comprised the group and often of how they participated within it, and what they did. Due to the totalitarian government, only close friends and acquaintances of Collective Actions were invited to their staged actions and private exhibitions—there was a need for the activities to remain somewhat obscure under the purview of the official systems of art, as punishments, though no longer deadly, could be severe.[23] Thus Collective Actions carefully maintained an archive of documents, perhaps in anticipation of the time when public recognition of their work would not cause any negative repercussions.

The collective TODT, on the other hand, had no overt risk of punishment, but chose to eliminate all signs of individuality. The group takes its name from the old German word meaning 'dead' but can be pronounced 'tot' to suggest a child, or as a reference to the Nazi officer and engineer, Fritz Todt. The collaborative consists of three men and one woman who remain unidentified, making TODT "both a brand name and a statement."[24] Two members of the group are married to each other and the third is the brother of one of those two. Exactly what about their personal and biological connections influenced their actions is unclear, but the suggestion that their familial relationship affects their working relationship remains consistent in the scholarship on the group. Furthermore, an allusion to clans suggests a primal relationship between the members that extends their creative potential.[25] The search or unlocking of the primal was also one of the key subjects of investigation by artists of the New York School. However, TODT does not make the same claims of autonomy for its individual members.[26] When discussed or quoted in texts, they are named as 'TODT member' and not identified according to their given or surname. This is unique to this artist collective as far as I have been able to determine. Other groups, such as Art & Language, have members identified by their proper names when discussed or quoted.[27] Mothers and Fathers do not go to the extreme erasure of identity as TODT does, but what can be learned from this comparison is that Mothers and Fathers, when presenting their work, speak from the position of "Mothers and Fathers" that is a sublimation their individual identity. In other words, any individual member, who maintains the plural identities of self, mother, artist, wife, father, husband, etc., assumes an artist-parent identity when making as part of the group Mothers and Fathers. This hybrid identity, as the cultural theorists Stuart Hall and Néstor García Canclini have noted, exists as an "organic formulation resulting from the dynamic that takes place when trajectories of cultural production, social interaction and symbolic capital overlap."[28] As such, the mother identity of an artist results from the cultural expectations of two different trajectories—women and artists: the social interaction with other parents and artists, and the symbolic significance of 'mother.' Thus, as the individual identities of the two women members of Mothers and Fathers often fall back, their personal experiences as mothers and artists unite to engender their poignant discourse on parenting. The same, of course, holds true for the male members—they sublimate their identities as musicians, sculptors, fathers, husbands, and teachers to privilege 'father' when making work for the group.

This analysis of the workings of Mothers and Fathers' unique formation suggests a solution for life after collaborative work, as their model shows that a particular aspect of one's identity becomes omitted, supplanted, or replaced by another. This, of course, does not solve the institutional problem of labeling, cataloging, and categorizing an object. But, this model does suggest that collaborative artists, and ex-collaborators, perhaps ask questions of themselves and their art that foresee their changing identities. In today's society, individuals are under pressure to change their careers if the economic sector collapses, or their identities after a divorce (or the death of children or a spouse), clearly indicating that such questions are not moot.

This very condition is performed in the project *What Would We Be Without Children?*, exhibited in 2007 at Gallery C2C in Prague (Plate 13). For this project, each artist cast his or her own body in plaster twice, thus immediately making the works self-referential and *individual*. After casting their own bodies, the artists then sanded, carved, and molded their likenesses into their ideal, non-parent selves. Though they remained unpainted and ghosts of the individuals, both the finished and unfinished works have the potential to be read as bodies of parents and non-parents. Though indexical and mimetic of the artist's body, the works do not represent the personal identities of each.

The viewer is asked to consider the casts solely in a parental vision and determine the answer to the exhibition title's query: What would the artists be without their children? Is the cast of the male torso with the visible seams, and a rough and gritty finish the person without children? Or can one find the non-parent in the second version, which has a smooth, youthful and classically rendered appearance? Both are incomplete, but in differing ways (Plate 14). Each artist's variations are deeply personal and individual by the very nature of the introspective title, *What Would [I] Be without Children?*, but reveals little other than physical traits. In relation to the probing question of the project and exhibition, one might again consider the situation of Tracey Emin. Emin, who publicly denounced motherhood in return for wealth and art world-success has found herself middle-aged and without any offspring and reevaluating the choices she made when she was young and pregnant.[29] In her work, *Everyone I Have Ever Slept With 1963–1995* (1995), Emin appliqued the names of 102 individuals inside of a tent. The names illustrated people with whom she had shared a sleeping space, and two document the fetuses she terminated. Emin's decision to include "Fetus 1" and "Fetus 2" among the names served as a public acknowledgment of her decisions to not have children.[30] Though Emin can now claim great artistic success, the question can be similarly turned around to ask, what would she be with children? Could Emin have had children and become the artist she is today? Such queries are impossible to answer, though Marina Abramović controversially claimed in 2015 that her success as a performance artist laid in the fact that she never had children, which would have divided her energy.[31]

Though not related to one's parental role, Mothers and Fathers' *What Would We Be Without Children?* bears similarities to Janine Antoni's *Lick and Lather* (1993–94), a series of fourteen busts, seven in chocolate and seven in soap, that are based on Antoni's own image. Once cast, Antoni obsessively licked (the chocolate) and lathered (the soap) to personally confront what the mimetic image actually means—does cleansing do more to destroy the image than eating (licking) too much? Antoni's rigorous process, like the works by Mothers and Fathers, upends the notion of the portrait and what it suggests. Antoni effectively interrogates the female identity, ideals of beauty, and female purity through this project. She suggests that neither soap (with its connotations of cleanliness and purity), nor chocolate (which is often associated with women's indulgences) will truly comprise one's identity. In an interview with Antoni, Stuart Horoder commented that people feel close to her "because of the body-generated" nature of her work, yet it "doesn't reveal autobiographical information."[32] Mothers and Fathers, akin to Antoni, investigate how one who has children might feel. The group suggests that the child is an "obvious reason of unachieved aims, unfulfilled dreams or dissatisfaction with [their] own efforts, not only in art."[33] But it isn't entirely clear which of the two images represents the artist with or without children, if it can represent him or her at all. The casts are traces or indices of the body, but as philosopher Charles Sanders Peirce reminds us, the index functions as a remnant of a physical event and can never fully represent the event itself.[34] Thus while each artist of Mothers and Fathers takes their personal identity, full of their unrealized hopes and dreams, as the site of investigation, the resultant works and exhibition *Co Bychom Byli Bez Děti?* presented only the parental identity and revealed little of personal aspiration.

Artist groups have and had a fairly consistent, though mostly subdued, presence in the Czech Republic. The group format offered security and camaraderie in a society that was and is still somewhat skeptical and unsupportive of contemporary art.[35] Support for contemporary art has not received the level of public, private financial, and government support that has been seen in other Eastern-Central European countries, such as Poland, which has several internationally recognized contemporary art museums and centers within its borders.[36] Given the Czechoslovak post-World War I history, the creation of the Warsaw Pact saw the establishment of the Eastern Bloc, which in turn led to the Soviet invasion after the Prague Spring of 1968. Twenty-one years of normalization followed, which liquidated anti-socialist and anti-revolutionary forces resulting in the suppression of—sending them underground or completely prohibiting—dissenting voices.[37] The root of much of this 'evil' was also seen in Western consumerism and capitalism, which led to governmental blocking of direct access by Czech citizens to Western ideas and products.[38] After the Velvet Revolution in 1989, art ideas and objects from the West were slow to infiltrate the country, and few actually had the means to support the arts. As discussed in Chapter Three, much of the same occurred in Poland. But the Czech Republic continues to subsist its economy on the agrarian and industrial fruits of the land, while Poland has risen as an international business center, with what some consider one of the fastest growing economies in Central Europe.[39] And while the Czech Republic has grown economically since its split with the eastern portion, now known as the Slovak Republic (1993), public and governmental support for contemporary art and artists have been stagnant.[40] Even today the Czech public remains skeptical of the contemporary art world and is much more willing to support exhibitions highlighting the work of artists from the past or from other countries.[41]

Czechoslovakian artists such as Skupina Ra and Skupina 42 formed groups in the 1940s to resist socialism and support each other against the threats of the State and continue their art practice. Both groups focused on the tragedies of war, often making works with existentialist meanings using the language of surrealism.[42] In recent times, groups have formed on the grounds of a common interest, goal, or standpoint, choosing a name that demonstrates their "energy, irreconcilability, determination, and strength."[43] More recently, the groups Tvrdohlaví (The Hard-Headed or Stubborn), RAFANI (Werewolves), and Ztohoven (translating to The Way Out or 100 Shits, depending on how you place emphasis) formed to convey their members' frustration with the status quo. Tvrdohlaví formed in the mid-1980s and created works that played an "ironic game of empty symbols," that highlighted how "far removed the patriotic cliché of family, state, and nation was from their true content."[44] RAFANI, on the other hand, was founded in 2000 as an "open, democratic, and collective structure for artistic action within the society," creating works that highlight the communist history of the country. As a group of "young (angry) men" one of RAFANI's first projects, *Love* (November 14, 2000), consisted of members painting the Lennon Wall dark green, the color the communist police used to censor dissident messages and graffiti, and wrote the single word "love" to remind viewers of the values of democracy.[45] Ztohoven functions as a group of Czech guerrilla artists who stage "artistically motivated pranks," such as painting a large question mark on the twenty-meter-high, neon red, *Heart Over the Castle* done by artist Jiří David in 2002. The heart, erected at the Prague Castle, functioned as a symbol associated with Vaclav Havel's signature.[46] Ztohoven's intervention, which could be viewed from afar, publicly questions who would succeed Havel's presidency.

Despite the presence of these highly political groups, Pode Bal has proclaimed itself to be one of the first to politicize art in the post-socialist situation. They actively exhibit in a "totalitarian manner," and address issues that are historically and currently reflective of their Czech context, such as, "the link between the new ruling elite and collaborators of the former secret police, the forced departure of the Sudeten Germans from Czechoslovakia in the aftermath of World War II, anti-drug legislation, as well as criticism of the institution of the National Gallery."[47] Formed in 1998, Pode Bal could be considered an antecedent to Mothers and Fathers, for they are based in the same city and focus their activities within the local and national context, though none of the members has claimed this relationship. The artists surely know each other; the artists who comprise Pode Bal have run workshops in Prague, participated in exhibitions, and both groups have shown work on the *Artwall*, a public art space along the Vltava River in Prague. Pode Bal's membership, like many other collectives, is fluid, yet has retained three primary members, Petr Motyčka, Michal Šiml, and Antonín Kopp. Though the aims, longevity, and success of these various artist groups have varied over the years, they share the drive to form, group, and collectivize in efforts of survival, a notion that is not, however, altogether unique to the Czech situation.[48]

Examples of the collective structure and its benefits can also be found among feminist artists beginning in the 1970s and lasting through the 2000s. Feminist groups are an important counterpoint to Mothers and Fathers because they often came together for very specific personal reasons, such as their interest in gender issues or roles as mothers. Together they affirmed the importance of working together to develop a community for themselves to discuss issues often relegated to the private, domestic sphere. Mareia de Socorro, a member of the Hispanic-American muralist group, Co-Madras Artistas, has spoken quite eloquently on this subject: "Solo, we are not that important. But as Co-Madres, we are giants. We belong as a whole to the community."[49] Co-Madres Artistas, a group formed in 1992, use their work (typically easel paintings) to discuss pertinent issues of the Chicano community and the power of women.[50]

They, like the group, Mother Artists Making Art (M.A.M.A.), a collective based in the Los Angeles area, make the rights of women a primary concern. M.A.M.A.

members find sanctity within the group structure which, in turn, allows them to stage performances such as *Milkstained*, where a nude woman lies on a pedestal, her back turned toward the audience, all the while a white substance flows down her back to the sounds of a breast pump. Simultaneously other M.A.M.A. members read texts about their own experiences breast-feeding. This performance culminated with M.A.M.A. members expressing their own milk, filling plastic champagne glasses, and then offering them to audience members. Andrea Liss, who has written extensively on the group, proclaims this performance a "challenging gesture toward characterizations in the Western philosophical tradition of women's and mother's bodies as chaotic and disorderly because of our uncontrollable, hysterical fluids—blood, milk, emotions, tears."[51] Such a performance challenges not only the Western philosophical tradition, as Liss asserts, but also the boundaries of what is socially acceptable, particularly among a general public, or non-parents.

In focusing visually as well as verbally on the political interests of the family, Mothers and Fathers, like Co-Madres Artistas and M.A.M.A., attempt to create a community. By making the private and domestic—the parent and the family—a part of public discourse, the group structure forms a community, a support system for the artists that places the issue (whether breast-feeding, cleaning up after others, or gender roles within the home) into a greater public discourse. Communities, as Benedict Anderson argued, are imagined and perceived through mutual affinities.[52] They, like identities and language, are formed out of similarities and differences that are only evident when encountered with the 'other.' Mothers and Fathers distinguish themselves from other Czech artist groups like Pode Bal, Tvrdohlaví, RAFANI, and Ztohoven through their focus on the politicization of the family, the personal, and the domestic, rather than on the mainstream political issues that have affected the former Czech Republic.

On Naming and Authorship: Mothers and Fathers

The fundamental difference in comparing an artist duo to an artist group like Mothers and Fathers lies in the identity politics of naming. Take for example, Marina Abramović and Ulay, Anne and Patrick Poirier, or Jane and Louise Wilson, who retain their full identities; or Komar and Melamid who only use their surnames for their collaborative work, Gilbert & George, who only use their given names, and Boyle Family, which identifies according to both surname and the marker 'Family.'

With a collaborative like Gilbert & George, the removal of surnames is significant for the erasure of identity the artists strive to attain. Gilbert & George could be brothers, they could be lovers, or they could be a corporation, akin to what Green asserts about 'Christo.' Gilbert & George, one must keep in mind, aspired to be and maintain themselves as "living sculptures" in the 1970s and thus maintained a very strict manifesto filled with spelling errors. Their "Law of Sculptors," published in the May 1970 issue of *Studio International*, proclaimed:

1. Allways be smartly dressed, well groomed relaxed friendly polite and in complete control.
2. Make the world to believe in you and to pay heavily for this priviledge.
3. Never worry assess discuss or critisize but remain quiet respectful and calm.
4. The lord chisels still, so dont leave your bench for long.[53]

These actions mean to minimize the visibility of George (Passmore)'s and Gilbert (Proesch)'s individual personalities, preferences, and tastes. Gilbert & George may have different physical features, heights, and personal beliefs, but in their collaboration, their mannerisms were mimed or mitigated to nearly identical gestures to create the alternative identity Gilbert & George.[54] Similarly, Mothers and Fathers took on a new identity when they created objects for their exhibition *Mothers and Fathers Offer (Matky a Octové Nabízejí)* (2002), in which customers were able to purchase items such as dirty dishes. No longer do the singular identities of Lenka Klodová, Lucie Nepasická, Martin Péč, or Marek Rejent matter; what counts is their intention as mothers and fathers to provide a critical artistic discourse on the domestic to the public.

The choice to be called 'Mothers and Fathers' is telling. They are not simply 'Co-Mother Artists' as Co-Madres Artistas, or 'Mother Artists Making Art,' they are both mothers *and* fathers *and* artists. In one of the first texts to be published on the group, the Czech scholar, Radek Wohlmuth, commented, "They might have combined their names like ABBA. They might have created two typical non/functioning married couples," but they did not.[55] They chose 'Mothers and Fathers'; immediately the name draws upon the familiar, the family, and suggests something of the individual identities of its members, if not revealing them entirely. Mothers and fathers are people with whom others have intimate, loving, troubled, and sometimes antagonistic relationships. To take such a name for an art group significantly imbues the personal roles with public meaning. As Wohlmuth asserted,

> the group seems to, at least at first, assume avant-garde attitudes or convictions, but they also manage to appear to be sociological or biological. But this name should not immediately connote the sweet or saccharine as "mothers and fathers—the parents—always impl[y] supervision, suppression, danger, and hidden threat."[56]

Thus, Mothers and Fathers is not a name to disregard or dismiss. The group may sound like they are non-critical, but the issues they raise about domesticity and parenting are not—and as I have discussed, parenthood is not always perceived as a welcome, critical presence in art.[57]

Like Jabłońska's appropriation of the Polish Mother stereotype, Mothers and Fathers' appropriation of the gendered family terms 'mother' and 'father' inherently reference the power struggle within patriarchal systems. Are mothers and fathers equal in this collaboration? Does only the mother or father care for the rest of the family? As with many collectives, they are often identified, guided, or spoken for by one dominant, or more successful, member who can perhaps be viewed as the maternal or paternal member of the group. Art & Language, for example, is often discussed in relation to Joseph Kosuth, who is one of the more famous American members, or founding member Terry Atkinson, or Charles Harrison, who acted as the manager of the group for a period of time.[58] It seems that when discussing a collective, it becomes easier for others to relate to the idea, the concept of the group 'author,' if one mentions the most famous person to come out of the group. Importantly, these external choices of acknowledgment do not always translate into the way the collective operates. Michael Baldwin asserted in his co-authored text, "On Art & Language," that the collective "did not work as a group. … We sought, or perhaps I sought to blur the edges so that it would not be possible or necessary to decide who or what constituted the membership of Art & Language, not to be the authors of our work so much as agents in a practice that produced it."[59] Similarly, Mothers and Fathers did not always create works collaboratively, though their projects were mutually agreed upon. The members would typically meet for a few beers at a local pub, discuss their individual art projects and private lives, and through the nature of their conversation, they would come to an idea for an exhibition or project that would strike their communal interest.[60] The artists would then return to their respective studio spaces (they do not share a studio, though some have studios in the vicinity of each other) and create their agreed upon part of the project.[61] When completed, the works would be displayed as by Mothers and Fathers.

In this form of group authorship, Boyle Family provides a fascinating counterpoint to Mothers and Fathers. Boyle Family, like Mothers and Fathers, is a mixed-gendered group based on the family structure—they are all members of the same family. Unlike the participants in Mothers and Fathers, Boyle Family had a father, Mark Boyle, speak for the activities of the group. Mark Boyle and Joan Hills began collaborating in 1969. Their children Sebastian and Georgia joined in their artistic environmental studies and archival projects (they are most famous for their ongoing project *Journey to the Surface of the Earth*), and as they got older, they joined their parents to form the entity "Boyle Family."[62] However, in public discourse, Mark Boyle would take the primary role, explaining their work to the public, and often suggesting his ownership, or at least leadership of the group, using the pronouns 'I' or 'he' instead of 'we' or 'they.'[63] Mark Boyle effectively enacted his patriarchal role in the family and elided the role of the other members. Despite his spokesman role, Boyle asserted that Boyle Family was structured as a democratic, communal, artistic 'family.'[64] Akin to Boyle Family, Mothers and Fathers has a mother who does most of the speaking for the group: Lenka Klodová. Klodová, who has exhibited widely as a solo artist, maintains the group archive, and has claimed to be the driving force behind the group's inception. She has stated that she often includes works created by Mothers and Fathers when sending samples of her own work to curators.[65] This suggests that in contrast to Boyle Family, the group operates according to a matriarchal family structure, which, to some degree, parallels that of the Czech family structure. Hana Maříková noted that women typically have a lot of decision-making power within the family structure that borders on a matriarchal system.[66] As in Boyle Family, the group does not simply follow the lead of Klodová. Ideas are generated and refined by all members through lively banter and careful introspection. They similarly decided to pay homage to each member's personal history through a series of art projects for each other's village of residence. The first of these occurred in 2005, under the title *Vitrina (Showcase)*, in Marek Rejent's hometown of Proseč.[67] Rejent's task was to secure the exhibition space in the village while the other three members decided on the subject of the work itself. Rejent obtained permission to mount the Mothers and Fathers project on a public notice board (situated between two road maps of the region) while the members decided how to employ the space. They chose to create a poster-collage in celebration of a woman's first menstrual cycle.[68] Featuring photographs of groups of old and young women standing and seated around a table, Mothers and Fathers placed a distinctly private female-only experience, its associated celebrations, and their spaces into the public mixed-gendered realm. The occurrence of a woman's first menstrual cycle traditionally signifies a girl's entry to womanhood.

The discourse of menstruation in art has been famously present in contemporary art practice in the United States since the 1970s with projects like the *Menstruation Bathroom* (1973) by Judy Chicago in *Womanhouse* and Carolee Schneemann's *Blood Work Diary* (1971), in which Schneemann arranged bloodstained pieces of tissue in a grid format.[69] However both of these artists placed their works into art spaces, which is not quite the same as placing it into the public domain, where the non-art enthusiast must encounter it. Considering the relatively small populations of Czech villages, such projects are doubly risky when the artist lives in the village. One's fellow villagers could directly criticize such a choice in theme, and one would have to literally live with, or next to, the criticism. However, such a situation proves the power and potential of collective-based art-making: The individual artist is omitted and erased, while the group identity, Mothers and Fathers, has the voice to discuss what the individual may feel pressure to censure.

Thus, the difference between Art & Language, and Mothers and Fathers and collectives who use the artists' surnames or given names, lies in the power of *naming*. The power that names hold has been much contested by theorists—Stuart Mill argues that names "do not signify but point to a referent" which, applied to Mothers and Fathers, means that the name points to the idea of mothers and fathers' in a non-specific way.[70] To the linguistically inclined philosopher, Julia Kristeva, who has given the act of naming close scrutiny, it as

> a substantive of definite reference (therefore similar to the demonstrative) but of indefinite signification (cognitive as well as 'emotive') arising from an uncertain position of the speaking subject's identity and referring back to the pre-objectival state of naming.[71]

In other words, names have plural meanings that change and fluctuate according to the position of the person speaking. Thus, the members of Mothers and Fathers not only announce their biological roles as mothers and fathers, but also the potential of this role to function as the source of a critical artistic discourse with which the public can engage.

What is evident through this history of collaborations and collectives is that collaborations involve artists bringing their individual personalities to the group and retaining them to some effect—either through individual style or personal name. Collectives, on the other hand, can have a fluctuating cast of actors that continually operates under the group identity. Artist collaborations combine names or identifying marks, such as Kukryiniksy, for instance, the Russian group of Mikhail Kuprianov, Porfiry Krylov, and Nikolai Sokolov, taking part of their names to form a new entity; or Gilbert & George, who erase personality but would not exist if there were no George or Gilbert. These types of collaborations are what Arthur C. Danto terms a "conjunctive collaboration," in which all parties need to participate in order to assert the work as by that group.[72]

To illustrate how the conjunctive collaboration functions in Mothers and Fathers, in 2004, Mothers and Fathers organized the exhibition and performance, *Happy and Merry (Šťastní a Veselí)* at Gallery Tropic in Prague. The idea behind the exhibition was to celebrate the artists', and their partners', suffering for their art actions. Each artist was to ask his or her partner to pose for the camera being crucified on the cross. This image was then enlarged and made into a photographic silhouette that would be then hung from the gallery ceiling in conjunction with the live crucifixion performance of the artists themselves (they stood on a ledge built into the crucifix and had their arms outstretched). Rejent's wife, however, refused to participate in the work. The celebration of being a spouse of an artist, according to Marek Rejent, was not something she for which she wanted to be known, despite the group's intentions.[73] In lieu of her image, the group hung a blank silhouette to record her absence. This action thus completed the representation of the spouses, and revealed the complicated nature of collective artistic actions and the balance of domestic life. Is the work authored by Mothers and Fathers if only three or two of the members participate? If one considers the project *Štastní a Veselí*, each member must contribute to the project in some way for it to be a work by the group.

To further develop the complicated nature of the identity politics of Mothers and Fathers, one must also consider the issue of language, abbreviation, and limitation. Mothers and Fathers are comprised of Czech artists, thus their name is naturally written in the Czech language, a complicated and relatively obscure language in terms of global discourse. Employing a language that is foreign to most of the international art world suggests that their primary audience is a local one; however the group also frequently translates their name to English which enables the non-Czech speaker to understand, to identify, the group and their art. Yet, given the Czech Republic's location within the continent, it would have just as easily been translated into German or Russian, which are both commonly heard and spoken tongues in the Czech Republic. The choice to translate the group identity to the English translation recognizes and places the group within the most frequently used language of global contemporary art discourse. In 2000, Susan Snodgrass remarked on Czech artists' desire to enter the international stage and that to translate one's name certainly aids that goal.[74]

Mothers and Fathers also commonly abbreviate their name to "M+O" or "M&O" which, like Art & Language or Gilbert & George, incorporates the corporate entity, making it seem like Mothers and Fathers is a business and the works that will be seen and produced will be commercialized, ready for consumer consumption, and without sentiment (the latter being far from the truth). To add to this plural Mothers and Fathers identity, sometimes the group adds the acronym, "ltd." to the end of their name. This addition, according to Wohlmuth, modifies the preceding terms, suggesting that, "the abilities of everyone are limited."[75] While Wohlmuth's interpretation certainly has its merits, I suggest another interpretation. According to the Oxford English Dictionary, "Ltd." is a term typically added to business names to denote "the position or state of being legally responsible only to a limited extent (usually the amount of one's stock or shares) for the debts of a trading company of which one is a member." If one considers this association, questions regarding the capital Mothers and Fathers have invested in the corporate identity *Mothers and Fathers, Ltd* arise. For which aspects of their art practice do they become "legally responsible?" They shroud themselves from individual blame in the project of Mothers and Fathers, and it seems to me, protect their ability to speak from a "parental point of view."[76] The individual is protected through quasi-anonymity and can speak of the parental problems often left unsaid for artists and non-artists alike, though they may be criticized or condemned for doing so. The group members are able to do much more together than they would be able to alone. They find mutual solace in their roles as parents, as artists, and have found a means to continue their activity. Torn down as they may have been as individuals, their identity as *Mothers and Fathers, Ltd* protects them and pushes them to investigate greater depths of the artist-parent problem.

Selling Domesticity: Consumption, Parenting, and Family Life in the Post-Socialist Czech Republic

The status of the artist-parent is widely ignored in broader public and artistic discourse in the Czech Republic. Indeed, maternal and paternal issues have only recently arisen as issues worth discussing in the public arena. After the fall of the Socialist enterprise in 1989, women's and parents' rights took a fascinating turn that was not expected by western scholars. In terms of feminism and the definition of private life, scholars based in the former socialist countries have recently made strides acknowledging the ironic transitions, public opinions, and perceptions that occurred between the years 1990 and 2010. During the communist period, women were praised as workers but were also expected to perform all the household duties. Even in dissident circles, "women's work was made invisible because it was doubly privatized as the household (private) was split into political activities (public) and basic maintenance."[77] In this negation of women's work, family and domestic duties were kept separate especially when the home became the place of dissident discourse and thus a type of public forum. The relationship between public and private and the domestic has always been somewhat conflicted. Mothers and Fathers capitalize on and investigate these aspects of everyday life in their country. They attempt to make the private issues of family public through three very specific projects: *Mothers and Fathers Offer* (2002), *Family Art Crimes* (2006), and *Bared!* (2009). These projects engage private concerns and attempt to push notions of domesticity, family, and parenting as critical topics for public discourse.

The Czech Republic's transition from a communist to capitalist society has been felt very strongly by its citizens. The ability to buy items from the west, as has been evidenced through the studies of several scholars, has transformed the way in which societies function, and ultimately influenced family life.[78] Mothers and Fathers witnessed this transition in their lifetime and one of their first projects together, *Mothers and Fathers Offer (Matky a Octové Nabízejí)* (2002), took mass consumption as its subject (Plate 15). Visitors to the exhibition could purchase items inspired by the household rubbish and problems of everyday life: *Dishes (to Wash)*—a plastic-wrapped pack of dirty dishes (Plate 16); *Father: Decoration*, a plastic-formed model of a father or *Mother*, a plastic-formed model of a mother (Figure 5.2); *Ružena: Bra*

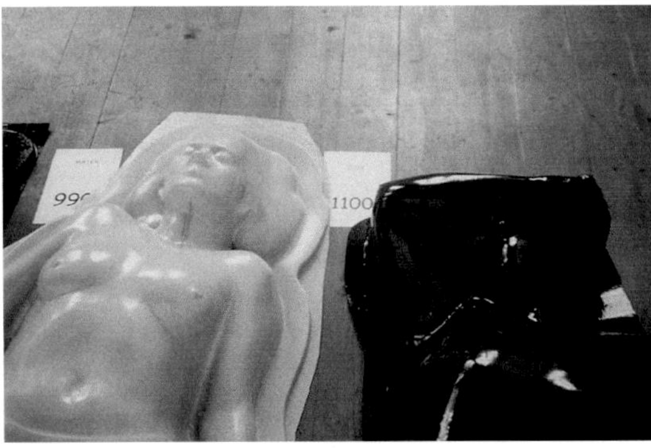

Figure 5.2 Mothers and Fathers, *Father: Decoration* and *Mother*, from *Mothers and Fathers Offer*, 2002. Plastic vacuum-formed molds. Courtesy the artists.

for after Children, bras that make your breasts sag as they do after having children (in size 80B); *Child Pillows*, pillows in the shape of children to sleep in bed with you; *Old Doll; Undressing: Decoration*, boxers and pants held in the shape you would find them on the floor; *Sand*, a parcel of sand cast in resin holding children's sandbox toys; *Mother Sleeping Bag*, sleeping bags with a woman's face on it; *Emergency Light*, emergency lights with messages which state: "clean it," "finish it," "slippers" and "brush your teeth"; and *CD hudební*, a self-produced *Mothers and Fathers Band* compact disc of lullabies.[79] These items, according to Wohlmuth, draw upon both the Duchampian readymade and Warholian pop art for their multiplication, perfect packaging, and premade nature.[80] While this relationship is certainly apparent, I contend that this exhibition project by the group is more akin to Claes Oldenburg's *The Store* (1961) in function, meaning, and visual traits than to Warhol's style of Pop art.

In 1961, Oldenburg opened a small shop in the Lower East Side of Manhattan. In this space, he created plaster sculptures of everyday objects—such as socks, underwear, pieces of pie, fruit. Displayed in a disorganized array akin to the other over-filled shops in the neighborhood, Oldenburg sold them for somewhat reasonable, high-art prices. Though not the bargain prices a typical shopper would expect in a Lower East Side store, items such as *9.99*, a free-hanging sign, or *Dress Jacket*, were available for $399.95 and $49.95, respectively.[81] Prices were always set at "x" number of dollars and sixty-nine, ninety-five, ninety-eight, or ninety-nine cents, demonstrating a keen awareness of the consumer model; the idea is that people will pay $49.95 but not $50 is asserted through the ubiquity of ninety-nine cent values and thus, Oldenburg never rounded up his prices to an even number. Very clearly set on capitalist models of consumption and everyday life, Oldenburg chose to dismantle the New York artist-gallery-collector system, and achieved it through his easy-to-consume pricing and presentation. Critic Jill Johnson remarked in a 1963 review, "most of [Oldenburg's] products simulate the original enough to the point of arousing the same desire associated with the original," noting that the critical process of art collecting, observing, and admiring have been conflated with consumer practices and desires.[82] The exhibition project, *Mothers and Fathers Offer*, is clearly akin to *The Store* in its clear relationship to capitalism and consumer-based social practices. The items are for sale at reasonable prices: a bra, 329 kč ($10.44); sets of dishes, cups, or bowls, from 140 kč ($4.44); and the child pillows, from 69 kč ($2.19).[83]

Items in both stores were viewed according to existing store, rather than art, display techniques; items were cluttered, set on the floor, or on plates (if food items), in *The Store*. In *Mothers and Fathers Offer*, objects were set upon their packaging boxes, on pallets, hung from racks, or displayed on stands, such as Mothers and Fathers' *Kinder Surprise*, which displayed modified milk-and-white chocolate Kinder Eggs (sold by the Italian manufacturer Ferraro). These popular candies were adorned with various phrases revealing their 'child surprise' pasted over the wrappers. Set in their original packaging, Mothers and Fathers supplemented the branding power of Kinder, which widely appeals to children, by advertising the eggs as a "Surprise for Mothers and Fathers" and giving the potential-parents news of their future: "you have hope," "you have twins," "you have a girl," "you have nothing" (with an image of a condom), "you have a boy," or "you have nothing" (with an image of a female's underwear and an object that is akin to an intra-uterine device).[84] Selling for 39 kč ($1.24), the group played with the very nature of this object—the child's treat in egg form with the inner baby—the 'surprise' toy—and made it like a pregnancy test or a future-telling device for the buyer. Each consumer must purchase the egg to determine their parent future—boy, girl, twins, hope, or nothing. Making the very act of consumption about biological reproduction was a theme common among several objects in offering.

Among the objects for sale, the most expensive item at the Mothers and Fathers exhibition was the plastic father at 988 kč, which according to exchange rates for 2002, roughly translated to $32. Similarly, the most expensive item at *The Store* was listed at $899.95, a free-standing *Bride Mannikin* (1961), which suggests that both sets of artists recognized the higher consumer value for domestic partners.[85] Indeed, in his essay "Consumer Society," Jean Baudrillard posited the relationship between consumption and the kinship system articulated by Claude Lévi-Strauss. Baudrillard claimed that both the social system of marriage and the cycle of consumption produce languages of communication, of social allegiance that are posited to keep the individual within the social system.[86] Both Mothers and Fathers and Oldenburg conflate these systems of signs, taking the "sociological system" and "substitut[ing] [it] for a bio-functional and bio-economic system of commodities and products." That is, they provide biologically and sociologically inspired commodities which can be perceived as desirable by those who do not already have them. For example, Mothers and Fathers pushes the bio-functional and bio-economic system with their Kinder Eggs. They reference the economic model of fertility treatments and surrogacy by allowing one to 'buy' their children.[87] Similarly, one can purchase the plastic vacuum-formed models *Otec* and *Matka* or Oldenburg's *Bride Mannikin*, an expressionist-style painted plaster-covered muslin creation, from Oldenburg, to participate in the consumer cycle and humorously enter the social world.

With the vast variety of items Oldenburg offered in *The Store* he seemed to have no specific sector of the consuming public in mind.[88] Mothers and Fathers' products, on the other hand, appear to have been intended for the non-high art consumer partially because of the dearth of contemporary collectors and the pricing model of their works. Their ideal audience consisted of families, married couples, and single parents who could humorously supplement or, perhaps, replace elements missing or in abundance in their domestic lives. For example, a single parent could purchase an *Otec* and place him in their bed for companionship; on the couch, to make him appear as if lounging on the couch and doing nothing; or underneath a car, suggesting he is either fixing it or he has met his end through it. Indeed, these are the very scenarios Mothers and Fathers used to promote the work.[89] Alternatively, a woman who has yet to bear and breastfeed children can buy *Ružena: podprsenka po dětech* so she can experience what it feels like to be Ružena and have breasts that hang down to her belly (or alternatively, a male could purchase these items to experience this).[90] These objects draw upon the larger cultural perceptions of domestic life in the Czech Republic. Feminist scholars have remarked upon the clear gender roles that men and women fulfilled after 1989. After the fall of communism, Western feminist ideas came into the country. These ideas spurred criticism of the new gender roles being established—women were often working full-time along with their spouses, but also doing all the cooking, cleaning, and child rearing, allowing for the male to visit the local pub, pursue a hobby, or lounge around the house. However, Czech politicians encouraged women to return to the household. This move was viewed as 'exactly what women wanted' and significantly, as progress.[91] And as these ideas were verbally exchanged in the political arena, tangible changes such as the closure of nurseries and kindergartens transformed the structure of care and women's work. This was partially due to the lack of funding after the fall of communism, but also aligned with the popular notion that "children were happiest at home with their mothers."[92] Women were in many ways forced to return to the home and assume domestic duties, such as cleaning dirty dishes, picking up dirty boxers from the floor, and dealing with the present, yet unhelpful, male in the household. *Otec* clearly draws on this situation in his frozen position. With one arm over his eyes as if to block the light and legs akimbo, he appears fully relaxed and, if viewed on the exhibition poster, lying on a chaise lounge, sleeping.

And though forty-one years apart, the *Store* and *Mothers and Fathers Offer* reflect the economic situations occurring in each country and a similar interest regarding the role of the consumer.[93] The post-World War II situation led to a financial boom in the American economy. America was a 'superpower' and supermarket and mass media consumption were on a steady incline.[94] Artists responded to this phenomenon in great number, and in 1964 a group of artists, including Oldenburg and Andy Warhol, staged an updated and more collaborative version of *The Store, The American Supermarket* at 16 East 78th St. in New York. This exhibition combined art objects with real market items and displayed them in supermarket shelf arrangements. The exhibition, according to *Life* magazine reporter, Calvin Tomkins, existed in the "no man's land between art and life," and *The New York Times* reported that "prices were rather 'horrendous,' starting with $2 for an egg, $12 for a paper bag with silk-screened Campbell's Tomato Soup motif by Andy Warhol or a turkey motif by Roy Lichtenstein, $27 for a fake sirloin steak by Mary Inman and going up to $125 for one of Watts' chrome cantaloupes."[95] The consumer supermarket and the art market were conflated to the point that women, attempting to buy their family groceries, found themselves baffled by what they saw when they entered the store.

Certainly, the exhibition invitation for *The American Supermarket* aided in the potential consumer's confusion; drawing on the existing style of supermarket flyers, items were offered for various prices, including a Sirloin Steak offered for $27.50, Spring Lamb Chops at $12.00, and Andy Warhol's Shopping Bags for $12.00. Deceiving the reader, the hand-drawn star-shaped forms on the 'exhibition announcement' both include and exclude the author, or make it appear to be a brand name: for example, the "Andy" part of "Andy Warhol's Shopping Bags" is excluded, and the lines of the star partially block out "Warhol." In the lower right portion of the invitation, "Farm's eggs from 2.00" is circled and the author, "Watt's" is placed just to the left and only slightly enters the form. Such play of authorship and confusion between art and product point to the problems of the overlapping boundaries of consumption, consumerism, and art. Mothers and Fathers' own exhibition announcement employs very similar techniques. It features seven items available for purchase in a floating monochromatic field, using horizontally distorted star shapes to highlight prices (the largest and boldest text), title of item (in all capitals), and item description, if any (in lowercase letters). For the first exhibition in Prague, the flyer included the title "Mothers and Fathers Offer," as the headline, yet information regarding time, place, and location is otherwise omitted.[96] For the second, at Galerie U Mloka in Olomouc, the title is removed, and only the gallery information is provided. Thus, both subvert the consumer model by not revealing where the sale will occur, in the first instance, or what the premise of the sale is, in the second. It cannot be determined if these choices were intentionally made to reflect the market economy, the rising costs of consumer products and produce, or consistently low wages which had left consumption practices very conservative—and based on acquiring the best 'deal.' While better than waiting in lines for the few goods available, as many did during the communist era, the free market has not been kind to the Czech people. Very few can afford to collect 'high art' or even express interest in its possibility because the need to buy necessities with their money predominates. Thus, while Oldenburg aimed to subvert the gallery system and entice the everyday person by making his objects at *The Store* more affordable than the fine art that could be purchased at the major galleries, Mothers and Fathers placed their work in a gallery aiming to generate budding art collections, as well as to provide access to the ironic, tedious, and frustrating aspects of domestic life.[97]

The ability to purchase these items at a fairly reasonable cost, and the fact that some were apparently used, or in states of disuse, also references the principles of Oldenburg's *Store* as well as the American phenomenon of garage and sidewalk sales, where items are highly discounted to a fraction of their cost or simply given away.[98] Advertising and potential affordability may have driven potential consumers through the doors of *The Store, The American Supermarket*, Gallery One at the Academy of Applied Arts in Prague, and Gallery U Mloka in Olomouc, but what they encountered in each was something that challenged their consumption habits.[99] Potential buyers of *Mothers and Fathers Offer* in Prague encountered some surprise when entering the exhibition—many of the prices were slightly higher than advertised. Bras cost 540 kč ($17.13) rather than 329 kč ($10.44); *Otec* cost 1100 kč ($34.91) as opposed to the 988 kč ($31.36) for which it was advertised (*Matka* was slightly cheaper, and closer to the original price at 990 kč ($31.42)); and sleeping bags were 864 kč ($27.42) rather than 460 kč ($14.60), nearly double their price.[100] In Olomouc there was significantly less choice among the objects for purchase. Wohlmuth nicknamed this the "M+O Bulk Discount" exhibition, as Mothers and Fathers brought the remaining items and grouped them together in two small niches and did not have the large-scale arrangement of objects on pallets and packing boxes of the first show.[101] In one, bras and a sleeping bag were hung from laundry lines, child-pillows were clumped together in a pile on the ground, old dolls were arranged together, and there were only two remaining Kinder Surprises and a few underwear/pants, which were placed atop one of two packing boxes. In the other, one set of dirty dishes sat in the center of the niche; two squares of resin-cast sand, and another sleeping bag, were laid to the right; and to the left were two more pieces of crumpled pants and underwear. Propped up against the walls were the *Mother* and *Father* objects, a significant change from the always-prostrate-on-the-couch or bed position seen in the previous exhibition, and next to them, placed on the wall, the last emergency light. The effect of this exhibition was that of the liquidation sale—items haphazardly arranged and are somewhat unappealing, in either their singularity or low level of repetition. Perhaps to compensate for the lack of items available, or to articulate more precisely the premise of the exhibition, Mothers and Fathers staged an "action" to explain their domestic perspective. In unison, spaced next to each other to form a half circle, the artists took off their shoes, unbuttoned and unzipped their pants, and pulled down their pants and underwear at the same time. Carefully stepping out of their outer layer of clothing (they were fully dressed beneath the performance clothing), each artist performed an act of their parental and spousal frustration—they left the clothing on a floor for others to pick up. This action also explained one of the items for sale, *Undressing, Decoration*, which, in resin form, captures the shape of one's pants and underwear when they have been absentmindedly stripped off and left on the floor. As a permanent emblem of the parental and spousal frustration of picking up after each other, this object—as much as the performance by the group—speaks to domestic concerns, and publicly engages with them.[102]

Perhaps like Oldenburg and the artists who contributed work to *The American Supermarket*, Mothers and Fathers critique the practices of consumption. The group satirizes the family and humorously offers domesticity to those who do not have it. In these two exhibitions, Mothers and Fathers take the specific place of the family within Czech culture to the public forum, ironically advertising it as an object to be consumed—and wryly suggesting that one may not want this burden. The artists allow you to buy elements that represent their frustration with the family.

Though placed within the gallery setting, Mothers and Fathers found a way to reach the public with their concerns about the domestic. This concern is only heightened in later projects. Their commitment to the public engagement of the private roles of mothers and fathers in the post-socialist era breathes new life into debates regarding the family. Mothers and Fathers' 2006 project, *Family Art Crimes*, the subject of the next section, takes a critical stance on the social role of the family and the kitsch label it generates.

Confronting Kitsch: Making the Family Criminal and Public

Mothers and Fathers' public art project, *Family Art Crimes*, involves taking something 'criminal'—graffiti—and attempting to make it domestic, and vice versa.[103] In this installation, Mothers and Fathers adopt a new style for their work, one that is not their own or even their group 'signature'—graffiti—and impregnate it with the theme of the family. The artists, interested in commenting upon the specificity of their local culture, decided that the style of graffiti would be the best way to convey the potential for the family to be safe and comforting, and at the same time, threatening. The *Artwall*, a span of the Kapitan Jaroš Embankment in Prague, which supports the Letná Gardens on the Western side of the Vltava River, is an area laden with a political meaning (Figure 5.3). When the country was under Soviet occupation, this embankment, with its evenly spaced niches, was a place of Soviet political propaganda, as well as the supporting foundation for the monumental statue of Josef Stalin in the gardens.[104] In 2000, the American artist Barbara Benish, who moved to the Czech Republic after the Velvet Revolution, realized her project, *Flower Power*, on the wall, which stimulated artists' interest in this public forum for art and discussion. For the Czech Republic, much like Poland, the creation of public space via the *ArtWall* project provided the artists an opportunity to expose both Czech citizens and tourists to Czech contemporary art.[105] Organized through the Center for Contemporary Arts in Prague, and in existence from 2005 to 2008, fifteen exhibitions were mounted in the predetermined niches, with varying themes and results.[106] The *Artwall* became the successful method of introducing contemporary artists and ideas to a large portion of the population without forcing them into a museum or art gallery. The viewer is intended to be a person riding on the tramway, in the car, or on a boat in the river, moving from the outer parts of the city to the center and vice versa.

Using an artistic style thought of as a criminal activity and which is also often present on the Letná Gardens walls, Mothers and Fathers used the power of language couched in graffiti art to establish the larger political content of their work.[107] Graffiti is highly prevalent in the city, much to the public's disapproval. Anti-graffiti laws in the Czech Republic are often considered to be some of the strictest, and graffiti-focused

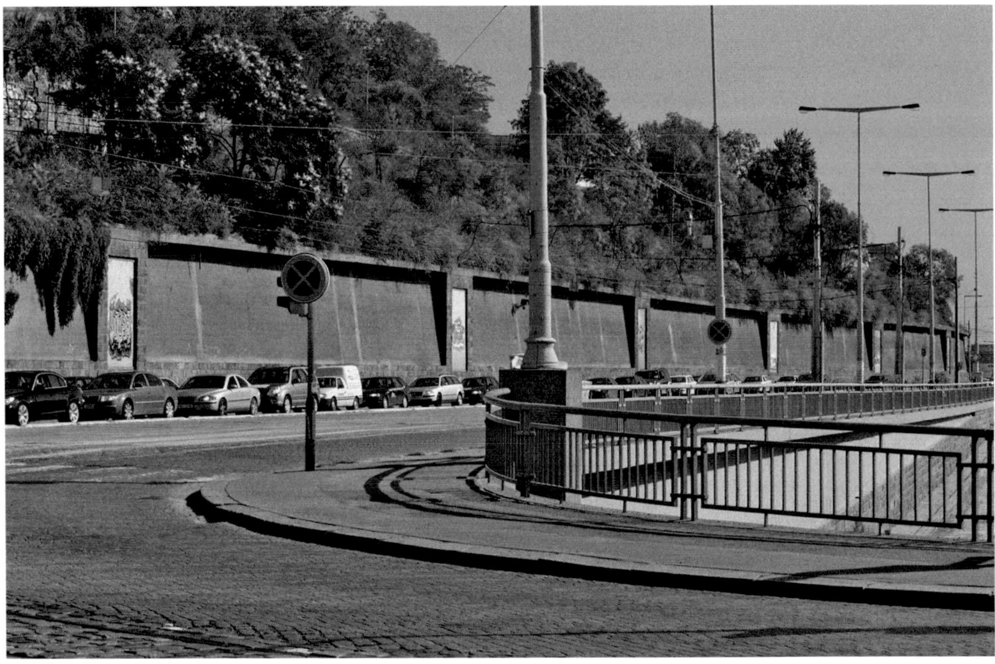

Figure 5.3 Mothers and Fathers, *Family Art Crimes*, 2006, digital prints. ArtWall public art installation, Prague, CZ. Courtesy the artists.

websites have claimed that police are especially violent when catching writers (the nomenclature typically employed to identity graffiti artists).[108] Graffiti art has had somewhat of a revival in recent years mostly due to the popularity and propaganda of artists like Banksy and on which Czech graffitists have capitalized. Although the Czech public largely considers graffiti to be an eyesore and a violation of historical integrity (especially when placed on buildings of historical or architectural significance), street art has had a home in Prague for some time: the Lennon Wall remains one of the most famous and consistent spaces of graffiti.

The Lennon Wall, located on the south wall of the building owned by the Knights of the Maltese Cross, and which faces the *Velkopřevorské náměstí* (Grand Priory Square), became a site dedicated to the memory of John Lennon in 1980 immediately after his murder. When the messages (typically dedications to Lennon) first appeared, the government, then under the communist leadership of Gustav Husak, had the wall whitewashed. By the next morning, the wall was once again covered with messages of love and peace.[109] This form of writing became a site of public outcry against the state, but also formed a place of community engagement. Though the messages on this wall are not all by highly skilled writers, this wall continues to exist in Prague as a unique site of sanctioned graffiti and one that has been recognized as having meaning greater than just simply writing one's street name.[110] However, the Lennon Wall is not the only sanctioned site for graffiti; the Names Street Art Fest was instituted in 2008, where a variety of international street artists were given spaces throughout the city to create a piece (short for "masterpiece"), some of which were retained for several years.[111]

Though the festival post-dates the Mothers and Fathers project, it does reveal that there has been a significant change of support for public art projects over the years.

While recent scholarship has asserted the importance of street art, popular opinion continues to consider graffiti to be the work of young and uninformed teenagers.[112] Mothers and Fathers attempted to find a common language to communicate the importance of family—how "cool" it can be and perhaps what repercussions it could have—when they took the terms for domestic life and the family—*Tat'ka* (*Daddy*), *Mami* (*Mom*), *Sourozenci* (*Siblings*), *Babička* (*Grandma*), *Vánoce* (*Christmas*), *Kaše* (*Mash*), and *Výprask* (*Whipping* or *Beating*)—and adopted a specific tag style for each. The group remarked on the difficulty of unlearning their own style and adopting a foreign tagging technique. They created several mock-ups, though they never used the tools of 'real' graffiti artists—that is, the group never employed spray paint. Instead, the artists used pastels and pencils to create the mock-ups that would be enlarged to fit the niche on the wall.

As they are more familiar to the trained artist, the pencils gave them greater control to create the variation of tone, depth, and symbolism for each familial word. Written in a strong three-dimensional and angular style that is reminiscent of shattered stone shards, *Tat'ka* is rendered in bright red and orange colors, suggesting the figure's fiery or eruptive demeanor (plate 17). Similarly, *Sourozenci* is written with each letter appearing like a piece of stone. The word rests on a green and purple island and has a purple shadow extending beyond each letter. *Mami* is written in baby blue bubble-letters, with bubbles floating around the word, providing it a sweet and almost saccharine connotation. *Babička,* on the other hand, is transcribed in strong block letters in bright pink. Thick hard lines outline the word, which has been split into almost a grid formation "babi" comprising the top, and "čka" the lower portion, recalling the emotive formation of the word "love" by Robert Indiana and the politically charged adaption "AIDS" by Gran Fury. Surrounding the term, there are three phrased: "bab" on the upper right, "babička" on the lower right, and illegible initials on the lower left. These letters frame the edges of the word-grid, acting as the artist's signature or possibly placing the term 'grandma' in a relationship of words, suggesting the ubiquity of graffiti art. Unexplainably, the term dědeček (grandfather), remains unvisualized, suggesting a minute importance for this family member, an absence, perhaps common for men of this generation of whom many would have participated in World War II, or even, a matriarchal family structure.

In accordance with the street-art style appropriated, Mothers and Fathers evoked the appearance of abandoned spaces by tearing the papers used for the exhibition. The act of tearing, especially associated with poster art, evokes the works of the *Affichistes*, such as, Jacques de la Villeglé and Raymond Hains, whose *Ach Alma Manétro* (1949) displayed the strategically torn, ripped, discarded, and overlapped posters in abandoned public arenas. The newly exposed layers of paper and wall transformed the original posters into artistic projects that investigated the internal nature of the aesthetic object as well as opening an aperture into the history of public events in the city. Like *L'Affichistes*, the destruction of the paper by Mothers and Fathers was a strategic technique used to inform new meanings. In *Tat'ka*, the paper has been torn away just below the text perhaps suggesting that a father can rise above destruction; *Sourozenci* has strategic places of wear in the top left corner and upper right, suggesting the strength of siblings to overcome adversity; *Mami*, surprisingly, is relatively untouched. A few horizontal cracks appear like varicose veins or wrinkles to suggest age and wear, but the text and rest of the poster are unscathed. And perhaps obviously, *Výprask* has the most violent tearing and largest spans of loss. Written in an active rectangular style, *Výprask* is enclosed by an orange-blocked frame and a splatter-style red field, as if the word was harshly thrown on a pool of red ink, transmitting the violence that the word connotes. Placed low on the field of the poster, this violence is reinforced by the great loss of the paper. It has been unevenly torn from the upper edge down to the image itself. With the rip damaging part of the outline, the play of words and images abounds. This tear might be the result of an angry burst, as easily as it could suggest a criticism of that type of parenting—to beat one's children, to inflict corporal punishment, remains one of the few domestic and social issues unreformed in the Czech Republic, in both school and the home.[113]

While choosing to highlight the names of family members clearly displays an interest in the structure of the family and its critical possibilities, the decision not to employ proper names to identify specific people in their tags is particularly striking. Rather, family roles are identified and terms related to family life are represented—*Kaše*, as in mashed potatoes, a common Czech meal; *Vánoce*, the Christian and consumption-based holiday; and *Výprask*, connoting the action of being punished.[114] These three posters convey terms about the dynamics of the family. One returns home for a meal, for Christmas, and if one misbehaves—or perhaps, is caught writing graffiti—he or she might receive a *výprask*. These domestic terms transform the project about the family to *Family Art Crimes*, demonstrating the criminal activity on many levels. On the one hand, these parents are creating the work of vandals, on the other, Mothers and Fathers assert that the real crimes are those of missing, ignoring, or whitewashing (as would be done with graffiti placed elsewhere) those moments of family interaction, both positive and negative. Of these images, Zuzana Štefková writes:

> [Mashed potatoes] and celebrating Christmas together will become a thing of the past one day and the only link which can stand the intergeneration alienation thus remains the ability to see one's own role—of children and parents, mothers and fathers—with a distance.[115]

Mothers and Fathers urge the viewer on the tram, car, or boat to see these images and be outraged, yet not for the graffiti aspect, for what the viewer may be missing as a mother, father, or grandparent, for the loss of the cohesive family life, taking a very private matter and placing it in the public sphere.

American feminism in the 1970s asserted that the "personal is political," a statement which combined the domestic with the public. Western-based feminist scholars often assume that this statement has universal applicability and is a means to exert critique of existing patriarchal structures. However, Eastern European scholars, such as Jiřina Šilková, Marie Čermáková, and Hana Havelková, have asserted that during the socialist era, the importance of the family was institutionalized, and the strict boundaries between public (political) and private (family) activities were conflated.[116] They assert that this situation made the family a compulsory space for female power and control, thus rendering the phrase, the 'personal is political' as moot for Czech women. However, as anthropologist Rebecca Nash has recounted, as these scholars posit that women were central, and the most authoritative figures in the home, they claim that women also were able to refrain from political activity "because motherhood and child-rearing were excuses for not joining the Communist Party."[117] Summarizing the work of Šilková, Čermáková, and Havelková from the 1990s, Nash asserts that these scholars posited the family structure as a retreat from corrupt socialist politics and created a safe environment for every member.[118] Given the perks families were provided under socialism, such as larger apartments and higher incomes, the end of the socialist regime (and thus the end of special perks for families) left the family structure less desirable for younger generations.

Mothers and Fathers affirm the applicability of the 'personal is political' statement in the Czech Republic in the 2000s. As mentioned previously, feminist ideas did not have their renaissance in the Czech Republic until the early 2000s, as women in the first decade after the end of the Socialist regime treated feminism with skepticism, doubt, and outright hostility.[119] By the late 1990s, Czech scholars' idealization of the family and descriptions of the woman's place in utopian language had significantly fallen off.[120] By the 2000s, the Czech Republic was assimilating Western culture, and as a result found that the dynamics of the family were shifting from tradition-centered to progressively modern, following Western feminist sensibility.[121] Women before and during socialism often were married and had children at a young age; however, by the 2000s they began to actively seek higher education and careers, postponing motherhood and sometimes moving away from their home village, somewhat destabilizing the family structure. Sociologist Herwig Reiter has asserted that "the postponement of motherhood, and the eventual resulting childlessness, is a phenomenon with an external, social cause that can find expression in individual behavior, attitudes and values, but without entirely losing its 'collective' characteristics."[122] Reiter, thus, on the one hand attributes historical circumstance and economic changes to this decline, and on the other, individual choice and preference.[123] Reiter concludes by noting that, "postponed motherhood cannot … be studied comprehensively by assuming clear-cut relationships between factors and variables," as multiple factors go into each woman's decision to put off motherhood.[124] The lack of children suggests the emphasis on work, and thus less time spent with one's family. As such, this delayed family has caused some to note the distancing of families. *Family Art Crimes* recognizes the private dissolution of family life, and attempts to bring it to public discourse. In a sense, it urges the viewer to remember the shared meal of mashed potatoes, the excitement of Christmas, and even, the nostalgia of being whipped by a parent or being a parent who punished their child. They are begged, in a sense, to remember both good and bad reasons why family is and was central to identity formation—that even though aspects of them are problematic, kinship systems are integral to social life, personal development, and our future as a culture.[125]

Other projects that were a part of the *Artwall* frequently introduced children, or the prospect of children, affirming the cultural importance of the family. Children seem to provide the means to generate a critical discourse that is otherwise omitted. In 2005, Klodová exhibited her solo project, *Victors*, in which she digitally altered images of sportswomen at their moment of victory to make them appear as if pregnant. According to Klodová, they are pregnant with their athletic prowess and potential for motherhood. She writes,

> Although it seems like there is nothing more simple than childbirth, for both parents it is rather like winning a race, for which they have strenuously trained both physically and mentally. Delivering a child is no less demanding than participating in a world tournament such as the Olympic Games. It is like winning a golden medal.[126]

In this instance, Klodová attributes the family to the already public figure and posits potential for women athletes to be celebrated as mothers, as well as mothers to be celebrated for the feat of giving birth.[127] This individual project considers the family, but in its infancy, so to speak. Other *Artwall* exhibitions by the group Pode Bal, or individuals such as Míla Preslová, prominently feature elements of the domestic to illustrate their political potential.

Mothers and Fathers are not alone in the present-day Czech Republic in their desire to make domestic tension along with family members the topic of their art. Like *Family Art Crimes*, Preslová's installation *Rituál* (2006) highlighted the desire for and tension of family bonds. She employed photographs of her family members, such as her son's face bound by a red nylon rope and white tape and her husband's arms bound and pulling on the very same red rope, to suggest that one's binding or suffering is always related to another member of the family. The rope can easily be read as an object that assists or prevents faltering, as the hands are reaching up, as if pulling one to safety, or tormenting, as if someone else is tightening the ropes and causing pressure on her husband's (and her son's) body. Preslová visually and figuratively renders the family as a network of associations, an interconnected structure that causes security and pain in seven simple images.

The use of the visual power of the language of contemporary graffiti distinguishes Mothers and Fathers' project from Preslová's, as one must visually infer the meaning of her images and infer the meaning related to the series title *Rituál*. Both, however, have a connection to collective Pode Bal's *Flagelanti (Flagellants)* (2006). Pode Bal's photographic project features children, but not their own, with handwritten signs around their necks to reveal the cruel secrets of the country's history. Messages such as, "You no longer need to suffer the fact that we denunciated one another during the normalization. I will suffer for you" and "You no longer need to suffer that we have handed over weapons to Hitler. I will suffer for you" address the viewer directly, and cause the viewer to read the secrets as if directly affecting the children pictured. Pode Bal aims to draw on the sordid aspects of Czechoslovak history such as the provision of arms to Hitler, the confinement of Gypsies in concentration camps, or the support of Husak, the communist leader of the 1980s. Children function as a medium to convey the messages—as people will be more likely to pay attention to images of children—which are quite poignant to Czech's history of normalization, where Czechs denounced each other in order to preserve their status as good citizens. On the subject of this exhibition, critic Klára Vomáčková wrote: "In the pre-election visual raid of stupid messages, these seven burning sentences work as a grounding blow—it stopped the voter's hand with the envelope, reminded, hurt a bit," suggesting that these crimes, like those highlighted by Mothers and Fathers, are still very real and present in Prague.[128] By employing children's relations to the family's elders, each of these artists poignantly discuss the personal and the political, bringing to light private memories, cultural history, and shame, into the public sphere.

Using their group anonymity, Mothers and Fathers expose the significant issues of family life. In sum, *Family Art Crimes* can be interpreted in several ways. The mothers and fathers are the threatening actors in the family structure, but they can also be viewed as the ones trying to make the public remember their families, and are perhaps desperately attempting to connect with the younger generation—a generation that has transformed due to the radical political and economic changes from the Eastern Bloc, to an independent Czechoslovakia, and finally to the Czech Republic. Alternatively sharp, bubbly, violent, and comforting, the language used by Mothers and Fathers captures the private family experience and attempts to generate public discourse. The success of this however may have been too great—several commuters believed that the panels of *Family Art Crimes* were actual graffiti, and this often obscured the deeper personal meaning individuals were intended to gain.[129]

Domesticity Runs Skin Deep

Making the private public is a recurrent theme in the oeuvre of Mothers and Fathers. In 2009, the group created *Bared!* (2009), a project that consists of photographs of their temporary ballpoint pen tattoos on their semi-naked bodies. The subjects of their "ink" initially cause the viewer to react with laughter, yet on closer introspection, one finds that there is nothing to laugh about. Their tattoos, which were highlighted in the "Family" issue of the Czech magazine, *Fotograf*, engage with culturally accepted ideas of the domestic gender roles of men and women—cooking, cleaning, education, and virility—as they pertain to the family. In each of these markings, the artist uses his or her own body to confront the stereotypical, but still active, gender issues artist-parents must confront—the woman-specific role of cleaning and cooking; the male-specific question of virility and fatherhood; and the parent-oriented (both male and female) question of, and responsibility for, children's education. The interrogation of the masculine and feminine roles is not uncommon within contemporary artistic practice; male and female artists continually explore the how, what, and why of what it means to be masculine and feminine; however what makes Mothers and Fathers unique is the equally divided attention to the stereotypes of both men and women.

The project's title suggests many things. Bared can mean, "not clothed or covered" or it can suggest being "unconcealed or undisguised." These definitions resonate in the exposed skin and underwear of the artists, and in the idea that the tattoos reveal the artists' participation and inclusion in a deviant subculture. In Czech, "bared" takes on another meaning, that of a child's corporal punishment—to get "bared" is to get smacked on one's bare buttocks, and endure pain.[130] This plurality of the project's meaning transforms the images from simply acknowledging the artists' relative state of undress, to drawing out questions of gender roles, parenting, and identity that arise due to the very subjects of their 'ink.'

Each member is shown semi-permanently tattooed with a blue ink pen displaying figurative and verbal elements that highlight domestic concerns: Klodová has the traditional Czech meal of a roast duck, cabbage, and dumplings emblazoned on her chest (plate 18); Nepasická has a mop drawn across her body from her chest to her right calf; Rejent has a suggestive electrical plug dangling down his thigh; and Péč has his son's school report card transferred to his chest and back. In each of the markings, I argue, the artists use their own bodies to highlight the negotiation that occurs between social expectations and private reality.

Tattoos, as anthropologist Clinton R. Sanders has recounted, mark one's physical appearance in a way that affects one self-definition, identity, and ultimately, how one is perceived by others.[131] Initially, Sanders argues, tattoos in Western society were a way of performing one's uniqueness or marginality, but they have become so popular that now those who wish to mark themselves in this way must resort to more extreme forms of body modification to "generate 'conspicuous outrage' among members of conventional society."[132] The designs chosen typically relate to one's connection to others, definition of self, and sometimes, desire to beautify the body. If these factors are considered in relation to *Bared!*, the designs the artists chose for their bodies convey very poignant meanings for their identities as artist-parents.

The women, Klodová and Nepasická, deal with their maternal identities and the responsibilities women generally assume. Despite the strides made for women to remain in the workforce as equals, domestic duties, like cooking and cleaning, remain the woman's responsibility in the Czech Republic. Klodová's tattooed image of a roast duck acts like a badge of pride or alternatively, as a burden, symbolizing the domestic duty continually attributed to women: cooking. This traditional meal takes several hours to prepare, from the slow roasting of the duck, preparation of the dumplings, and braising of the cabbage, all of which should be consumed at lunch, the most substantial meal of the day in traditional Czech culture. To have a meal ready by the noon hour, the mother (Klodová) must rise early in the morning, thus this meal becomes a particularly onerous burden. However, the preparation of food, and the eager consumption of it by others, including the family, has significant positive attributes as well. Frequently women's magazines remark that the preparation of food develops a means for women to create self-worth. Though the mother may not enjoy the cooking process, seeing her children and spouse consume these meals, grow strong from them, and possibly enjoy them, brings about a positive feeling or energy. In this line of thinking, only bad mothers do not cook for their children.

In the image reproduced in the magazine, Klodová's face and body is aggressively cropped so the lens only captures the area between her bra and chin. Breasts and duck distorted, it appears that the work is not being performed properly. (Klodová appears to be lying down with one arm above her body in a pose somewhat akin to that of *Father: Decoration* from the *Mothers and Fathers Offer* exhibition). This image reduces her identity, so that she becomes nothing beyond her potential to cook and nurse children. The bra, decorated with pink polka dots and various forms of ice cream desserts—cones, bars, and sundaes—suggests a kitschy, saccharine maternal nature and may be an intentional, ironic choice. A second image includes more of Klodová's body, forming a bust-type of portrait, though it was clearly taken from a higher vantage point, focused squarely on her chest. In this photograph, the tattoo of the duck appears clearly legible and her breasts are evenly contained within her bra. Klodova, however, with her half-smiling, oblique gaze into the distance suggests once again, that her duty regarding this meal is branded to her skin, to her body, but that her repeated performance of it is not voluntary. The framing devices, as well as her gaze, intone subservience, a submission to the domestic that suggests that this role has and has not defined her identity.

The images documenting Nepasická's *Mop* are similar in this regard. She has been branded with a mop that traverses her body, suggesting on the one hand, that she *is* a mop and that she is tied to her domestic cleaning duties (Figure 5.4). These two distinctions, while similar to the ideas addressed in Klodová's tattoo, champion the mother as the protector of the home while simultaneously the victim of it. The purpose of mopping is to clean floors or soak up an excess of fluid, which ultimately protects, maintains, and cleanses the home. However, it can also enslave one to the home. Feminist artists, such as Ukeles, have long investigated such "women's work" or labor, visualizing the unseen labor of the mother/wife/woman and transforming it to art in the space of the institution.

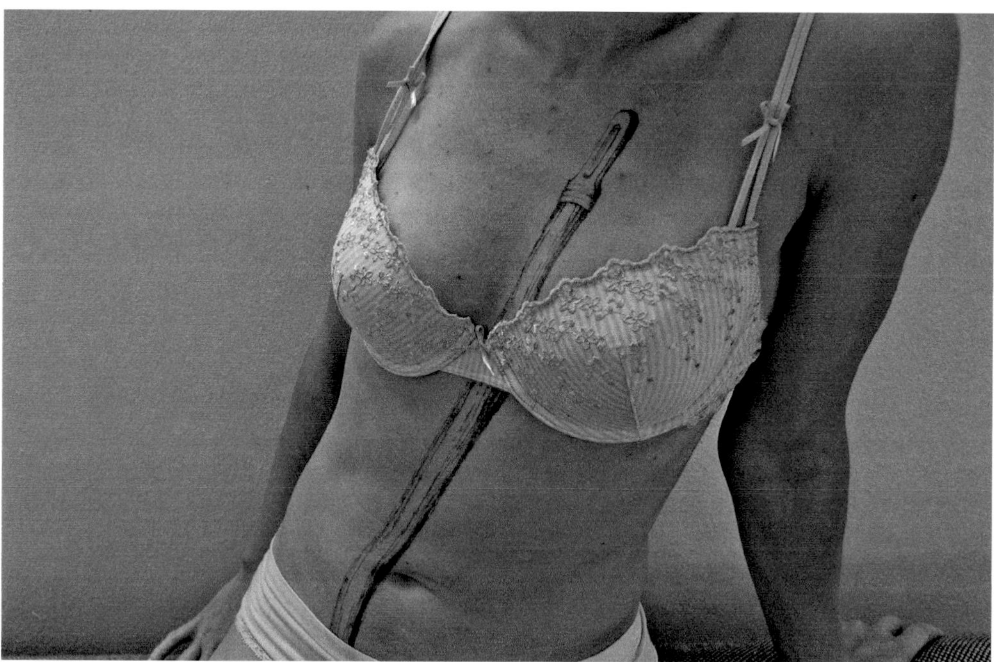

Figure 5.4 Mothers and Fathers, *Mop*, from *Bared!*, 2009, photographic project for *Fotograf* magazine. Courtesy the artists.

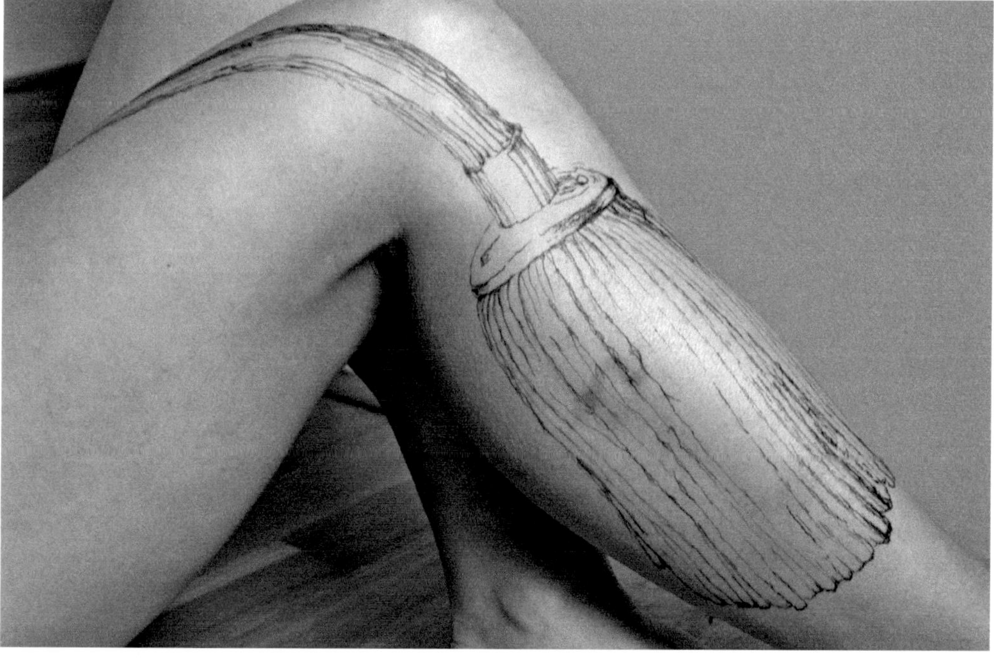

Figure 5.5 Mothers and Fathers, *Mop*, from *Bared!*, 2009, photographic project for *Fotograf* magazine. Courtesy the artists

Similarly, Mothers and Fathers attempt to draw awareness to such connections between motherhood and art. As such, the handle of the mop begins on Nepasická's chest slightly above and between her breasts and traverses diagonally down her stomach and ultimately to her right calf muscle (Figure 5.5). To have this instrument of domesticity branded across the body ultimately marks the female body as the site of the domestic, whether or not she is actually in the act of home-making. This association between the female body and the domestic has been a central issue within feminist discourse around the world. Women protested their relegation to the home, and sought ways to confront such oppression.[133] Women artists, over the decades, similarly confronted these ideas through their art projects—particularly in the United States. For example, another early project by Ukeles consisted of a series of photos taken by her husband, Jack Ukeles, which were published along with her Maintenance Art Manifesto in the pages of *Artforum* in January 1971. These images highlight Ukeles performing the female duties of "Dusting a Baffle," "Rinsing a B.M. Diaper," and "Mopping the Floor."[134] In "Mopping the Floor" Ukeles cleans the floor, knees slightly bent and barefoot. She, like Nepasická, effectively embodies the mop, and in their similar reproduction in print sources, they bring the private labor of women into the public realm. While Ukeles and other feminist artists from the West provide significant comparative ideas to both Nepasická's and Klodová's tattoos, it would be remiss to think of these images solely in terms of Western feminism. What Western feminists consider a universal battle for women's rights and equality has in truth been very different in the Czech Republic. From the pre-Socialist period, women were granted equal access to the workforce under the "feminist President" Tomáš Garrigue Masaryk, who implemented pro-women legislation while in office. Most of this carried over through the Normalization period.[135] Women thus never had to fight for their rights as suffragettes did elsewhere. While this fact does not negate the importance of feminism in the twenty-first century, women's access to the workforce comprises one reason why Czech women remain skeptical of feminism. As sociologists Marianne Ferber and Phyllis Raabe have recounted, women consider men as partners who support women's issues, despite the fact that they do little in terms of housework. In a 2003 study, Ferber and Raabe assert that, "Czech women take pride in being both homemakers and breadwinners, and strongly identify with both these roles."[136] Thus the interpretation that these tattoos symbolize badges of honor becomes less suspect, as they reaffirm the very identity asserted by my larger project—that of the artist-parent. These women assert their creative identities with the hand-drawn images marking their skin and, at the same time, allow those images to reveal the important duties they perform at home, for art and parenting.

The tattoos selected by the men similarly engage the artist-parent identity and reveal an even less researched aspect of Czech culture: that of the father. Rejent and Péč chose images that investigate the social expectations men encounter regarding paternity. Rejent's "jack plug" tattoo, on his thigh, erupts from underneath his shorts, suggesting the phallic and electric potential of his manhood (Figure 5.6). In the image selected for reproduction, Rejent leans against the wall, effectively lifting the cuff of his right short, exposing more of the plug and more aggressively suggesting his sexual potency. In a patriarchal society, the father should earn, create, and project his energy, and the failure to do so connotes not only his failure as a father, but also as man. Even in Czech society, men are largely held to their provider roles—they should financially support the family, have prowess, and not succumb to domestic duties. However, Czech men earn relatively low wages in comparison to other Eastern European countries, and

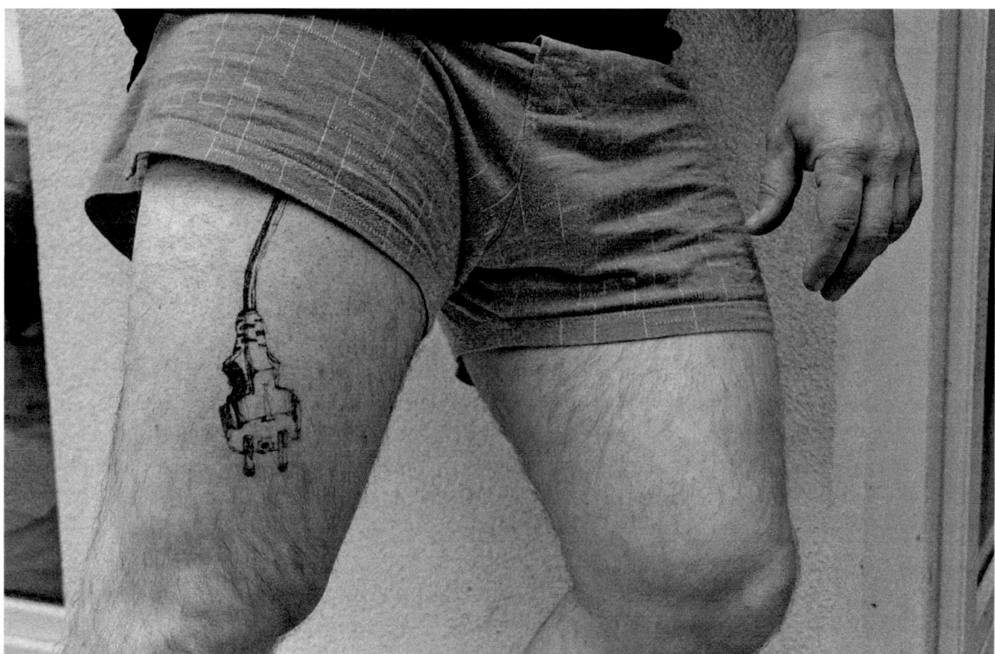

Figure 5.6 Mothers and Fathers, *Plug*, from *Bared!*, 2009, photographic project for *Fotograf* magazine. Courtesy the artists.

thus what Western feminists champion, Czech men may condone—Czech women must work to help the family survive.[137] Therefore, as Rejent employs this phallic symbol to humorously suggest his prowess, it simultaneously reminds the viewer of the cultural pressure put on men to provide, much akin to the presence of the penis in Ben-Ner's early work. Like the photographs of Klodová, the lens fragments Rejent's body, capturing only his waist down, effectively sexualizing and depersonalizing him. Though Rejent does not expose his genitals to the camera, this image recalls Robert Mapplethorpe's *Polyester Suit* in its framing and emphasis on the stereotype of the male body. Like in Mapplethorpe's image, only the lower portions of Rejent's body are captured, as if knowing the man behind the instrument is not necessary. The plug also infers that Rejent, the father, functions akin to an appliance, that is plugged in and turned on when needed. Thus, the father becomes an object that is kept in the home, collecting dust until needed, secondary to the family unit. It is striking that we do not see the 'tool' that is attached to the plug—it suggests a fluidity of items—it could be the cord to an iron or a vacuum—but it remains unknown. This secretive aspect could suggest that one kind of labor has the potential to be electrified in the Czech Republic. Rejent suggests this notion, but leaves it to the viewer to decide.

While Klodová, Nepasická, and Rejent become somewhat anonymous in the photographs, Péč does not. Choosing to highlight his son's school report card on his chest and back, Péč confronts the camera, asserting a very different statement about fatherhood. As in Ben-Ner's *Wild Boy*, Péč's tattoo focuses on the paternal duty to educate his son. In an unpublished image, Péč, bare-chested with arms behind his back, gazes confidently at the camera with a grim expression, as if his son's academic progress has been dissatisfactory, or perhaps, as if this report card truly is a reflection of Péč as a father. On closer inspection, one finds that the marks are good—Jóchym Péč earned the highest score in all subjects. An alternate view documents the opposite side of the report with Péč's back decorated with final comments, the emblems of the Czech Republic, and reports for non-academic items, like behavior and citizenship (Plate 19). However, it is the third, much different, photograph which was published and distributed in *Fotograf*: the image returns the focus on Péč's chest, this time face cropped, shirt unbuttoned and a three-quarter view—the viewer becomes enticed to peak beneath the shirt as if these grades are really part of Péč's skin and his identity as a father (Figure 5.7). His face and personal identity no longer matter; he will be defined by his son's actions and success.

In sum, Mothers and Fathers' project, *Bared!*, takes the gendered stereotypes of both men and women and explores whether they are truly 'skin deep' or if they go beyond the skin. While the tattoos and stereotypes they address are only temporary, Mothers and Fathers assert that the duties, pressures, and pain of parenting and domestic life remain. By engaging with tattoo culture, they use a transgressive form of art to subvert established notions of the family, and the kitsch it often connotes. They remind the viewer that parenthood, domestic duties, and the families become marked on the body and one's identity, regardless if one can visibly see them or not. By exposing them, they suggest that such gendered identities are ironic and passé.

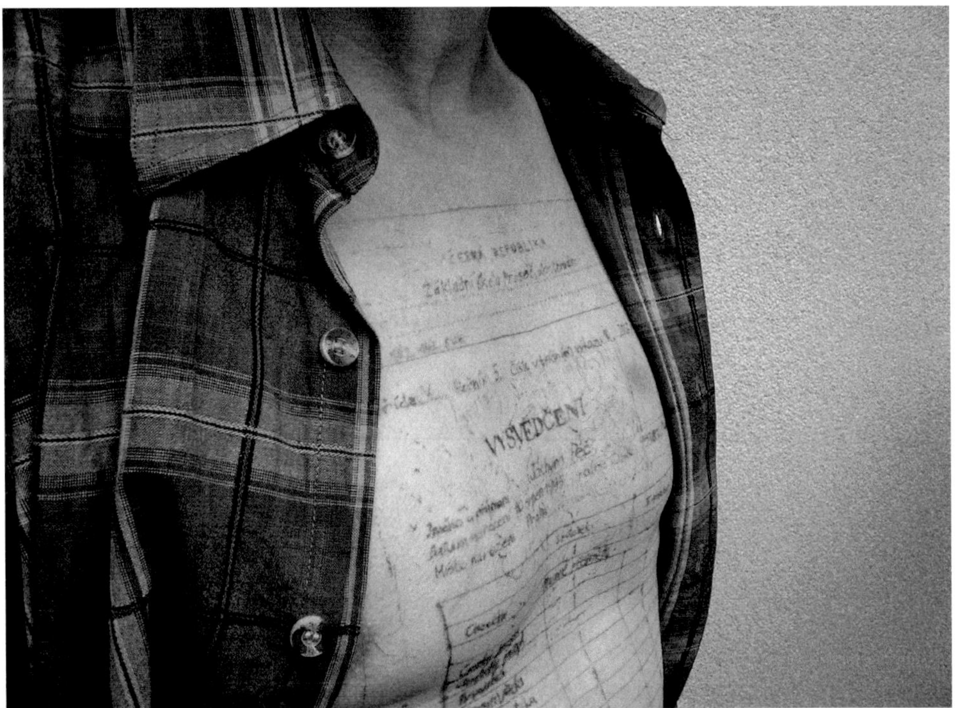

Figure 5.7 Mothers and Fathers, *Report Card (front)*, from *Bared!*, 2009, photographic project for Fotograf magazine. Courtesy the artists.

Fluid Identities

The collective identity of Mothers and Fathers has provided Lenka Klodová, Lucie Nepasická, Martin Péč, and Marek Rejent an effective means to bring into the public the domestic and gender issues which feminist and gender scholars are still struggling to incorporate into political and social rhetoric. This assumed identity builds upon their personal interests and situations, yet as in the case of *What Would We Be Without Children?* or *Bared!*, the artists' own personal identities have been sublimated to privilege a more universalist view of parenting. And in accordance with scholars who have remarked that theories of universalism in art history are often fraught with specific definitions of what constitutes "universal," the universal for Mothers and Fathers is tied very specifically to the post-socialist, white, middle-class Czech Republic.[138] They attempt, however, to convey not only personal and natural parenting concerns, but also those that potentially afflict all parents.

While still considered an active affiliation, Mothers and Fathers do not meet on a regular basis. When meeting the group in January 2011, it had been the first time in nearly a year that they had all gathered together to conceive of a new project. Each has been pursuing their individual art practices, which are not always concerned with the issues of the mother-father-artist problem. However, as I have demonstrated throughout this chapter, when brought together, the members of Mothers and Fathers interrogate these interests and assume the artist-parent identity. They employ this identity as the primary voice from which to speak and continually interrogate what it means to be a mother, father, husband, and wife in the post-socialist landscape of the Czech Republic. Their projects, while varying in media and artistic inspiration, always attempt to have a universal appeal to the general public—they speak artistically of the dilemmas of the husband, wife, mother, father, and parent, and attempt to form a community discourse on the subject.

Though they continually remain true to the particularities of their specific cultural context and their identity as artist-parents in the Czech Republic, they have inspired artists in other countries, such as Great Britain, to form artist-parent groups. In 2008, Rachel Howfield formed the online group, "Artist Parents Talking" (APT), citing Mothers and Fathers as an inspiration.[139] Though not a collective in the sense of Mothers and Fathers, APT became an international support system for artists who are parents, and who are trying to balance work, art-making, and childrearing. Ultimately, Mothers and Fathers have had quite an impact on the international community of artist-parents.

Notes

1 Emma Amos quoted in "Forum on Motherhood, Art, and Apple Pie," in *M/E/A/N/I/N/G: An Anthology of Artist's Writings, Theory, and Criticism*, Mira Schor and Susan Bee, eds. (Durham: Duke University Press, 2000), 254.

2 It is imperative to note that in some cultures, *not* having children acts as a source of isolation. Sociologist Margaret K. Nelson, for example, discusses the isolation of families as part of the cause of over-anxious parenting in her book, *Parenting Out of Control: Anxious Parents in Uncertain Times* (New York: NYU Press, 2010).

3 Sara Keating, "If You Want to Be an Artist with a Career, Don't Have Children," *The Irish Times*, May 27, 2019, www.irishtimes.com/culture/if-you-want-to-be-an-artist-with-a-car eer-dont-have-children-1.3895632?mode=amp.

4 While many materials published on the artists utilize the artist's married name, Krecjová, the artist divorced from her husband sometime around 2009. The artist thereafter returned

to her maiden name, Nepasická, and this is the name by which the artist will be referred to hereon.

5 The actual formation of the group is somewhat fuzzy to the members. Martin Péč remembers that Klodová was invited or taking part in an exhibition in which she invited the other, soon-to-be, members to join her. Martin Péč, conversation with author, January 8, 2011, Prague.

6 Klodová and Nepasická, conversation with the author, January 8, 2011, Prague.

7 "Mothers and Fathers," Mothers and Fathers archive, courtesy Lenka Klodová, Prague.

8 Mothers and Fathers name themselves an "art-social group" in their self-produced documents. In Czech they are called a "skupina," a term employed for both artistic collaborations and musical bands. It simply translates to "group," "party," or "team." The plurality of the term "skupina" also reflects notions of the "contemporary" and "contemporary art." Referenced in footnote 5, Terry Smith's article, "The State of Art History: Contemporary Art," which explores the meaning of "contemporary" in artistic practice. Richard Meyer's text, *What Was Contemporary Art?*, also promises to provide a fruitful discussion of the periodization of art. See: Richard Meyer, *What Was Contemporary Art?* (Cambridge, The MIT Press, 2013).

9 These exhibitions reflect what one could call a self-consciously "collaborative" movement in the late 80s and early 90s. Some of the artists highlighted continued to work collaboratively, but it was no longer new. By the 2000s scholars began thinking in terms of relational aesthetics and participation, which can be partly considered as collaborative practices.

10 See The Ruth & Harold D. Uris Center for Education. *Collaborations: Artists Working Together* (New York: Metropolitan Museum, 1983); Susan Sollins and Nina Castelli Sundell, *Team Spirit* (New York: Independent Curators, 1990).

11 See for example, Charles Green, *The Third Hand: Collaboration in Art from Conceptualism to Postmodernism* (Minneapolis: University of Minnesota Press, 2001); the exhibition catalog by Cynthia Jaffee McCabe, *Artistic Collaboration in the Twentieth Century* (Washington DC: Smithsonian Institution Press, 1984), which includes essays by McCabe, Robert C. Hobbs, and David Shapiro; Grant H. Kester's *The One and the Many: Contemporary Collaborative Art in a Global Context* (Durham: Duke University Press, 2011); and Reva Wolf, "Collaboration as Social Exchange: Screen Tests/A Diary by Gerard Malanga and Andy Warhol," *Art Journal* 52 no. 4 (Winter 1993): 59–66.

12 Green, *Third Hand*, x.

13 The work has been alternatively called *Svačina*, which means "snack."

14 Ellen Mara De Wachter, *Co-Art: Artists on Creative Collaboration* (London: Phaidon, 2017), 7.

15 Glenn Zorpette, "Dynamic Duos: Artists Are Teaming Up in Growing Numbers," *Art News* 93 no. 6 (Summer 1994): 167.

16 A third type of collaboration exists in the elaborate creation of a fictive artist identity, for example: Seymour Likely or Claire Fontaine.

17 Zorpette, "Dynamic Duos," 167.

18 Robert L. Pincus notes that Kienholz made the collaboration statement in 1981 in an exhibition catalog, though both artists began co-signing works in 1979. See Robert L. Pincus, *On A Scale that Competes with the World: The Art of Edward and Nancy Reddin Kienholz* (Berkeley: University of California Press, 1990), 77.

19 Green notes that this decision was made at the urging of the artists' son. Green, *Third Hand*, 129.

20 Ibid.

21 Ibid., 69.

22 The constant activity, Matthew Jesse Jackson notes, also nearly destroyed the group. See Matthew Jesse Jackson, *The Experimental Group: Ilya Kabakov, Moscow Conceptualism, Soviet Avant-Gardes* (Chicago: University of Chicago Press, 2010).

23 During Stalin's regime, artists who refused to follow the official policies lost their jobs, were murdered, or sent to the Gulag. After Stalin's death in 1953, official art policies were maintained, but penalties were made less severe. By 1976, Nikita Khrushchev had denounced Stalin's practices, attended at least one nonconformist exhibition, and reduced the punishments for dissident artists to the denial of their admittance to the union. For

more, see Alla Rosenfeld and Norton T. Dodge, eds., *Nonconformist Art: The Soviet Experience, 1956–1986* (New York: Thames and Hudson in association with the Jane Voorhees Zimmerli Art Museum, 1995), 36–41.

24 James K. Kettlewell, "TODT: An Artist Collaborative," TODT, 2018, http://todt. us/?page_id=13.

25 In 1989 Eleanor Heartney noted the biological relationship among the members and suggested that this made them "more of a clan than a collaboration." Eleanor Heartney, "Combined Operations," *Art in America* 77 (June 1989): 143.

26 Kettlewell, "TODT: An Artist Collaborative."

27 For example, here are two texts written by Art & Language members: Michael Baldwin and Mel Ramsden, "On Art & Language," *Art and Text* no. 35 (Summer 1990): 23–37; and Charles Harrison, *Essays on Art & Language* (Cambridge, MA and Oxford: Blackwell, 1991).

28 Néstor García Canclini, "The State of War and the State of Hybridization," in *Without Guarantees: In Honour of Stuart Hall*, ed. Paul Gilroy, et al. (London: Verso, 2000), 38–39.

29 Emin has made many statements on this subject in her online column for the London paper *The Independent*. In particular, consult the entry titled, "I felt that, in return for my children's souls, I have been given my success," *The Independent,* January 29, 2009, http:// www.independent.co.uk/voices/columnists/tracey-emin/tracey-emin-i-felt-that-in-return-fo r-my-childrens-souls-i-had-been-given-my-success-1518934.html

30 Neal Brown, *Tracey Emin* (London: Tate, 2006), 83.

31 Marina Abramović interview with *Tagesspiegel*, quoted in Henri Neuendorf, "Marina Abramović Says Children Hold Back Female Artists," *Art News*, July 25, 2016, https ://news.artnet.com/art-world/marina-abramovic-says-children-hold-back-female-artists-575150.

32 Stuart Horoder and Janine Antoni, "Janine Antoni," *BOMB* no. 66 (Winter 1999): 50.

33 Mothers and Fathers archives, courtesy of Lenka Klodová, Prague, CZ.

34 For more on Peirce's theories, see Max Fisch, *Writings of Charles S. Peirce: A Chronological Edition*, 6 vols. (Bloomington: Indiana University Press, 1982); and James Hoopes, ed. *Pierce on Signs: Writings on Semiotic* (Chapel Hill: University of North Carolina Press, 1991).

35 Even during Vaclav Havel's tenure as president in Czechoslovakia (1989–92) and the Czech Republic (1993–2003), the visual arts were not as prominently supported as the literary arts and theater. In his assessment, "Six Asides About Culture," Havel asserted that despite governmental suppression or lack of official support, the cultural community did not cease to exist. See Vaclav Havel, "Six Asides About Culture," *Cardozo Studies in Law and Literature* 2 no. 1 (Spring 1990): 44.

36 As illustrated in Chapter 2, Poland boasts several cities with important contemporary art museums and spaces, including Warsaw, Gdansk, Poznań, and Toruń.

37 Martina Pachmanová, "The Politicization of the Private, or the Privatization of Politics? A View of Recent Czech Art by Women," *Art Margins: Contemporary Central & East European Visual Culture* (January 27, 2000), https://artmargins.com/the-politicization-of-the-private-or-the-privatization-of-politics-a-view-of-recent-czech-art-by-women/.

38 Susan Snodgrass recounts the status of culture and the arts in the Czech Republic in "Towards a New Bohemia," *Art in America* 88 no. 4 (April 2000): 86–94.

39 At present, Poland's economy is rising, however it was in a much more difficult position, economically and politically than the Czech Republic in the late 1980s and early 1990s. The country itself is much larger than the former Czechoslovakia and has a larger and poorer agricultural population. For more information, consult Robert R. Kaufman, "Market Reform and Social Protection: Lessons from the Czech Republic, Hungary, and Poland," *East European Politics and Societies* 21 no. 1 (2007): 111–25.

40 This is a perspective held in particular by the group. Mothers and Fathers, in conversation with the author, January 8, 2011, Prague. A similar, yet more optimistic assessment was highlighted in a travel guide published in *The New York Times*; see Evan Rail, "Gallery Crawling in Prague? Get Out the G.P.S.," *The New York Times*, July 16, 2009, http://tra vel.nytimes.com/2009/07/19/travel/19cultured.html?pagewanted=all.

41 In January 2011, the National Gallery of Prague held a retrospective exhibition of Czech Baroque painter Karel Škéta at the Valdštejnská jízdárna; it had recently closed a widely popular Monet to Warhol exhibition at its Veletržní Palace exhibition—one that highlighted "modern masters," but notably, no Czech artists.

42 Alena Potůčková, *...o lidech...Několik pohledů na současné české výtvarné umění.* [...On People...Many Views on Contemporary Czech Fine Art.] (Praha: Česke muzeum výtvarných umění v Praze, červen-září, 2001), np.

43 Radek Wohlmuth, "Family Bonds Mothers and Fathers, Ltd." *Umělec* 1 (2005), http://div us.cc/berlin/de/article/family-bonds-mothers-and-fathers-ltd.

44 Potůčková, *...o lidech...*, np.

45 The Lennon Wall will be discussed in greater detail later in this chapter. Also, Kristofer Paetau claims that RAFANI welcomed women, despite their identity as "angry men." Kristofer Paetau, "Rafani," March 2005, http://www.paetau.com/downloads/Friends/Rafani.html.

46 Silvia Van Espen, "Jiří David: Too Light...Vertigo...Panic...Stendhal Syndrome...Local Anaesthesia...Geopornography," Zarhorian Gallery, April 27–June 9, 2012, http://www .zahoriangallery.com/new/en/vystava-prilis-lahka/.

47 Jiří Ševčík, *Pode Bal 1998–2008* (Prague: Divus, 2008), iii. Pode Bal member Michal Šiml claims that Pode Bal is, "likely the art group that has received the most media coverage in the Czech Republic." Michal Šiml, "That's Not Art, It's Political Art," in *Pode Bal 1998–2008*, 238–39.

48 In architecture, Philip Johnson has said as much of The Five (architects Peter Eisenman, Michael Graves, Charles Gwathmey, John Hejduk, and Richard Meyer): "They no doubt felt they would collectively receive more exposure as five than as five ones. They were right. As five, they have been attacked and defended, praised and vilified." Philip Johnson, "Postscript," in *Five Architects: Eisenman, Graves, Gwathmey, Hejduk, Meier* (New York: Oxford University Press, 1975), np.

49 María Ochoa, *Creative Collectives: Chicana Painters Working in the Community* (Albuquerque: University of New Mexico Press, 2003), 84.

50 Ibid., 60.

51 Liss, *Feminist Art and the Maternal*, 76.

52 See Benedict Anderson, *Imagined Communities: Reflections on the Origin and Spread of Nationalism* (London: Verso, 1991).

53 Gilbert & George, "Law of Sculptors," *Studio International* (May 1970), reprinted in Green, *Third Hand*, 148.

54 For more, see Chapter Seven of Green, *Third Hand*, 139–55.

55 Wohlmuth, "Family Bonds Mothers and Fathers, Ltd."

56 Ibid.

57 This could be applied to cultural workers more broadly as well.

58 For more on Art & Language, see Chapter Two of Green, *Third Hand*, 25–56.

59 Michael Baldwin quoted in "On Art & Language," 26–27.

60 This type of event began to occur during my meeting with the artists in January 2011, in Prague. They began to brainstorm ideas for new projects.

61 Mothers and Fathers, in conversation with the author, January 8, 2011, Prague.

62 See Green, "Memory, Ruins, and Archives: Boyle Family," in *Third Hand*, 59–74; Nina Castelli Sundell and Susan Sollins, *Team Spirit* (New York: Independent Curators, 1990); and *Beyond Image: Boyle Family* (London: Hayward Gallery, 1986).

63 Green, *Third Hand*, 67.

64 Ibid.

65 Eastern European art historians Martina Pachmanová and Charlotta Kotik have both written of Klodová as the central force behind the group. See Martina Pachmanová, *Klodová: Pregnant Songs* (Prague: Divus, 2004); Charlotta Kotik, "Post-Totalitarian Art: Eastern and Central Europe," in *Global Feminisms: New Directions in Contemporary Art* (London and New York: Merrell and the Brooklyn Museum of Art, 2007), 157. Klodová remarked that she sent works by Mothers and Fathers when curator Felicita Rauschling asked to submit work for the exhibition, "Mothering, Domestic and Private," (or alternatively titled, "Beyond RE Production. Mothering. Dimensions of Social Reproduction During

Neo-Liberalism") at the Kunstraum Kreuzberg/Bethanien at the Kunstquartier Bethanien in Berlin (February 25–April 25, 2011). This exhibition included work by Klodová, Margi Geerlinks, Elżbieta Jabłońska, and Tracey Moffatt, among others. Klodová, in conversation with the author, January 8, 2011, Prague.

66 Hana Maříková, "The Czech Family at Present and in the Recent Past," in *Families in Eastern Europe*, ed. Mihaela Robila (Oxford: Elsevier, 2004), 29–47.

67 This project has yet to be completed for each member. As of this writing, only the version in Rejent's hometown has occurred. Mothers and Fathers, conversation with author, January 8, 2011, Prague.

68 Mothers and Fathers archive, Prague.

69 Schneemann's *Blood Work Diary* (1971) notably is not one of Schneemann's more famous works, yet it is reproduced in Linda Weintraub, *Art on the Edge and Over: Searching for Art's Meaning in Contemporary Society* (Litchfield, CT: Art Insights, Inc., 1996), 165–66.

70 Julia Kristeva, "Place Names," in *Desire in Language*, 290.

71 Ibid.

72 Arthur C. Danto, "K.O.S. and the Art History of Collaboration," in *Amerika: Tim Rollins and K.O.S.*, ed. Gary Garrels (New York: Dia Art Foundation, 1989), 60.

73 Rejent and Nepasická, in conversation with the author, January 8, 2011, Prague. Both Rejent and Nepasická commented that their spouses resent their activity as artists and with Mothers and Fathers.

74 Snodgrass, "Towards a New Bohemia," 89.

75 Wohlmuth, "Family Bonds Mothers and Fathers, Ltd."

76 This phrase is commonly used when seeking advice from other parents, and as mentioned in the introduction, this is a phrase Gayle Clemans employs for her dissertation on American artist-parents.

77 Susan Gal and Gail Klingman cited in Bojana Pejic, "Proletarians of All Countries, Who Washes Yours Socks? Equality, Dominance, and Difference in Eastern European Art," in *Gender Check*, 24.

78 See for example, Maříková, "The Czech Family at Present and in the Recent Past," 29–47; and Joseph Hraba, Frederick O. Lorenz, and Zdeňka Pechačová, "Family Stress During the Czech Transformation," *Journal of Marriage and Family* 26 no. 2 (May 2000): 520–31.

79 Title translations by the author.

80 Wohlmuth, "Family Bonds Mothers and Fathers, Ltd."

81 Claes Oldenburg, *Store Days: Documents from* The Store *(1961) and* Ray Gun Theater *(1962)*. Selected by Claes Oldenburg and Emmett Williams. Photographs by Robert R. McElroy (New York: Something Else Press, Inc., 1967), 31. Cécile Whiting has written on the type of consumer who frequented the shops in the Lower East Side of New York as the "bargain hunter." See Cécile Whiting, *A Taste for Pop: Pop Art, Gender and Consumer Culture* (Cambridge: Cambridge University Press, 1997), 27–30.

82 Jill Johnson, "The Artist in a Coca-Cola World," *The Village Voice*, January 31, 1963, 24; quoted in Whiting, *A Taste for Pop*, 29.

83 These and all subsequent currency conversions of the Czech Koruna to US Dollars were calculated using an 1% interbank rate for September 19, 2002, listed at 1 CZK=0.03 USD. Consult http://www.oanda.com.

84 Translations by the author from documentary photograph of exhibition. Original text reads as follows: "Překvapení pro Matky a Otce: Máte Naději! Máte Dvojčátka! Máte Holčičku! Nemáte Nic..., Máte Chlapečka!, Nemáte Nic...."

85 Oldenburg's *Bride Mannikin* (1961) now resides in the collection of the Museum of Contemporary Art, Los Angeles.

86 Baudrillard writes, "Consumption can be compared with the kinship system, which is not determined in the final analysis by consanguinity and filiation, by a natural given, but rather by the arbitrary regulation of classification. ... Rules of marriage represent the multiple ways of assuring the circulation of women within the social group. It is the replacement of a consanguineous system of relations of biological origin by a sociological system of alliance. Thus, rules of marriage and kinship systems can be seen as a kind of language, that is, a set of operations intended to assure, between individuals and groups, a certain kind of communication. The same is true for consumption: a sociological system of

signs (the level characteristic of consumption) is substituted for a bio-functional and bio-economic system of commodities and products (the biological needs and subsistence). And the essential function of the regulated circulation of objects and commodities is the same as that of women and words." See Jean Baudrillard, "Consumer Society," in *Jean Baudrillard: Selected Writings*, ed. Mark Poster (Stanford: Stanford University Press, 2001), 50.

87 As mentioned in the introduction, this is a topic similarly broached by Martha Rosler in *Born to Be Sold: The Strange Case of Baby M*, 1988.

88 Though it could be argued that Oldenburg intended for the affluent high art consumer to venture to the Lower East Side.

89 See: *Matky a Octové Nabizeji*, pamphlet, 2002, and Wohlmuth, "Family Bonds Mothers and Fathers, Ltd."

90 Ružena is a woman's name that derives from the Czech word for 'rose,' which also doubles as a reference to the color of the bra. A second bra, in white, was also available. It was called *Bĕla*, a woman's name and derived from an old Slavic word meaning 'white.'

91 These ideas are further explored in two gender studies published in 2010 by the Heinrich Böll Foundation, which is attempting to document and monitor the progress of Central-Eastern European country's implementation of European Union standards. In these collection of studies, Czech scholars, Nina Bosničová, Kristýna Ciprová, Alexandra Jachanová-Doleželová, Kateřina Machovcová, and Linda Sokčévá noticed that while feminist ideas began to seem enticing in the 2000s in the Czech Republic, women who thought themselves feminists, or "new women" would, instead of marrying a Czech man, marry a foreigner and do those same things for him or reject feminism outright. See Nina Bosničová, Kristýna Ciprová, Alexandra Jachanová-Doleželová, Kateřina Machovcová, and Linda Sokčévá, "Gender Changes in the Czech Republic after 1989," in *Gender Issues 2009*, 11–35.

92 Petra Hůlová, "Happiness Short of Sean Connery," in *Women in Times of Change, 1989–2009* (Warsaw: Heinrich Böll Stiftung, 2010), 62.

93 Attempts to determine whether the group knew about Oldenburg's project when they set upon their project have been unsuccessful, but it seems unlikely that the artists would not be aware of his project.

94 Whiting, *A Taste for Pop*, 31.

95 Calvin Tomkins and *New York Times* quoted in Christoph Grunenberg, "The American Supermarket," in *Shopping: A Century of Art and Consumer Culture*, Christoph Grunenberg and Max Hollein, eds. (Ostfildern-Ruit: Hatje Cantz, 2002), 171–72.

96 The other side of the announcement provided the pertinent exhibition data.

97 Mothers and Fathers note that this exhibition, while encountered with some skepticism initially, was widely popular. Several items were purchased, though the artists did not keep records of who actually took these items home. Klodová, in conversation with the author, January 8, 2011, Prague.

98 On the subject of American garage sales, see Gretchen M. Herrmann, "Gift or Commodity: What Changes Hands in the U.S. Garage Sale?" *American Ethnologist* 24 no. 4 (1997): 910–30.

99 The Galerie U Mloka is a unique venue for such an exhibition. It is part of a larger non-profit, non-governmentally mandated treatment facility for those battling addiction. As a part of its facilities, Galerie U Mloka functions as a space to draw a wider public so those who enter as a part of drug treatment do not feel stigmatized.

100 The artists note that it was production costs that drove up the prices of many of the items. Nepasická and Klodová, in conversation with the author, January 8, 2011, Prague.

101 Wohlmuth asserts that the first exhibition was actually like a "50% liquidation" of other "'clearance sale' exhibitions," with the exhibit like "discount stores in bulk on racks, in cardboard boxes or on palettes [sic] in the middle of the gallery"; however it is my opinion that the exhibition operated like a store and the second like a liquidation sale. See Wohlmuth, "Family Bonds Mother and Fathers, Ltd."

102 Mothers and Fathers' first exhibitions, *Mothers and Father in Action (Matky a Octové v Akci)* and *Ashore (Na souši)*, included concerts of the *MaO* band; Nepasická, vocals and lead guitar; Klodová, vocals and keyboard; Rejent, drums; and Péč, bass guitar. Songs performed were a mix of lullabies and rock tunes. They wrote lyrics about domestic troubles

(washing the dishes, doing the laundry, etc.) written to the tunes of Iggy Pop songs for *Na souši*, which was a project about living with handicaps. Both women wore mermaid fins and crawled around the performance space, while the men wore humorous elements: Péč wore a frog mask and Rejent wore arm flotation devices while playing the drums with toilet bowl scrubbers. Mothers and Fathers archives, Prague.

103 For this project, the group chose the *Family Art Crimes* as the project title, and referred to it in English even in Czech publications.

104 Barbara Benish, "ArtWall as Installation: A Short History," *ArtWall*, ed. Ludviík Hlaváček (Prague: Centrum Pro Současné Umění Praha, 2006), np [18].

105 Hlaváček, *ArtWall*, np [1].

106 In May 2008 the Municipality of Prague withdrew the Center for Contemporary Art Prague's lease of the Letná Wall due to its disapproval of the "Collective Identity" exhibition by Guma Guar, a group of Czech artists. This exhibition was unveiled on May 16, 2008 and on the evening of May 29, someone censored all but one of the images with black asphalt. See www.artwall.cz for more information.

107 Indeed, when the author was in Prague in January 2011, graffiti was found on the wall.

108 This information is found on the www.graffiti.org website's page "Art Crimes: Trains 62: El Nino, Czech Republic," www.graffiti.org/trains/trains_62.html.

109 For more information regarding the Lennon Wall, see Petr Blažek, Roman Laube, a Filip Pospíšil, *Lennonova zed' v Praze: Neformální shromáždění mládeže na Kampě 1980-1989 (The Lennon Wall in Prague: An Informal Gathering of Youth in Kampa 1980–1989)*, (Praha: Ústav pro soudobé dějiny AV ČR, 2003).

110 According to weburbanist.com, there is a hierarchy of street art which begins with a simple "tag" that consists of the artist using spray paint, markers, or pens to write their street name; a "throw-up," which is more complicated with two to three colors and use bubble letters; a "stencil," which is the use of stencils to create more complicated images; "wild-style," which is a more complicated form of writing, often with a three-dimensional often illegible result; and the most daring, "piece," which displays careful execution, planning, time, and a variety of colors. "Graffiti Designs + Styles: Tagging, Bombing, Painting," posted by user Delana, http://weburbanist.com.

111 One piece in particular, by Blu, was still visible on a wall in the Narodni Trida area of Prague, in January 2011.

112 The critical acclaim of artists such as Keith Haring and Jean-Michel Basquiat in the 1980s brought a combination of graffiti and pop art into the mainstream art world. Similarly, in 2010 when the street artist Banksy released the documentary film *Exit Through the Gift Shop*, graffiti art gained another moment of popularity. Capitalizing on this moment, from April 17 to August 8, 2011 the Museum of Contemporary Art in Los Angeles hosted an exhibition titled "Art in the Streets," highlighting and thereby officially sanctioning graffiti as a high art. The museum's interpretation of the history of graffiti was controversial, as many critics noted. See, for example: Christopher Knight, "MOCA's 'Art in the Streets' Gets the Big Picture Wrong," *Los Angeles Times*, May 29, 2011, http://articles.lati mes.com/2011/may/29/entertainment/la-ca-kinght-graffiti-notebook-20110529; or, Adam Nagourney, "Admirers Call it Art, But the Police Call it a Problem," *The New York Times*, April 22, 2011, http://www.nytimes.com/2011/04/23/us/23graffiti.html.

113 Despite the efforts of grassroots organizations like the Global Initiative to End All Corporeal Punishment of Children, the Czech Republic remains one of the two countries in the EU (the other France), which has no law against corporeal punishment in schools. A large portion of the Czech population considers corporeal punishment necessary in some situations, and many do not consider smacking or slapping as corporeal punishment. For more information see: Global Initiative to End All Corporeal Punishment of Children, "Czech Republic - Country Report," 2020, https://endcorporalpunishment.org/.

114 This word has been translated to mean "porridge" or "pudding" by a few authors, but these are mistranslations. Czechs do not commonly eat or make porridge, and "pudding" is typically called "pudding," even in Czech. "*Kaše*" is a common short-term for "*bramborova kaše*" or mashed potatoes.

115 Štefková translates "*kaše*" here as "semolina pudding," yet, as mentioned in the note above, this is a mistranslation, or a secondary, less common meaning of the term. Zuzana

Štefková, "Artists on the Track of Crime," *Respekt* (September 10, 2006) reprinted in Hlaváček, *Art Wall,* np [24].

116 Rebecca Nash traces the scholarship of Šilková, Čermáková, and Havelková in relation to the pre- and post-socialist conditions and Western feminism, and engages ideas of why Czechs accept "gender studies" as opposed to feminist studies. See Rebecca Nash, "Exhaustion from Explanation: Reading Czech Gender Studies in the 1990s," *European Journal of Women's Studies* 9 no. 3 (2002): 300.

117 Ibid., 301.

118 Ibid.

119 Nina Bosničová, Kristýna Ciprová, Alexandra Jachanová-Doleželová, Kateřina Machovcová, Linda Sokčévá, "Gender Changes in the Czech Republic after 1989," in *Gender Issues 2009*, 13.

120 Nash attributes this partially to the economic conditions of the country, which became more visible after 1997. Nash, "Exhaustion from Explanation," 303.

121 A fascinating dialogue between scholars of Central-Eastern Europe has articulated the East–West dilemma in terms of postcolonial discourse. They largely assert that Central and Eastern European countries can, by no means, be called the "Other" in the twenty-first century; however they are certainly not part of the "West." They have articulated the idea of these countries being "in-between" and being a powerful position from which to speak. Postcolonial and cultural theorists such as, Rasheed Araeen, Stuart Hall, Edward Said, and Gayatri Spivak have articulated this. A worthy topic of further research, however, it falls beyond the scope of this study. See Susan Snodgrass, et al., "Central and East European Art and Culture, 1945–Present," *Art Margins: Contemporary Central & East European Visual Culture*, online journal (October 15, 2001), https://artmargins.com/central-and-east-europ ean-art-and-culture-1945-present/.

122 Herwig Reiter, "Beyond the Equation Model of Society—the Postponement of Motherhood in Post-State Socialism in an Interdisciplinary Life-Course Perspective," *Innovation: The European Journal of Social Science Research* 22 no. 2 (2009): 236.

123 Ibid., 240.

124 Ibid., 241.

125 This idea returns to the work of Claude Levi-Strauss. See Claude Levi-Strauss, *Structural Anthropology* (New York: Basic Books, 1963–1976).

126 Lenka Klodová, "Vítězky," in Hlaváček, *Art Wall*, np [3].

127 The athlete-mother role has gained interest with the growing number of high-profile athletes such as Kara Goucher, Gwen Jorgensen, Paula Radcliffe, and Serena Williams, having children.

128 Pode Bal's *Artwall* exhibition concurred with the elections. Klára Vomáčková, "Searching Our Conscience at the Wall," *Weekly A2* (June 2006), reprinted in Ševčík, *Pode Bal 1998–2008*, 224.

129 The artists noted that friends and colleagues were not aware that this was their art project and rather they believed that graffiti artists had transgressed into the spaces of these niches. The artists were genuinely surprised at the level of dissimulation their work received. Nepasická, in conversation with the author, January 8, 2011, Prague.

130 The artists made a point of highlighting this dual meaning. Nepasická and Klodová, in conversation with the author, January 8, 2011, Prague.

131 Clinton R. Sanders and D. Angus Vail, *Customizing the Body: The Art of Culture and Tattooing*, second edition, (Philadelphia: Temple University Press, 2008), 1.

132 Ibid., 165.

133 Although, as discussed below, this is not necessarily true of Czech women.

134 See Liss, *Feminist Art and the Maternal*, 53.

135 Tomáš Garrigue Masaryk is a noted Austro-Hungarian and Czechoslovak politician who notably took his wife's last name as his middle name upon their marriage. For more on Masaryk and his policies, see H. Gordon Skilling, *T.G. Masaryk: Against the Current, 1882–1914* (University Park, PA: Pennsylvania State University Press, 1994).

136 Marianne A. Ferber and Phyllis Hutton Raabe, "Women in the Czech Republic: Feminism, Czech Style," *International Journal of Politics, Culture and Society* 16 no. 3 (Spring 2003): 423.

137 Ibid., 413.
138 On the dismantling of universalism, see Ann Gibson, "Universality and Difference in Women's Abstract Painting: Krasner, Ryan, Sekula, Piper, and Streat," *The Yale Journal of Criticism* 8 (1995): 103–32.
139 Previous to January 2011, the group was unaware that Howfield has found their formation and activities inspirational.

6   The Future of Artist-Parents in Contemporary Art

While I was working on this project, every few months, it seemed, someone would contact me about a new controversy highlighted in media related to artist-parents. The news source, blog, or journal often exposed 'inappropriate' or 'offensive' projects by artists that engaged issues of parenting, or featured one's children. These timely controversies only reinforced the importance of this project and the possibilities a discussion of artist-parents could hold for contemporary art historical discourse. Slowly, this transitioned to greater and greater discussion of what it meant to be an artist and mother and/or father, and an artist-parent.

Parenthood is a fundamental part of human nature, and artists, individuals who are interested in uncovering, revealing, and dissecting the human condition, offer some of the most provocative and challenging assertions to our understanding of it. For example, in April 2008 the Yale University undergraduate art major Aliza Shvarts claimed to artificially inseminate herself "as often as possible" and periodically take abortifacient drugs for her senior art project. Challenging the boundaries of art and the acts that she could undertake as a student—Yale officials claimed that the project was a ruse and that they would not have allowed such a violation of "ethical standards" to take place.[1] The question of how far the institution can reach into one's path to parenthood is continually challenged in contemporary politics across the world. Had Yale officials known about Shvarts artificial insemination attempts, what legal rights would they have to stop her from taking the abortion drugs? She has a right to choose to terminate the pregnancy. However, for countries like Poland that outlaw abortion, the question becomes more about sustainability. What provisions or latitude does the government, society, and culture offer women who attempt to balance raising children, being a proper Polish Mother, and also work?

Jabłońska's photographs, installations, and performances revealed that dominant, popular thinking expects women to do all—to conform to traditional values, be modern, and raise their children to be active culture workers—in other words, to be *superwomen*. We saw how the mytho-history of the Polish Mother, merging with particular notions of the Virgin Mary, affects ideals of motherhood and family life in Poland and that these issues continue to dominate the country's perception of motherhood as it struggles to retain its conservative Catholic values and enter the global economy. However, Jabłońska's projects also suggest that there is a power in *thinking maternally*. This power, when utilized among both men and women, can ensure the creation and care of a community of individuals and move a nation forward to prosperity.

The post-communist national context had much to do with the way that Jabłońska engaged with and articulated her artist-parent identity. For Mothers and Fathers, the post-communist and anti-feminist context of the Czech Republic caused the group to explore the gendered issues of the family and domestic work much later than their American counterparts. For Ben-Ner, the politics of nation is not dominant, but is a detectable undercurrent throughout his work. His interest in fatherhood and parenting are couched in references to actors, artists, and films from the West, yet they are made with subtle references to the history of Israel as a promised land for those of the Jewish faith.

Despite these politically charged national histories, it would be remiss to label these artists as political. But this is not true of all artist-parents. In March 2010, Danish artist Nina Maria Kleivan was criticized in the media for dressing up her four-month-old daughter Faustina as ruthless dictators, including Hilter, Stalin, Ayatollah Khomenei, and Augusto Pinochet, among others in the series, *Potency*. Kleivan justified her project by claiming that we all have a "little evil in us."[2] While the works are clearly meant to be incendiary, Kleivan's decision to utilize her daughter in her art stems from similar reasons as those of Ben-Ner: She was bound to her home and could not access her studio.[3]

Interestingly, unlike the works by Ben-Ner featured in this text and Jabłońska's *Supermother* series, the projects by Mothers and Fathers only occasionally featured their children. As such, the work they produced suggests that they were more interested in interrogating what their roles as parents meant in terms of identity when the children were not present. Each of these artists suggests that parenting or the state of parenthood may indeed be a type of life-long performance in which one can engage, but none go to the extent of Marni Kotak. In 2011, New York-based artist Marni Kotak converted the Microscope Art Gallery into a home birthing center and then gave birth to her son, Ajax, as the performance project, *The Birth of Baby X*. In this performance, Kotak associates the creation of life with her artistic oeuvre, further bending the boundaries between art and life.[4] Upon birth, Kotak initiated the project, *Raising Baby X*, which she characterized as "the ongoing performance of motherhood as art until my child grows into adulthood, roughly age eighteen."[5] While evoking a durational similarity to Gellert's thirteen year project, *CarlVision*, Kotak's work is inspired by Mary Kelly and Mierle Laderman Ukeles, and aligned with the conceptual frame of Jabłońska's practice of art making from a parental point of view.

While Kotak's performance as an artist-parent clearly relies on the biological condition of being or becoming a parent, I would like to reiterate that this is not a requirement for the artist-parent identity. It is true that Elżbieta Jabłońska, Guy Ben-Ner, and the members of Mothers and Fathers decided to engage with the issues of parenting because of their own personal experiences of it, but biological reproduction does not necessitate one's ability to visually investigate parenting. For example, many of the works from Tracey Emin's two-year (2009–10) collaboration with Louise Bourgeois evince the sense of isolation, loneliness, and fear for (or of) the expectant mother. To engage the artist-parent identity, one must be interested in engaging the discourse on parenthood, domesticity, and gender.

To this end, networks are being developed to provide community, support, and resources for artist-parents. In 2008, contemporary British artist-parent Rachel Howfield aimed to create a support network for artists who are parents through an online blog forum titled, "Artist Parents Talking." While the blog is now defunct (or transformed into another venue), Howfield's attempt to create an artistic community by capitalizing on the accessibility and community the internet provides is not wasted. In 2016, Lenka

Clayton initiated her *An Artist Residence in Motherhood*, in which she provided an online toolkit for artists to examine "the usually separated roles of parenting and art-making."[6] Based on her own self-created residency from 2013–15, Clayton's project provides a framework for hundreds of individuals to explore the intersection of art and parenting in their own homes. In 2018, the artist KimyiBo instituted a collective art practice known as IOMA – the Institute of Mothering Artists, which advances a "new definition of the word 'mother' where the work of caring does not assume the body of women." According to the IOMA manifesto, the term 'mother' becomes a verb; 'to mother' means to take care of or to protect someone or something."[7] The group, originally consisting of the artist's friends, both male and female parents, came together with their children to reconsider the relationship between artwork, care, and relationships in general.[8] Similarly, other opportunities are developing for artist-parents, such as critique groups and retreats organized by Kaylan Buteyn, host of the *Artist/Mother Podcast*, which are aimed at creating a supportive community for practicing artists. While many of these opportunities are identified by the term *mother*, which may preclude men and non-gender-conforming artist-parents from participating, it is evidence that the discourse of art and parenting is growing exponentially.

Through this examination of artist-parents, we begin to see the social, political, economic, and artistic pressures that circumscribe contemporary parenting. The contemporary parent must confront a diverse set of social stigmas that become heightened when one attempts to engage them in a cultural discourse. As discussed, Elżbieta Jabłońska, Guy Ben-Ner, and the members of Mothers and Fathers bravely enter this discourse in order to attempt to make sense of their own identities, of their own roles as cultural workers and parents, and to show that art about children, the domestic, and parenting need not be kitschy, sentimental, or saccharine. Collectively, their works show that art about these topics can be perceived as reflections of some of the most critical national, social, and cultural issues of our time. Thankfully, current trends show that these issues are gaining prevalence and acceptance within the art world and artistic discourse more broadly.

Notes

1 For more information, consult "Aliza Shvarts' Insists Miscarriage Art Project is Real," *Huffington Post*, first posted April 25, 2008, updated November 17, 2011.
2 "Baby Hitler Artist Explains 'We Have Evil in All of Us,'" Metro online, March 18, 2010.
3 See: Morten Berthelsen, "In Pictures: Danish Artist Dresses Her Baby as Hitler, Exploring the Meaning of Evil," Haaretz.com, March 16, 2010.
4 Kotak was accused of narcissism, exploiting her unborn child, and even endangering his life—issues that clearly merit further investigation. Consult Maura Judkis, "Live Birth Performance Artist Marni Kotak Delivers Healthy Baby Boy," *Washington Post* online, *The Style Blog*, October 26, 2011.
5 Marni Kotak statement in interview with Niku Kashef in "The Durational Performance of the Parent-Artist," eds. Rachel Epp Buller and Charles Reeve, *Inappropriate Bodies: Art, Design, and Maternity* (Bradford, ON: Demeter Press, 2019), 157.
6 Lenka Clayton, statement, *An Artist Residence in Motherhood*, 2016.
7 Institute of Mothering Artists, Manifesto, https://www.kimyibo.com/imofa#/manifesto -ioma
8 See KimyiBo, "The personal is political: Refuting the images through the personal: artist, mother, color and how care has a roll in all of that," (Master of Fine Art Thesis, Seoul National University, 2008), 67–68.

Bibliography

Allara, Pamela. "'Matter' of Fact: Alice Neel's Pregnant Nudes." *American Art* 8, no. 2 (Spring 1994): 6–31.

Anderson, Benedict. *Imagined Communities: Reflections on the Origin and Spread of Nationalism*. London: Verso, 1991.

Anzaldúa, Gloria. *Borderlands: The New Mestiza*, 4th edition. San Francisco: Aunt Lute Books, 2007.

Armstrong, Carol and M. Catherine de Zegher, eds. *Women Artists at the Millennium*. Cambridge, MA: The MIT Press, 2006.

Atlan, Eva, ed. *Access to Israel 1: Israeli Contemporary Art*. Köln: Walther König, 2008.

Babin, Sylvette, ed. *Eating the Universe*. Köln: Dumont, 2009.

Baggesen, Lise Haller. *Mothernism*. Chicago/Oak Park: Green Lantern Press/Poor Farm Press, 2014.

Bain, Alex. *The Jewish Question: Biography of a World Problem*. Translated by Harry Zohn. New York: Herzl Press, 1990.

Baker, Steve. *Picturing the Beast: Animals, Identity, and Representation*. Urbana: University of Illinois Press, 2001.

Baldwin, Michael and Mel Ramsden. "On Art & Language." *Art and Text* no. 35 (Summer 1990): 23–37.

Banai, Nuit. "Guy Ben-Ner: Tel Aviv." *Art Papers* 30, no. 4 (July/August 2006): 71.

Baraitser, Lisa. *Maternal Encounters: The Ethics of Interruption*. London/New York: Routledge, 2009.

Baudelaire, Charles. "The Painter of Modern Life." *Figaro* (1863). In *The Painter of Modern Life and Other Essays*, edited by Jonathan Mayne, 1–40. London: Phaidon Press, 1964.

Baudrillard, Jean. *Jean Baudrillard: Selected Writings*. Edited by Mark Poster. Stanford: Stanford University Press, 2001.

Beauvoir, Simone de. *The Second Sex*. Translated by Constance Borde and Sheila Malovany-Chevaillier. Introduction by Judith Thurman, 1949. Reprint, New York: Vintage Books, 2011.

Beck, James H. "Joan Brown." *Art News* 63, no. 1 (March 1964): 10.

Bergan, Ronald, ed. *François Truffaut: Interviews*. Jackson: University Press of Mississippi, 2008.

Berkeley, George. *An Essay Towards a New Theory of Vision*. 1732. Facsimile of the fourth edition. Edited by David R. Wilkins, 2002. http://www.maths.tcd.ie/~dwilkins/Berkeley/Vision/.

Bernadac, Marie-Laure and Hans-Ulrich Obrist, eds. *Louise Bourgeois: Destruction of the Father Reconstruction of the Father: Writings and Interviews 1923–1997*. Cambridge, MA: The MIT Press, 1998; second printing, 2000.

Berwick, Carly. "Guy Ben-Ner." *ARTnews* 105, no. 9 (October 2006): 176.

Bhabha, Homi. *The Location of Culture*. London: Routledge, 1994.

Bishop, Claire. "Antagonism and Relational Aesthetics." *October* 110 (Fall 2004): 51–79.
Bishop, Claire. *Artificial Hells: Participatory Art and the Politics of Spectatorship*. New York: Verso, 2012.
Bishop, Claire and Marta Dziewańska, eds. *1968–1989. Political Upheaval and Artistic Change*. Warsaw: Museum of Modern Art, 2009.
Boardman, Michael M. *Defoe and the Uses of Narrative*. New Brunswick, NJ: Rutgers University Press, 1983.
Borkowski, Grzegorz, Monika Branicka, and Adam Mazur. *Nowe zjawiska w sztuce polskiej po 2000*. (New phenomena in Polish art after 2000). Warsaw: Centrum Sztuki Współczesnej Zamek Ujazdowski, 2007.
Bourdieu, Pierre. *The Logic of Practice*. Translated by Richard Nice. Stanford: Stanford University Press, 1990.
Bourriaud, Nicholas. *Relational Aesthetics*. Dijon: Les Presses du reel, 2002.
Brannen, Julia and Margaret O'Brien, eds. *Children in Families: Research and Policy*. Washington, DC: Falmer Press, 1996.
Brown, Joan. Interview with Paul Karlstrom. 1 July 1975. Archives of American Art. Washington, DC: Smithsonian Institution.
Brown, Neal. *Tracey Emin*. London: Tate, 2006.
Bruzzi, Stella. *Bringing Up Daddy: Fatherhood and Masculinity in Post-War Hollywood*. London: British Film Institute, 2005.
Bryan-Wilson, Julia. *Art Workers: Radical Practice in the Vietnam War Era*. Berkeley: University of California Press, 2009.
Bulawka, Hanna. "Locating the Female Identity in the Polish Media: A Feminist Critical Discourse Study." PhD dissertation. University of Birmingham, 2011.
Buller, Rachel Epp and Charles Reeve, eds. *Inappropriate Bodies: Art, Design, and Maternity*. Bradford, ON: Demeter Press, 2019.
Butler, Cornelia and Lisa Gabrielle Mark, eds. *WACK!: Art and the Feminist Revolution*. Cambridge, MA: The MIT Press, 2007.
Carnevale, Fulvia and John Kelsey. "Art of the Possible: An Interview with Jacques Rancière." *Artforum International* 45, no. 7 (March 2007): 256–269.
Carr, Carolyn. *Alice Neel: Women*. New York: Rizzoli Publishing, 2002.
Carr, Carolyn. "The Generation Gap: Three Performers and a Waterbed." *The Village Voice*. July 11, 2000. http://www.villagevoice.com/2000-07-11/news/the-generation-gap/1/.
Cart, Ashley Weeks. "(M)Other Work: Feminist Maternal Performance Art." MA thesis, University of Southern California, 2010.
Caws, Peter. *Sartre*. New York: Routledge, 2008.
Certeau, Michel de and Luce Giard. "The Nourishing Arts." In *Food and Culture: A Reader*, 2nd ed., edited by Carole Counihan and Penny Van Esterick, 67–77. New York: Routledge, 2008.
Certeau, Michel de, Luce Giard and Pierre Mayol. *The Practice of Everyday Life, Volume 2: Living & Cooking*. Translated by Timothy J. Tomasik. Minneapolis: University of Minnesota Press, 1998.
Chave, Anna. "Minimalism and Biography." *The Art Bulletin* 82, no. 1 (March 2000): 149–163.
Chave, Anna. "Pollock and Krasner: Script and Postscript." *Res* 24 (Autumn 1993): 95–111.
Chicago, Judy. "The Birth Project Newsletter." Fall 1981. Judy Chicago Papers. Schlesinger Library, Radcliffe Institute for Advanced Study, Harvard University, Cambridge, MA. 57.28.
Chicago, Judy. Interview with John W. Whitehead. "Women and Art." *Gadfly*. Online magazine. (November/December 1999). http://gadflyonline.com/archive/NovDec99/archive-judychicago.html.
Chris, Cynthia. *Watching Wildlife*. Minneapolis: University of Minnesota Press, 2006.
Cichocki, Sebastian. *Elżbieta Jabłońska: Supermatka*. Bialystok: Galeria Arsenal, 2003.

Cichocki, Sebastian. *Sztuka domowa: cała prawda o planecie X* (Home art or the entire truth about planet x). Katowice: Górnośląskie Centrum Kultury, 2002.

Ciesielska, Jolanta, red. *Między naturą a kulturą.* Bielsko-Biała: Galeria Bielska BWA, 2002.

Clemans, Gayle. "Parental Points of View: Photographic and Filmic Acts in Contemporary Art." PhD dissertation. University of Washington, 2011.

Corrin, Chris, ed. *Superwomen and the Double Burden: Women's Experience of Change in Central and Eastern Europe and the Former Soviet Union.* Toronto: Second Story Press, 1992.

Crowley, David, Zofia Machnicka, and Andrzej Szczerski, eds. *The Power of Fantasy—Modern and Contemporary Art from Poland.* New York: Prestel, 2011.

Dardis, Tom. *Keaton: The Man Who Wouldn't Lie Down.* New York: Scribners, 1979.

Davies, Jon. "Family Romance: IKEA Sets the Stage for Israeli Artist Guy Ben-Ner's Household Politics." *C Magazine* no. 96 (Winter 2008): 10–13.

De Wachter, Ellen Mara. *Co-Art: Artists on Creative Collaboration.* London: Phaidon, 2017.

Dezeuze, Anna, ed. *The 'do-it-yourself' Artwork: Participation from Fluxus to New Media.* Manchester, UK: Manchester University Press, 2010.

DiPaolo, Marc. *War, Politics, and Superheroes: Ethics and Propaganda in Comics and Film.* Jefferson, NC: McFarland & Co., 2011.

Doucet, Andrea. *Do Men Mother? Fathering, Care, and Domestic Responsibility.* Toronto: University of Toronto Press, 2006.

Edelsztein, Sergio, and Daria Kassovsky. *Guy Ben-Ner: Self-Portrait as a Family Man.* Tel Aviv: Hakibbutz Hameuchad Publishing House, 2005.

Elkins, James. *On the Strange Place of Religion in Contemporary Art.* New York: Routledge, 2004.

Ettinger, Bracha. *The Matrixial Borderspace.* Minneapolis: University of Minnesota Press, 2006.

Ferber, Marianne A. and Phyllis Hutton Raabe. "Women in the Czech Republic: Feminism, Czech Style." *International Journal of Politics, Culture and Society* 16, no. 3 (Spring 2003): 407–430.

Filipovic, Elena, and Joanna Mytkowska. *Alina Szapocznikow: Sculpture Undone, 1955–1972.* New York: Museum of Modern Art, 2011.

Foucault, Michel. "Of Other Spaces." Translated by Jay Miskowiec. *Diacritics* 16, no. 1 (Spring 1986): 22–27.

Freud, Sigmund. *The 'Wolfman' and Other Cases.* New York: Penguin Classics, 2003.

Funk, Nanette and Magda Mueller, eds. *Gender Politics and Post-Communism.* London/New York: Routledge, 1993.

Gajewska, Bożena and Jerzy Hanusek. *Maria Pinińska-Bereś: 1931–1999.* Kraków: Galeria Sztuki Współczesnej Bunkier Sztuki, 1999.

Gal, Susan and Gail Kligman, eds. *Reproducing Gender: Politics, Publics, and Everyday Life After Socialism.* Princeton: Princeton University Press, 2000.

Garrels, Gary, ed. *Amerika: Tim Rollins + K.O.S.* New York: Dia Art Foundation, 1989.

Pejic, Bojana, ed. *Gender Check: Femininity and Masculinity in the Art of Eastern Europe.* Wien: Museum Moderner Kunst Stiftung Ludwig/Cologne: Walther König, 2009.

Gibson, Ann Eden. *Abstract Expressionism: Other Politics.* New Haven: Yale University Press, 1997.

Gibson, Ann Eden. "Color and Difference in Abstract Painting: The Ultimate Case of Monochrome." In *The Feminism and Visual Culture Reader,* edited by Amelia Jones, 192–204. New York: Routledge, 2003.

Gibson, Ann Eden and Lucia Palmer. "George Berkeley's Visual Language and the New England Portrait Tradition." *The Centennial Review* 31, no. 2 (Spring 1987): 122–145.

Gilroy, Paul, Lawrence Grossberg, and Angela McRobbie, eds. *Without Guarantees: In Honour of Stuart Hall.* London: Verso, 2000.

Global Initiative to End All Corporal Punishment of Children. "Czech Republic - Country Report." Last updated January 2020. https://endcorporalpunishment.org/.

Godelier, Maurice. *The Enigma of the Gift*. Translated by Nora Scott. Chicago: University of Chicago Press, 1999.

Godmilow, Jill and Ann-Louise Shapiro. "How Real Is Reality in Documentary Film?" *History and Theory* 36, no. 4, Theme Issue 36: Producing the Past: Making Histories Inside and Outside the Academy (December 1997): 82–85.

Gorenberg, Gershom. *The Accidental Empire: Israel and the Birth of the Settlements, 1967–1977*. New York: Times Books, 2006.

Green, Charles. *The Third Hand: Collaboration in Art from Conceptualism to Postmodernism*. Minneapolis: University of Minnesota Press, 2001.

Grzybek, Agnieszka, ed. *Women in Times of Change, 1989–2009*. Warsaw: Heinrich Böll Foundation, 2009.

Gumbs, Alexis Pauline, China Martens, and Mai'a Williams. *Revolutionary Mothering: Love on the Front Lines*. Oakland, CA: PM Press, 2016.

Grunenberg, Christoph and Max Hollein. *Shopping: A Century of Art and Consumer Culture*. Ostfildern-Ruit: Hatje Cantz, 2002.

Gunning, Tom. "Lost in Play: Adapting the Zone of Imagination in the Works of Guy Ben-Ner." *Adaptation*. Smart Museum of Art. Chicago: University of Chicago, 2008. https://smartmu seum.uchicago.edu/adaptation/2008/03/31/lost-in-play-adapting-the-zone-of-imagination -in-the-works-of-guy-ben-ner/

Halberstam, J. Jack. *Gaga Feminism: Sex, Gender, and the End of Normal*. Boston: Beacon Press, 2012.

Harrison, Jane. "Joan Brown." *Arts Magazine* 38 (March 1964): 64.

Havel, Vaclav. "Six Asides About Culture." *Cardozo Studies in Law and Literature* 2, no. 1 (Spring 1990): 43–52.

Heartney, Eleanor. "Combined Operations." *Art in America* 77 (June 1989): 140–147.

Heiss, Alanna. *And the Mind Grew Fingers: Dennis Oppenheim: Selected Works 1967–90*. New York: Harry N. Abrams, 1992.

Herrmann, Gretchen M. "Gift or Commodity: What Changes Hands in the U.S. Garage Sale?" *American Ethnologist* 24, no. 4 (1997): 910–930.

Hirsch, Marianne. *Family Frames: Photography, Narrative, and Postmemory*. Cambridge: Harvard University Press, 1997.

Hirsch, Marianne, ed. *The Familial Gaze*. Hanover: Dartmouth College, 1999.

Hlaváček, Ludvík, ed. *ArtWall*. Prague: Centrum Pro Současné Umění Praha, 2006.

Hobson, Barbara, ed. *Making Men into Fathers: Men, Masculinities, and the Social Politics of Fatherhood*. Cambridge: Cambridge University Press, 2002.

Hochschild, Arlie. *The Second Shift*. New York: Avon Books, 1989.

Hopkins, David. *Dada's Boys: Masculinity After Duchamp*. New Haven/London: Yale University Press, 2002.

Horak, Jan-Christopher. "Wildlife Documentaries: From Classical Forms to Reality TV." *Film History* 18, no. 4, Documentary Before Verité (2006): 459–475.

Horoder, Stuart and Janine Antoni. "Janine Antoni." *BOMB* no. 66 (Winter 1999). http://bom bsite.com/issues/66/articles/2191.

Hraba, Joseph, Frederick O. Lorenz, and Zdeňka Pechačová. "Family Stress During the Czech Transformation." *Journal of Marriage and Family* 26, no. 2 (May 2000): 520–531.

Huyghe, Pierre. Interview with Hans-Ulrich Obrist. *Point of View: An Anthology of the Moving Image*. Electronic Arts Intermix. DVD, 2004.

Ishizuka, Karen L. and Patricia R. Zimmermann, eds. *Mining the Home Movie: Excavations in Histories and Memories*. Berkeley: University of California Press, 2008.

Jabłońska, Elżbieta. *Elżbieta Jabłońska: (Un)usually Successful*. Olsztyn, Poland: Galeria Sztuki, 2011.

Jabłońska, Elżbieta. Untitled Text. nd. Elżbieta Jabłońska's Archive, Bydgoszcz, Poland.

Jackson, Matthew Jesse. *The Experimental Group: Ilya Kabakov, Moscow Conceptualism, Soviet Avant-Gardes*. Chicago: University of Chicago Press, 2010.

Johnson, Philip. *Five Architects: Eisenman, Graves, Gwathmey, Hejduk, Meier*. New York: Oxford University Press, 2003.

Jones, Amelia. *Body Art/Performing the Subject*. Minneapolis: University of Minnesota Press, 1998.

Jones, Amelia, ed. *Sexual Politics: Judy Chicago's Dinner Party in Feminist Art History*. Los Angeles: University of California Press, 1996.

Jones, Caroline. *Machine in the Studio: Constructing the Postwar American Artist*. Chicago: University of Chicago Press, 1996.

Jones, Jonathan. "The Myth-Maker." *The Guardian*. October 16, 2002. http://guardian.co.uk/film/2002/oct/16/artsfeatures/print.

Katz, Melissa R. and Robert A. Orsi. *Divine Mirrors: The Virgin Mary in the Visual Arts*. New York: Oxford University Press, 2001.

Kaufman, Robert R. "Market Reform and Social Protection: Lessons from the Czech Republic, Hungary, and Poland." *East European Politics and Societies* 21, no. 1 (2007): 111–125.

Keaton, Buster. *My Wonderful World of Slapstick*. London: George Allen & Unwin, 1960.

Kelly, Mary. *Post-Partum Document*. London/Boston/Melbourne/Henley: Routledge & Kegan Paul, 1983.

Kester, Grant H. *The One and the Many: Contemporary Collaborative Art in a Global Context*. Durham: Duke University Press, 2011.

Kettlewell, James K. "TODT: An Artist Collaborative." *TODT*. Last modified 2018. http://todt.us/?page_id=13.

Kowalczyk, Izabela. "Iza Kowalczyk rozmawia z Elą Jabłońską: Supermenka w krainie codzienności." *Artmix, sztuka feminism kultura wizualna*. February 16, 2011. http://free.art.pl/artmix (site discontinued).

Krajewski, Marek. "Distanced Towards One's Role. On Ela Jabłońska's Art." n.d. Elżbieta Jabłońska Archive, Bydgoszcz, Poland.

Kristeva, Julia. *Desire in Language: A Semiotic Approach to Literature and Art*. Edited by Leon S. Roudiez. New York: Columbia University Press, 1980.

Lambert-Beatty, Carrie. "Against Performance Art." *Artforum International* 48, no. 9 (May 2010): 208–212.

Lach-Lachowitz, Natalia. *Natalia LL: Teksty*. Bielsko-Biało: Galeria Bielska-BWA, 2004.

Levi-Strauss, Claude. *Structural Anthropology*. New York: Basic Books, 1963–1976.

Lippard, Lucy. "The Pains and Pleasures of Rebirth: European and American Women's Body Art." *Art in America* 64, no. 3 (May-June 1976): 73–81.

Lippard, Lucy. *The Pink Glass Swan: Selected Feminist Essays on Art*. New York: The New Press, 1995.

Liss, Andrea. *Feminist Art and the Maternal*. Minneapolis: University of Minneapolis Press, 2009.

Loiperdinger, Martin. "Lumière's Arrival of the Train: Cinema's Founding Myth." *Moving Image* 4, no. 1 (Spring 2004): 89–118.

Lorde, Audre. *Sister Outsider*. Berkeley: Crossing Press, 1984.

Lutz, Helma. "At Your Service Madam! The Globalization of Domestic Service." *Feminist Review* 70 (2009): 89–104.

MacDonald, Scott. "Up Close and Political: Three Short Ruminations on Ideology in the Nature Film." *Film Quarterly* 59, no. 3 (Spring 2006): 4–21.

Malti, Tina, Michaela Gummerum, Monika Keller, and Marlis Buchmann. "Children's Moral Motivation, Sympathy, and Prosocial Behavior." *Child Development* 80, no. 2 (March/April 2009): 442–460.

Margolles, Teresa. "Santiago Sierra." *BOMB* 86 (Winter 2004). http://bombmagazine.org/articl es/santiago-sierra.

Marinetti, Filippo Tommaso. *The Futurist Cookbook*. Translated by Suzanne Brill. Introduction by Lesley Chamberlain. San Francisco: Bedford Arts, 1989.

Marotti, William. "Political Aesthetic: Activism, Everyday Life, and Art's Object in 1960s' Japan." *Inter-Asia Cultural Studies* 7, no. 4 (2006): 606–618.

Maříková, Hana. "The Czech Family at Present and in the Recent Past." In *Families in Eastern Europe*, edited by Mihaela Robila, 29–47. Oxford: Elsevier, 2004.

Masters, HG. "Solitary Refinement: Guy Ben-Ner." *ArtAsiaPacific* 66, (November/December 2009). http://artasiapacific.com/Magazine/66/SolitaryRefinmentGuyBenNer.

May, Pamela. *Child Development in Practice: Responsive Teaching and Learning from Birth to Five*. New York: Routledge, 2011.

Mayer, Musa. *Night Studio: A Memoir of Philip Guston by His Daughter*. New York: Knopf, 1988.

Mayeroff, Milton. *On Caring*. New York: Harper Row, 1971.

Mazierska, Ewa and Elżbieta Ostrowska. *Women in Polish Cinema*. New York: Berghahn Books, 2006.

Mazur, Adam. "Supermatki gry domowe." *Foto Tapeta*. May-June 2002. http://fototapeta.art. pl/2002/ejb.php.

McCabe, Cynthia Jaffee. *Artistic Collaboration in the Twentieth Century*. Washington, DC: Smithsonian Institution Press, 1984.

Melville, Herman. *Moby-Dick*. Edited and Introduction by Tony Tanner. Oxford: Oxford University Press, 1998. Originally published London: Harper & Brothers, 1851.

Merewether, Charles and Rika Iezumi Hiro, eds. *Art, Anti-Art, Non-Art: Experimentations in the Public Sphere in Postwar Japan, 1950–1970*. Los Angeles: Getty Research Institute, 2007.

Montessori, Maria. *The Discovery of the Child*. Translated by M. Joseph Costelloe, SJ. Notre Dame, IN: Fides Publishers, 1967.

Molesworth, Helen. "House Work and Art Work." *October* 92 (Spring 2000): 71–97.

Morgan, Jessica. "From Out There to Down Here." *Parkett* 87 (2010): 34–39.

Mosquera, Gerardo. "Good-Bye Identity, Welcome Difference." *Third Text* 15, no. 56 (September 2001): 25–32.

Munro, Eleanor. *Originals: American Women Artists*. New York: Da Capo Press, 2000.

Munroe, Alexandra. *Japanese Art After 1945: Scream Against the Sky*. New York: Harry N. Abrams, 1996.

Nash, Rebecca. "Exhaustion from Explanation: Reading Czech Gender Studies in the 1990s." *European Journal of Women's Studies* 9, no. 3 (2002): 291–309.

Neel, Andrew. *Alice Neel*. DVD. SeeThink, 2007.

Nelson, Margaret K. *Parenting Out of Control: Anxious Parents in Uncertain Times*. New York: NYU Press, 2010.

Nemser, Cindy. *Art Talk: Conversations with 12 Women Artists*. New York: Charles Scribner's Sons, 1975.

Nixon, Mignon. *Fantastic Reality: Louise Bourgeois and a Story of Modern Art*. Cambridge, MA: The MIT Press, 2005.

Nochlin, Linda. "Why Have There Been No Great Women Artists?" *Art News* 69 (January 1971): 22–39.

Notermans, C. "Local and Global Icons of Mary: An Ethnographic Study of a Powerful Symbol." *Anthropos* 103, no. 2 (2008): 471–481.

O'Reilly, Andrea. "'I Envision a Future in Which Maternal Thinkers Are Respected and Self-Respecting:' The Legacy of Sara Ruddick's 'Maternal Thinking.'" *Women's Studies Quarterly* 37, no. 3/4, Mother (Fall–Winter 2009): 295–298.

Ochoa, María. *Creative Collectives: Chicana Painters Working in the Community*. Forward by Amalia Mesa-Bains. Albuquerque: University of New Mexico Press, 2003.

Oldenburg, Claes. *Store Days: Documents* from *The Store* (1961) and *Ray Gun Theater* (1962). Photographs by Robert R. McElroy. New York: Something Else Press, Inc., 1967.

Oppenheim, Dennis. *Dennis Oppenheim: Retrospective-Works 1967–77*. Montreal: Musée d'art contemporain, 1978.

Orem, R.C., ed. *Montessori: Her Method and the Movement: What You Need to Know*. New York: Putnam, 1974.

Orgeron, Davin Anthony and Marsha Gabrielle Orgeron. "Eating Their Words: Consuming Class á la Chaplin and Keaton." *College Literature* 28, no. 1 (Winter 2001): 84–104.

Pachmanová, Martina. *Behind the Velvet Curtain: Seven Women Artists from the Czech Republic*. Washington, DC: American University Museum at the Katzen Arts Center, 2009.

Pachmanová, Martina. *Klodová: Pregnant Songs*. Prague: Divus, 2004.

Pachmanová, Martina. "The Politicization of the Private, or the Privatization of Politics? A View of Recent Czech Art by Women." *Art Margins: Contemporary Central & East European Visual Culture*. January 27, 2000. http://artmargins.com/index.php/2-articles/427-the-poli ticization-of-the-private-or-the-privatization-of-politics-a-view-of-recent-czech-art-by-w omen.

Paetau, Kristofer. "Rafani." March 2005. *Pateau.com* http://www.paetau.com/downloads/Fri ends/Rafani.html.

Park, Shelley. *Mothering Queerly, Queering Motherhood:Resisting Monomaternalism in Adoptive, Lesbian, Blended, and Polygamous Families*. Albany: State University of New York Press, 2013.

Pelikan, Jaroslav. *Mary Through the Centuries: Her Place in the History of Culture*. New Haven: Yale University Press, 1996.

Pincus, Robert L. *On A Scale that Competes with the World: The Art of Edward and Nancy Reddin Kienholz*. Berkeley: University of California Press, 1990.

Piotrowski, Piotr. "How to Write a History of Central-East European Art?" *Third Text* 23, no. 1 (2009): 5–14.

Pomerance, Murray and Frances Gatward, ed. *Where the Boys Are: Cinemas of Masculinity and Youth*. Detroit: Wayne State University Press, 2005.

Poprzęcka, Maria. "Czy będzie jedzenie?" *Arteon – magazyn o sztuce* 72, no. 4 (April 2006). http://www.atlassztuki.pl/pdf/jablonska1.pdf.

Porter, Brian. "Hetmanka and Mother: Representing the Virgin Mary in Modern Poland." *Contemporary European History* 14, no. 2 (2005): 151–170. doi: 10.1017/S0960777305002298

Potůčková, Alena. *...o lidech...Několik pohledů na současné české výtvarné umění.* [...On People...Many Views on Contemporary Czech Fine Art.] Praha: Česke muzeum výtvarných umění v Praze, červen-září, 2001.

Rancière, Jacques. *Dissensus: On Politics and Aesthetics*. Edited and Translated by Steven Corcoran. New York: Continuum, 2010.

Rancière, Jacques. "The Emancipated Spectator." *Artforum International* 45, no. 7 (March 2007): 271–280.

Rancière, Jacques. *The Ignorant Schoolmaster: Five Lessons in Intellectual Emancipation*. Translated with an Introduction by Kristin Ross. Stanford: Stanford University Press, 1991.

Rancière, Jacques. *The Politics of Aesthetics*. Translation and Introduction by Gabriel Rockhill. New York: Continuum, 2004.

Reilly, Maura and Linda Nochlin, eds. *Global Feminisms: New Directions in Contemporary Art*. London: Merrell/New York: Brooklyn Museum of Art, 2007.

Reiter, Herwig. "Beyond the Equation Model of Society—The Postponement of Motherhood in Post-State Socialism in an Interdisciplinary Life-Course Perspective." *Innovation: The European Journal of Social Science Research* 22, no. 2 (2009): 233–246.

Risman, Barbara J. "Can Men 'Mother'? Life as a Single Father." *Family Relations* 35, no. 1 (January 1985): 85–102.

Risman, Barbara J. *Gender Vertigo: American Families in Transition*. New Haven: Yale University Press, 1998.

Robinson, Julia. "The Sculpture of Indeterminacy: Alison Knowles's Beans and Variations." *Art Journal* 63, no. 4 (Winter 2004): 96–115.

Rosenberg, Harold. "Introduction to 'Six American Artists.'" *Possibilities* 1, no. 1 (Winter 1947–48): 75.

Rosenberg, Karen. "Guy Ben-Ner: Postmasters." *Artforum International* 42, no. 9 (April 2005): 189.

Rosenfeld, Alla and Norton T. Dodge, eds. *Nonconformist Art: The Soviet Experience, 1956–1986*. New York: Thames and Hudson in association with the Jane Voorhees Zimmerli Art Museum, 1995.

Rosler, Martha. *Decoys and Disruptions: Selected Writings, 1975-2001*. Cambridge, MA: The MIT Press, 2004.

Ross, John Munder. *What Men Want: Mothers, Fathers, and Manhood*. Cambridge: Harvard University Press, 1994.

Rousseau, Jean-Jacques. *Emile or On Education*. Introduction, Translation and Notes by Allan Bloom. New York: Basic Books, 1979.

Ruddick, Sara. *Maternal Thinking: Towards a Politics of Peace*. New York: Ballantine Books, 1989.

Ruddick, Sara. "On 'Maternal Thinking.'" *Women's Studies Quarterly* 37, no. 3/4, Mother (Fall–Winter 2009): 305–308.

Rzepecki, Adam. *Adam Rzepecki, 2016 Portfolio*. Warsaw: Dawid Radziszewski Gallery, 2016.

Saltz, Jerry. "Artist in Residence: When Guy Ben-Ner Goes to Ikea, He's Not There for the Meatballs." *New York Magazine*, January 31, 2008. http://nymag.com/arts/art/reviews/43567.

Sanders, Clinton R. and D. Angus Vail. *Customizing the Body: The Art of Culture and Tattooing*. Philadelphia: Temple University Press, 2008.

Sanders, Judith and Daniel Lieberfeld. "Dreaming in Pictures: The Childhood Origins of Buster Keaton's Creativity." *Film Quarterly* 47, no. 4 (Summer 1994): 14–28.

Sartre, Jean-Paul. *Saint Genet: Actor and Martyr*. New York: New American Library, 1971.

Scapp, Ron and Brian Seitz, eds. *Eating Culture*. Albany: State University of New York Press, 1998.

Schillebeeckx, Edward and Catharina Halkes. *Mary: Yesterday, Today, Tomorrow*. New York: Crossroad, 1993.

Schor, Mira and Susan Bee, eds. *M/E/A/N/I/N/G: An Anthology of Artists' Writings, Theory, and Criticism*. Durham: Duke University Press, 2000.

Schriver, Juliea. "Images of Pregnancy in Alice Neel's Paintings." MA thesis. California State University, Fullerton, 2004.

Schwendener, Martha. "Family Guy: The Domestic Fantasies of Guy Ben-Ner." *Tablet Magazine*, April 16, 2008. http://www.tabletmag.com/arts-and-culture/732/family-guy/.

Schwendener, Martha. "Guy Ben-Ner: Postmasters." *Artforum International* 46, no. 8 (April 2008): 369.

Ševčík, Jiří. *Pode Bal 1998-2008*. Prague: Divus, 2008.

Sieglohr, Ulrike. *Focus on the Maternal: Female Subjectivity and Images of Motherhood*. London: Scarlet Press, 1998.

Sienkiewicz, Karol. "Julita Wójcik: Peeling Potatoes." *Culture.pl*, March 2011. Edited and translated by Sylwia Wojda, July 2011.

Sitegallery. "Guy Ben-Ner Interview." YouTube Video, 6:56, March 10, 2011. http://youtu.be/MSbz9G-qRqs.

Skilling, H. Gordon. *T.G. Masaryk: Against the Current, 1882–1914*. University Park, PA: Pennsylvania State University Press, 1994.

Smith, Jeremy Adam. *The Daddy Shift: How Stay-at-Home Dads, Breadwinning Moms, and Shared Parenting Are Transforming the American Family.* Boston: Beacon Press, 2009.

Smith, Joe and Petr Jehlička, "Stories Around Food, Politics and Change in Poland and the Czech Republic." *Transactions of the Institute of British Geographers* 32, no. 3 (September 2007): 395–410.

Smith, Stephanie. "Interview: Guy Ben-Ner and Stephanie Smith." *Adaptation.* University of Chicago, 2008. https://smartmuseum.uchicago.edu/adaptation/artists/ben-ner/interview/index.html

Smith, Terry. "The State of Art History: Contemporary Art." *The Art Bulletin* 92, no. 4 (December 2010): 366–383.

Smolak, Anna. *Happy Birthday: Katarzyna Górna 1994-2004.* Kraków: Galeria Sztuki; Bunkier Sztuki, 2004.

Snodgrass, Susan. "Central and East European Art and Culture, 1945-Present." *Art Margins: Contemporary Central & East European Visual Culture,* online journal (October 15, 2001). Accessed June 16, 2011. http://artmargins.com/ /index.php/5-interviews/410-central-and-east-european-art-and-culture-1945-present.

Snodgrass, Susan. "Toward a New Bohemia." *Art in America* 88, no. 4 (April 2000): 86–94.

Solomon, Matthew, ed. *Fantastic Voyages of the Cinematic Imagination: George Méliès's Trip to the Moon.* Albany: State University Press, 2011.

Spence, Jo and Patricia Holland, eds. *Family Snaps: The Meanings of Domestic Photography.* London: Virago Press, 1991.

Spence, Rachel. "The Art of Guy Ben-Ner." *Jewish Quarterly* 52, no. 2 (Summer 2005): 25–28. doi:10.1080/0449010X.2005.10706923

Spencer, Catherine. "Acts of Displacement: Lea Lublin's *Mon fils*, May '68, and Feminist Psychosocial Revolt." *Oxford Art Journal* 40, no. 1 (March 2017): 65–83.

Spivak, Gayatri. *A Critique of Postcolonial Reason: Toward a History of the Vanishing Present.* Cambridge: Harvard University Press, 1999.

Spock, Benjamin. *Baby and Child Care.* New and Enlarged Edition. London: Bodley Head, 1958.

Stewart, Susan. *On Longing: Narratives of the Miniature, The Gigantic, The Souvenir, The Collection.* Durham: Duke University Press, 1993.

Storr, Robert. *Elizabeth Murray.* New York: Museum of Modern Art, 2005.

Sundell, Nina Castelli and Susan Sollins. *Team Spirit.* New York: Independent Curators, 1990.

Szczerski, Andrzej. "Why the PRL Now? Translations of Memory in Contemporary Polish Art." *Third Text* 23, no. 1 (2009): 85–96.

Sznajder, Michal and Benjamin Senauer. "The Changing Polish Food Consumer." Working Papers 14306. The Food Industry Center. St. Paul: University of Minnesota, 1998. doi: 10.22004/ag.econ.14306.

Szylak, Aneta. *Architectures of Gender, Contemporary Women's Art in Poland.* Long Island City: Sculpture Center, 2003.

Szylak, Aneta. "Have Billboards Changed the Meaning of Public Space in Poland?" *M/E/A/N/I/N/G Online* 1 (July 2005). http://writing.upenn.edu/pepc/meaning/01/anetaszylak.html

Tarkowska, Elżbieta. "Poverty and Education Risk of 'Inheritance' of Poverty in the Former State Farms in Poland." *Polish Sociological Review* no. 138 (2002): 203–215.

Taylor, Kate. "Artist's Daughter Wants Videos Back." *New York Times.* July 7, 2010.

Temkin, Ann. *Alice Neel.* New York: Harry N. Abrams in association with the Philadelphia Museum of Art, 2000.

Tiravanija, Rirkrit. *Rirkrit Tiravanija: Cook Book.* Bangkok: River Books, 2010.

Treacher, Amal. "Children's Imaginings and Narratives: Inhabiting Complexity." *Feminist Review* 82, no. 1, Everyday Struggling (2006): 96–113.

Tolnay, Alexander. *Biały Mazur.* Berlin/Warsaw: Neuer Berliner Kunstverein, 2004.

Ujma, Magdalena. "A Child to Be Proud Of." nd. Elżbieta Jabłońska Archive, Bydgoszcz, Poland.

Ujma, Magdalena. "Katarzyna Górna." In *Katarzyna Górna.*, ed. Program Art Gallery. Warsaw: Program Art Gallery, 2006.

Van Espen, Silvia. "Jiří David: Too Light… Vertigo…Panic…Stendhal Syndrome…Local Anaesthesia…Geopornography." *Zarhorian Gallery*, April 27–June 9, 2012. Accessed October 6, 2012. http://www.zahoriangallery.com/new/en/vystava-prilis-lahka/.

Vaughan, Dai. *For Documentary: Twelve Essays.* Berkeley: University of California Press, 1999.

Wagner, Anne M. "'Alice Neel: Painted Truths' Whitechapel Gallery, London." *Artforum International* 49, no. 4 (December 2010): 206–207.

Wagner, Anne M. *Mother Stone: The Vitality of Modern British Sculpture.* New Haven/London: Yale University Press, 2005.

Wark, Jayne. "Conceptual Art and Feminism: Martha Rosler, Adrian Piper, Eleanor Antin, and Martha Wilson." *Woman's Art Journal* 22, no. 1 (Spring-Summer 2001): 44–50.

Wark, Jayne. "Martha Wilson: Not Taking It at Face Value." *Camera Obscura* 15, no 3 (2001): iv–33.

Watson, Peggy. "Eastern Europe's Silent Revolution: Gender." *Sociology* 27, no. 3 (August 1993): 471–87. doi: 10.1177/0038038593027003008.

Wead, George. *Buster Keaton and the Dynamics of Visual Wit.* New York: Arno Press, 1976.

Whiting, Cécile. *A Taste for Pop: Pop Art, Gender and Consumer Culture.* Cambridge: Cambridge University Press, 1997.

Wilkin, Karen. "Not-So-Great New York 2005." *The New Criterion* 23, no. 9 (May 2005): 43–47.

Williams, Joan. *Unbending Gender: Why Family and Work Conflict and What to Do About It.* Oxford/New York: Oxford University Press, 2000.

Winnicott, D.W. *Dreaming, Fantasying and Living in Playing and Reality.* London: Routledge, 1996.

Winston, Helena. "Guy Ben-Ner: Postmasters." *ArtUS* no. 14 (July/September 2006): 46.

Włodarczyk, Justyna, ed. *Gender Issues 2009: Gender Equality Discourse in Times of Transformation, 1989–2009. The Czech Republic, Poland, Slovakia and Ukraine.* Warsaw: Heinrich Böll Foundation, 2010.

Wohlmuth, Radek. "Family Bonds Mothers and Fathers, Ltd." *Umělec* 1 (2005) http://divus.cc /berlin/de/article/family-bonds-mothers-and-fathers-ltd.

Wójick, Julitą. "Rozmawia with Małgorzata Lisiewicz, Obieranie ziemniaków." *Magazyn Sztuki* 26 (2001). http://www.magazynsztuki.eu/old/archiwum/nr_26/archiwum_nr26_teks t_4.htm

Wolf, Reva. "Collaboration as Social Exchange: Screen Tests/A Diary by Gerard Malanga and Andy Warhol." *Art Journal* 52, no. 4, Interactions between Artists and Writers (Winter 1993): 59–66.

Woolf, Virginia. *A Room of One's Own.* London: Leonard and Virginia Woolf at the Hogarth Press, 1929.

Young, Craig and Sylwia Kaczmarek. "Changing the Perception of the Post-Socialist City: Place Promotion and Imagery in Łódź, Poland." *The Geographical Journal* 165, no. 2, The Changing Meaning of Place in Post-Socialist Eastern Europe: Commodification, Perception and Environment (July 1999): 183–191.

Załuski, Tomas. "Zależy mi znalezieniu małej szczeliny, która powoduje chwilowy zwrot akcji, wprowadza zamęt, a czasem zadziwia z Elżbietą Jabłońską rozmawia Tomas Załuski." *Arteon – magazyn o sztuce* 72, no. 4 (April 2006). http://www.atlassztuki.pl/ pdf/jablonska3.pdf.

Zaya, Octavio. *Del Revés: Artistas contemporáneos de Israel. (Inside-Out: Contemporary Artists from Israel).* Vigo: Museo de Arte Contemporánea de Vigo, 2006.

Zegher, Catherine de, ed. *Martha Rosler: Positions in the Life World.* Cambridge, MA: The MIT Press, 1998.
Zimmermann, Patricia R. *Reel Families: A Social History of Amateur Film.* Bloomington/ Indianapolis: Indiana University Press, 1995.
Zoja, Luigi. *The Father: Historical, Psychological and Cultural Perspectives.* Translated by Henry Martin. Philadelphia: Brunner-Routledge, 2001.
Zorpette, Glenn. "Dynamic Duos: Artists Are Teaming Up in Growing Numbers." *Art News* 93, no. 6 (Summer 1994): 164–69.

Index

Note: Page numbers in *italics* indicate figures and page numbers in **bold** indicate tables.

2-Stage Transfer Drawing (Advancing to a Past State) (Oppenheim) 92, *93*
83 Waiters and a Helper (Jabłońska) 47–48, *48*
250 cm Line Tattooed on Six Paid People (Sierra) 53
303 Gallery 49

abortion 9–10, 44, 62n83, 154
Abramović, Marina 104, 116, 120, 123
Accidental Pleasure (Jabłońska) 46
Acconci, Vito 75, 84–85, 104
Ach Alma Manétro (Villeglé and Hains) 135
Aesop's Fables 95
L'Affichistes 135
Aguilar, Alberto 2–3
A.I.R. Gallery 1
Akasegawa, Genpei 85
Algar, James 97
Allara, Pamela 9
"Ambivalent Beauty, The" (Kowalczyk) 43
American Family Series, The (Cox) 21
American Supermarket, The 131–33
Amos, Emma 8, 115
Analysis of a Phobia in a Five-Year-Old Boy (Freud) 74
Anderson, Benedict 123
Anderson, Bridget 53
Anna Leonowens Gallery 15
Antoni, Janine 120–21
Anzaldúa, Gloria 4
Arad, Boaz 68, 77–78, 102
L'Arrivee d'un Train a la Cioat 96
art: children in 5, 16–18; democratic 49; fatherhood and 2–3; food-based 40–49; menstruation in 33, 125–26; motherhood and 1–4, 16, 18, 32, 142; parenting and 5, 11, 18–19; political 122; pregnancy in 9, 11, 14, 17, 23n15, 137; relational aesthetics and 39–40, 49, 51, 63n111; religious 31; sentimentality/kitsch label 9,

15, 19, 57, 68, 83, 96, 156; Virgin Mary iconography and 30–33
Art & Language 116, 119, 124–26
artist couples 118–19, 123–24
artist groups: collaboration and 121–25, 146n9; collectives and 123; Czech Republic 121–23; matriarchal structure in 125; mixed gender in 118, 125; naming and 123–26; participation of all members in 127; patriarchal structure in 125
Artist is Present, The (Abramović) 104
Artist/Mother Podcast 156
artist-mothers: as bad parent 19; birth images and 12; collective groups and 21; depiction of children by 9, 28–29; depiction of families and 21; identity and 21–22; multiple demands on 29; perceived as dilettantes 8, 10, 22n9, 68; performance of 52; sentimentality/kitsch label 9, 15, 19, 57, 68; as superheroes 36–38
Artist Parent Index 2
artist-parents: caring and 53; children and 14–19, 154–55; collectives and 22, 145, 155–56; community support for 155–56; contemporaneity and 4; defining 3–4; domestic duties and 20; exhibits and 1–2; hybrid identity and 4, 12, 74; identity and 1–6, 20–22, 27, 76, 142, 155; isolation and 115; masculinity and 3, 75, 82; national context and 154–55; parental gaze and 6n7; political state and 154–55; sentimentality and 1, 83, 96, 156
Artist Parents Talking (APT) 145, 155
Artist Residence in Motherhood, An (Clayton) 156
artists: collaboration and 116–19, 121–22; consumer culture and 128–33; identity and 20; isolation and 21; male identity and 117–18; masculine/feminine roles and 139; role of parents and 14–15; solo identity and 117–18; studios and 20–21, 25n64

Art Marketing Syndicate S.A. (AMS) 37
Art of Breastfeeding, The 2
Artwall 122, 133, 137–38
Atkinson, Terry 124
Atlas Sztuki Gallery 47
Autobiographical Series (Bourgeois) *12*
Awakening (Jabłońska) 53–55
Aya & Gal 68

Babička (*Grandma*) (Mothers and
    Fathers) 135
Baggesen, Lise Haller 1
Baker, Steve 98
Baldwin, Michael 124
Banai, Nuit 72–73
BANK 117
Banksy 134, 151n112
Baraitser, Lisa 3, 4
Bared! (Mothers and Fathers) 128, 139–40,
    144–45
Barney, Matthew 68
Baudrillard, Jean 130
Beam (Murray) 11
beauty 43
Beauvoir, Simone de 66
Becher, Bernd 116
Becher, Hilla 116
Beck, James H. 10
Benish, Barbara 133
Ben-Ner, Guy: *Aesop's Fables* and 95; as
    artist-parent 1, 66–67, 70, 74, 76, 96, 105;
    body art and 70–71, 75, 84–86; critical
    response to 105; critique of family use 103;
    documentary aesthetic 98–99, 101, 103;
    domesticity and 5, 71, 78; family ideology
    and 99, 102; father-daughter relationship
    and 80–81, 88; fatherhood and 66–70, 76,
    78, 86; father-son relationship and 88–96;
    home studio and 67–68, 104; identity and
    67, 156; Jewish faith and 76–77, 87, 102,
    113n167; kitchens and 69, 104–5; as male
    mother 97, 99–100; masculinity and 69–
    71, 73–76, 83, 105; maternal thinking and
    100; parenting and 86, 100; perception
    and 75; political state and 19, 67–68,
    86–87, 102, 155; punishment and reward
    87–88; relocation to New York 97, 99,
    101–2; sexual imagery 70, 74–75; slapstick
    and 70, 76, 79–85, 104–5; survival and
    101–2; use of children in art 66–67, 70–84,
    86, 88–100, 102–5; vaudeville model
    and 88; video art and 67–68; wildlife
    documentaries and 97–99
Ben-Ner, Guy. Works: *Berkeley's Island* 67–
    68, 70, 72, 73–75, 78–79, 86; *Elia* 67, 69,
    73, 88, 97–101, *101*, 102, 105; *Friday the
    12th* 2; *House Hold* 78; *I'd Give It to You*
    If I Could But I Borrowed It 102; *Karaoke*
    70, 74; *Moby Dick* 67, 69, 73–74,
    76–81, *81*, 82–88, 105; *Second Nature* 95;
    Stealing Beauty 102, *103*; *Treehouse Kit*
    102; *Untitled (Forked)* 70, 74–75; *Untitled
    (Rolling Pin)* 70; *Wild Boy* 74, 86, 88–91,
    91, 92, 94, 95, 100
Berkeley, George 71, 75
Berkeley's Island (Ben-Ner) 67–70, 72,
    73–75, 78–79, 86
Bernadac, Marie-Laure 12
Betterton, Rosemary 2
Bhabha, Homi 4
billboards: *Home Games* exhibition 30;
    Polish art and 37–38; public discourse and
    37–38; *Supermother* (Jabłońska) 28, 34,
    36–37
Birth of Baby X, The (Kotak) 155
Birth Project, The (Chicago) 11
Bishop, Claire 49, 53, 54
Blood Ties (Kozyra) 37
Blood Work Diary (Schneemann) 126
body art: Acconci and 85, 104; Ben-Ner and
    70–71, 84–86; Hendricks and 85; Murray
    and 11; Oppenheim and 70, 75, 85–86,
    92–93; slapstick and 84–85
Body/Hair (Hendricks) 85
Born to Be Sold (Rosler) 18, *18*
Bourdieu, Pierre 50
Bourgeois, Louise 12, *12*, 14, 155
Bourriaud, Nicholas 49
Boyle, Georgia 125
Boyle, Mark 125
Boyle, Sebastian 125
Boyle Family 123, 125
Bread (Chleba) (Mothers and Fathers)
    117, *117*
Bride Mannikin (Oldenburg) 130
Bride Stripped Bare by her Bachelors, The
    (Duchamp) 75
Brooklyn Museum of Art 1
Brown, Joan 10–11, 19, 69
Bruzzi, Stella 66, 80, 89
Buller, Rachel Epp 2
Buñuel, Luis 50, 61n65
Buschmann, Renate 46
Buteyn, Kaylan 156

Canclini, Néstor García 119
CARE exhibition 15
Cargol, Jean-Pierre 89–91
caring: as artistic practice 56–57; artist-
    mothers and 52–53; defining 4; families
    and 4; food preparation and 40, 45, 52;
    mothering and 45, 156; supermother and 36
CarlVision (Gellert) *13*, 14, 155
Cart, Ashley Weeks 44–45

Casagemas, Carlos 18
Catholicism 19, 31–33
Cattelan, Maurizio 48
CD hudebni (Mothers and Fathers Band) 129
Center for Contemporary Arts (Prague) 133
Centre Pompidou 1
Čermáková, Marie 136–37
Certeau, Michel de 40
Chaplin, Charlie 79–82, 84
Chapman, Dinos 118
Chapman, Jake 118
Chauvinistic Pieces (Wilson) 15
Chave, Anna 20, 28
Chernick, Myrel 2
Chicago, Judy 11–12, 15, 126
Child Pillows (Mothers and Fathers) 129
children: aesthetic value and 73, 107n30; in art
    5, 16–18; artist-parents and 14–19, 154–55;
    Artwall and 137–38; cultural history and
    138; in Israel 83; parent dependence on
    100; security/stability and 77–78; used in art
    66–67, 70–84, 88–100, 102–5, 111n112,
    155; women artists and 8–9
Children Meeting (Murray) 11
Chris, Cynthia 99
Christo 116, 118
Chukhrov, Kati 16
Cichocki, Sebastian 29, 32, 34–35, 45
Ciesielska, Jolanta 37
Clayton, Lenka 156
Clemans, Gayle 6n7
Clothespins Assert Churning Action
    (Nakaniski) 85
Club Mózg 55
Co-Art (De Wachter) 118
Colab 116
collaboration: artist couples and 118–19;
    artist groups and 121–25, 146n9; artists
    and 116–19; family relationships and
    118–19; feminist artists 122–23; mixed
    gender in 118; naming and 123–24
*Collaborations: Artists Working
    Together* 116
Collective Actions 21, 116, 119
collectives: artist-parents and 22, 145,
    155–56; artists and 116, 119, 123; art
    prizes and 118; benefits of 122; group
    identity and 126; *habitus* and 50; mothering
    and 156; naming and 126; social history
    and 116; spokesperson for 124; women
    artists and 21, 122; *see also* artist groups
Color Application for Chandra
    (Oppenheim) 104
Co-Madras Artistas 122–23
"Conceptual Art...The NSCAD Connection,
    1967–73" 15
Consumer Art (LL) 26

"Consumer Society" (Baudrillard) 130
consumption 128–33, 149n86
contemporaneity 4
Converting, Domesticating, Taming
    (Sawicka) 37
Corrin, Chris 36
Cox, Renée 8, 21
Cremaster Cycle (Barney) 68
Czech Republic: anti-graffiti laws in 133–34;
    artist groups in 121–23, 125–26; artist-
    parents in 115–16, 128; Communist
    history of 116, 122; consumer culture in
    128, 133; corporal punishment in 139,
    151n113; cultural history and 138; families
    and 136–38; fatherhood and 142–43;
    feminism and 128, 130, 137, 142; food
    consumption in 140; gender roles in 130–
    31, 139–40, 142; language of artworks
    in 127; matriarchal family structure in
    125; motherhood and 130–31, 136–37,
    140, 142; normalization period 138, 142;
    parenting practices and 136; public spaces
    for art in 133–35; street art in 134–35;
    support for art in 121–22, 132, 147n35;
    universal and 145; Western influences in
    41, 121, 128, 130; women in 128, 130–31,
    136–37, 142–43

Daddy Shift, The (Smith) 68
Dakota's Red (Murray) 11
Danto, Arthur C. 126
David, Jiří 122
Davies, Jon 75, 80
da Vinci, Leonardo 32
Defoe, Daniel 70–71, 75
democratic art 49
De Wachter, Ellen Mara 118
Dinner Party, The (Chicago) 11
Dishes (to Wash) (Mothers and Fathers) 128
documentary films 97–99, 101
Documentation I (Kelly) 15
Domestic (Opie) 22
domesticity: Ben-Ner and 5, 71, 78; female
    body and 142; isolation and 71; Jabłońska
    and 28–29, 32–43, 46, 51; male artists and
    69; male impotence and 70; masculinity
    and 69–70, 74–75, 78; Mothers and
    Fathers 128, 131–33, 139–40, 142;
    parenting and 78
domestic workers 52–53
Donoghue, Deirdre 1
Double Pregnancy (Rzepecki) 17
Doucet, Andrea 66, 100
Duchamp, Marcel 21, 75
Dueul Lusky, Aim 86
Dziamski, Grzegorz 33
Dzividzinska, Zenta 18, 25n59

Eastern Europe: art of women and children in 18, 25n59; feminist art in 16; food culture in 46; institutionalization of families and 136–37; postcolonial discourse and 152n121; St. Nicholas' Day 55; support for art in 121; Western influences in 46, 57, 121; women in 128
Eat Art Banquets (Spoerri) 46
Eat Art Gallery 46
Edelson, Mary Beth 11
Edelsztein, Sergio 67–68, 74, 76, 84, 85, 104
ejaculatory iconography 75
Elia (Ben-Ner) 67, 69, 73, 88, 97–101, *101*, *102*, 105
Elkins, James 31
Elles 1
Emergency Light (Mothers and Fathers) 129
Emile (Rousseau) 95
Emin, Tracey 10, 120, 155
L'Enfant sauvage (Truffaut) 89–92
Engels, Frederick 102
Enríquez, Carlos 9
Ettinger, Bracha 2
Every Person I Have Ever Slept With 1963–1995 (Emin) 10, 120

Familial Gaze, The (Hirsch) 2
families: caring and 4; Eastern European institutionalization of 136–37; feminism and 136; gendered constructions of 96–97, 99; heteronormativity and 3; illusion of unity and 14; male artists and 18; representation of 2; street art and 137–38
Family Art Crimes (Mothers and Fathers) 128, 133, *134*, 136–39
Family Frames (Hirsch) 2
Family IV 1983–1995 (Stacho) 17
Father: Decoration (Mothers and Fathers) 128, *128*
fatherhood: art and 2–3; caregiving and 68, 106n13; in critical discourse 3; domesticity and 75; Enlightenment concept of 88; in film 89; Freud on 94–95; good/bad 13, 68, 74, 104; male artists and 13–14, 17–18; masculinity and 66, 70–71, 73–74, 100, 105; social expectations and 142–44; stereotypes of 66; *see also* artist-parents
feminism: artist identity and 20; art world bias and 104, 117–18; Christianity and 33; critique of patriarchy 136; Czech Republic and 128, 130, 137, 142; male caretaking and 68, 106n13; Poland and 49; women artists and 8, 12, 16
Feminist Art and the Maternal (Liss) 2, 21
feminist artists 16, 75, 122–23, 142
feminist movement 8–9, 12–13, 119
Ferber, Marianne 142

Fitzsimmons, Jim 8
Flagelanti (Flagellants) (Pode Bal) 138
Flower Power (Benish) 133
food art 40–49
food consumption: artist-mothers and 38–42; beauty standards and 44; caloric content and 43–44; Czech culture and 140; men and 45; mothering and 38; Polish culture and 41, 46–47; as private affair 50; public spaces and 50, 64n125, 64n127; as social interaction 40–42, 45–46, 48–50; women and 44–45, 51; women's labor and 40, 42, 49, 51
For Documentary (Vaughan) 98
Forgács, Péter 103
Francis, Connie 74
Freud, Sigmund 73–74, 94
Friday the 12th (Ben-Ner) 2
Fritsch, Katharina 30
Futurist Cookbook, The (Marinetti) 40

gaga feminism 3–4
Gallery 400 2
Gallery C2C 120
Gallery One 132
Gallery Tropic 126
Gallery U Mloka 131–32
Garbuz, Yair 67
Gaudreault, André 79
Gebauer, Kurt 16
Geis, Deborah R. 50
Gellert, Carl *13*, 14
Gellert, Vance 2, 13, *13*, 14, 155
Gender Check exhibition 18
gender identity 16, 31, 44, 104
Genet, Jean 71
George Staempfli Gallery 10
Gerlovin, Valery 16
Gerlovina, Rimma 16
Getter, Tamar 67
Giard, Luce 40
Gibson, Ann E. 20, 75
Giddens, Anthony 52
Gilbert & George 116, 123–24, 126
Ginzel, Andrew 118
Giotto 30
Giza-Poleszczuk, Anna 31, 34, 59n25
Global Feminisms 1
globalization 52
Godelier, Maurice 55
Godmilow, Jill 101
Gold Rush, The 82, 84
Górna, Katarzyna 32–33
graffiti 133–39, 151n112
Gran Fury 116, 135
Grant, Carson 97
Green, Charles 117, 123

Gruault, Jean 89
Guerrilla Girls 116
Gumbs, Alexis Pauline 3
Gunning, Tom 81–82, 86, 96
Guston, Philip 13

habitus 50
Hains, Raymond 135
Halberstam, J. Jack 3–4
Hall, Stuart 119
Happy and Merry (Mothers and Fathers) 126–27
Harrison, Charles 124
Harrison, Jane 10
Hartford Wash (Ukeles) 16, 42, 62n73
Hartigan, Grace 9
Havel, Vaclav 122
Havelková, Hana 136–37
Heart Over the Castle (David) 122
Heis, Alanna 103
Helping (Jabłońska) 5, 27–28, 52–55
Help Yourself (Jabłońska) 53
Hendricks, Geoff 85
Hepworth, Barbara 8–9
Hershman Leeson, Lynn 104
heteronormativity 3
Hills, Joan 125
Hi Red Center 85
Hirsch, Marianne 2, 14
Hobbs, Robert 117
Hochschild, Arlie 4
Holy Virgin Mary (Ofili) 30
Home Games exhibition 30
home movies 70, 73, 76, 92, 103, 107n29
Hopkins, David 75
Horak, Jan-Christopher 98–99
Horoder, Stuart 121
House Hold (Ben-Ner) 78
Howfield, Rachel 145, 155
Husak, Gustav 134
Hutton, Will 52
Huyghe, Pierre 21

identity politics 4, 123, 127
I'd Give It to You If I Could But I Borrowed It (Ben-Ner) 102
Ignorant Schoolmaster, The (Rancière) 95
Immediate Family (Mann) 19
Immigrant, The 80–81, 84
Inappropriate Bodies (Buller and Reeve) 2
Indiana, Robert 135
Inman, Mary 131
Institute of Mothering Artists (IOMA) 156
Irvin, Sarah 2, 4
Is a Woman a Human Being? (Pinińska-Bereś) 26
Israel: artist studios in 106n11; childhood and 83; cultural history and 83, 87; Jewish faith and 87–88, 110n83, 155; Jewish settlements and 102; male identity and 83; political state and 76, 86; video art in 67–68, 106n6
Itard, Jean 89–90, 92, 94
I've Got It All (Emin) 10

Jabłońska, Elżbieta: as artist-mother 1, 3, 26–28, 38, 49–50, 52–53, 58; background of 26; billboards and 36–38; caring and 52–54, 56–58; Catholicism and 19, 31–33; domesticity and 28–29, 32–43, 46, 51; domestic workers and 52–53; food preparation/consumption 38–47, 49–51, 61n65; giving and 55–56; helping and 53–56, 63n105; home artmaking and 26–27, 68; maternal identity and 27–30, 32–33, 36, 38, 57, 156; maternal practice and 38–47, 51–52, 55, 155; maternal subjectivity of 27, 38, 40–41, 56–57; maternal thinking and 28, 41, 58, 154; nationalism and 19; participatory art and 39–41, 45, 49–50; as Polish Mother 19, 27, 38, 43, 46, 49–50, 53, 58; popular culture and 28–29, 31–32; relational aesthetics and 39–40, 49, 51; social interaction and 48–49, 55–56; studio space and 21; superhero portrayal by 29, 32–36, 59n11; as supermother artist 5, 34, 36–37, 45, 56, 58, 68, 154; Virgin Mary iconography and 29–33, 68; women's labor and 47–48, 52–54
Jabłońska, Elżbieta. Works: 83 Waiters and a Helper 47–48, *48*; *Accidental Pleasure* 46; *Awakening* 53–55; *Helping* 5, 28, 52–55; *Help Yourself* 53; *Kitchen* 38, 40–43, 45, 47, 51–52; *Line of Art* 55; Łódź banquet performance 47; *Meeting* 47–48; *New Life* 27, 57, *57*, 58; *Polish Mother Presents No. 1, Home Stories* 27, 38; *Supermother* 5, 27–30, 33–34, *34*, 36–37, 155; *Supermother, Home Games* 37; *Through the Stomach to the Heart* 5, 27–28, 38–39, *39*, 40, 42, 44, 47, 51–53, 55–56; *When Antek Sleeps* 26; *Woman Has a Soul* 53–54; *Women's Day* 53–55; *Zasiedzenie* 38
Jacotot, Louis 95–96
Javacheff, Christo *see* Christo
Jeanne-Claude 116, 118
Jehlička, Petr 41
Jenks, Chris 77, 83
Johanson, Patricia 10
John Paul II 33, 48
Johnson, Jill 129
Jones, Caroline 20–21
Jones, Kristen 118

Karaoke (Ben-Ner) 70, 74
Kaše (Mash) (Mothers and Fathers) 135–36
Keaton, Buster 83–84, 89
Kelly, Mary 14–15, 155
Kester, Grant 49, 117
Khrushchev, Nikita 69
Kienholz, Ed 118
Kienholz, Nancy Reddin 118
KimyiBo 156
Kitchen (Jabłońska) 38, 40–43, 45, 47, 51–52
kitchens: avant-garde visualizations of 69;
    as fantasyland 86; as feminine space 69;
    male appropriation and 104–5; as place
    for children 87–88, 91; as private space
    38, 42, 45, 52, 61n68; video art in 68–70,
    74, 77, 80, 84, 86, 106n15; women artists
    and 69
Klein, Jennie 2
Kleivan, Nina Maria 155
Klodová, Lenka: as artist-parent 115;
    domesticity and 140; group identity and
    124–25, 143, 145; maternal identity and
    139–40, 142; as spokesperson 125; *Victors*
    137–38
Knowles, Alison 45, 51
Komar 123
Kopp, Antonín 122
Kosuth, Joseph 124
Kotak, Marni 155
Kowalczyk, Izabela 35, 43–44, 49, 56
Kozyra, Katarzyna 37
Krajewski, Marek 37, 50, 56
Krasner, Lee 20
Kristeva, Julia 11, 126
Krylov, Porfiry 126
Kukryiniksy 126
Kuprianov, Mikhail 126
Kwon, Miwon 47

Lambert-Beatty, Carrie 104
Lampe & Bouche (Illuminated Lips)
    (Szapocznikow) 26
La Vie (Picasso) 18
Lavie, Raffi 67
"Law of Sculptors" (Gilbert & George) 123
Léaud, Jean-Pierre 90
Lennon, John 134
Lennon Wall 122, 134
Lévi-Strauss, Claude 130
Lichtenstein, Roy 131
Lick and Lather (Antoni) 120
Lin, Hilla Lulu 68
Line of Art, The (Jabłońska) 55
Lippard, Lucy 8, 11, 16, 21
Liss, Andrea 2, 8, 21, 123
Living Desert, The 98
LL, Natalia 26

Locke, John 95
Loiperdinger, Martin 96
Lorde, Audre 4
Love (RAFANI) 122
Loveless, Natalie 1
Lubin, Siegmund 99
Lublin, Léa 16, 21
Lumière, Louis 96
Lutz, Helma 52–53

MacDonald, Scott 99
Machine in the Studio (Jones) 20
Madonna and Child imagery *see* Virgin Mary
    iconography
Madonnas (Górna) 32–33
Madonnenfigur (Fritsch) 30
"Maintenance Art Manifesto" (Ukeles)
    15–16, 142
Make a Salad (Knowles) 45
male artists: depiction of children by 5,
    16–17; depiction of families and 18;
    domestic appropriations 69, 104–5;
    ejaculatory iconography of 75;
    fatherhood and 13–14, 17–18, 20;
    impact of feminist movement on 13;
    maternity and 17; parenting and 3,
    12–13; studios and 20–21, 25n64; *see also*
    artist-parents
Mami (Mom) (Mothers and Fathers) 135
Mann, Sally 2, 19
Mapplethorpe, Robert 143
Maříková, Hana 125
Marinetti, Filippo Tammaso 40
Marody, Mira 31, 34, 59n25
Martens, China 3
Masaryk, Tomáš Garrigue 142
masculinity: artistic identity and 67, 76;
    artist-parents and 3, 75, 82; domesticity
    and 69–70, 74–75, 78; fatherhood
    and 66, 70–71, 73–74, 100, 105; food
    consumption and 45; Israelis and 83
MassMOCA 2
Maternal Bodies in the Visual Arts
    (Betterton) 2
Maternal Metaphors 1
maternal subjectivity 27, 38, 40–41, 56–57,
    61n67
maternal thinking 3, 28, 41, 58, 100, 154
Maternal Thinking (Ruddick) 3, 100
Matisse, Henri 21
Matrixial Borderspace, The (Ettinger) 2
Mayer, Musa 13
Mayeroff, Milton 4
Meeting (Jabłońska) 47–48
Melamid 123
Méliès, Georges 79
Melville, Herman 76, 78, 82, 86–87

men: as artist-parents 13; as "big child"
31, 59n25; food consumption and 45;
mothering and 67, 96, 99–100; parenting
and 3–4, 13, 100, 106n14; *see also*
masculinity
menstruation 33, 125–26
Menstruation Bathroom (Chicago) 126
Microscope Art Gallery 155
Migrant Domestic Workers (Anderson and
Phizacklea) 53
Mikołaj 55
Milkstained (M.A.M.A.) 123
Mill, Stuart 126
Moby Dick (Ben-Ner) 67, 69, 73–74, 76–81,
81, 82–88, 105
Moby Dick (Melville) 76, 86–87
MOMA PS.1 1
Mon Fils (Lublin) 16
Montessori, Maria 43
Mop (Mothers and Fathers) 140, *141*
M/Other 2
Mother (Mothers and Fathers) 128
Mother Art 21
mother-artist 2–3, 21, 29, 50, 56; *see also*
artist-mothers; artist-parents
Mother Artists Making Art (M.A.M.A.) 21,
122–23
motherhood: art and 1–4, 16, 18, 32, 142;
Catholicism and 19; as critical position
27–29, 41; Czech Republic 130–31,
136–37, 140, 142; good/bad 35;
limitations of 12; as mode of practice
38–40; nationalism and 19; performance
of 155–56; Poland and 27–29, 154; social
expectations and 8, 22n8, 52; stereotypes
of 19; superheroes and 35–36; video art
and 18; Virgin Mary iconography and
32–33; women artists and 8–12, 16,
23n15, 28, 120
mothering: artist-parents and 3; collectives
and 156; defining 3; food consumption and
38; maternal thinking and 3, 41; men and
67, 99–100; in Poland 38; women artists
and 2–3, 9, 12, 16
Mother/Mother 1
Mothers and Fathers: as artist-parents 1, 5–6,
115–17, 119–21; collaboration and 116–
20, 125–27, 146n8; community-building
and 123; consumer culture and 128–33;
Czech culture and 116; Czech language
and 127; domesticity and 128, 131–33,
139–40, 142; families and 135–40,
142–44; fatherhood and 143–44; feminist
artists and 122; formation of 115, 146n5;
on gender roles 139–40, 142–44, 155;
graffiti art and 133–39; group identity and
116–21, 126–27, 138, 145, 156; identity

politics and 127; individual identity and
117–21, 125, 140, 145; making the private
public 139–40, 142; matriarchal structure
in 125; mixed gender in 118; motherhood
and art 142; naming and 124–27; parental
identity and 121; torn paper and 135–36;
universal and 145; use of children in
art 155
Mothers and Fathers. Works: *Babička*
(*Grandma*) 135; *Bared!* 128, 139–40,
144–45; *Bread* (*Chleba*) 117, *117*; *CD
hudebni* 129; *Child Pillows* 129; *Dishes (to
Wash)* 128; *Emergency Light* 129; *Family
Art Crimes* 128, 133, *134*, 136–39; *Father:
Decoration* 128, *128*; *Happy and Merry*
126–27; *Kaše* (*Mash*) 135–36; *Mami*
(*Mom*) 135; *Mop* 140, *141*; *Mother* 128;
Mothers and Fathers Offer 124, 128–32;
Mother Sleeping Bag 129; *Old Doll* 129;
Plug 143; *Report Card* 144; *Ružena* 128,
130; *Sand* 129; *Sourozenci* (*Siblings*)
135; *Tat'ka* (*Daddy*) 135; *Undressing:
Decoration* 129, 132; *Vánoce* (*Christmas*)
135–36; *Výprask* (*Whipping*) 135–36;
What Would We Be Without Children?
117, 120–21, 145
Mothers and Fathers Band 129
Mothers and Fathers Offer (Mothers and
Fathers) 124, 128–32
Mother Sleeping Bag (Mothers and Fathers)
129
Mother Stone (Wagner) 9
Motyčka, Petr 122
Moves on a Human Scale (Aguilar) 2
Munro, Eleanor 9
Murray, Elizabeth 10–11, 24n34
Musée d'Art Moderne de la Ville de Paris 16
Museum Moderner Kunst Stiftung Ludwig
Wien 18
M Word, The (Chernick) 2

Na'aman, Michal 67
Nakaniski, Natsuyuki 85
Names Street Art Fest 134
naming 123–27
Nanas (Saint Phalle) 9
Nash, Rebecca 136–37
nationalism 19, 30–31
nature documentaries 97–99
Nauman, Bruce 74
Neel, Alice 8–9
Nepasická, Lucie: as artist-parent 115;
domesticity and 140, 142; group identity
and 124, 143, 145; maternal identity and
139–40
Neri, Manuel 10
Neuer Berliner Kunstverein 52

New Life (Jabłońska) 27, 57, *57*, 58
New Maternalisms (Loveless) 1
New York School 119
Night Studio, The (Mayer) 13
Ninth Hour, The (Cattelan) 48
Nixon, Richard 69
Nochlin, Linda 8, 12, 22n1
Noel and Bob (Brown) 10
Noel in the Kitchen (Brown) 69

Obrist, Hans-Ulrich 21
Ofili, Chris 30
Ognissanti Madonna (Giotto) 30
Old Doll (Mothers and Fathers) 129
Oldenburg, Claes 69, 129–33
Olmsted, Frederick Law 99
One Week 83
On the Strange Place of Religion in Contemporary Art (Elkins) 31
Openings (Acconci) 84
Opie, Catherine 21–22
Oppenheim, Dennis: *2-Stage Transfer Drawing (Advancing to a Past State)* 92, *93*; body art and 70, 75, 85–86, 92–93; parent imagery and 11; *Reading Position for Second Degree Burn* 70; *Transfer Drawings* 14, 89, 103; use of children in art 14, 92–93, 103–4, 111n112
O'Reilly, Andrea 2, 3
Originals (Munro) 9
Origin of the Family, Private Property and the State, The (Engels) 102
Ostrich Farm at Pasadena 99
Ostrowksa, Elżbieta 31
"Outdoor Gallery" (Galeria Zewnetrzna) 37
Oxytocin symposia 2

"Pains and Pleasures of Rebirth, The" (Lippard) 21
Palmer, Lucia 75
parenting: art and 5, 18–19; body action and 86; contemporary pressures on 156; defining 3; domesticity and 78; Enlightenment concept of 95; expectant mothers and 155; good/bad 13, 19, 35, 68, 74, 104; heteronormativity and 3; isolation and 115; as long-term performance 86, 155; maternal thinking and 100, 155; men and 4; politics of 19
Park, Shelley 3
Parsons, Betty 20
participatory art 39–41, 45, 49–50
Péč, Jóchym 144
Péč, Martin 115, 124, 139, 142–45
Peeling Potatoes (Wójcik) 48
Peirce, Charles Sanders 121
Phantom of Liberty, The 50, 61n65
Phizacklea, Annie 53

Picasso, Pablo 18, 21
Pinińska-Bereś, Maria 26
Plug (Mothers and Fathers) *143*
Pode Bal 122–23, 138
Poirier, Anne 123
Poirier, Patrick 123
Poland: art controversies in 30, 33, 48–49; billboard art and 37–38; Catholicism and 33; domestic workers from 52–53; expectations for women in 28–29, 34, 36, 38, 42–44, 49; feminism and 49; food consumption in 40–42; food culture in 46–47, 62n95; gender relations in 31, 59n23, 59n25; helping art and 53–54; *Mikołaj* 55; motherhood and 27–29, 154; Polish Mother stereotype in 27, 30–31, 36, 38, 42; post-Communist 37, 57–58; public spaces in 37; support for art in 121; Virgin Mary iconography and 30, 33; Western influences in 29, 41, 46, 57; women artists in 26; women in 28
Polish Mother: art and 52; brave victim identity and 31, 34, 59n25; consumer culture and 44; expectations for 17, 42–43; home cooking and 42–43, 46; Jabłońska as 19, 27, 36, 43, 46, 49–50, 58; nationalism and 31; performance of 42–43; sacrifice and 31, 42, 53–54, 56; as superhero 37–38, 44; Virgin Mary iconography and 30–31
Polish Mother Presents No. 1, Home Stories, The (Jabłońska) 27, 38
Pollock, Jackson 20
*Polyester Suit (*Mapplethorpe) 143
Pop Art movement 69, 129, 151n112
Poprzęcka, Maria 40–41
Porter, Brian 30
poster art 135
Post-Partum Document (Kelly) 14–15
Potency (Kleivan) 155
Pousette-Dart, Richard 20
Poznański, Izrael Kalman 47, 63n106
Poznański Palace 47, 63n106
pregnancy: in art 9, 11, 14, 17, 23n15, 137; male body and 17; women artists and 8–11, 16, 120, 137, 154
Preslová, Míla 138
private space: domesticity and 51; food consumption and 50; kitchens and 38, 42, 45, 52, 61n68; public performance and 50; symbolic 49
Procreate Project 2
Project of the Father Pole Memorial (Rzepecki) 17, *17*
public spaces 28, 30, 37, 50, 133

Raabe, Phyllis 142
RAFANI 122–23

Raising Baby X (Kotak) 155
Rancière, Jacques 49, 95–96
Reading Position for Second Degree Burn (Oppenheim) 70
Reconciling Art and Motherhood (Buller) 2
Reeve, Charles 2
Reiter, Herwig 137
Rejent, Marek: as artist-parent 115, 124, 139; fatherhood stereotypes and 139, 142–43; group identity and 128, 145; *Happy and Merry* 127–28; individual identity and 124; *Vitrina (Showcase)* 125
relational aesthetics 39–40, 49, 51, 63n111
religious art 31
reperformance 109n78
Report Card (Mothers and Fathers) 144
Reproduction Drawings (Saville) 32
Reproductive Media 4
Reticent Child, The (Bourgeois) 14
Revolutionary Mothering (Gumbs and Martens) 3
Rituál (Preslová) 138
Rivers, Clarice 9
Robinson Crusoe (Defoe) 70–71, 75–76
Rosenberg, Harold 21
Rosenberg, Karen 105
Rosler, Martha 18, *18*, 19, 25n60, 69
Ross, John Munder 94–95
Rottenberg, Anda 48
Rousseau, Jean-Jacques 88, 95
Ruddick, Sara 3, 4, 41, 99–100
Ružena: Bra for after Children (Mothers and Fathers) 128, 130
Rzepecki, Adam 17, *17*

Ságlová, Zorka 18
Saint Genet (Sartre) 71
Saint Phalle, Niki de 9
Saltz, Jerry 104–5
Sand (Mothers and Fathers) 129
Sanders, Clinton R. 139
Sartre, Jean-Paul 71
Saville, Jenny 32
Sawicka, Jadwiga 37
Schneemann, Carolee 126
Schwendener, Martha 104
Second Nature (Ben-Ner) 95
Second Sex, The (Beauvoir) 66
Seedbed (Acconci) 75
Self-Portrait/Nursing (Opie) 21
Self-Portrait/Pervert (Opie) 22
Semiotics of the Kitchen (Rosler) 69
Shapiro, David 117
Shoot Paintings (Saint Phalle) 9
Shvarts, Aliza 154
Sicard, Roch-Ambroise Cucurron 89
Sienkiewicz, Karol 48

Sierra, Santiago 53, 54, 56
Šilková, Jiřina 136–37
Šiml, Michal 122
Situationist International 21
Skillin-Brauchle, Cayla 4
Skupina 42 121
Skupina Ra 121
slapstick: Ben-Ner and 70, 76, 79–85, 104–5; body art versus 85–86
Smith, Jeremy Adam 66, 68
Smith, Joe 41
Smith, Stephanie 90
Smith, Terry 4
Smithson, Robert 20
Snodgrass, Susan 127
Sobczyk, Marek 37
Socorro, Mareia de 122
Sokolov, Nikolai 126
Sollins, Susan 116
Sound of Music, The 89
Sourozenci (Siblings) (Mothers and Fathers) 135
Spence, Jo 2
Spivak, Gayatri 4
Spock, Benjamin 70
Spoerri, Daniel 45–46, 51
Stacho, L'ubo 17–18
Staempfli, George 10
Starn Twins 118
Stealing Beauty (Ben-Ner) 102, *103*
Štefková, Zuzana 136
Stella, Frank 20
Stern, Elizabeth 19
Stern, William 19
Stewart, Susan 73
St. Nicholas' Day 55
Store, The (Oldenburg) 69, 129–32
street art 134–35, 151n110
studios 20–21, 25n64
Sundell, Nina Castelli 116
superheroes: artist-mothers as 36–38; Jabłońska portrayal of 29, 32–36, 59n11; Polish Mother as 37–38, 44; supermother as 35–37; symbolism of 34–35, 59n13, 60n41; Virgin Mary iconography and 31–33
Supermother (Jabłońska) 5, 27–30, 33–34, *34*, 36, 155
Supermother, Home Games (Jabłońska) *37*
Świtek, Gabriela 48
Szapocznikow, Alina 26

Takamatsu, Jiro 85
Tamir, Tali 83
Tat'ka (Daddy) (Mothers and Fathers) 135
tattoos 139–40, 142–44
Team Spirit 116

Tel Aviv Cinematheque 68
Terrible Turkish Executioner, The (Méliès) 79
Through the Stomach to the Heart
    (Jabłońska) 5, 27–28, 38–39, *39*, 40, 42,
    44, 47, 51–53, 55–56
Tiravanija, Rirkrit 49–51
Titkow, Anna 43
TODT 119
To Kill a Mockingbird 89
Tokyo Metropolitan Art Museum 85
Tomkins, Calvin 131
Transfer Drawing Series (Oppenheim) 14,
    89, 103
Trap Pictures (Spoerri) 46
Treacher, Amal 82
Treehouse Kit (Ben-Ner) 102
True-Life Adventure films 97–98
Truffaut, François 89–92
Tvrdohlaví 122–23

Ujma, Magdalena 33, 36, 38, 56–57
Ukeles, Jack 142
Ukeles, Mierle Laderman 15–16, 21, 42,
    62n73, 142, 155
Ulay 116, 123
Undressing: Decoration (Mothers and
    Fathers) 129, 132
universalism 145
Untitled (Forked) (Ben-Ner) 70, 74–75
Untitled (Free) (Tiravanija) 49
Untitled (Rolling Pin) (Ben-Ner) 70

Vainstein, Moysey 18
Vánoce (Christmas) (Mothers and Fathers)
    135–36
Vaughan, Dai 98, 101
Victors (Klodová) 137
video art: fantastic actions in 79; in Israel
    67–68, 106n6; kitchens and 68–70, 74, 77;
    parenting and 18–19; slapstick and 81–82
Villeglé, Jacques de la 135
*Virgin and Child with St. Anne and John the
    Baptist, The* (da Vinci) 32
Virgin Mary iconography: contemporary
    art and 32–33; context for 30, 59n15;
    Italian art and 30; Jabłońska and 29–33;
    motherhood and 33; Poland 30–31; public
    opposition to 33–34; superhero portrayal
    and 31–33
Vitrina (Showcase) (Rejent) 125
Vomkováčová, Klára 138
Výprask (Whipping) (Mothers and Fathers)
    135–36

WACK! Art and the Feminist Revolution 1
Wadsworth Atheneum (Hartford, Conn.)
    16, 42

Wagner, Anne M. 9
Walt Disney 97–98
Warhol, Andy 20, 69, 129, 131
Wark, Jayne 15
Watts, Robert 131
Wead, George 79
Weems, Carrie Mae 2
Weinstein, Mariano 101
Wesselmann, Tom 69
What Would We Be Without Children?
    (Mothers and Fathers) 117, 120–21, 145
When Antek Sleeps (Jabłońska) 26
White, Patrick E. 90
Whitehead, Mary Beth 18–19
Whiting, Cecile 69
"Why Have There Been No Great Women
    Artists?" (Nochlin) 8, 12
Wild Boy (Ben-Ner) 74, 86, 88–91, *91*, 92,
    94, 95, 100
wildlife films 97–99, 101
Wilkin, Karen 105
Wilson, Jane 118, 123
Wilson, Louise 118, 123
Wilson, Martha 15
Winnicott, D. W. 82
Winston, Helena 76
Wohlmuth, Radek 124, 127, 129
Wójcik, Julita 48–49, 51
Wolf, Reva 117
Woman Has a Soul, A (Jabłońska) 53–54
Womanhouse 11, 126
women: ambivalent notions of 43–44;
    in art 18, 30; beauty and 43; cultural
    expectations for 52; Czech Republic 128,
    130–31, 136, 142–43; food consumption
    and 43–45; food preparation by 42–43;
    motherhood and 44; parenting and 4, 100;
    payment for housework by 22n7; Poland
    28; Virgin Mary iconography and 29–30;
    see also Polish Mother
women artists: abortion and 9–10; art world
    bias and 104–5; censure of 19; collectives
    and 21, 122; creative spaces for 20; critic
    disdain for 10–12; denial of sentiment and
    15; domesticity and 142; exclusion from
    the academy 8; exhibits and 1; feminist
    16, 75, 122–23; gender identity and 16;
    identity and 8–9, 15; kitchens and 69;
    lack of scholarship on 8, 22n2; masculine
    attributes and 22n1; motherhood and
    8–12, 16, 23n15, 28, 120; parenting and 3;
    Polish 26; portrayal of housewife activities
    42–43, 50; pregnancy and 8–11, 16, 120,
    137, 154; as prize winners 118; public
    spaces and 50; rebellion and 22n1; support
    for family by 10–11; texts and 2; uterine
    shapes and 11, 24n34

!Women Art Revolution (Hershman Leeson) 104
Women's Building 21
Women's Day (Jabłońska) 53–55
Woolf, Virginia 20
Wyckoff, Danielle 4

Yo Mama! (Cox) 21

Zachęta National Gallery of Art 38, 48–49
Zasiedzenie (Jabłońska) 38
Zaya, Octavio 67
Zimmermann, Patricia 73
Zonshein, Dana 68
Zoo—Homo Sapiens (Gerlovina and Gerlovin) 16
Ztohoven 122–23